Patterns of Reflection

A Reader

Fifth Edition

Dorothy U. Seyler

Northern Virginia Community College

PEARSON
Longman

New York San Francisco Boston
London Toronto Sydney Tokyo Singapore Madrid
Mexico City Munich Paris Cape Town Hong Kong Montreal

Senior Vice President and Publisher: Joseph Opiela
Executive Marketing Manager: Ann Stypuloski
Media Supplements Editor: Nancy Garcia
Production Manager: Joseph Vella
Project Coordination, Text Design, and Electronic Page Makeup:
    Electronic Publishing Services Inc., N.Y.C.
Cover Design Manager: Wendy A. Fredericks
Cover Designer: Maria Ilardi
Cover Art: *Poplars on the Bank of the Epte River*, Claude Monet, 1891,
    39 $1/2$" x 25 $11/16$", oil on canvas. 1954-66-8, Philadelphia Museum of
    Art: Bequest of Anne Thompson in memory of her father, Frank
    Thompson, and her mother, Mary Elizabeth Clarke Thompson.
Manufacturing Manager: Dennis J. Para
Printer and Binder: R.R. Donnelly & Sons Company
Cover Printer: Coral Graphics Services

For permission to use copyrighted material, grateful
acknowledgment is made to the copyright holders on pp. 485–492,
which are hereby made part of this copyright page.

Library of Congress Cataloging-in-Publication Data

Patterns of reflection / Dorothy U. Seyler.—5th ed.
    p. cm
    Includes bibliographical references and index.
    ISBN 0-321-16516-0
    1. College readers.   2. English language—Rhetoric—Problems, exercises,
  etc.   3. Report writing—Problems, exercises, etc.   I. Seyler, Dorothy U.
  PE1417.P396   2004
  808'.0427—dc21

                                                 2003048204

Please visit us at www.ablongman.com

ISBN 0-321-16516-0

1 2 3 4 5 6 7 8 9 10—DOH—06 05 04 03

It is not enough to have a good mind.
The main thing is to use it well.

I like to find
What's not found
at once, but lies
within something of another nature
in repose, distinct.

Denise Levertov

Contents

3. Using Description: Reflecting on People and Places   76

6.   Using Process Analysis: How We Work and Play   **210**

**9.   Using Causal Analysis: Examining
Family and Community Issues   344**

Preface

What This Book Is About

Patterns of Reflection provides engaging selections on personal, social, and political concerns and issues, selections that also demonstrate varied uses of the major rhetorical strategies or patterns. The organizing of chapters by both rhetorical patterns and topics makes *Patterns of Reflection* a special text, both a practical guide to the various writing structures and purposes students will use in their college writing and a study of themes generating lively class discussions and personal reflections.

Patterns of Reflection asks students in its opening chapter to think about the challenges and rewards of reading and writing, both in an honest and helpful introduction and in three essays on issues such as writing anxiety and style. Each of the subsequent chapters illustrates one specific pattern or purpose, beginning with those strategies students are most comfortable with and then progressing to the more demanding ones: narration, description, comparison and contrast, explaining and illustrating, process analysis, division and classification, definition, causal analysis, and, finally, argument and persuasion. At the same time, each chapter's thematic core allows students to begin by reflecting on what is closest to them—their childhood, the people and places they know, the learning process—and then move beyond their immediate lives to their society—the media, working and playing, interpersonal relations, values, and social issues—and then to reflect on how they want to live as individuals, as members of a group, and as part of an interdependent environment.

Within the two broad organizational patterns are diverse works appealing to readers of varied backgrounds and interests. Instructors can skip some chapters and order others to meet their needs; students will have their favorite selections at the same time that they can be reminded of how much we all share as individuals who must grow up, learn, and prepare for work. Each chapter gains further diversity by:

- Essays of varied length
- A mix of essays and op-ed columns and excerpts from longer works
- The addition of a poem, short story, or visual
- The inclusion of five annotated student essays.

Patterns of Reflection is indeed a rich storehouse of opportunity.

Although the selections are preeminent, this is not just an anthology. It is a text, providing many aids to learning. Each chapter begins with a clear explanation of the strategy that includes specific guidelines for writing. Then the student is encouraged to "get started" by engaging in some reflecting and/or writing activity that can be used as a preparation for reading, as a class activity, or as a basis for journal writing. Following each selection are vocabulary exercises and questions that guide students from understanding to analyzing to responding to their reading. After all selections in a chapter, you will find "Making Connections," a section that helps readers to stretch their minds beyond one selection. These can be topics for discussion, research, writing, or all of these. Finally, each chapter concludes with topics for writing that are based on the chapter's readings and that will give practice in the chapter's rhetorical strategy. Topics are explained at length to help students reflect on and then plan their essays.

What's New in the Fifth Edition

This fifth edition offers some changes and additions that both instructors and students will appreciate. They include:

- Twenty-eight new works out of the 75 total.
- Three updated works by "old" authors because adopters said they wanted these authors kept in the text.
- The greatest number of new works in Chapter 10 on argument, to keep that chapter focused on current issues. The second greatest number of new works in Chapter 5 on media issues, again, to keep that chapter current.
- Two new pieces of art in the collection of 6 color reproductions in Chapter 3.

- More visuals throughout, some within essays, plus a cartoon and four advertisements in the media chapter.
- A new total of five student essays; three of the five are new to this edition.
- A new feature in each chapter, "Writing Focus," offers guidance on one key writing issue. Topics range from guidelines for summary to basic rules of punctuation to varying sentences for effect. The material on summary, analysis, and synthesis, formerly in Chapter 11, has become the Writing Focus of Chapter 1.
- Two questions about each selection now precede the work to serve as reading prompts.
- An expanded argument chapter with 10 essays organized into 5 point/counterpoint groups on: gun control, trying juveniles as adults, affirmative action in college admissions, immigration, and the environmental movement.
- New "Making Connections" topics in each chapter that invite a study of sources beyond the text, including the use of reference books and online sources.

Acknowledgments

No book of value is written alone. I am happy to acknowledge the help of friends and colleagues in preparing this new edition. Once again I am indebted to my daughter Ruth for her always-sound advice on selections. And thanks are due, as always, to the library staff at the Annandale Campus of Northern Virginia Community College, especially to Marian Delmore and Ruth Stanton, for their help in solving my research problems.

I remain grateful to Scott Rubin, Barbara Heinssen, Tim Julet, and Eben Ludlow for their help with the early editions of *Patterns of Reflection*. I would not be writing this preface to the fifth edition if it were not for the continued support, through four editions now, of my current editor, Joe Opiela. I also appreciate the many fine suggestions of the following reviewers: Jacqueline Farr, Bristol Community College; Frederic Giacobazzi, Kirtland Community College; Steve Katz, Southwest Tennessee Community College; Joyce Marie Miller, Collin County Community College; Karen Petit, Bristol Community College; Barbara L. Siek, Harold Washington College.

Finally, I want to give a special thank you to the five students who gave me permission to use their essays. They were hardworking and thoughtful writers who should be proud of their achievements. I hope they will find the same joy that I have in reaching out to students all over the country.

DOROTHY U. SEYLER

1

On Reading and Writing

You have purchased your texts and are ready to begin another English course. What papers will be assigned, you wonder, perhaps somewhat nervously. And why has this text of readings been assigned? After all, writing is difficult enough; must you read, too? Giving these questions some thoughtful analysis is a good place to start your journey through this text and course.

The Challenges and Rewards of Writing

Many people, of all ages, become nervous about writing; they experience what is called writing anxiety. Some are so anxious, as Gail Godwin observes in this chapter (see pp. 18–22), that they dream up all kinds of excuses to put off a writing task. If you have some anxiety about writing, you can take comfort in knowing that others share your nervousness, including professional writers who sometimes go through lengthy periods of writer's block. You can also take some comfort in recognizing the appropriateness of your feelings. When faced with a term of writing compositions, students can expect a degree of anxiety, because writing well is not easy.

Let's consider some realities of the writing process. First, writing is a skill, like dancing or riding a bike or playing tennis. You were not born knowing how to ride a bike. You had to learn, perhaps with some painful bumps and bruises to both bike and ego. To be a competent writer, you must develop your skills the same way tennis players develop a spin serve: good instruction, a strong desire to succeed, and practice, practice, practice. A second fact of writing is that some writers are more talented than others, just as Pete Sampras is a more talented tennis player than most. But Sampras's ability did not come from a genie in a bottle. The best in any field make their abilities look "like magic." You need to remember, however, that they also spend years of study, self-discipline, and practice to achieve their excellence. This text cannot give you a great tennis game, but it can help you to become, with practice and commitment on your part, a competent writer.

Even for those willing to practice, learning to write well is not easy because writing is a complex skill. Topics to write about, audiences to write for, and reasons to write cannot be completely catalogued, and the ways of choosing and combining words into sentences are infinite in their variety. Still, you can, through instruction and practice in this course, develop some good strategies for planning, organizing, drafting, and revising your writing. In addition, this text will provide opportunities for thinking about issues important to all of us and worthy of exploring through writing.

If learning to write well is difficult, why bother to try to develop your skills? For a good answer to this question, ask any student over twenty-five why he or she is now in college. Many "older" students are training for a second career, but many more want to improve basic skills so that they can advance in their current careers. They will assure you, from their experience in the workplace, that all language skills are essential: reading, speaking, listening, and writing. More immediate and personal goals for writing well can also be noted:

- The more you develop your awareness of the writing process, the better reader you will become. You will understand, from your own experience, how writers select and organize material to achieve their purpose.
- The more confident a writer you become, the more efficiently you will handle written assignments in your other college courses.
- Since writing is an act of discovery, the more you write, the more you will learn about who you are and what matters to you. After all, how accurately do you see your parents, your friends, your campus? Writing will sharpen your vision of the world around you and your understanding of the world inside you.

Good Reasons for Reading

Good writers make good readers. It is also true that reading well improves writing. The strong connection between reading and writing skills explains why students in reading courses are asked to write and students in writing courses are asked to read. Here are three specific uses of reading in a composition course.

Reading for Models

At times students are assigned readings to illustrate a type of writing: the personal essay, the book review, the scholarly report. Or, the readings may illustrate a strategy or purpose in writing: description, illustration, argument. Chapters 2 through 10 in this text contain readings grouped by a dominant writing pattern or purpose. If you are assigned Tracy Kidder's description of Mrs. Zajac and then asked to write a descriptive essay of someone you know, you have been asked to use Kidder's essay as a model for your assignment.

Readings can also be studied as models of effective writing. They can illustrate clever openings, the use of transitions, varied sentence patterns, and effective metaphors. Read, then, not just for what the work says but for what kind of writing it represents and for what writing techniques it illustrates. Questions on strategies and style following each reading will guide your study of the work's special merits. Remember: In the broadest sense, reading contributes to language development. You learned your first language by imitating the speech you heard around you. Imitate the readings in this text to improve your writing skills.

Reading for Information and Insight

You may also be asked to read for information: for facts, for new ideas, for startling analyses. Even when you are reading for models, you will have the chance to explore many subjects, some new to you. Reading, as syndicated columnist Robert Samuelson has observed, "allows you to explore new places, new ideas and new emotions." In this text when you read, you can travel with Lance Morrow to Africa, understand with Linda Waite the ways that marriage improves people's lives, and contemplate with John Ciardi the meaning of happiness. When preparing reading assignments, be sure to think about the questions asking for your reactions. Approach each reading assignment as an opportunity to grow in knowledge, understanding, and imagination.

Reading for Writing

One of the interesting effects of reading is that it produces writing, more works to read and react to in a never-ending chain reaction. A columnist writes about assault weapons. A reader responds with a letter to the editor opposing the banning of such guns. A student, to complete an argument assignment, writes a refutation of the letter. At times writing assignments in this course may call for a response to reading. You may be asked to summarize an essay, analyze a writer's use of details, or contrast writers' differing views on a subject. When writing about reading, you will need to show both skill in writing and understanding of the reading, a challenging task.

Guidelines for Active Reading

When first looking over library materials or texts for courses, you are wise to begin by skimming to see how the material is put together and what, in general, it is about. But, once you become engaged in a particular work that you need to know well, accuracy—not speed—is your goal. You can improve your reading skills by becoming an active, engaged reader who follows a clear reading strategy. A good reading strategy calls for the following preparation, reading, and responding steps.

Prepare

1. *Prepare to become a part of the writer's audience.* Not all writers write with each one of us in mind. Some writers prepare scholarly reports for other specialists. Some scholars, such as Linda Waite (see pages 364–376), present the results of research to a more generally educated audience. Writers of the past wrote for readers in their time, readers who may be expected to know their times or other works with which you may be unfamiliar. So, prepare yourself to join the writer's audience by learning as much as you can about each of the following:

   - the writer
   - the time in which the work was written
   - the kind of work it is (a textbook chapter, a newspaper editorial, a personal narrative)
   - the writer's anticipated audience.

For writings in the text, you will be aided in this step by introductory notes. Be sure to study them. *Never start to read words on a page without first knowing what you are reading!*

2. *Prepare to read with an open mind.* Good readers seek new knowledge and ideas. They do not "rewrite" a work to suit themselves. Keep in mind that not all who write will share your views or express themselves as you do. Read what is on the page, giving the writer a fair chance to develop ideas, giving yourself the thoughtful reflection needed to understand those ideas. Remember: You are in a college course to learn, not to be entertained. So, stick to the task of reading with understanding, not complaining that you didn't "like" this work or that the assignment was "boring." If the reading is difficult for you, look up words or references you do not know and be prepared to read a second time to really learn the material.

3. *Prepare by prereading.* To be prepared to read with understanding, you need to skim the selection to see what kind of work you are about to read (#1 above), to get some idea of the author's subject, and to start thinking about what you already know on that topic. Follow these steps:

- Read all introductory notes or biographical notes provided about the author.
- Consider the title. What clues in the title reveal the work's subject and perhaps the writer's approach to or attitude about that subject?
- Read the opening paragraph and then skim the rest of the work, noting in particular any subheadings and/or graphics.
- Ask yourself: "What do I already know about this subject?" and "What do I expect to learn—and what will I need to know—from reading this work?"
- From your prereading, raise two or three questions about the subject that you hope to find answers to by reading the work.

Read Actively

4. *Read with concentration.* Your goal is understanding, not completing an assignment as quickly as possible, so read as slowly as necessary to achieve comprehension. Maintain concentration. Avoid reading a page and then gazing out the window or getting a snack. You will have to go back to the beginning to really know what you have read if you

keep interrupting the reading process. Read an entire essay
or story or poem or chapter (or several related sections in
one chapter) at one time.

5. *Use strategies for understanding words and references.* Reading
a work containing words you do not know is like trying to
play tennis with some of the strings missing from your rack-
et. When you come to a word you do not know, begin by
studying the sentence in which it appears. You may be able
to guess the word's meaning from its context. If context clues
do not help, study the parts that make up the word. Many
words are combinations of words or word parts (roots, pre-
fixes, and/or suffixes) that appear in other words that you
do know. For example, take the word *autobiography.* This is
made up of *auto,* a root meaning self (*auto*mobile), *bio,* a root
meaning life (*bio*logy), and *graph,* a root meaning writing
(auto*graph*). You can understand many longer words if you
think about their parts. Often these strategies will allow you
to keep reading rather than interrupting the process to turn
to a dictionary. But, be sure to look up words that you
cannot figure out. You should also use a dictionary or encyclopedia to learn about writers an author refers to. Understanding references to people, places, and other written
works is essential for full comprehension.

6. *Be alert to the use of figurative language and other writing strategies.* Figures of speech such as metaphors, irony, and understatement help shape a writer's tone and convey a writer's
attitude to his or her topic. Use the Glossary if necessary
to check the definitions of these terms.

7. *Annotate or make notes as you read.* Studies have demonstrated that students who *annotate* (underline key passages
and make notes in the margin) their texts get higher grades
than those who do not annotate. So, to be a successful student, develop the habit of reading with pen in hand. As you
read, underline key sentences such as each paragraph's
topic sentence and the writer's thesis, if stated. When you
look up a definition or reference, write what you learn in
the margin so that you can reread that section with understanding. When you underline a writer's thesis, note in the
margin that this is the main idea. When you see a series of
examples or a list, label it as examples (exs) or list and then

number each one in the margin. If you read that there are *three* reasons for this or *four* ways of doing that, be sure to find all three or all four in the passage and label each one. Put a question mark next to a difficult passage—and then ask about it in class. Pay attention to transition words and phrases; these are designed to show you how the parts of the work fit together. Draw arrows to connect example to idea. Create your own abbreviations and symbols; just use them consistently. Become engaged with the text, as illustrated by the sample annotation in Figure 1.

8. *As you read and annotate, think about the writer's primary purpose in writing and the structures or strategies being used.* Keep in mind the strategies examined in Chapters 2 through 10 in this text as you read and identify the primary strategy

---

Johnson?
Descartes?

Thesis—
advan-
tages
of journal
writing

Thoreau—
example
of journal
writer

interesting
simile

"I write, therefore I am," wrote Samuel Johnson, altering   1
Descartes' famous dictum: "I think, therefore I am."

When writing in my journal, I feel keenly alive and some-how   2
get a glimpse of what Johnson meant.

My journal is a storehouse, a treasury for everything in my   3   ①
daily life: the stories I hear, the people I meet, the quotations I
like, and even the subtle signs and symbols I encounter that
speak to me indirectly. Unless I capture these things in writing,
I lose them.

All writers are such collectors, whether they keep a journal or   4
not; they see life clearly, a vision we only recognize when reading their books. Thoreau exemplifies the best in journal writing—
his celebrated *Walden* grew out of his journal entries.

By writing in my own journal, I often make discoveries. I see   5   ②
connections and conclusions that otherwise would not appear
obvious to me. I become a craftsman, like a potter or a carpen-
ter who makes a vase or a wooden stoop out of parts. Writing
is a source of pleasure when it involves such invention and
creation.   *meaning?*

I want to work on my writing, too, hone it into clear, read-   6   ③
able prose, and where better to practice my writing than in my
journal. Writing, I'm told, is a skill and improves with practice.
I secretly harbor this hope. So my journal becomes the arena
where I do battle with the written word.

Figure 1.   Sample annotation of first six paragraphs of Joseph Reynolds's "I Think (and Write in a Journal), Therefore I Am."

that gives the work its structure and/or purpose. Consider, as well, if the writer's primary purpose is to share feelings and experiences, to inform readers, or to argue for a claim. However, also keep in mind that writers can—and usually do—mix strategies and may have more than one purpose. For example, a writer using a contrast pattern can develop the points of contrast by providing examples. The writer's primary purpose may be to persuade, but at the same time readers are informed about a topic.

9. *Keep a reading journal.* In addition to annotating to aid reading comprehension, you may want to develop the habit of writing regularly in a journal. A reading journal records your responses to reading assignments but is more informal and personal than class notes. Keeping a journal gives you the chance to list impressions and feelings in addition to ideas that you may use in your next paper. Develop the habit of writing regularly and often. Chances are that both your reading and writing skills will improve.

Respond

10. *Review your reading.* To aid memory, review your reading immediately and then periodically. After finishing an assignment in this text, you can review by answering the questions following each selection. Then, look over your annotations and your reading journal shortly before class discussion of the assigned selection. *Warning: When you are called on, the instructor does not want to hear that you read the selection but cannot remember enough to answer the question!*

11. *Reflect.* In addition to reviewing to check comprehension, reflect on your reading and connect it to other parts of the course and other parts of your life. Remember that reading is not "drill." It is one of the most important ways that we gain new knowledge and new insights into ourselves and our world.

Guided Reading

Read the following article (published August 27, 1994), practicing all the guidelines for active reading. Remember to prepare, to read actively, and then to respond to your reading. Use the questions to the right of the article to guide your reading and thinking. Add your own annotations to the left.

Learning to Brake for Butterflies

ELLEN GOODMAN

Ellen Goodman (b. 1941) has been a syndicated columnist since 1976. Her columns have appeared in over 250 newspapers, and she has won a Pulitzer Prize for distinguished commentary. Although Goodman has written many thoughtful columns during her career, among her most memorable are those written from her summer home in Maine, reminding us of our need to slow down and reconnect to the natural world.

Casco Bay, Maine—I arrive here coasting on the 1 fumes of hioctane anxiety. The split-second timing of my daily life has adhered to my mood like a watch strapped to a wrist.

1. Where has the author gone? What has she tried to accomplish? Has she succeeded?

Behind me is a deadline met by the skin of my 2 teeth. A plane was late. A gas tank was empty. A boat was missed.

The carry-on baggage of my workaday life has 3 accompanied me onto the island. An L. L. Bean bag full of work, a fax machine, a laptop with a modem. I have all sorts of attachments to the great news machine that feeds me its fast-food through the electronic stomach tube.

Fully equipped this way, I tell myself that I can 4 get an extra week away. And so I spend that week wondering why I cannot get away.

For days I perform the magic trick unique to 5 my species. My head and my body are in two different places.

Like some computer-generated animation, my 6 body is on an island where the most important news is the weather report. My head is on the mainland of issues, ideas, policies. My body is

dressed in shorts, T-shirt, baseball cap. My mind
is in a suit, pantyhose, heels.

7   I am split across the great divide between this
place and the other. Neither here nor there. The
desk chair is full, the hammock empty. On the
road, I am able to see the brown-eyed Susans and
Queen Anne's lace only in my peripheral vision.
My focus remains elsewhere.

2. Why can't the author see the flowers?

8   I feel like a creature of the modern world who
has learned to live much—too much—of the time
on fast-forward and to pretend that it is a natural rhythm.

9   What would Charlie Chaplin make of these
Modern Times? Our impatience when the computer or the ATM machine "slows" down, or
when the plane is late? The way many of us have
to do two things at once, to ratchet up our productivity, that buzzword of the era, as if life were
an assembly line?

10   In some recess of this modern times mind-set,
I thought I could be on vacation and at work.
Instead, these two masters wrangle for custody
over me and I learned that there are two things
you cannot do at once: something and nothing.

3. What is Goodman's subject? Taking a vacation? Something else?

11   But finally, this morning, walking down the
country road at a distracted, aerobic, urban speed,
I brake for butterflies.

12   I am aware suddenly of four monarchs in full
orange and black robes at their regal work. They
have claimed a weedy plot of milkweeds as their
territory.

13   As I stand absolutely still, these four become
eight and then 12. My eye slowly adjusts to monarchs the way it adjusts to the dark or the way you
can gradually see blueberries on a green bush.

4. What is the effect on Goodman of standing in the midst of the butterflies?

14   There are 20 butterflies harvesting a plot no
bigger than my desk. Here are 30 in a space smaller than my office. The flock, the herd, has followed its summer taste buds onto my island the
way native tribes once came here for the clams.
They leave as suddenly as summer people.

The monarchs allow me, a commoner, to stand 15 among them in the milkweeds while they work. I feel foolishly and deliciously like some small-time anthropologist, some down-home Jane Goodall,[1] pleased to be accepted by the fluttering royals.

I am permitted to watch from inches away. For 16 half a minute, one monarch chooses my baseball cap as his throne. For half an hour I am not an intruder but part of the native landscape.

I remember now the lines of poetry I read in the 17 icy dead of last winter. After watching two mockingbirds, spinning and tossing "the white ribbons of their songs into the air," Mary Oliver wrote, "I had nothing/better to do/than listen./I mean this/seriously."

Such moments are rare in our world of Rapid 18 Eye Moments. We have been taught to hurry, to scan instead of read, to surf instead of watch.

5. What does the experience teach Goodman? What is her thesis? What does she want readers to understand?

We can go from zero to 100 miles an hour in 19 seconds—but only by leaving the natural world in the dust.

We pride ourselves on speed—and forget 20 that time goes by fast enough. The trick is to slow down long enough to listen, smell, touch, look, live.

At long last, the faxes and phones and ties all 21 disconnect. And for a summer afternoon, surrounded by monarchs, I know this: I have nothing better to do than watch. I mean this seriously.

6. Are many of us living much as the author does? Is this a problem in your view? Reflect on her ideas.

WRITING FOCUS:
USING SUMMARY, ANALYSIS, AND SYNTHESIS

You will have many occasions, in your composition class, in other classes, and in the workplace, to write using summary, analysis, and synthesis. The book review, for example, combines all three.

[1]Famous for her observations of chimpanzees in Africa.

Summary

Whether it is paragraph length or a few pages, a *summary* is a condensed, nonevaluative restatement of a writer's main ideas.

To prepare a good summary, read carefully and then follow these guidelines for writing:

1. Maintain a direct, objective style without using overly simplistic sentences.
2. Begin with the author's thesis and then present additional key points.
3. Exclude all specific examples, illustrations, or background sections. However, you may want to indicate the kinds of evidence or methods of development used.
4. Combine main ideas into fewer sentences than were used in the original article or book.
5. Select precise, accurate verbs (*asserts, argues, concludes*) rather than vague verbs (*says, talks about*) that provide only a list of ideas. Pay attention to word choice to avoid such judging words as: "Jones then develops the *silly* idea that . . ."

With these guidelines in mind, read the following summary of Isaac Asimov's "Science and the Sense of Wonder" (pp. 463–467) and consider why it needs revision.

Summary #1

In "Science and the Sense of Wonder," Isaac Asimov quotes Whitman's poem "When I Heard the Learn'd Astronomer." He says that Whitman's view of science is convenient and agrees that the night sky is beautiful. Asimov then talks about what he sees in the night sky—planets and the stars that are really suns. He then says that the Milky Way—our galaxy—has more stars in it than we can see, and beyond it are many galaxies that we can't see either. All of this was discovered after Whitman died.

We can agree that the writer of this summary has read Asimov's essay, but we can also assert that the summary lacks focus and may even be misleading in places. The writer has gone through the essay, picked out some ideas, and strung them together. One result is no clear statement of Asimov's main idea. Another result is the implication (in sentence 2) that Asimov agrees with Whitman's view of both the night sky and science, a misrepresentation of Asimov's position. Here is a much-improved version.

Summary #2

In "Science and the Sense of Wonder," Isaac Asimov challenges Whitman's view that scientists, reducing nature to charts and numbers, miss the beauty of nature. Asimov, quoting Whitman's poem "When I Heard the Learn'd Astronomer," uses the astronomer and the beautiful night sky as his examples. He argues that it is the sky of the astronomer that produces the greater sense of wonder and awe. When we understand what we are looking at—not bright lights but planets and suns—and when we understand just how huge the "sky" really is—not just our own galaxy but thousands of galaxies—we will recognize that Whitman's view was "a stultified and limited beauty." Asimov concludes that modern science has given us a vision almost beyond our ability to imagine.

Analysis

The process of analysis is not new to you. You will find chapters on process analysis and causal analysis in this text. The process of comparison (or contrast) is also analysis. To establish some guidelines for writing analysis, let's consider one paragraph in an essay that analyzes a writer's style.

Suppose your thesis is that the writer uses connotative words, clever metaphors, and ironic understatement to convey her attitude. You will need a paragraph on each element of style: word choice, metaphors, irony, and understatement. Follow these guidelines for each paragraph.

1. Have a *topic sentence* that conveys the paragraph's subject and ties the paragraph to the essay's thesis.
2. Quote or paraphrase to present *examples* of the element of style, at least three examples taken from throughout the work.
3. *Explain* how the examples support the paragraph's topic sentence and hence your thesis. This is your

analysis, the "glue" that holds the paragraph together and makes your point.

4. Use the correct tense. Analyze style in the *present tense*.

Here is one paragraph from student Alan Peterson's style analysis of an essay by Ellen Goodman.

Analysis

Perhaps the most prevalent element of style present in Goodman's article, and a dominant characteristic of her essay style, is her use of metaphors. From the opening sentences through to the end, this article is full of metaphors. Keeping with the general focus of the piece (the essay appeared on Thanksgiving day), many of the metaphors liken food to family. Her references include "a cornucopia of family," "chicken-sized households" and "a turkey-sized family," people who "feast on the sounds as well as the tastes," and voices that "add relish to a story." She imparts that a politician can use the word "family" like "gravy poured over the entire plate." Going to the airport to pick up members of these disjointed American families has become "a holiday ritual as common as pumpkin pie." Goodman draws parallels between the process of "choosing" people to be with us and the simple ritual of passing seconds at the table. Indeed, the essay's mood emphasizes the comparison of and inextricable bond between food and family.

Synthesis

There are many reasons for drawing on two or more sources to develop your own piece of writing, and there is more than one way to acknowledge sources to readers. But what you must do, whether with a formal pattern of documentation or informally including details of author and title in your essay, is *always* let readers know where ideas and information not original with you have been found. Follow these general guidelines for creating synthesis.

1. Have a clear topic sentence in each paragraph. Material from sources is used to support an idea; it is not just "filler."

2. Combine information/ideas from several sources. If you devote each paragraph to only one source,

you are writing a series of summaries. You are not synthesizing.

3. Put most of the borrowed material in your own words. When necessary, use brief quotations.
4. Make the sources of your borrowed material absolutely clear throughout. Use introductory tags; guide your reader through the material.
5. Explain and discuss the material. Do not just dump material from sources on your reader. The result is a list, not a synthesis.

The following paragraph, part of a documented report on theories of dinosaur warmbloodedness, illustrates one student's command of synthesis. (The essay concludes with a "works cited" page that includes the sources cited after the paragraph.)

Synthesis

The body weight of a dinosaur provides one of the arguments supporting the assertion that some dinosaurs were endotherms. Don Lessem reports that one reason for paleontologists' change of thinking arose in 1964 from Dr. John Ostrom's discovery of *Deinonchyus*, "terrible claw," in central Montana (43). Christopher Lampton argues that since *Deinonchyus* had large claws on its feet and was only as tall as a human, it must have been endothermic to remain active enough to flee from larger predators and to attack its own prey with its terrible claw (90). Lampton quotes Ostrom in further support of *Deinonchyus's* endothermy: "'It does not surprise us to see a hawk slash with its talons. . . . Reptiles are just not capable of such intricate maneuvers, such delicate balance'" (88–89). Lampton concludes that *Deinonchyus* could not have been coldblooded and still remain an aggressive predator that actively hunted by slashing with the claws on its feet (89). The evidence suggests that at least this one dinosaur was warmblooded.

Works Cited

Lampton, Christopher. *New Theories on Dinosaurs*. New York: Watts, 1989.

Lessem, Don. *Dinosaurs Rediscovered: New Findings Which Are Revolutionizing Dinosaur Science*. New York: Simon, 1992.

Getting Started

Read the following poem by Richard Wilbur; it is not a difficult poem to read, I promise! Enjoy his images and metaphors as you picture the scene he re-creates. Then think about what Wilbur has to say about the writing process. Use these questions to guide your reading and thinking:

1. What is his daughter doing in her room? Why are there silences in between the periods of typing?
2. Five stanzas are about a bird trapped in his daughter's room. What does this story have to do with his daughter's current activity?
3. What does he wish for his daughter? Why, at the end of the poem, does he wish her the same thing—but harder?
4. What would you say is the basic meaning or point of the poem?
5. Why has this poem been included in this chapter?

Did you like this poem? If so, do you think you can use it as a useful reminder or as a guide through this writing course? If not, why not? You may want to answer these questions in a journal entry or have answers ready for class discussion.

The Writer

RICHARD WILBUR

Born in New York City, Richard Wilbur (b. 1921) attended Amherst College and fought in World War II. He then taught at several colleges, including Harvard and Smith. He has several collections of poetry and has published literary criticism and children's books. His books have led to two Pulitzer Prizes and a National Book Award. The following poem is from his collection *The Mind Reader* (1971).

In her room at the prow of the house
Where light breaks, and the windows are tossed with linden,
My daughter is writing a story.

I pause in the stairwell, hearing
From her shut door a commotion of typewriter-keys   5
Like a chain hauled over a gunwale.*

Young as she is, the stuff
Of her life is a great cargo, and some of it heavy:
I wish her a lucky passage.

But now it is she who pauses,
As if to reject my thought and its easy figure.
A stillness greatens, in which

The whole house seems to be thinking,   10
And then she is at it again with a bunched clamor
Of strokes, and again is silent.

I remember the dazed starling
Which was trapped in that very room, two years ago;
How we stole in, lifted a sash   15

And retreated, not to affright it,
And how for a helpless hour, through the crack of the door,
We watched the sleek, wild, dark

And iridescent creature
Batter against the brilliance, drop like a glove   20
To the hard floor, or the desk-top,

And wait then, humped and bloody,
For the wits to try it again; and how our spirits
Rose when, suddenly sure,

It lifted off from a chair-back,   25
Beating a smooth course for the right window
And clearing the sill of the world.

It is always a matter, my darling.
Of life or death, as I had forgotten. I wish
What I wished you before, but harder.   30

*Upper edge of the side of a boat, pronounced gün′əl

The Watcher at the Gates

GAIL GODWIN

With degrees from the Universities of North Carolina and Iowa, Gail Godwin (b. 1937) began her career as a journalist and English instructor before becoming primarily a fiction writer. She has published a collection of short stories and several novels, including her 1982 best-seller *A Woman and Two Daughters*. In the following essay, published in 1977 in the *New York Times Book Review*, Godwin examines the sources of writer's block and offers some solutions to the problem.

Questions to Guide Your Reading

1. How did reading about a Watcher at the Gates make the author feel?
2. What two unpleasant traits do most Watchers have?

---

1   I first realized I was not the only writer who had a restraining critic who lived inside me and sapped the juice from green inspirations when I was leafing through Freud's *Interpretation of Dreams* a few years ago. Ironically, it was my "inner critic" who had sent me to Freud. I was writing a novel, and my heroine was in the middle of a dream, and then I lost faith in my own invention and rushed to "an authority" to check whether she could have such a dream. In the chapter on dream interpretation, I came upon the following passage that has helped me free myself, in some measure, from my critic and has led to many pleasant and interesting exchanges with other writers.

2   Freud quotes Schiller, who is writing a letter to a friend. The friend complains of his lack of creative power. Schiller replies with an allegory. He says it is not good if the intellect examines too closely the ideas pouring in at the gates. "In isolation, an idea may be quite insignificant, and venturesome in the extreme, but it may acquire importance from an idea which follows it. . . . In the case of a creative mind, it seems to me, the intellect has withdrawn its watchers from the gates, and the ideas rush in pell-mell,

and only then does it review and inspect the multitude. You are ashamed or afraid of the momentary and passing madness which is found in all real creators, the longer or shorter duration of which distinguishes the thinking artist from the dreamer . . . you reject too soon and discriminate too severely."

So that's what I had: a Watcher at the Gates. I decided to get   3
to know him better. I discussed him with other writers, who told me some of the quirks and habits of their Watchers, each of whom was as individual as his host, and all of whom seemed passionately dedicated to one goal: rejecting too soon and discriminating too severely.

It is amazing the lengths a Watcher will go to keep you from   4
pursuing the flow of your imagination. Watchers are notorious pencil sharpeners, ribbon changers, plant waterers, home repairers and abhorrers of messy rooms or messy pages. They are compulsive looker-uppers. They are superstitious scaredy-cats. They cultivate self-important eccentricities they think are suitable for "writers." And they'd rather die (and kill your inspiration with them) than risk making a fool of themselves.

My Watcher has a wasteful penchant for 20-pound bond   5
paper above and below the carbon of the first draft. "What's the good of writing out a whole page," he whispers begrudgingly, "if you just have to write it over again later? Get it perfect the first time!" My Watcher adores stopping in the middle of a morning's work to drive down to the library to check on the name of a flower or a World War II battle or a line of metaphysical poetry. "You can't possibly go on till you've got this right" he admonishes. I go and get the car keys.

Other Watchers have informed their writers that: 6

"Whenever you get a really good sentence you should stop   7
in the middle of it and go on tomorrow. Otherwise you might run dry."

"Don't try and continue with your book till your dental   8
appointment is over. When you're worried about your teeth, you can't think about art."

Another Watcher makes his owner pin his finished pages to   9
a clothesline and read them through binoculars "to see how they look from a distance." Countless other Watchers demand "bribes" for taking the day off: lethal doses of caffeine, alcoholic doses of Scotch or vodka or wine.

10   There are various ways to outsmart, pacify or coexist with your Watcher. Here are some I have tried, or my writer friends have tried, with success:

11   Look for situations when he's likely to be off guard. Write too fast for him in an unexpected place, at an unexpected time. (Virginia Woolf captured the "diamonds in the dustheap" by writing at a "rapid haphazard gallop" in her diary.) Write when very tired. Write in purple ink on the back of a Master Charge statement. Write whatever comes into your mind while the kettle is boiling and make the steam whistle your deadline. (Deadlines are a great way to outdistance the Watcher.)

12   Disguise what you are writing. If your Watcher refuses to let you get on with your story or novel, write a "letter" instead, telling your "correspondent" what you are going to write in your story or next chapter. Dash off a "review" of your own unfinished opus. It will stand up like a bully to your Watcher the next time he throws more obstacles in your path. If you write yourself a good one.

13   Get to know your Watcher. He's yours. Do a drawing of him (or her). Pin it to the wall of your study and turn it gently to the wall when necessary. Let your Watcher feel needed. Watchers are excellent critics after inspiration has been captured; they are dependable, sharp-eyed readers of things already set down. Keep your Watcher in shape and he'll have less time to keep you from shaping. If he's really ruining your whole working day sit down, as Jung did with his personal demons, and write him a letter. On a very bad day I once wrote my Watcher a letter. "Dear Watcher," I wrote, "What is it you're so afraid I'll do?" Then I held his pen for him, and he replied instantly with a candor that has kept me from truly despising him.

14   "Fail," he wrote back.

Expanding Vocabulary

1. In her essay Godwin refers to four people and one work. She does not identify them because she expects her readers to know them. Find the people and book and identify each one in a sentence. Use your dictionary or a biographical dictionary in your library or online.

2. Match each word in column A with its definition in column B. When in doubt, first find the word in the essay and look for con-

text clues to aid your understanding of the word's meaning. Then, if necessary, use your dictionary to complete the matching exercise. The number in parentheses is the number of the paragraph in which the word appears.

Column A	Column B
restraining (1)	note differences
sapped (1)	those who strongly dislike
allegory (2)	deadly
duration (2)	liking
discriminate (2)	holding back
severely (2)	symbolic story
notorious (4)	work
abhorrers (4)	frankness
eccentricities (4)	weakened or cut off
penchant (5)	calm down
begrudgingly (5)	reluctantly
admonishes (5)	length of time in an activity
lethal (9)	famous in a negative way
pacify (10)	warns
opus (12)	seriously or harshly
candor (13)	oddities

Understanding Content

1. Where did Godwin find the idea of a Watcher at the Gates?
2. What are some of the tricks Watchers use to keep us from writing?
3. What do Watchers fear? Why do many writers have a Watcher at the Gates problem?
4. What are some ways writers can outsmart their Watchers?

Drawing Inferences about Thesis and Purpose

1. What is a Watcher at the Gates? That is, what problem does the Watcher stand for?
2. What is Godwin's primary purpose in writing? To develop the idea of the Watcher? To offer some understanding of writing anxiety? To explain ways to get rid of writing anxiety?

Analyzing Strategies and Style

1. What strategy does Godwin use when she calls a restraining critic a Watcher at the Gates and suggests that writers get to know him or her? What is effective about this strategy, this approach to her subject?

2. Godwin opens with a metaphor: "sapped the juice from green inspirations." Explain the metaphor.
3. Godwin's piece is a good example of a personal essay. On the basis of your study of this essay, list the characteristics of a personal essay.

Thinking Critically

1. Follow Godwin's suggestion about getting to know your Watcher. Begin by drawing, as best you can, a picture of your Watcher. Then write a brief description of this person or thing.
2. What are some of your favorite excuses for avoiding writing? Now pretend that you are Gail Godwin; how might she tell you to get around these excuses and go on to write?

On Reading and Becoming a Writer

TERRY MCMILLAN

African-American writer Terry McMillan (b. 1951) has published several novels, including *Disappearing Acts* (1989), *Waiting to Exhale* (1992), and *How Stella Got Her Groove Back* (1996). An instructor in writing at the University of Arizona, McMillan has also edited *Five for Five: The Films of Spike Lee* (1991) and *Breaking Ice: An Anthology of Contemporary African-American Fiction* (1990). The following excerpt, from the introduction to *Breaking Ice*, recounts McMillan's exciting discovery of black writers and her development as a writer.

Questions to Guide Your Reading

1. What does McMillan confess to lacking when she was young?
2. What did she learn from her college course in African-American literature?

1   As a child, I didn't know that African-American people wrote books. I grew up in a small town in northern Michigan, where the only books I came across were the Bible and required reading for school. I did not read for pleasure, and it wasn't

until I was sixteen when I got a job shelving books at the public library that I got lost in a book. It was a biography of Louisa May Alcott. I was excited because I had not really read about poor white folks before; her father was so eccentric and idealistic that at the time I just thought he was crazy. I related to Louisa because she had to help support her family at a young age, which was what I was doing at the library.

Then one day I went to put a book away, and saw James   2
Baldwin's face staring up at me. "Who in the world is this?" I wondered. I remember feeling embarrassed and did not read his book because I was too afraid. I couldn't imagine that he'd have anything better or different to say than Thomas Mann, Henry Thoreau, Ralph Waldo Emerson, Nathaniel Hawthorne, Ernest Hemingway, William Faulkner, etc. and a horde of other mostly white male writers that I'd been introduced to in Literature 101 in high school. I mean, not only had there not been any African-American authors included in any of those textbooks, but I'd never been given a clue that if we did have anything important to say that somebody would actually publish it. Needless to say, I was not just naïve, but had not yet acquired an ounce of black pride. I never once questioned why there were no representative works by us in any of those textbooks. After all, I had never heard of any African-American writers, and no one I knew hardly read *any* books.

And then things changed.   3

It wasn't until after Malcolm X had been assassinated that I   4
found out who he was. I know I should be embarrassed about this, but I'm not. I read Alex Haley's biography of him and it literally changed my life. First and foremost, I realized that there was no reason to be ashamed of being black, that it was ridiculous. That we had a history, and much to be proud of. I began to notice how we had actually been treated as less than human; began to see our strength as a people whereas I'd only been made aware of our inferiorities. I started thinking about my role in the world and not just on my street. I started *thinking*. Thinking about things I'd never thought about before, and the thinking turned into questions. But I had more questions than answers.

So I went to college. When I looked through the catalog and   5
saw a class called Afro-American Literature, I signed up and couldn't wait for the first day of class. Did *we* really have

enough writers to warrant an entire class? I remember the text-book was called *Dark Symphony: Negro Literature in America* because I still have it. I couldn't believe the rush I felt over and over once I discovered Countee Cullen, Langston Hughes, Ann Petry, Zora Neale Hurston, Ralph Ellison, Jean Toomer, Richard Wright, and rediscovered and read James Baldwin, to name just a few. I'm surprised I didn't need glasses by the end of the semester. My world opened up. I accumulated and gained a totally new insight about, and perception of, our lives as "black" people, as if I had been an outsider and was finally let in. To dis-cover that our lives held as much significance and importance as our white counterparts was more than gratifying, it was exhilarating. Not only had we lived diverse, interesting, provocative, and relentless lives, but during, through, and as a result of all these painful experiences, some folks had taken the time to write it down.

6   Not once, throughout my entire four years as an under-graduate, did it occur to me that I might one day *be* a writer. I mean, these folks had genuine knowledge and insight. They also had a fascination with the truth. They had something to write about. Their work was bold, not flamboyant. They learned how to exploit the language so that readers would be affected by what they said and how they said it. And they had talent.

7   I never considered myself to be in possession of much of the above, and yet when I was twenty years old, the first man I fell in love with broke my heart. I was so devastated and felt so helpless that my reaction manifested itself in a poem. I did not sit down and say, "I'm going to write a poem about this." It was more like magic. I didn't even know I was writing a poem until I had written it. Afterward, I felt lighter, as if something had happened to lessen the pain. And when I read this "thing" I was shocked because I didn't know where the words came from. I was scared, to say the least, about what I had just experienced, because I didn't understand what had happened.

8   For the next few days, I read that poem over and over in dis-belief because *I* had written it. One day, a colleague saw it lying on the kitchen table and read it. I was embarrassed and shocked when he said he liked it, then went on to tell me that he had just started a black literary magazine at the college and he wanted to publish it. Publish it! He was serious and it found its way onto a typeset page. Seeing my name in print excited me. And

from that point on, if a leaf moved on a tree, I wrote a poem about it. If a crack in the sidewalk glistened, surely there was a poem in that. Some of these verbose things actually got published in various campus newspapers that were obviously desperate to fill up space. I did not call myself a poet; I told people I wrote poems. Years passed.   9

Those poems started turning into sentences and I started get-   10
ting nervous. What the hell did I think I was doing? Writing these little go-nowhere vignettes. All these beginnings. And who did I think I was, trying to tell a story? And who cared? Even though I had no idea what I was doing, all I knew was that I was beginning to realize that a lot of things mattered to me, things disturbed me, things that I couldn't change. Writing became an outlet for my dissatisfactions, distaste, and my way of trying to make sense of what I saw happening around me. It was my way of trying to fix what I thought was broken. It later became the only way to explore personally what I didn't understand. The problem, however, was that I was writing more about ideas than people. Everything was so "large," and eventually I had to find a common denominator. I ended up asking myself what I really cared about: it was people, and particularly African-American people.

The whole idea of taking myself seriously as a writer was ter-   11
rifying. I didn't know any writers. Didn't know how you knew if you "had" it or not. Didn't know if I was or would ever be good enough. I didn't know how you went about the business of writing, and besides, I sincerely wanted to make a decent living. (I had read the horror stories of how so few writers were able to live off of their writing alone, many having lived like bohemians.) At first, I thought being a social worker was the right thing to do, since I was bent on saving the world (I was an idealistic twenty-two years old), but when I found out I couldn't do it that way, I had to figure out another way to make an impact on folks. A positive impact. I ended up majoring in journalism because writing was "easy" for me, but it didn't take long for me to learn that I did not like answering the "who, what, when, where, and why" of anything. I then—upon the urging of my mother and friends who had graduated and gotten "normal" jobs—decided to try something that would still allow me to "express myself" but was relatively safer, though still risky: I went to film school. Of course what was inherent

in my quest to find my "spot" in the world was this whole notion of affecting people on some grand scale. Malcolm and Martin caused me to think like this. Writing for me, as it's turned out, is philanthropy. It didn't take years for me to realize the impact that other writers' work had had on me, and if I was going to write, I did not want to write inconsequential, mediocre stories that didn't conjure up or arouse much in a reader. So I had to start by exciting myself and paying special attention to what I cared about, what mattered to me.

12   Film school didn't work out. Besides, I never could stop writing, which ultimately forced me to stop fighting it. It took even longer to realize that writing was not something you aspired to, it was something you did because you had to. . . .

13   I've been teaching writing on the university level now for three years, and much to my dismay, rarely have I ever had an African-American student. I wish there were more ways to encourage young people to give writing a shot. Many of them still seem to be intimidated by the English language, and think of writing as "hard"—as in Composition 101–hard. So many of them are set on "making it" (solely in material terms) that we find many of our students majoring in the "guaranteed" professions: the biological sciences, law, engineering, business, etc. If I can make an appeal to those who will read this anthology, I would like to say this to them: If for whatever reason you do not derive a genuine sense of excitement or satisfaction from your chosen field, if you are majoring in these disciplines because of a parent's insistence, if you are dissatisfied with the world to any extent and find yourself "secretly" jotting it down whenever or wherever you can; if you don't understand why people (yourself included) do the things that they do and it plagues you like an itch—consider taking a fiction writing course. Find out if there are African-American writing groups or *any* workshops that are available in your area. Then write. Read as much "serious" fiction as you can—and not just African-American authors. Then, keep writing. "Push it," says Annie Dillard. "Examine all things intensely and relentlessly. Probe and search . . . do not leave it, do not course over it, as if it were understood, but instead follow it down until you see it in the mystery of its own specificity and strength."

14   Persist.

Expanding Vocabulary

Determine the meaning of each of the following words either from its context in this essay or from studying your dictionary. Then select five of the words and use each one in a separate sentence of your own. The number in parentheses is the number of the paragraph in which the word appears.

eccentric (1)	bohemians (11)
exhilarating (5)	philanthropy (11)
provocative (5)	inconsequential (11)
flamboyant (6)	mediocre (11)
verbose (8)	conjure (11)
vignettes (10)	specificity (13)

Understanding Content

1. In what way did the author identify with Louisa May Alcott?
2. What writers was McMillan introduced to in high school? What writers were not part of her required reading?
3. How did McMillan come to write and publish her first poem? Why did she not want to call herself a poet? What seems to have been her attitude toward writers and writing?
4. What were her reasons for writing fiction? How did she narrow and focus her writing?
5. Why did she go to film school? What was the result?
6. What dismays McMillan as a college teacher? What reasons does she offer for students' not taking a fiction writing course? What advice does she give to potential African-American writers?

Drawing Inferences about Thesis and Purpose

1. What is McMillan's purpose in writing?
2. From your reading of this essay, what sort of person do you imagine McMillan to be? Describe her personality.

Analyzing Strategies and Style

1. How would you characterize the style in which this essay is written? (Style is shaped from word choice and sentence structure.) List examples of McMillan's word choice and sentence patterns that help to create the essay's style.
2. What is McMillan's tone? That is, what voice do you hear? How does she create that tone?

Thinking Critically

1. McMillan presents a list of writers in paragraph 2 and another list in paragraph 5. How many writers from the first list do you know? How many from the second list? From your own survey (or the class's as a whole), would you conclude that students today are more familiar than McMillan was with African-American authors, or has the situation not changed much?
2. McMillan believes that students think of fiction writing as "hard" in the same way that freshman composition is hard. Which course do you think would be harder for you? Why?
3. The author concludes with advice directed to the expected audience for *Breaking Ice*, African-American students, some of whom may possibly become writers. How can her advice be applied to composition writers as well as to fiction writers? Explain.

How to Write with Style

KURT VONNEGUT

Kurt Vonnegut (b. 1922) is one of the most popular contemporary novelists. A former employee of General Electric in public relations, Vonnegut is now famous for such novels as *Cat's Cradle* (1963), *Slaughterhouse Five* (1969), and, most recently, *Timequake* (1993). The following advice on style was published by International Paper Company as one of a series of articles used as ads on the "Power of the Printed Word."

Questions to Guide Your Reading

1. What is the most compelling element in a writer's style?
2. What will happen when you break rules, give new meanings to words, or try to create an avant-garde style?

1   Newspaper reporters and technical writers are trained to reveal almost nothing about themselves in their writings. This makes them freaks in the world of writers, since almost all of the other ink-stained wretches in that world reveal a lot about themselves to readers. We call these revelations, accidental and intentional, elements of style.

These revelations tell us as readers what sort of person it is 2
with whom we are spending time. Does the writer sound ignorant or informed, stupid or bright, crooked or honest, humor-
less or playful—? And on and on.

Why should you examine your writing style with the idea 3
of improving it? Do so as a mark of respect for your readers,
whatever you're writing. If you scribble your thoughts any
which way, your readers will surely feel that you care nothing
about them. They will mark you down as an egomaniac or a
chowderhead—or worse, they will stop reading you.

The most damning revelation you can make about yourself 4
is that you do not know what is interesting and what is not.
Don't you yourself like or dislike writers mainly for what they
choose to show you or make you think about? Did you ever
admire an empty-headed writer for his or her mastery of the
language? No.

So your own winning style must begin with ideas in 5
your head.

1. Find a Subject You Care About

Find a subject you care about and which you in your heart 6
feel others should care about. It is this genuine caring, and not
your games with language, which will be the most compelling
and seductive element in your style.

I am not urging you to write a novel, by the way—although 7
I would not be sorry if you wrote one, provided you genuine-
ly cared about something. A petition to the mayor about a pot-
hole in front of your house or a love letter to the girl next door
will do.

2. Do Not Ramble, Though

I won't ramble on about that. 8

3. Keep It Simple

As for your use of language: Remember that two great mas- 9
ters of language, William Shakespeare and James Joyce, wrote
sentences which were almost childlike when their subjects were
most profound. "To be or not to be?" asks Shakespeare's Hamlet.

The longest word is three letters long. Joyce, when he was frisky, could put together a sentence as intricate and as glittering as a necklace for Cleopatra, but my favorite sentence in his short story "Eveline" is this one: "She was tired." At that point in the story, no other words could break the heart of a reader as those three words do.

10   Simplicity of language is not only reputable, but perhaps even sacred. The *Bible* opens with a sentence well within the writing skills of a lively fourteen-year-old: "In the beginning God created the heaven and the earth."

4. Have the Guts to Cut

11   It may be that you, too, are capable of making necklaces for Cleopatra, so to speak. But your eloquence should be the servant of the ideas in your head. Your rule might be this: If a sentence, no matter how excellent, does not illuminate your subject in some new and useful way, scratch it out.

5. Sound Like Yourself

12   The writing style which is most natural for you is bound to echo the speech you heard when a child. English was the novelist Joseph Conrad's third language, and much that seems piquant in his use of English was no doubt colored by his first language, which was Polish. And lucky indeed is the writer who has grown up in Ireland, for the English spoken there is so amusing and musical. I myself grew up in Indianapolis, where common speech sounds like a band saw cutting galvanized tin, and employs a vocabulary as unornamental as a monkey wrench.

13   In some of the more remote hollows of Appalachia, children still grow up hearing songs and locutions of Elizabethan times. Yes, and many Americans grow up hearing a language other than English, or an English dialect a majority of Americans cannot understand.

14   All these varieties of speech are beautiful, just as the varieties of butterflies are beautiful. No matter what your first language, you should treasure it all your life. If it happens not to be standard English, and if it shows itself when you write standard English, the result is usually delightful, like a very pretty girl with one eye that is green and one that is blue.

I myself find that I trust my own writing most, and others 15
seem to trust it most, too, when I sound most like a person from
Indianapolis, which is what I am. What alternatives do I have?
The one most vehemently recommended by teachers has no
doubt been pressed on you, as well: to write like cultivated Eng-
lishmen of a century or more ago.

6. Say What You Mean to Say

I used to be exasperated by such teachers, but am no more. 16
I understand now that all those antique essays and stories with
which I was to compare my own work were not magnificent for
their datedness or foreignness, but for saying precisely what
their authors meant them to say. My teachers wished me to
write accurately, always selecting the most effective words, and
relating the words to one another unambiguously, rigidly, like
parts of a machine. The teachers did not want to turn me into
an Englishman after all. They hoped that I would become
understandable—and therefore understood. And there went
my dream of doing with words what Pablo Picasso did with
paint or what any number of jazz idols did with music. If I broke
all the rules of punctuation, had words mean whatever I wanted them to mean, and strung them together higgledy-piggledy,
I would simply not be understood. So you, too, had better avoid
Picasso-style or jazz-style writing, if you have something worth
saying and wish to be understood.

Readers want our pages to look very much like pages they 17
have seen before. Why? This is because they themselves have a
tough job to do, and they need all the help they can get from us.

7. Pity the Readers

They have to identify thousands of little marks on paper, and 18
make sense of them immediately. They have to *read*, an art so
difficult that most people don't really master it even after having studied it all through grade school and high school—twelve
long years.

So this discussion must finally acknowledge that our stylis- 19
tic options as writers are neither numerous nor glamorous, since
our readers are bound to be such imperfect artists. Our audience requires us to be sympathetic and patient teachers, even

willing to simplify and clarify—whereas we would rather soar high above the crowd, singing like nightingales.

20   That is the bad news. The good news is that we Americans are governed under a unique Constitution, which allows us to write whatever we please without fear of punishment. So the most meaningful aspect of our styles, which is what we choose to write about, is utterly unlimited.

8. For Really Detailed Advice

21   For a discussion of literary style in a narrower sense, in a more technical sense, I commend to your attention *The Elements of Style*, by William Strunk, Jr., and E. B. White (Allyn & Bacon, 2000). E. B. White is, of course, one of the most admirable literary stylists this country has so far produced.

22   You should realize, too, that no one would care how well or badly Mr. White expressed himself, if he did not have perfectly enchanting things to say.

Expanding Vocabulary

Match each word in column A with its definition in column B. When in doubt, first find the word in the essay and look for context clues to aid your understanding of the word's meaning. Then, if necessary, use your dictionary to complete the matching exercise. The number in parentheses is the number of the paragraph in which the word appears.

Column A	Column B
egomaniac (3)	having many complexly arranged parts
chowderhead (3)	moving, expressive language use
intricate (9)	iron or steel with zinc coating
reputable (10)	appealingly provocative
eloquence (11)	one who is pretty dense, like a thick soup
piquant (12)	particular style of speaking
galvanized (12)	angrily impatient
locutions (13)	one who has an obsessive focus on ✓ the self
exasperated (16)	in utter disorder
higgledy-piggledy (16)	esteemed, of good reputation

Understanding Content

1. How will readers respond to you if you "scribble your thoughts any which way"?
2. A winning style begins with what?
3. List the specific guidelines Vonnegut provides, each in a separate sentence.
4. Explain Vonnegut's rule for cutting.
5. Why is it best to sound like yourself?

Drawing Inferences about Thesis and Purpose

1. What is Vonnegut's topic?
2. More than anything else, what does your style tell readers?
3. What, for Vonnegut, is the most important "element of style"?

Analyzing Strategies and Style

1. The author has little to say about his second point. What does he gain by his brevity?
2. Find some examples of clever word choice or metaphors. Explain why they are effective.

Thinking Critically

1. Which of Vonnegut's points do you think is most important for writers? Why? Which point is most important for *you* to focus on as you work on your writing? Why?
2. Vonnegut writes that simplicity is "perhaps even sacred." Explain how simple language can be called sacred. Is this a new idea for you? Does it make sense?
3. Vonnegut begins and ends emphasizing the importance of having something to say. Do you agree with him that this is the most important element of style? Why or why not?

MAKING CONNECTIONS

---

1. Several writers in this chapter refer to other writers in their essays. Select a writer referred to in this chapter about whom you know little and read about that writer in at least two sources in your library or online. (Your library will own several biographical indexes, both in paper and electronic

formats.) Then prepare a short biography (that includes a list of the author's major works) for your class.

2. Godwin, Vonnegut, and McMillan are all authors of novels. After becoming acquainted with each of these writers through their essays in this chapter, which one's novels do you most want to read? Be prepared to defend your choice. Alternatively, read a novel by the writer of your choice and prepare a two-page summary and evaluation of the novel for your class.

3. We all understand that both our reading and our writing skills improve with an expanded vocabulary. Explore various online dictionaries and thesauruses to find one you like. Use one not just for reference but to build your vocabulary. The *Merriam-Webster Online Dictionary* has a Word Game of the Day (*www.mw.com*); Thesaurus.com has a word-of-the-day e-mail service (*www.thesaurus.com*). Check out at least one of these.

TOPICS AND GUIDELINES FOR WRITING

---

1. Terry McMillan offers some insight into how she creates her literature. How do you get started on a piece of writing? How do ideas come to you? What strategies do you use? In an essay explain the ways you get started on a piece of writing. Your purpose in writing should be either to offer your strategies as a useful way to get started or to offer your approach as a way to avoid because, on reflection, you have decided that your approach is not effective.

2. How have you learned to fool your Watcher at the Gates (see Godwin, p. 18–22)? In an essay give your advice to anxious writers for avoiding writer's block, based on techniques that have worked for you. Think of your essay as possibly a feature article in your college paper. (Remember: If you use the term "Watcher at the Gates," give Godwin credit.)

3. What kind of reading do you enjoy most? Do you like science fiction, romance novels, the newspaper, magazines devoted to a special interest or hobby? In an essay explain why you

enjoy the kind of material you usually read. Illustrate your reasons with specific examples from your reading.

4. Terry McMillan advises future writers to read as much fiction as they can. What are good reasons for reading? In an essay explain and support reasons for encouraging college students to read more.

5. This chapter's introduction offers some reasons for writing. Why should adults become competent writers? Why should an engineer, a banker, or a teacher be able to write? In an essay answer these questions. Focus either on the practical considerations of a particular job or on more philosophical reasons having to do with personal growth and discovery or general career needs. Remember to explain and illustrate each reason.

2

Using Narration

Growing Up, Growing Wiser

"Once upon a time there lived a princess"—so the fairy tale begins. A story, or narrative, relates a series of events in time sequence. If the narrative relates events that are made up out of the writer's imagination, then the narrative is *fiction*. If the narrative relates events that have taken place, it is *nonfiction*. Nonfiction narratives are found in histories, biographies, newspaper articles, and essays that use narration as a development strategy.

In some writing, distinction between fiction and nonfiction blurs. The historical novel, for example, is fiction bound by the author's research of a particular time and place. Many feature articles in newspapers and magazines reveal the use of such story elements as conflict and point of view. Santha Rama Rau's "By Any Other Name" is a good example of nonfiction that strikes us as very much like a story.

When to Use Narration

Your instructor may ask you to write a story, a narrative account drawn, perhaps, from some incident in your life, complete with characters and dialogue. More likely, you will be asked to draw on incidents from your life to develop a narrative essay. This means that narration will be used as a technique for developing a main idea or thesis. Your purpose in writing may be to share experiences or inform readers of a different time, place, or culture, or some blending of both purposes. (In other classes, you may use narrative to answer test questions, especially in history classes.) However you see your primary purpose in writing, the incidents you select, the way you tell about them, and the reflective comments you include will add up to a statement (or strong implication) of the main point you want to make.

How to Use Narration

Purpose and Thesis

The fewer observations you make about the significance of the events you narrate, the more you need to rely on the telling of the events to carry your meaning. Rau, for example, tells her story with only the briefest of comments about the significance of one's first day at school. Gaye Wagner, on the other hand, reflects on the events she narrates, observing in paragraph 4, "With the death of a comrade, I understood that I was inside the fence." Only you can decide just how much comment you want in a given narrative essay and where those comments should be placed to greatest effect. But first, and most important, have a clear sense of purpose and thesis. An unfocused retelling of some event in your life does not become a polished essay.

When thinking about experiences you might use in a narrative essay, reflect on your purpose and subject as a way to decide on a thesis. Ask, "Why do I want to tell readers about a particular incident?" "What insights into human life do I find in the incident?" Try analyzing your experiences as potential stories shaped by a central conflict that is resolved in some way. But remember that resolution does not necessarily mean a happy ending. Often the only resolution to some experiences is a lesson, bitterly learned. Growing up seems, all too often, to be filled with such painful lessons. Fortunately, they can become the topics of good stories and essays.

Organization and Details

After selecting your topic and deciding on a tentative thesis, think about the shape of your essay. The good narrative essay does not include every stray telephone call that you received the day of the big game. Select the details that are truly significant, that will carry the meaning of the experience for readers. Make your writing vivid through the use of concrete details, but be sure that they are details that contribute to the support of your thesis.

Usually narratives are presented in chronological order, but you may want to consider beginning at the end of the event and then going back to recount the events leading up to the key moment. For example, Gaye Wagner begins with her feelings after an officer's death and then goes back in time to recount his death and funeral before going forward to tell of the event after his death that altered her thinking. Varying time sequence requires careful attention to verb tenses and transition words and phrases so that readers can follow the shifts in time. Some transition words you may need to use include *first, next, then, after, the following day (week, etc.), meanwhile, at the same time.* You will find other examples in the essays in this chapter and in Chapter 5's **Writing Focus** that lists many transition words.

Another choice you must make is the perspective or point of view from which the incident will be told. Most narrative essays are told in the first person. Some writers prefer to use the third person (he, she, they) even though they are writing about their own experiences. Another choice to make is the vantage point of the narrator or essayist. Do you want to take your reader into the event at the time it occurred in your life? That is, should you tell it as if it is occurring as you write? Or, should you select the distance of the adult voice reflecting back on a childhood experience? When Elizabeth Wong writes: "At last I was one of you; I wasn't one of them. Sadly, I still am," we hear the voice of the adult thinking back to her experience with Chinese school.

Keep in mind these several steps when planning your narrative essay. We all have stories to tell, experiences worth sharing with others. The key is to shape those experiences into a composition that brings readers into our lives and makes them want to know us and understand us, and thereby to understand better what they share with us.

WRITING FOCUS:
PREPARING YOUR ESSAY FOR READERS

Your instructor has probably emphasized the writing process early in your course. You may have reviewed invention strategies, ways to state a good thesis, and tips for revising and editing drafts. These steps are important, but also important is preparing your essay to meet the expectations of readers. Here are basic guidelines that will usually work. List in the margin any variations required by your instructor.

1. Always type (keyboard) papers not written in class.
2. Double-space throughout, with 1-inch margins.
3. Use a 12-point font and a standard form of type, such as Times New Roman or Courier. Never use unusual type or a script type; these are hard to read.
4. Indent paragraphs 5 spaces. Do not quadruple space between paragraphs.
5. Modern Language Association style guidelines call for placing your name, the date, and course information (e.g., English 111) in the upper left of your paper. Starting at the left margin on the first line, place your name. Put the date and course information on separate lines following your name.
6. Center your title and capitalize appropriately. (Capitalize first and last words and all other words except articles, conjunctions, and prepositions of five letters or less.) Do not underline the title or put it in quotation marks. *Remember:* Every essay has a title. "Essay #1" is not an effective title. Make your title clever if you can—but not "cutesy." Clear and direct are always good goals for titles.
7. Refer to Chapter 9's *Writing Focus* (p. 347) for handling references to people and titles and for handling direct quotations.

Getting Started: Reflections on Growing Up

Think back over your growing-up years. What periods in your life, particular events, or individuals come to mind as having had an impact on you, perhaps moving you closer to adulthood, to a clearer understanding of yourself and of life? What, on reflection, was an important period in your life? What was an event that changed you in some way? Who was an influential person? Why was he or she important? Write some of your reflections on these questions in a journal entry. Keep your reflections in mind as you read the essays in this chapter, thinking as you read about ways you might use your experiences in an effective narrative essay.

The Struggle to Be an All-American Girl

ELIZABETH WONG

A native of Los Angeles and graduate of the University of Southern California, Elizabeth Wong (b. 1958) began her career as a journalist in southern California. She has written several plays and screenplays, including *Kimchee and Chitlins: A Serious Comedy about Getting Along* (1996), and *Letters to a Student Revolutionary* (1996). In the following article, published originally in the *Los Angeles Times,* Wong examines her attitudes toward growing up Chinese in American society.

Questions to Guide Your Reading
1. What is Wong's subject?
2. What point does she make about her subject? (Wong does not state a thesis; you will have to write one for the essay when you finish your reading and reflecting.)

1   It's still there, the Chinese school on Yale Street where my brother and I used to go. Despite the new coat of paint and the high wire fence, the school I knew ten years ago remains remarkably, stoically the same.

2   Every day at 5 P.M., instead of playing with our fourth- and fifth-grade friends or sneaking out to the empty lot to hunt ghosts and animal bones, my brother and I had to go to Chinese school. No amount of kicking, screaming, or pleading could dissuade my mother, who was solidly determined to have us learn the language of our heritage.

3   Forcibly, she walked us the seven long, hilly blocks from our home to school, depositing our defiant tearful faces before the

stern principal. My only memory of him is that he swayed on his heels like a palm tree, and he always clasped his impatient twitching hands behind his back. I recognized him as a repressed maniacal child killer, and knew that if we ever saw his hands we'd be in big trouble.

We all sat in little chairs in an empty auditorium. The room   4
smelled like Chinese medicine, an imported faraway mustiness. Like ancient mothballs or dirty closets. I hated that smell. I favored crisp new scents. Like the soft French perfume that my American teacher wore in public school.

There was a stage far to the right, flanked by an American   5
flag and the flag of the Nationalist Republic of China, which was also red, white and blue but not as pretty.

Although the emphasis at the school was mainly language—   6
speaking, reading, writing—the lessons always began with an exercise in politeness. With the entrance of the teacher, the best student would tap a bell and everyone would get up, kowtow, and chant, "Sing san ho," the phonetic for "How are you, teacher?"

Being ten years old, I had better things to learn than ideo-   7
graphs copied painstakingly in lines that ran right to left from the tip of a *moc but,* a real ink pen that had to be held in an awkward way if blotches were to be avoided. After all, I could do the multiplication tables, name the satellites of Mars, and write reports on *Little Women* and *Black Beauty.* Nancy Drew, my favorite book heroine, never spoke Chinese.

The language was a source of embarrassment. More times   8
than not, I had tried to disassociate myself from the nagging loud voice that followed me wherever I wandered in the near-by American supermarket outside Chinatown. The voice belonged to my grandmother, a fragile woman in her seven-ties who could outshout the best of the street vendors. Her humor was raunchy, her Chinese rhythmless, patternless. It was quick, it was loud, it was unbeautiful. It was not like the quiet, lilting romance of French or the gentle refinement of the Amer-ican South. Chinese sounded pedestrian. Public.

In Chinatown, the comings and goings of hundreds of Chi-   9
nese on their daily tasks sounded chaotic and frenzied. I did not want to be thought of as mad, as talking gibberish. When I spoke English, people nodded at me, smiled sweetly, said

encouraging words. Even the people in my culture would cluck and say that I'd do well in life. "My, doesn't she move her lips fast," they would say, meaning that I'd be able to keep up with the world outside Chinatown.

10   My brother was even more fanatical than I about speaking English. He was especially hard on my mother, criticizing her, often cruelly, for her pidgin speech—smatterings of Chinese scattered like chop suey in her conversation. "It's not 'What it is,' Mom," he'd say in exasperation. "It's 'What *is* it, what *is* it, what *is* it!'" Sometimes Mom might leave out an occasional "the" or "a," or perhaps a verb of being. He would stop her in mid-sentence: "Say it again, Mom. Say it right." When he tripped over his own tongue, he'd blame it on her: "See, Mom, it's all your fault. You set a bad example."

11   What infuriated my mother most was when my brother cornered her on her consonants, especially "r." My father had played a cruel joke on Mom by assigning her an American name that her tongue wouldn't allow her to say. No matter how hard she tried, "Ruth" always ended up "Luth" or "Roof."

12   After two years of writing with a *moc but* and reciting words with multiples of meanings, I finally was granted a cultural divorce. I was permitted to stop Chinese school.

13   I thought of myself as multicultural. I preferred tacos to egg rolls; I enjoyed Cinco de Mayo more than Chinese New Year.

14   At last, I was one of you; I wasn't one of them.

15   Sadly, I still am.

Expanding Vocabulary

Match each word in column A with its definition in column B. When in doubt, first find the word in the essay and look for context clues to aid your understanding of the word's meaning. Then, if necessary, use your dictionary to complete the matching exercise. The number in parentheses is the number of the paragraph in which the word appears.

Column A	Column B
stoically (1)	insane
dissuade (2)	meaningless talk
defiant (3)	obscene
maniacal (3)	not showing emotion, impassive
kowtow (6)	corresponding to pronunciation

phonetic (6)	convince not to do something
ideographs (7)	agitated
raunchy (8)	simplified version of one language with
	some elements of a second language
pedestrian (8)	rebellious
frenzied (9)	intolerant
gibberish (9)	lacking distinction
fanatical (10)	bow in subservience
pidgin (10)	picture symbols used to make words

Understanding Content

1. What details of American culture does Wong provide to establish contrast and reveal her preference?
2. What is Wong's attitude toward the Chinese language? What was her brother's attitude toward speaking English?
3. When Wong says that Chinese sounded "pedestrian," "frenzied," and like "gibberish,"how are we to understand her statements? Do these judgments tell us about Chinese or about Wong's feelings?
4. Wong was finally freed from attending Chinese school. How did she feel at the time?

Drawing Inferences about Thesis and Purpose

1. Wong thought of herself as "multicultural." Explain her meaning.
2. Explain the essay's last sentence.

Analyzing Strategies and Style

1. In the opening paragraphs, Wong describes the Chinese school that she attended. List all the words and phrases that express her feelings about the school. (Note: Some are direct, others more subtle. Look at her description of the teacher, for example.)
2. Wong describes her Chinese principal as a "repressed maniacal child killer." How are we to understand her description? What does the author accomplish with this description?
3. In paragraph 4, the author uses two sentence fragments. What do they contribute to the paragraph? How are they effective?
4. Wong also uses several metaphors. Find two, expressed as similes. Explain each one.

Thinking Critically

1. Have you ever been embarrassed by something a parent said or did, or the way he or she spoke or dressed? If so, how old were

you? Do children and adolescents usually outgrow these feelings? Why do so many young people experience them? What are some situations in which children embarrass parents?

2. Were you required to do something as a child that was different from what your classmates or friends did? (For example, take violin lessons when none of your friends did.) If so, how did you feel about it then? Have your attitudes changed? If so, in what way?

3. Should children be forced to attend a school or participate in an activity that they do not want to attend or participate in? Why or why not?

By Any Other Name

SANTHA RAMA RAU

Santha Rama Rau (b. 1923) was born in India and lived her early years there, during British colonial rule of India. She has also been educated in England and at Wellesley College in the United States. A novelist, essayist, and travel writer, Rama Rau's books include *Home to India* (1945) and *Gifts of Passage* (1961). "By Any Other Name," a recounting of her experience at a British-run school in India, was first published in 1951 in *The New Yorker*.

Questions to Guide Your Reading

1. How did the author feel when she was asked to tell the class her name? How do you know?

2. How would you describe the tone of this essay? Is the author angry or bitter or nostalgic or happy or something else?

1   At the Anglo-Indian day school in Zorinabad to which my sister and I were sent when she was eight and I was five and a half, they changed our names. On the first day of school, a hot, windless morning of a north Indian September, we stood in the headmistress's study and she said, "Now you're the *new* girls. What are your names?"

2   My sister answered for us. "I am Premila, and she"—nodding in my direction—"is Santha."

The headmistress had been in India, I suppose, fifteen years or   3
so, but she still smiled her helpless inability to cope with Indian
names. Her rimless half-glasses glittered, and the precarious bun
on the top of her head trembled as she shook her head. "Oh, my
dears, those are much too hard for me. Suppose we give you pretty English names. Wouldn't that be more jolly? Let's see, now—
Pamela for you, I think." She shrugged in a baffled way at my
sister. "That's as close as I can get. And for *you*," she said to me,
"how about Cynthia? Isn't that nice?"

My sister was always less easily intimidated than I was, and   4
while she kept a stubborn silence, I said, "Thank you," in a very
tiny voice.

We had been sent to that school because my father, among   5
his responsibilities as an officer of the civil service, had a tour of
duty to perform in the villages around that steamy little provin-
cial town, where he had his headquarters at that time. He used
to make his shorter inspection tours on horseback, and a week
before, in the stale heat of a typically postmonsoon day, we
had waved good-by to him and a little procession—an assistant,
a secretary, two bearers, and the man to look after the bedding
rolls and luggage. They rode away through our large garden,
still bright green from the rains, and we turned back into the
twilight of the house and the sound of fans whispering in every
room.

Up to then, my mother had refused to send Premila to school   6
in the British-run establishments of that time, because, she used
to say, "you can bury a dog's tail for seven years and it still
comes out curly, and you can take a Britisher away from his
home for a lifetime and he still remains insular." The examinations and degrees from entirely Indian schools were not, in
those days, considered valid. In my case, the question had never
come up, and probably never would have come up if Mother's extraordinary good health had not broken down. For the
first time in my life, she was not able to continue the lessons she
had been giving us every morning. So our Hindi books were put
away, the stories of the Lord Krishna as a little boy were left
in mid-air, and we were sent to the Anglo-Indian school.

That first day at school is still, when I think of it, a remark-   7
able one. At that age, if one's name is changed, one develops
a curious form of dual personality. I remember having a certain

detached and disbelieving concern in the actions of "Cynthia," but certainly no responsibility. Accordingly, I followed the thin, erect back of the headmistress down the veranda to my class-room feeling, at most, a passing interest in what was going to happen to me in this strange, new atmosphere of School.

8   The building was Indian in design, with wide verandas opening onto a central courtyard, but Indian verandas are usu-ally white-washed, with stone floors. These, in the tradition of British schools, were painted dark brown and had matting on the floors. It gave a feeling of extra intensity to the heat.

9   I suppose there were about a dozen Indian children in the school—which contained perhaps forty children in all—and four of them were in my class. They were all sitting at the back of the room, and I went to join them. I sat next to a small, solemn girl who didn't smile at me. She had long, glossy-black braids and wore a cotton dress, but she still kept on her Indian jewelry—a gold chain around her neck, thin gold bracelets, and tiny ruby studs in her ears. Like most Indian children, she had a rim of black kohl around her eyes. The cotton dress should have looked strange, but all I could think of was that I should ask my mother if I couldn't wear a dress to school, too, instead of my Indian clothes.

10   I can't remember too much about the proceedings in class that day, except for the beginning. The teacher pointed to me and asked me to stand up. "Now, dear, tell the class your name."

11   I said nothing.

12   "Come along," she said, frowning slightly. "What's your name, dear?"

13   "I don't know," I said, finally.

14   The English children in the front of the class—there were about eight or ten of them—giggled and twisted around in their chairs to look at me. I sat down quickly and opened my eyes very wide, hoping in that way to dry them off. The little girl with the braids put out her hand and very lightly touched my arm. She still didn't smile.

15   A lot of that morning I was rather bored. I looked briefly at the children's drawings pinned to the wall, and then concen-trated on a lizard clinging to the ledge of the high, barred win-dow behind the teacher's head. Occasionally it would shoot out

its long yellow tongue for a fly, and then it would rest, with its eyes closed and its belly palpitating, as though it were swallowing several times quickly. The lessons were mostly concerned with reading and writing and simple numbers—things that my mother had already taught me—and I paid very little attention. The teacher wrote on the easel black-board words like "bat" and "cat," which seemed babyish to me; only "apple" was new and incomprehensible.

When it was time for the lunch recess, I followed the girl with braids out onto the veranda. There the children from the other classes were assembled. I saw Premila at once and ran over to her, as she had charge of our lunchbox. The children were all opening packages and sitting down to eat sandwiches. Premila and I were the only ones who had Indian food—thin wheat chapatties, some vegetable curry, and a bottle of buttermilk. Premila thrust half of it into my hand and whispered fiercely that I should go and sit with my class, because that was what the others seemed to be doing. 16

The enormous black eyes of the little Indian girl from my class looked at my food longingly, so I offered her some. But she only shook her head and plowed her way solemnly through her sandwiches. 17

I was very sleepy after lunch, because at home we always took a siesta. It was usually a pleasant time of day, with the bedroom darkened against the harsh afternoon sun, the drifting off into sleep with the sound of Mother's voice reading a story in one's mind, and, finally, the shrill, fussy voice of the ayah waking one for tea. 18

At school, we rested for a short time on low, folding cots on the veranda, and then we were expected to play games. During the hot part of the afternoon we played indoors, and after the shadows had begun to lengthen and the slight breeze of the evening had come up we moved outside to the wide courtyard. 19

I had never really grasped the system of competitive games. At home, whenever we played tag or guessing games, I was always allowed to "win"—"because," Mother used to tell Premila, "she is the youngest, and we have to allow for that." I had often heard her say it, and it seemed quite reasonable to me, but the result was that I had no clear idea of what "winning" meant. 20

21   When we played twos-and-threes that afternoon at school, in accordance with my training, I let one of the small English boys catch me, but was naturally rather puzzled when the other children did not return the courtesy. I ran about for what seemed like hours without ever catching anyone, until it was time for school to close. Much later I learned that my attitude was called "not being a good sport," and I stopped allowing myself to be caught, but it was not for years that I really learned the spirit of the thing.

22   When I saw our car come up to the school gate, I broke away from my classmates and rushed toward it yelling, "Ayah! Ayah!" It seemed like an eternity since I had seen her that morning—a wizened, affectionate figure in her white cotton sari, giving me dozens of urgent and useless instructions on how to be a good girl at school. Premila followed more sedately, and she told me on the way home never to do that again in front of the other children.

23   When we got home we went straight to Mother's high, white room to have tea with her, and I immediately climbed onto the bed and bounced gently up and down on the springs. Mother asked how we had liked our first day in school. I was so pleased to be home and to have left that peculiar Cynthia behind that I had nothing whatever to say about school, except to ask what "apple" meant. But Premila told Mother about the classes, and added that in her class they had weekly tests to see if they had learned their lessons well.

24   I asked, "What's a test?"

25   Premila said, "You're too small to have them. You won't have them in your class for donkey's years." She had learned the expression that day and was using it for the first time. We all laughed enormously at her wit. She also told Mother, in an aside, that we should take sandwiches to school the next day. Not, she said, that *she* minded. But they would be simpler for me to handle.

26   That whole lovely evening I didn't think about school at all. I sprinted barefoot across the lawns with my favorite playmate, the cook's son, to the stream at the end of the garden. We quarreled in our usual way, waded in the tepid water under the lime trees, and waited for the night to bring out the smell of the jasmine. I listened with fascination to his stories of ghosts and demons, until I was too frightened to cross the garden alone

in the semidarkness. The ayah found me, shouted at the cook's son, scolded me, hurried me in to supper—it was an entirely usual, wonderful evening.

It was a week later, the day of Premila's first test, that our   27
lives changed rather abruptly. I was sitting at the back of my class, in my usual inattentive way, only half listening to the teacher. I had started a rather guarded friendship with the girl with the braids, whose name turned out to be Nalini (Nancy, in school). The three other Indian children were already fast friends. Even at that age it was apparent to all of us that friendship with the English or Anglo-Indian children was out of the question. Occasionally, during the class, my new friend and I would draw pictures and show them to each other secretly.

The door opened sharply and Premila marched in. At first,   28
the teacher smiled at her in a kindly and encouraging way and said, "Now, you're little Cynthia's sister?"

Premila didn't even look at her. She stood with her feet plant-   29
ed firmly apart and her shoulders rigid, and addressed herself directly to me. "Get up," she said. "We're going home."

I didn't know what had happened, but I was aware that it   30
was a crisis of some sort. I rose obediently and started to walk toward my sister.

"Bring your pencils and your notebook," she said.   31

I went back for them, and together we left the room. The   32
teacher started to say something just as Premila closed the door, but we didn't wait to hear what it was.

In complete silence we left the school grounds and started   33
to walk home. Then I asked Premila what the matter was. All she would say was "We're going home for good."

It was a very tiring walk for a child of five and a half, and I   34
dragged along behind Premila with my pencils growing sticky in my hand. I can still remember looking at the dusty hedges, and the tangles of thorns in the ditches by the side of the road, smelling the faint fragrance from the eucalyptus trees and wondering whether we would ever reach home. Occasionally a horse-drawn tonga passed us, and the women, in their pink or green silks, stared at Premila and me trudging along on the side of the road. A few coolies and a line of women carrying baskets of vegetables on their heads smiled at us. But it was nearing the hottest time of day, and the road was almost deserted. I walked more and more slowly, and shouted to Premila, from

time to time, "Wait for me!" with increasing peevishness. She spoke to me only once, and that was to tell me to carry my notebook on my head, because of the sun.

35   When we got to our house the ayah was just taking a tray of lunch into Mother's room. She immediately started a long, worried questioning about what are you children doing back here at this hour of the day.

36   Mother looked very startled and very concerned, and asked Premila what had happened.

37   Premila said, "We had our test today, and she made me and the other Indians sit at the back of the room, with a desk between each one."

38   Mother said, "Why was that, darling?"

39   "She said it was because Indians cheat," Premila added. "So I don't think we should go back to that school."

40   Mother looked very distant, and was silent a long time. At last she said, "Of course not, darling." She sounded displeased.

41   We all shared the curry she was having for lunch, and afterward I was sent off to the beautifully familiar bedroom for my siesta. I could hear Mother and Premila talking through the open door.

42   Mother said, "Do you suppose she understood all that?"

43   Premila said, "I shouldn't think so. She's a baby."

44   Mother said, "Well, I hope it won't bother her."

45   Of course, they were both wrong. I understood it perfectly, and I remember it all very clearly. But I put it happily away, because it had all happened to a girl called Cynthia, and I never was really particularly interested in her.

Expanding Vocabulary

Determine the meaning of each of the following words either from its context in this essay or from studying your dictionary. Then select five of the words and use each one in a separate sentence of your own. The number in parentheses is the number of the paragraph in which the word appears.

precarious (3)	ayah (18)
intimidated (4)	wizened (22)
insular (6)	sari (22)

kohl (9)	tepid (26)
palpitating (15)	tonga (34)
incomprehensible (15)	coolies (34)
chapatties (16)	peevishness (34)

Understanding Content

1. Why did Rama Rau and her sister start attending the Anglo-Indian day school? What was the author's mother's view of the British?
2. What happened to the author and her sister at the beginning of their first day?
3. What did Rama Rau have to learn about games?
4. What happened the day her sister had a test?
5. What was Rama Rau's reaction, at five, to her school experience?

Drawing Inferences about Thesis and Purpose

1. What was the author's reaction to her first day of school?
2. What is the author's purpose in writing? What does she want readers to understand from her experience? Write a thesis for the essay.

Analyzing Strategies and Style

1. Look at Rama Rau's description of the headmistress (paragraph 3). What do the details tell us about the author's view of this woman?
2. What differences in cultures are revealed by the details of afternoons at schools and afternoons and evenings at home?

Thinking Critically

1. What, if any, details of Indian culture are new to you? Has Rama Rau captured the Indian—and Anglo-Indian—life effectively? What details are most important in creating this glimpse of Indian culture?
2. Santha and Premila respond differently to the discrimination they experience. Do you think that one strategy is better than the other? Defend your views.
3. Should students from other cultures change their names—or the pronunciation of their names—to fit in better in U.S. schools? Why or why not?

The End of My Childhood

N. SCOTT MOMADAY

For many years an English professor at the University of Arizona, N. Scott Momaday (b. 1934) is an artist, poet (*The Gourd Dancer*), Pulitzer Prize–winning novelist (*House Made of Dawn*), and author of a much-praised autobiography, *The Names: A Memoir,* published in 1976. Momaday, whose father was a Kiowa, explores this heritage in his memoir, capturing the American Indian's sense of harmony with the Earth. The following excerpt from *The Names* recounts Momaday's loss of childhood innocence.

Questions to Guide Your Reading

1. When stretched across the rocky chute, what does Momaday think about initially? Then what happens to him?
2. How is the narrative organized? What is Momaday's point of view, the perspective from which the event is presented to readers?

1   At Jemez I came to the end of my childhood. There were no schools within easy reach. I had to go nearly thirty miles to school at Bernalillo, and one year I lived away in Albuquerque. My mother and father wanted me to have the benefit of a sound preparation for college, and so we read through many high school catalogues. After long deliberation we decided that I should spend my last year of high school at a military academy in Virginia.

2   The day before I was to leave I went walking across the river to the red mesa, where many times before I had gone to be alone with my thoughts. And I had climbed several times to the top of the mesa and looked among the old ruins there for pottery. This time I chose to climb the north end, perhaps because I had not gone that way before and wanted to see what it was. It was a difficult climb, and when I got to the top I was spent. I lingered among the ruins for more than an hour, I judge, waiting for my strength to return. From there I could see the whole valley below, the fields, the river, and the village. It was all very beautiful, and the sight of it filled me with longing.

3   I looked for an easier way to come down, and at length I found a broad, smooth runway of rock, a shallow groove wind-

ing out like a stream. It appeared to be safe enough, and I started to follow it. There were steps along the way, a stairway, in effect. But the steps became deeper and deeper, and at last I had to drop down the length of my body and more. Still it seemed convenient to follow in the groove of rock. I was more than halfway down when I came upon a deep, funnel-shaped formation in my path. And there I had to make a decision. The slope on either side was extremely steep and forbidding, and yet I thought that I could work my way down on either side. The formation at my feet was something else. It was perhaps ten or twelve feet deep, wide at the top and narrow at the bottom, where there appeared to be a level ledge. If I could get down through the funnel to the ledge, I should be all right; surely the rest of the way down was negotiable. But I realized that there could be no turning back. Once I was down in that rocky chute I could not get up again, for the round wall which nearly encircled the space there was too high and sheer. I elected to go down into it, to try for the ledge directly below. I eased myself down the smooth, nearly vertical wall on my back, pressing my arms and legs outward against the sides. After what seemed a long time I was trapped in the rock. The ledge was no longer there below me; it had been an optical illusion. Now, in this angle of vision, there was nothing but the ground, far, far below, and jagged boulders set there like teeth. I remember that my arms were scraped and bleeding, stretched out against the walls with all the pressure that I could exert. When once I looked down I saw that my legs, also spread out and pressed hard against the walls, were shaking violently. I was in an impossible situation: I could not move in any direction, save downward in a fall, and I could not stay beyond another minute where I was. I believed then that I would die there, and I saw with a terrible clarity the things of the valley below. They were not the less beautiful to me. It seemed to me that I grew suddenly very calm in view of that beloved world. And I remember nothing else of that moment. I passed out of my mind, and the next thing I knew I was sitting down on the ground, very cold in the shadows, and looking up at the rock where I had been within an eyelash of eternity. That was a strange thing in my life, and I think of it as the end of an age. I should never again see the world as I saw it on the other side of that moment, in the bright reflection of time lost. There are such reflections, and for some of them I have the names.

Expanding Vocabulary

Examine the following words in their contexts in the essay and then write a brief definition or synonym for each one. (Do not use a dictionary; try to guess the word's meaning from its context.) The number in parentheses is the number of the paragraph in which the word appears.

mesa (2)
negotiable (3)
chute (3)
optical illusion (3)

Understanding Content

1. What were the circumstances that led Momaday to the event at Jemez?
2. Momaday presents dramatic details of the incident. Where was he climbing? What could he see at the top of his climb? How did the view make him feel?
3. Why did Momaday choose to come down a different way? After starting down, what decision did he have to make?
4. How did that decision turn out to be critical? What situation did it lead to?
5. When stretched across the rocky chute, what does Momaday think about initially? Then what happens to him?

Drawing Inferences about Thesis and Purpose

1. Momaday says that this experience marked "the end of an age." Why? Why will he "never again see the world as I [he] saw it on the other side of that moment"? What did Momaday have to face on the rocky chute?
2. What is Momaday's thesis?

Analyzing Strategies and Style

1. Analyze Momaday's style of writing. Is his word choice mostly informal or formal, concrete or abstract? Are his sentences mostly simple or complex, short or long, straightforward or highly qualified? Do the choices seem right for the telling of this narrative? What does he gain by his choice of style?
2. Momaday uses an effective metaphor in the middle of paragraph 3: "jagged boulders set there like teeth." Explain the comparison and its emotional effect.

Thinking Critically

1. Momaday took his climb "to be alone with my [his] thoughts" before his move to a new state and school. Why is it good to take time for reflection before major changes in our lives? Do you take time for reflection, for time alone, on a regular basis? Why or why not?

2. Many people like to test themselves physically, believing that such activities build character as well as muscles. Do you enjoy some strenuous physical activity? If so, what are your reasons for the activity? What do you think you have gained?

Always Running

LUIS J. RODRIGUEZ

Luis Rodriguez (b. 1954), a poet, journalist, and community activist, grew up poor in Los Angeles, struggled with drugs and gangs, and held many odd jobs before and during his years at East Los Angeles College, Berkeley, and UCLA. He has served as a facilitator for various writing workshops and has published two books of poems, *Poems Across the Pavement* (1989) and *The Concrete River* (1991). In the following (an excerpt from Chapter 2 of Rodriguez's memoir *Always Running* [1993]), observe how the author combines descriptive details and dialogue—and uses restraint effectively.

Questions to Guide Your Reading

1. Why does Rodriguez begin with the "barrio" quotation? What does it contribute to the essay?
2. When the police officers arrive, what does Tino recommend? Why does he choose his course of action?

"If you ain't from no barrio, then you ain't born."

—a 10-year-old boy from South San Gabriel

One evening dusk came early in South San Gabriel, with   1
wind and cold spinning to earth. People who had been sitting
on porches or on metal chairs near fold-up tables topped with

cards and beer bottles collected their things to go inside. Others put on sweaters or jackets. A storm gathered beyond the trees.

2   Tino and I strolled past the stucco and wood-frame homes of the neighborhood consisting mostly of Mexicans with a sprinkling of poor white families (usually from Oklahoma, Arkansas and Texas). *Ranchera* music did battle with Country & Western songs as we continued toward the local elementary school, an oil-and-grime stained basketball under my arm.

3   We stopped in front of a chain-link fence which surrounded the school. An old brick building cast elongated shadows over a basketball court of concrete on the other side of the fence. Leaves and paper swirled in tiny tornadoes.

4   "Let's go over," Tino proposed.

5   I looked up and across the fence. A sign above us read: NO ONE ALLOWED AFTER 4:30 PM, BY ORDER OF THE LOS ANGELES COUNTY SHERIFF'S DEPARTMENT. Tino turned toward me, shrugged his shoulders and gave me a who-cares look.

6   "Help me up, man, then throw the ball over."

7   I cupped my hands and lifted Tino up while the boy scaled the fence, jumped over and landed on sneakered feet.

8   "Come on, Luis, let's go," Tino shouted from the other side.

9   I threw over the basketball, walked back a ways, then ran and jumped on the fence, only to fall back. Although we were both 10 years old, I cut a shorter shadow.

10   "Forget you, man," Tino said. "I'm going to play without you."

11   "Wait!" I yelled, while walking further back. I crouched low to the ground, then took off, jumped up and placed torn sneakers in the steel mesh. I made it over with a big thud.

12   Wiping the grass and dirt from my pants, I casually walked up to the ball on the ground, picked it up, and continued past Tino toward the courts.

13   "Hey Tino, what are you waiting for?"

14   The gusts proved no obstacle for a half-court game of B-ball, even as dark clouds smothered the sky.

15   Boy voices interspersed with ball cracking on asphalt. Tino's lanky figure seemed to float across the court, as if he had wings under his thin arms. Just then, a black-and-white squad car cruised down the street. A searchlight sprayed across the school

yard. The vehicle slowed to a halt. The light shone toward the courts and caught Tino in mid-flight of a lay-up.

The dribbling and laughter stopped. 16

"All right, this is the sheriff's," a voice commanded. Two 17 deputies stood by the fence, batons and flashlights in hand.

"Let's get out of here," Tino responded. 18

"What do you mean?" I countered. "Why don't we just stay 19 here?"

"You nuts! We trespassing, man," Tino replied. "When they 20 get a hold of us, they going to beat the crap out of us."

"Are you sure?" 21

"I know, believe me, I know." 22

"So where do we go?" 23

By then one of the deputies shouted back: "You boys get over 24 here by the fence—now!"

But Tino dropped the ball and ran. I heard the deputies yell 25 for Tino to stop. One of them began climbing the fence. I decided to take off too.

It never stopped, this running. We were constant prey, and 26 the hunters soon became big blurs: the police, the gangs, the junkies, the dudes on Garvey Boulevard who took our money, all smudged into one. Sometimes they were teachers who jumped on us Mexicans as if we were born with a hideous stain. We were always afraid. Always running.

Tino and I raced toward the dark boxes called classrooms. 27 The rooms lay there, hauntingly still without the voices of children, the commands of irate teachers or the clapping sounds of books as they were closed. The rooms were empty, forbidden places at night. We scurried around the structures toward a courtyard filled with benches next to the cafeteria building.

Tino hopped on a bench, then pulled himself over a high 28 fence. He walked a foot or two on top of it, stopped, and proceeded to climb over to the cafeteria's rooftop. I looked over my shoulder. The deputies weren't far behind, their guns drawn. I grabbed hold of the fence on the side of the cafeteria. I looked up and saw Tino's perspiring face over the roof's edge, his arm extended down toward me.

I tried to climb up, my feet dangling. But then a firm hand 29 seized a foot and pulled at it.

30   "They got me!" I yelled.

31   Tino looked below. A deputy spied the boy and called out: "Get down here . . . you *greaser!*"

32   Tino straightened up and disappeared. I heard a flood of footsteps on the roof—then a crash. Soon an awful calm covered us.

33   "Tino!" I cried out.

34   A deputy restrained me as the other one climbed onto the roof. He stopped at a skylight, jagged edges on one of its sides. Shining a flashlight inside the building, the officer spotted Tino's misshapen body on the floor, sprinkled over with shards of glass.

Expanding Vocabulary

Study the contexts in which the following words are used, or study their definitions in your dictionary, and then use each word in a separate sentence. The number in parentheses is the number of the paragraph in which the word appears.

elongated (3)	smudged (26)
scaled (7)	hauntingly (27)
obstacle (14)	irate (27)
interspersed (15)	scurried (27)

Understanding Content

1. Briefly summarize the situation of the narrative by answering the reporter's questions: who, what, where, when.
2. What happens to Tino?

Drawing Inferences about Thesis and Purpose

1. Although both Tino and Luis are 10 years old, their relationship does not seem quite equal. Which one seems to be the leader? How do you know?
2. Since Tino is already on the court, why does Luis say, in paragraph 13, "What are you waiting for?" What does he want to accomplish?
3. What is Rodriguez's purpose in writing? What is his thesis?

Analyzing Strategies and Style

1. Examine the author's opening three paragraphs. What do we learn about the narrator from the opening? What tone do the paragraphs establish?

2. Rodriguez includes several metaphors and images in his writing. Find three and explain each one's meaning and contribution.

Thinking Critically

1. Are you surprised by Tino's assertion that the police will beat the boys if they are caught? Do you think that he overstates and over-reacts? If you think so, how would you explain your views to Rodriguez? If you agree with Rodriguez, do you have evidence to support your views?
2. Rodriguez writes that the many "hunters" blur into one. Included are teachers "who jumped on us Mexicans." Does this statement surprise you? Why or why not?
3. What are some strategies young people can use to try to cope with gangs, with drug dealers, and with prejudiced teachers?

Death of an Officer

GAYE WAGNER

Gaye Wagner (b. 1955) is a detective with the child abuse unit in the San Diego Police Department. She holds a master's degree and previously worked in children and youth services in New Hampshire. "Death of an Officer" was first published in *The American Enterprise* magazine in May 1995. Through narration Wagner examines issues of a police officer's commitment and perspective and shows us how we can learn and grow through reflection on telling moments in our lives, regardless of our age.

Questions to Guide Your Reading

1. How did Officer Wagner feel after Officer Davis's death? What was the difference between her training experience and this experience?
2. Why does the author include many of the students' letters? What do they contribute to the essay?

When Officer Ron Davis was shot in the dark, foggy predawn   1
of September 17, 1991, I momentarily lost my perspective on
why I've chosen to do what I'm doing. For a time, I focused on

just one dimension of my job as a police officer: the possibility of a violent death, for me or people I care about.

2   Despite the graphic slides and blow-by-blow descriptions of on-duty deaths that we sat through in the Academy, I still must have believed deep down that I, and those alongside me, were invincible. Then the faceless gloom of mortality took the place of a fallen comrade. The streets became an evil, threatening place.

3   Before I felt the blow of a co-worker's death, I looked on each shooting, stabbing, and act of violence as any rubbernecker would—with a certain detachment. I was living the ultimate student experience: Social Wildlife 101. What better way to understand problems of crime and justice than to immerse yourself in the 'hood. I was there, but I was still an onlooker peering inside some kind of fence. I watched, probed each tragic or bizarre incident with curiosity, and pondered the problems I faced.

4   With the death of a comrade, I understood that I was inside the fence. I'm no longer an outsider looking in. The shadow of death stalks all of us who walk in the valley of drugs, guns, alcohol, hopelessness, and hate. Police, addicts, hustlers, parents trying to build futures for their children, good people struggling—we all risk falling into the firing line of desperation, apathy, or corruption.

5   For a while, my response to the new threats I saw around me was to treat all people like they were the enemy. Since an "us" and "them" mentality can be a self-fulfilling prophecy, some of my contacts with people were a little bumpy. Normally my approach is courteous, in one of several variations: either as sympathizer, "just the facts, Bud" chronicler, or all-ears naive airhead who can hardly believe that you, yes you, could do a dastardly deed . . . ("how did this all happen my friend?").

6   But suddenly I just wasn't as enamored with this job as I had been. Let's face it, a sense of contributing to society, the excitement of racing cars with lights and sirens, helping folks, and the drama of never knowing what's next place a poor second to living long enough to count grey hairs and collect Social Security.

I had trouble getting an impersonal all-units bulletin about someone I knew out of my head. I read these bulletins every day, but the words now stung: "187 Suspect . . . Arrest in Public for 187 P.C.—Homicide of a Police Officer . . . Suspect Description: Castillo, Arno . . . On September 17, 1991, at 05:15 hours, Castillo was contacted by two officers in regard to a domestic violence call. As the officers approached, Castillo opened fire with a .45 cal. automatic weapon, fatally wounding one officer."

It was a routine incident that any one of us could have gone to, in an apartment complex that we've all been to. A victim mired in her own problems—a broken collar bone and a life crushing down around her—forgot to tell officers that her crazed, abusive boyfriend had fled with a gun. What followed happened fast. Thick fog and darkness shrouded the complex parking lot where Davis and his partner stopped to contact a driver backing out of the lot.

Ron took a bullet in the neck as he stepped out of his passenger side door. The bullet bled him faster than any resuscitating efforts could counteract. He died while his partner hopelessly tried to breathe life back into his bloody, weakening body. Medics said that even if they'd been there when it happened, there would have been nothing they could do to save his life.

The next week brought a crush of support for our division. The chief, the field operations commander, psychological services counselors, and peer support counselors all came to our lineups to say we're here man, and we know it doesn't feel good. The lineup room looked like a wake with its display of food, flowers, and cards that showered in from other divisions, other departments, and the citizens of our division.

Ron's squad was placed on leave, so officers came from other divisions to help us cover manpower shortages. And on the day of the funeral, officers volunteered from all over the city to cover our beats so that everyone in our division could go to the service.

The funeral procession filled the three miles from Jack Murphy Stadium to the church with bumper-to-bumper police units flashing red and blue overhead lights. Police cars came from San

7

8

9

10

11

12

Diego, the Border Patrol, the U.S. Marshals, El Cajon, La Mesa, Chula Vista, National City, Riverside, Los Angeles, seemingly everywhere. The sight we made sent chills up my spine.

13   For the breadth of that three-mile procession, for a few minutes at least, drivers couldn't keep racing in their usual preoccupied frenzy. Traffic had to stop. In those frozen freeway moments, a tiny corner of the world had to take time out to notice our mourning at the passing of Ronald W. Davis, age 24, husband, father of two, San Diego police officer. The citizens held captive by the procession responded with heart. There was no angry beeping, there were no cars nosing down breakdown lanes. Drivers turned off ignitions in anticipation of a long wait and watched patiently. Many got out of their cars and waved or yelled words of sympathy.

14   The pastor's words at the funeral have stayed with me, because he began stretching my perspective back to a more fruitful, hopeful size. "Life is not defined by the quantity of years that we are on this earth, but by the quality of the time that we spend here."

15   I never cried at the funeral. I cried three weeks later in front of a second grade class.

16   Staring at the bulletin board one day drinking my coffee, I noticed a sheaf of papers with big, just-learned-to-write letters on them. The papers were letters to the Officers of Southeastern from Ms. Matthews's second grade class at Boone Elementary:

Dear Friends of Officer Davis,

We hope this letter will make you feel better. We feel sad about what happened to Officer Davis. We know he was a nice man and a good cop. We thank you for protecting our neighborhood. We know you try to protect every one of us. We know Officer Davis was a good father. We're sorry.

Your friend, Jeffrey

Dear Friends of Officer Davis,

We feel sorry about Officer Davis. I know you feel sorry for what happened when the bad guy killed your friend, Officer

Davis. Thank you for protecting us. I know that he's dead and I know you feel sorry about it. I'm glad you got the bad guy. Do you think this would happen again? I'm sure not. Please protect yourself.

Your friend,

Henry

P.S. I live in Meadowbrook apartments.

Thank you.

Dear Friends of Officer Davis,

We feel sad about Officer Davis being killed. The man that killed Officer Davis got killed right behind our house. We live in front of Meadowbrook apartments. It is really sad that Officer Davis got killed. Last year when my brother was in sixth grade and he was playing basketball with his friends, two kids came and took the ball away. They broke his basketball hoop. Officers helped find the two kids. We are thankful you are trying to protect us.

Your friend,

Travis

Dear Friends,

I hope you will feel better. I know how you feel, sad. Was Officer Davis your friend? Well, he was my friend, too. When I saw the news I felt very sad for him. When I grow up, I might be a police officer. I'll never forget Officer Davis. I know how losing a friend is. When you lose a friend you feel very sad. I know how losing a friend is cause my best friend moved away to Virginia. They wrote to me once and I still miss her and I miss Officer Davis, too.

Your Friend,

Jennifer L.

Dear Officers,

I hope you feel a little better with my letter. We feel sorry that Officer Davis was killed. I heard that he got shot on his neck when he was just getting out of his car. I also heard that Officer Davis was an officer for two years and that he has two children. That one is one years old and the other five years old. I want to say thank you for protecting us and for helping us. We all wish that Officer Davis was still alive.

Your friend always,

Arlene

Dear Officers,

We were so sad that your friend Officer Davis died. Last night on 9-17-91 I couldn't sleep because I was thinking all about your friend Officer Davis. When I heard about Officer Davis getting shot I was so sad. I know how it feels when a friend is gone. I wish that Officer Davis could hear this but he can't right now. Officer Davis and the rest of the force do a great job.

Sincerely,

Jasper

17   Those letters brought feelings up from my gut. The next day I visited Room B-17 to deliver thank you notes to the authors. Ms. Matthews was so excited with my visit that she asked me to speak to the class. She explained that the letters were a class exercise to help the students deal with fears they had expressed to her after the shooting. Because many of her students lived in the apartments where Ron was shot, the shooting was very personal to them. Some couldn't sleep, others were afraid to walk to school, and some were shocked at the realization that the "good guys" get killed too.

18   I hadn't expected to give a speech, and wasn't really ready to give one on this particular topic. When I faced the class, I saw 32 sets of Filipino, Latino, white, and African-American eyes fixed on me. Their hands all sat respectfully in their laps. In those young faces, I saw an innocence and trust that I didn't want to shake. I thought of the sympathy in their letters; I pic-

tured them passing by the large, dark stain of Officer Davis's blood that still scarred the parking lot pavement; and I wondered what young minds must think when a force of blacked-out SWAT officers sweeps through nearby homes in search of the "bad guy" who shot the "good guy."

I wondered how many of the children had been home look- 19
ing out their windows when the suspect, Arnanda Castillo, was shot by a volley of officers' gunfire as he sprung out of his hiding place in the late afternoon of September 17. I couldn't imagine what these children must be thinking, because a second grader growing up in rural New Hampshire in 1962 didn't witness such events. I could only think that second graders of any generation in any place in the world shouldn't have to witness or ponder the senselessness of human violence.

When I finally opened my mouth to speak, my eyes watered 20
and no words would come out. I could say nothing. Each time I tried to push my voice, my eyes watered more. I looked helplessly at Ms. Matthews and the vice principal, who had come to listen to me. Ms. Matthews came to my rescue by starting to talk to the class about strong feelings and the importance of letting feelings out so we don't trap sadness inside ourselves. "Even police officers know that crying can be a strong thing to do." Her reassurances to them reassured me and made me smile at the image of myself, "the big, brave cop" choked up by a second grade class.

We talked for a time about the shooting, about having some- 21
one to talk to about scary things, and about how important their thoughtful letters had been in a time of sadness. By the time I left, they were more enchanted with my handcuffs and nun-chakus than they were concerned by death. Ahhh, the lure for us kids of all ages conjured up by cops and robbers, catching bad guys, rescuing good guys, and having a belt full of cop toys. Through Ron's death, I grew to have a more mature, realistic view of my job.

Through the eyes of the pastor at the funeral and Ms. 22
Matthews's second grade class, I recovered perspective and belief in the value of what I do. It's important for me to live my life doing something I believe is important for this thing we call humanity. And I believe that what I do is important because of people like Henry, Jasper, Jennifer L., Jeffrey, Travis, Arlene, Ms. Matthews, and all of the kids in Room B-17.

Expanding Vocabulary

Examine the following words in their contexts in the essay and then write a brief definition or synonym for each one. (Do not use a dictionary; try to guess the word's meaning from its context.) The number in parentheses is the number of the paragraph in which the word appears.

invincible (2)	shrouded (8)
rubbernecker (3)	resuscitating (9)
bizarre (3)	nunchakus (21)
dastardly (5)	conjured (21)
enamored (6)	

Understanding Content

1. Where does the author work, and what does she do?
2. What was her initial response to Officer Davis's death?
3. What did she do in response to reading the students' letters? Then what happened?

Drawing Inferences about Thesis and Purpose

1. What did the author receive from the young students? How did they help her change her thinking?
2. What is Wagner's thesis?

Analyzing Strategies and Style

1. Describe Wagner's chronology. How could the order be altered? What does Wagner gain with her chronology?
2. Near the end, Wagner writes that the students seem most interested in her "cop toys." What does she gain by including this detail?

Thinking Critically

1. Have you experienced violence in your family, neighborhood, or school? If so, how did the experience make you feel? If not, can you describe how you think the second graders from the neighborhood where Officer Davis was shot may have felt?
2. Has it occurred to you that police officers may doubt their commitment or fear for their safety? Should officers express their feelings as Wagner has? Why or why not?
3. Is it fair to say that there are some truths we have to "learn" several times before we really understand? Is there any age limit to

learning tough truths? How hard is it to learn, to gain perspective, to grow wiser? Be prepared to discuss your answers to these questions.

How Mr. Dewey Decimal Saved My Life

BARBARA KINGSOLVER

Barbara Kingsolver (b. 1955) grew up in rural Kentucky, obtained a degree from DePauw University, worked abroad, settled in Tucson, Arizona, and obtained an MA degree in biology from the University of Arizona. As a novelist she draws on her rural roots, her time spent living abroad, and the southwestern world of her adult years. Her first big novel was *Pigs in Heaven* (1994), and she received much acclaim for *The Poisonwood Bible* (1999) as well. The following essay comes from her collection of essays, *High Tide in Tucson: Essays from Now or Never* (1994).

Questions for Guided Reading

1. Who or what is Dr. Dewey Decimal?
2. Why does Kingsolver want to throw her arms around every librarian?

A librarian named Miss Truman Richey snatched me from   1
the jaws of ruin, and it's too late now to thank her. I'm not the first person to notice that we rarely get around to thanking those who've helped us most. Salvation is such a heady thing the temptation is to dance gasping on the shore, shouting that we are alive, till our forgotten savior has long since gone under. Or else sit quietly, sideswiped and embarrassed, mumbling that we really did know pretty much how to swim. But now that I see the wreck that could have been, without Miss Richey, I'm of a fearsome mind to throw my arms around every living librarian who crosses my path, on behalf of the souls they never knew they saved.

I reached high school at the close of the sixties, in the Com-   2
monwealth of Kentucky, whose ranking on educational spending was I think around fifty-first, after Mississippi and whatever

was below Mississippi. Recently Kentucky has drastically changed the way money is spent on its schools, but back then, the wealth of the county decreed the wealth of the school, and few coins fell far from the money trees that grew in Lexington. Our county, out where the bluegrass begins to turn brown, was just scraping by. Many a dedicated teacher served out earnest missions in our halls, but it was hard to spin silk purses out of a sow's ear budget. We didn't get anything fancy like Latin or Calculus. Apart from English, the only two courses of study that ran for four consecutive years, each one building upon the last, were segregated: Home Ec for girls and Shop for boys. And so I stand today, a woman who knows how to upholster, color-coordinate a table setting, and plan a traditional wedding— valuable skills I'm still waiting to put to good use in my life.

3   As far as I could see from the lofty vantage point of age sixteen, there was nothing required of me at Nicholas County High that was going to keep me off the streets; unfortunately we had no streets, either. We had lanes, roads, and rural free delivery routes, six in number, I think. We had two stoplights, which were set to burn green in all directions after 6 P.M., so as not, should the event of traffic arise, to slow anybody up.

4   What we *didn't* have included almost anything respectable teenagers might do in the way of entertainment. In fact, there was one thing for teenagers to do to entertain themselves, and it was done in the backs of Fords and Chevrolets. It wasn't upholstering skills that were brought to bear on those backseats, either. Though the wedding-planning skills did follow.

5   I found myself beginning a third year of high school in a state of unrest, certain I already knew what there was to know, academically speaking—all wised up and no place to go. Some of my peers used the strategy of rationing out the Science and Math classes between periods of suspension or childbirth, stretching their schooling over the allotted four years, and I envied their broader vision. I had gone right ahead and used the classes up, like a reckless hiker gobbling up all the rations on day one of a long march. Now I faced years of Study Hall, with brief interludes of Home Ec III and IV as the bright spots. I was developing a lean and hungry outlook.

6   We did have a school library, and a librarian who was surely paid inadequately to do the work she did. Yet there she was, every afternoon, presiding over the study hall, and she noticed

me. For reasons I can't fathom, she discerned potential. I expect she saw my future, or at least the one I craved so hard it must have materialized in the air above me, connected to my head by little cartoon bubbles. If that's the future she saw, it was riding down the road on the back of a motorcycle, wearing a black leather jacket with "Violators" (that was the name of our county's motorcycle gang, and I'm not kidding) stitched in a solemn arc across the back.   7

There is no way on earth I really would have ended up a Violator Girlfriend—I could only dream of such a thrilling fate. But I was set hard upon wrecking my reputation in the limited ways available to skinny, unsought-after girls. They consisted mainly of cutting up in class, pretending to be surly, and making up shocking, entirely untrue stories about my home life. I wonder now that my parents continued to feed me. I clawed like a cat in a gunnysack against the doom I feared: staying home to reupholster my mother's couch one hundred thousand weekends in a row, until some tolerant myopic farm boy came along to rescue me from sewing-machine slavery.   8

Miss Richey had something else in mind. She took me by the arm in study hall one day and said, "Barbara, I'm going to teach you Dewey Decimal."   9

One more valuable skill in my life.   10

She launched me on the project of cataloging and shelving every one of the, probably, thousand books in the Nicholas County High School library. And since it beat Home Ec III by a mile, I spent my study-hall hours this way without audible complaint, so long as I could look plenty surly while I did it. Though it was hard to see the real point of organizing books nobody ever looked at. And since it was my God-given duty in those days to be frank as a plank, I said as much to Miss Richey.   11

She just smiled. She with her hidden agenda. And gradually, in the process of handling every book in the room, I made some discoveries. I found *Gone With the Wind*, which I suspected my mother felt was kind of trashy, and I found Edgar Allan Poe, who scared me witless. I found that the call number for books about snakes is 666. I found William Saroyan's *Human Comedy*, down there on the shelf between Human Anatomy and Human Physiology, where probably no one had touched it since 1943. But I read it, and it spoke to me. In spite of myself I imagined the life of an immigrant son who believed human kindness was a tangible and glorious thing. I began to think about words like *tangible* and *glorious*. I read on. After I'd read all the good ones, I went back and read Human Anatomy and Human Physiology and found that I liked those pretty well too.

12   It came to pass in two short years that the walls of my high school dropped down, and I caught the scent of a world. I started to dream up intoxicating lives for myself that I could not have conceived without the books. So I didn't end up on a motorcycle. I ended up roaring hell-for-leather down the backroads of transcendent, reeling sentences. A writer. Imagine that.

Expanding Vocabulary

Match each word in column A with its definition in column B. When in doubt, first find the word in the essay and look for context clues to aid your understanding of the word's meaning. Then, if necessary, use your dictionary to complete the matching exercise. The number in parentheses is the number of the paragraph in which the word appears.

Column A	*Column B*
heady (1)	strategically superior
sideswiped (1)	out of one's good sense
decreed (2)	recognized, detected
missions (2)	hit with a glancing blow
vantage (3)	out loud
fathom (6)	thrilling, intoxicating
discerned (6)	comprehend, understand
surly (7)	special assignments, vocations
myopic (7)	exalted, mystical
audible (10)	established, determined
witless (11)	dizzying
transcendent (12)	ill-humored, nasty
reeling (12)	nearsighted

Understanding Content

1. What period in her life does the author discuss in this essay?
2. How does Kingsolver describe education at her school?
3. What did teens do for "entertainment" in the author's community?
4. What did the author initially yearn to be or do?
5. What did the high school librarian have Kingsolver do?
6. What was the consequence of this experience for Kingsolver?

Drawing Inferences about Thesis and Purpose

1. What can we conclude about the world the author grew up in?
2. Kingsolver sums up her Home Ec classes as having taught her "how to upholster, color-coordinate a table setting, and plan a traditional wedding—valuable skills I'm still waiting to put to good use in my life." What can we infer about her life? What seems to be Kingsolver's attitude toward her Home Ec education?

Analyzing Strategies and Style

1. Kingsolver uses several clever, perhaps unusual, expressions. Explain the idea in each of the following.
   a. "hard to spin silk purses out of a sow's ear budget" (2)
   b. "used the classes up, like a reckless hiker gobbling up all the rations on day one of a long march" (5)
   c. "I clawed like a cat in a gunnysack" (7)
   d. "in two short years . . . the walls of my high school dropped down" (12)
   e. "I ended up roaring hell-for-leather down the backroads of transcendent, reeling sentences" (12)

Thinking Critically

1. Have you had someone older, a teacher or friend's parent for example, significantly change the direction of your life? If so, what did they do to help you change?
2. When Kingsolver writes that reading books allowed her to catch "the scent of a world," what does she suggest that books give us?
3. Have you found some particular book or books that have given you "the scent of a world"? If so, what books did this for you—and what world did they show you?
4. Many young people are not reading much these days. Is this a problem? Why or why not? If it is a problem, what can we do to correct the problem?

Amtrak Subsidy Cartoon

TOM TOLES

Tom Toles is the political cartoonist for the *Washington Post*, with the demanding task of producing a new cartoon six days a week.

Tom Toles

His Amtrak subsidy cartoon reminds us that cartoons tell a story, just as fiction or narrative essays do. Use these questions to guide your reading and thinking about the cartoon.

1. What is the Amtrak subsidy represented by the woman?
2. What does the man want to happen to the woman whom he ties to the railroad tracks? What happens instead? What is ironic about the outcome?
3. What does the man's action represent symbolically? How is he depicted? Are we to identify with the man or the woman?
4. What point does Toles make in his cartoon? Do you agree with his position? Do you agree that his cartoon cleverly presents his view, even if you do not agree with his position? What makes the strategy of irony effective for writers—and cartoonists?

MAKING CONNECTIONS

1. How important are names? Do names help to shape our characters? Do you know people whose names do not seem to fit them? Do you think that your name fits you? Be prepared for a class discussion on the topic of "names."

2. Luis Rodriguez and N. Scott Momaday write of dangerous experiences that lead to greater awareness and a loss of innocence. Most of us, though, do not face such dramatic moments. We need to learn and grow from being made to feel different (Rau) or from experiences on the job (Wagner). Reflect on how we gain insight and mature from seemingly insignificant encounters with life. Why do some young people seem more grown up than others? What is required of us to grow from our experiences? What do the authors suggest on this subject? What can you add from your experience and reflection?

3. Elizabeth Wong and Santha Rama Rau write of the important role of language in fitting in or being in control of one's life. Compare their views and then reflect on the significance of language skills in growing up.

4. Luis Rodriguez, Santha Rama Rau, and N. Scott Momaday have written autobiographies. Select one from your library and read it. Think about what more you learn about the writer's life from reading the complete memoir. Prepare a two-page summary of the memoir.

5. Barbara Kingsolver had a kind of mentor in the school librarian, and she was helped enormously by this person. Would you like to be a mentor, to help a younger person? What mentoring programs are available on your campus or in your community? Schools and churches often provide mentoring opportunities. There is also the national Big Brother/Big Sister program. You can learn more about them at: *http://www.bbbsa.org*.

TOPICS AND GUIDELINES FOR WRITING

1. Several writers in this chapter write of dangerous experiences. Have you ever experienced a situation of physical danger? If so, what were your thoughts and feelings at the

time? What were your reactions to the experience after the danger had passed? Did the experience change you in any way? Select the important details of your experience, decide on a point of view, and write a narrative essay in which you let the details of the experience reveal much, if not all, of the effect of the experience on you. You may want to write from the perspective of the age you were at the time of the event, or you may choose to reflect back on the event from your current perspective.

2. Barbara Kingsolver reveals the influences in our society that affect us, especially when we are young and trying to find our way through adolescence: parents and peers. Do you have a story to tell about the influence of either parents or a social group or clique in your school or community? If so, select one narrative moment to retell to show the influence—or pressure to influence—you. Your essay can reveal how you resisted the influence and the consequences or how you were influenced and the consequences. Do not write in general about growing up and dealing with parents. Select one particular event to develop and carry your point.

3. Think of a situation, or period in your life, in which you felt unattractive or physically different from others in some way. (For example, you were big for your age, or short for your age, or had to wear braces.) How did the situation affect you at the time? Later? Reflect on what you might share from that time with readers and then plan your narrative essay to develop and support those reflections. Select significant details of the event or time, select a point of view, and use time words (e.g., *then, later*) to guide your reader through the situation. You may want to use metaphors that capture your emotions at the time.

4. Think of your years in school. Was there a special teacher who made a difference in your attitude toward education or about yourself? If so, reflect on the incidents involving that teacher and then select either several important moments in that teacher's class or one particular event to serve as a narrative basis for your reflections. Decide whether you want to take your reader back to that time to present only your understanding then, or whether you want to blend your emerging awareness at the time with your greater understanding as an adult.

5. If you came to America as a young person or were born here of parents who were recent immigrants, think of the stories you might tell of growing up in the midst of two cultures. Did you experience discrimination in any way? Did you experience feeling torn between two cultures? How did these situations make you feel then? Now? If you maintained elements of your family's culture, how has that benefited you? If you rejected your family's culture, what, from your perspective now, do you think you have lost? Reflect on these questions as a way to select your essay's subject and thesis. Resist the urge to write in general about your childhood. Rather, focus on one incident or short period and have one clear thesis.

6. Can you recall an incident in which one of your parents embarrassed you, or in which you embarrassed your parent? If you have experienced either one of these situations, think about your feelings both at the time and now. If you were embarrassed by a parent, do you think, on reflection, that you should have felt embarrassment? If you embarrassed a parent, were you aware of it at the time or only on looking back? What insights into the parent/child relationship or into the problems of growing up have you gained from reflecting on these incidents? Those insights can serve as the thesis of your narrative essay. Focus your retelling only on the important elements of the incident, those parts that will guide your reader to the insight you have gained.

7. Recall an event in your life from which you learned a lesson, perhaps a painful one. What was the lesson? How much did you understand at the time? Did you try to deny the lesson, or did you accept it? Construct your narrative so that your retelling carries your point. Offer some reflection but avoid stating the lesson as a simple moral, such as "I learned that one shouldn't steal."

8. Recall a particular event or period in your life that resulted in your losing some of your innocence, in your rather suddenly becoming much more grown up. What romantic or naive view of life did you lose? What more adult view was forced on you? You will probably want to place your reader back in that time of your growing up. Use chronological order and focus your attention on the key stages in the event that moved you from innocence to awareness.

3

Using Description

Reflecting on People and Places

Good writing is concrete writing. Good writers *show* readers what they mean; they do not just tell them. Vague and abstract words may be confusing and often fail to engage readers. "The tawny-colored cocker spaniel with big, floppy ears" has our attention in ways that "The dog" will never achieve. We can see the "spaniel"; what "dog" are we to imagine? Thus, descriptive details are a part of all good writing, whatever its primary purpose or form.

When to Use Description

Sometimes writers use description to make the general concrete and to engage readers. But sometimes, a writer's primary purpose is to describe—to show us—what a particular person, place, or thing looks like. Many instructors like to assign descriptive essays both because they are fun to write and because they provide good practice for using concrete language in other essays.

The descriptive essay can be viewed as a painting in words. (Not surprisingly, you will find some paintings reproduced in this chapter.) Like the artist who draws or paints, the artist working with words must be a perceptive observer. Some people actually see more than others. Can you close your eyes and "see" your writing classroom? The college library? Your history instructor?

How carefully have you looked at the world around you? Some people go to a restaurant because they are hungry. The food critic goes to a restaurant not just to have dinner but to observe the color of the walls, the politeness of the waiters, the taste of the food. The food critic does not want to write, in her Sunday column, that the service was "okay." She needs to decide whether the waiters were formally polite, chatty, intrusive, uninformed. To generate details for good essays you will need to see more of the world around you and to store those visual impressions in your memory.

How to Use Descriptive Details

Descriptive Language

Really seeing what you want to describe is the necessary first step to writing a good descriptive essay. But, just as the artist must transfer impressions into forms and colors on canvas, so you must transfer your impressions into words. To help your reader see what you see, you need to choose words that are accurate, concrete, and vivid. If you are describing your backyard, for example, you want descriptive details so precise that a reader could easily draw a picture of your yard. If you were to write that you have "a large yard that goes to a creek," you would not be helping your reader to see much. How large is large? To an apartment dweller, the fifteen-by-twelve-foot deck of a townhouse might seem large. Better to describe your backyard as "gently sloping seventy feet from the screened-in back porch to a narrow creek that marks the property line." Now we can begin to see—really to see—your yard.

Take time to search for just the right word. The food critic will soon lose her column if she writes that the walls of a restaurant are "a kind of beige with pink." She needs to write, instead, that they are "salmon-colored." Do not settle for describing a lake as "bluish green." Is the water aquamarine? Or a deeper turquoise? Is its surface mirror-like or opaque? You might notice that some of these examples are actually metaphors: "salmon-colored" and "mirror-like." Fresh, vivid comparisons (not worn-out clichés) will help readers see your world and will leave a lasting impression on them. Lance Morrow, describing an East African wildlife preserve, writes that "a herd of elephants moves like a dense gray cloud . . . a mirage of floating boulders" and "a lion prowls in lion-colored grasses."

Finding Unity

When your primary purpose is to write a description, one way to get started is to list all the details that come to mind. However, to shape those details into a unified essay, you will eventually want to eliminate some and develop others. Remember that a list of details, no matter how vivid, does not make an essay. First, select the *telling details*, the specifics that really work to reveal your subject. Second, be sure that your essay has a thesis. Select the details that, taken together, create a unified impression, that make a point. In an essay on her father, British novelist Doris Lessing wants to show that war kills the spirit if not the body of those who have to fight. To support her thesis, she first draws the portrait of her father as a vigorous young man, full of life, and then presents the unpleasant details of the angry, sick, shattered man whom she knew after the war.

Organization

Remember to organize details according to some principle so that readers can follow the developing picture. You need to decide on a perspective from which the details will be "seen" by the reader. In describing a classroom, for example, you could create the impression of someone standing at the door by presenting details in the order in which the person's eyes move around the room. Spatial patterns are numerous. You can move from foreground to background, from the center out, from left to right. Descriptions of people are sometimes more challenging to organize, because in addition to physical details you need possessions, activities, and ways of speaking—the telling details of character. You could take the perspective of a new acquaintance, presenting what one would see first and then what details of personality emerge as a relationship develops. Whatever pattern you choose, develop it consistently and use connecting words (e.g., *from* the left, *below* the penetrating eyes, *next* to the rose bushes) to guide your reader. It's your canvas; get to know your subject well, select your colors with care, and pay close attention to each brushstroke.

WRITING FOCUS:
IT'S ALL ABOUT WORDS

As we have noted, good writing is concrete and specific. In addition to taking time to search for vivid language, though, you need to be sure to select the *right* word. There are many simple, frequently used words that writers confuse. Learn to use the following words correctly. Consult a handbook for a longer list of words in each category.

Possessive Pronouns	*Contractions*
its *(Its message is clear.)*	it's *(it is)*
their *(Their books are on the table.)*	they're *(they are)*
whose *(Whose jacket is this?)*	who's *(who is)*
your *(Your time is up.)*	you're *(you are)*

Homonyms (Words that sound alike but are spelled differently and have different meanings.)

which *(one of a group)*	witch *(female sorcerer)*
roll *(move by turning over; bread)*	role *(part played)*
aisle *(passage between rows)*	isle *(island)*
bare *(naked)*	bear *(to carry; an animal)*
course *(path; part of a meal)*	coarse *(rough)*
cite *(refer to)*	sight *(vision)* site *(a place)*
capital *(major city; wealth)*	capitol *(government building)*
principal *(first; school head)*	principle *(basic truth/belief)*
stationery *(paper)*	stationary *(not moving)*
weather *(climatic condition)*	whether *(if)*

Pseudohomonyms (words that are similar in sound and often confused)

accept *(to receive)*	except *(other than)*
affect *(to influence)*	effect *(result; to bring into existence)*
then *(at that time; next)*	than *(in comparison with)*
allusion *(indirect reference)*	illusion *(misleading image, idea)*
conscience *(following sense of right behavior)*	conscious *(awareness; awake)*
loose *(not tight)*	lose *(to misplace)*
sense *(perception)*	since *(from then until now)*

Pieter Bruegel the Elder, *The Peasant Dance*, c. 1567. Approx. 45" x 65". Kunsthistorisches Museum, Vienna.

Pieter Bruegel the Elder (c. 1525-69) is viewed by many as the greatest Flemish painter of the sixteenth century. Take a close look at this apparently happy, robust festival gathering.

Francisco de Goya y Lucientes, *Third of May, 1808*, 1814. Approximately 8′ 8″ x 11′ 3″. Museo del Prado, Madrid, Spain. Copyright Scala/Art Resource, NY.

A Spaniard, Goya (1746–1828) lived and painted at the Spanish court of Charles II. His paintings reveal an unsentimental, tough-minded observation of human life.

Edgar Degas, *The Dance Class*, c. 1873–1876. Oil on canvas, 85 x 75 cm. Musée d'Orsay, Paris, France. Copyright Erich Lessing/Art Resource, NY.

One of the best known of the French Impressionists, Degas (1834–1917) is known for his interest in capturing movement, an interest that led to many studies of dancers and racehorses.

Vincent Van Gogh, *The Night Café*, 1888. Approx. 28 1/2" x 36 1/4". Yale University Art Gallery, New Haven, Connecticut (bequest of Stephen Carlton Clark, B.A., 1903).

Hollander Van Gogh (1853–90) spent most of his painting years either in Paris or the south of France. His paintings blend impressionistic techniques with an expressionistic use of color.

Pablo Picasso, *The Three Dancers*, 1925. Tate Gallery, London/Art Resource, NY. Copyright © 2003 Estate of Pablo Picasso/Artists Rights Society (ARS), New York.

Perhaps the best-known of twentieth-century painters, Picasso (1881–1973) was born in Spain but lived most of his life in France. His many canvases provide lessons in modern art's movements from Impressionism to Expressionism.

Salvador Dali, *The Persistence of Memory* [*Persistance de la mémoire*], 1931. Oil on canvas, 9-1/2" x 13" (24.1 x 33 cm). The Museum of Modern Art, New York. Given anonymously. Copyright © 2003 Salvador Dali, Gala-Salvador Dali Foundation/Artists Rights Society (ARS), New York.

Salvador Dali (1904–1989), a native of the Spanish province of Catalan, drew on dream imagery to create his surrealist canvases.

Getting Started: Reflections on a Painting

The preceding pages contain reprints of six paintings representing a range of time, styles, and subjects. Examine them, reflect on them, and then select the one you find most appealing or most startling. Write briefly (in your journal or class notebook), explaining what attracted you to the particular painting you selected. Then read at least one biographical entry about the painter (in an encyclopedia or art book—including online) and add a paragraph on the painter to your journal or notes. Your paragraph should include information that goes beyond the brief details included with the painting. Be prepared to share your information about the painter and your reactions to the work with classmates.

Mrs. Zajac

TRACY KIDDER

In his Pulitzer Prize–winning book *The Soul of a New Machine* (1981), Tracy Kidder (b. 1945) makes complex technical material about computers clear and interesting. He perfected his talent for clarity by writing articles on a variety of complex topics for the *Atlantic*, where he now serves as a contributing editor. His most recent book is *Old Friends* (1993). Kidder's portrait of Mrs. Zajac comes from his best-seller, *Among Schoolchildren* (1988), a compassionate study of a year in Mrs. Zajac's fifth-grade classroom. As you read, pay close attention to Kidder's telling details, the details that reveal character.

Questions to Guide Your Reading

1. What is the italic print of the opening paragraph designed to represent? What is effective about beginning this way?
2. What are three details that you would consider *telling* details?

Mrs. Zajac wasn't born yesterday. She knows you didn't do your 1
best work on this paper, Clarence. Don't you remember Mrs. Zajac
saying that if you didn't do your best, she'd make you do it over? As

for you, Claude, God forbid that you should ever need brain surgery. But Mrs. Zajac *hopes that if you do, the doctor won't open up your head and walk off saying he's* almost *done, as you just said when Mrs. Zajac asked you for your penmanship, which, by the way, looks like who did it and ran. Felipe, the reason you have hiccups is, your mouth is always open and the wind rushes in. You're in fifth grade now. So, Felipe, put a lock on it. Zip it up. Then go get a drink of water. Mrs. Zajac means business,* Robert. *The sooner you realize she never said* everybody *in the room has to do the work except for* Robert, *the sooner you'll get along with her. And . . .* Clarence. *Mrs. Zajac knows you didn't try. You don't just hand in junk to Mrs. Zajac. She's been teaching an awful lot of years. She didn't fall off the turnip cart yesterday. She told you she was an old-lady teacher.*

2   She was thirty-four. She wore a white skirt and yellow sweater and a thin gold necklace, which she held in her fingers, as if holding her own reins, while waiting for children to answer. Her hair was black with a hint of Irish red. It was cut short to the tops of her ears, and swept back like a pair of folded wings. She had a delicately cleft chin, and she was short— the children's chairs would have fit her. Although her voice sounded conversational, it had projection. She had never acted. She had found this voice in classrooms.

3   Mrs. Zajac seemed to have a frightening amount of energy. She strode across the room, her arms swinging high and her hands in small fists. Taking her stand in front of the green chalkboard, discussing the rules with her new class, she repeated sentences, and her lips held the shapes of certain words, such as "home-work," after she had said them. Her hands kept very busy. They sliced the air and made karate chops to mark off boundaries. They extended straight out like a traffic cop's, halting illegal maneuvers yet to be perpetrated. When they rested momentarily on her hips, her hands looked as if they were in holsters. She told the children, "One thing Mrs. Zajac expects from each of you is that you do *your* best." She said, "Mrs. Zajac gives homework. I'm sure you've all heard. The old meanie gives homework." *Mrs. Zajac.* It was in part a role. She worked her way into it every September.

4   At home on late summer days like these, Chris Zajac wore shorts or blue jeans. Although there was no dress code for teachers here at Kelly School, she always went to work in skirts or dresses. She dressed as if she were applying for a job, and hoped

in the back of her mind that someday, heading for job interviews, her students would remember her example. Outside school, she wept easily over small and large catastrophes and at sentimental movies, but she never cried in front of students, except once a few years ago when the news came over the intercom that the Space Shuttle had exploded and Christa McAuliffe had died—and then she saw in her students' faces that the sight of Mrs. Zajac crying had frightened them, and she made herself stop and then explained.

At home, Chris laughed at the antics of her infant daughter   5
and egged the child on. She and her first-grade son would sneak up to the radio when her husband wasn't looking and change the station from classical to rock-and-roll music. "You're regressing, Chris," her husband would say. But especially on the first few days of school, she didn't let her students get away with much. She was not amused when, for instance, on the first day, two of the boys started dueling with their rulers. On nights before the school year started, Chris used to have bad dreams: her principal would come to observe her, and her students would choose that moment to climb up on their desks and give her the finger, or they would simply wander out the door. But a child in her classroom would never know that Mrs. Zajac had the slightest doubt that students would obey her.

The first day, after going over all the school rules, Chris spoke   6
to them about effort. "If you put your name on a paper, you should be proud of it," she said. "You should think, This is the best I can do and I'm proud of it and I want to hand this in." Then she asked, "If it isn't your best, what's Zajac going to do?"

Many voices, most of them female, answered softly in uni-   7
son, "Make us do it over."

"*Make you do it over,*" Chris repeated. It sounded like a chant.   8

"Does anyone know anything about Lisette?" she asked   9
when no one answered to that name.

Felipe—small, with glossy black hair—threw up his hand.   10
"Felipe?"   11

"She isn't here!" said Felipe. He wasn't being fresh. On those   12
first few days of school, whenever Mrs. Zajac put the sound of a question in her voice, and sometimes before she got the question out, Felipe's hand shot up.

In contrast, there was the very chubby girl who sat nearly   13
motionless at her desk, covering the lower half of her face with

her hands. As usual, most of their voices sounded timid the first day, and came out of hiding gradually. There were twenty children. About half were Puerto Rican. Almost two-thirds of the twenty needed the forms to obtain free lunches. There was a lot of long and curly hair. Some boys wore little rattails. The eyes the children lifted up to her as she went over the rules— a few eyes were blue and many more were brown—looked so solemn and so wide that Chris felt like dropping all pretense and laughing. Their faces ranged from dark brown to gold, to pink, to pasty white, the color that Chris associated with sunless tenements and too much TV. The boys wore polo shirts and T-shirts and new white sneakers with the ends of the laces untied and tucked behind the tongues. Some girls wore lacy ribbons in their hair, and some wore pants and others skirts, a rough but not infallible indication of religion—the daughters of Jehovah's Witnesses and Pentecostals do not wear pants. There was a lot of prettiness in the room, and all of the children looked cute to Chris.

Expanding Vocabulary

Examine the following words in their contexts in the essay. Then write a brief definition or synonym for each one. (Do not use a dictionary; try to guess the word's meaning from its context.) The number in parentheses is the number of the paragraph in which the word appears.

projection (2)	egged . . . on (5)
karate (3)	unison (7)
maneuvers (3)	pretense (13)
perpetrated (3)	infallible (13)
holsters (3)	

Understanding Content

1. The excerpt you have read comes from the first four pages of Kidder's book. Why does Kidder begin his study in this way? What, exactly, does he accomplish in these opening pages?
2. What specific details do we get about Mrs. Zajac? List them. (Consider age, physical appearance, personality traits, values.)
3. Why does Mrs. Zajac go to school in a skirt or dress?
4. What details do we get about the children? List them.

Drawing Inferences about Thesis and Purpose

1. What is effective about Kidder's last sentence? What does it tell us about Mrs. Zajac's attitude toward teaching?
2. What can you conclude about the Kelly School neighborhood from details about the children?
3. What is the author's attitude toward his subject? Does he present Mrs. Zajac in a positive or negative way? As a good or bad teacher?

Analyzing Strategies and Style

1. Kidder offers some contrasts between Mrs. Zajac's classroom behavior and her behavior at home and with her children. How do these contrasts help us to understand Mrs. Zajac?
2. Can you find any sentences that contain general or abstract ideas?
3. What does your answer to question 2 tell you about Kidder's style of writing? Is this writing primarily general or specific? Abstract or concrete?

Thinking Critically

1. Would you have enjoyed being in Mrs. Zajac's fifth-grade class? Why or why not?
2. Mrs. Zajac emphasizes being proud of work you sign your name to. Is it ever too early to teach this idea? Is it ever too late?
3. Are you usually proud of the work you hand in? If not, why do you hand it in that way?
4. Mrs. Zajac believes in dressing properly for her job. Should students have a dress code or wear uniforms? How can clothes make a difference in the classroom or on the job?

Lost Lives of Women

AMY TAN

Amy Tan (b. 1952) was born in California shortly after her parents immigrated to the United States from China. Tan started a career in consulting on programs for disabled children and then turned to writing short stories, some of which became part of her first and best-selling novel *The Joy Luck Club*. Her second novel, *The Kitchen God's Wife*, appeared in 1991. In the following article, which appeared in the April 1991 issue of *Life* magazine, Tan captures the stories of several women, relatives of hers, grouped in an old photo.

Questions to Guide Your Reading

1. Tan tells us in paragraph 5 that the women in the photo "were not peasant women but big city people, very modern." Why does she include this comment? Why is this a telling detail?
2. What is Tan's thesis?

---

1   When I first saw this photo as a child, I thought it was exotic and remote, of a faraway time and place, with people who had no connection to my American life. Look at their bound feet! Look at that funny lady with the plucked forehead!

2   The solemn little girl is, in fact, my mother. And leaning against the rock is my grandmother, Jingmei. "She called me Baobei," my mother told me. "It means Treasure."

3   The picture was taken in Hangzhou, and my mother believes the year was 1922, possibly spring or fall, judging by the clothes. At first glance, it appears the women are on a pleasure outing.

4   But see the white bands on their skirts? The white shoes? They are in mourning. My mother's grandmother, known to the others as Divong, "The Replacement Wife," has recently died. The women have come to this place, a Buddhist retreat, to perform yet another ceremony for Divong. Monks hired for the occasion have chanted the proper words. And the women and little girl have walked in circles clutching smoky sticks of incense. They knelt and prayed, then burned a huge pile of spirit money so that Divong might ascend to a higher position in her new world.

5   This is also a picture of secrets and tragedies, the reasons that warnings have been passed along in our family like heirlooms. Each of these women suffered a terrible fate, my mother said. And they were not peasant women but big city people, very modern. They went to dance halls and wore stylish clothes. They were supposed to be the lucky ones.

6   Look at the pretty woman with her finger on her cheek. She is my mother's second cousin, Nunu Aiyi, "Precious Auntie."

You cannot see this, but Nunu Aiyi's entire face was scarred from smallpox. Lucky for her, a year or so after this picture was taken, she received marriage proposals from two families. She turned down a lawyer and married another man. Later she divorced her husband, a daring thing for a woman to do. But then, finding no means to support herself or her young daughter, Nunu eventually accepted the lawyer's second proposal—to become his number two concubine. "Where else could she go?" my mother asked. "Some people said she was lucky the lawyer still wanted her."

Now look at the small woman with a sour face (*third from left*). There's a reason that Jyou Ma, "Uncle's Wife," looks this way. Her husband, my great-uncle, often complained that his family had chosen an ugly woman for his wife. To show his displeasure, he often insulted Jyou Ma's cooking. One time Great-Uncle tipped over a pot of boiling soup, which fell all over his niece's four-year-old neck and nearly killed her. My mother was the little niece, and she still has that soup scar on her neck. Great-Uncle's family eventually chose a pretty woman for his second wife. But the complaints about Jyou Ma's cooking did not stop.

8   Doomma, "Big Mother," is the regal-looking woman seated on a rock. (The woman with the plucked forehead, far left, is a servant, remembered only as someone who cleaned but did not cook.) Doomma was the daughter of my great-grandfather and Nu-pei, "The Original Wife." She was shunned by Divong, "The Replacement Wife," for being "too strong," and loved by Divong's daughter, my grandmother. Doomma's first daughter was born with a hunchback—a sign, some said, of Doomma's own crooked nature. Why else did she remarry, disobeying her family's orders to remain a widow forever? And why did Doomma later kill herself, using some mysterious means that caused her to die slowly over three days? "Doomma died the same way she lived," my mother said, "strong, suffering lots."

9   Jingmei, my own grandmother, lived only a few more years after this picture was taken. She was the widow of a poor scholar, a man who had the misfortune of dying from influenza when he was about to be appointed a vice-magistrate. In 1924 or so, a rich man, who liked to collect pretty women, raped my grandmother and thereby forced her into becoming one of his concubines. My grandmother, now an outcast, took her young daughter to live with her on an island outside of Shanghai. She left her son behind, to save his face. After she gave birth to another son she killed herself by swallowing raw opium buried in the New Year's rice cakes. The young daughter who wept at her deathbed was my mother.

10   At my grandmother's funeral, monks tied chains to my mother's ankles so she would not fly away with her mother's ghost. "I tried to take them off," my mother said. "I was her treasure. I was her life."

11   My mother could never talk about any of this, even with her closest friends. "Don't tell anyone," she once said to me. "People don't understand. A concubine was like some kind of prostitute. My mother was a good woman, high-class. She had no choice."

12   I told her I understood.

13   "How can you understand?" she said, suddenly angry. "You did not live in China then. You do not know what it's like to have no position in life. I was her daughter. We had no face! We belonged to nobody! This is a shame I can never push off my back." By the end of the outburst, she was crying.

On a recent trip with my mother to Beijing, I learned that my 14
uncle found a way to push the shame off his back. He was the son
my grandmother left behind. In 1936 he joined the Communist
party—in large part, he told me, to overthrow the society that
forced his mother into concubinage. He published a story about
his mother. I told him I had written about my grandmother in a
book of fiction. We agreed that my grandmother is the source of
strength running through our family. My mother cried to hear this.

My mother believes my grandmother is also my muse, that
she helps me write. "Does she still visit you often?" she asked 15
while I was writing my second book. And then she added shyly,
"Does she say anything about me?"

"Yes," I told her. "She has lots to say. I am writing it down."

This is the picture I see when I write. These are the secrets I 16
was supposed to keep. These are the women who never let me 17
forget why stories need to be told.

Expanding Vocabulary

Define each of the following words and then use each one in a sentence.
The number in parentheses is the number of the paragraph in which
the word appears.

exotic (1)
heirlooms (5)
concubine (6)
shunned (8)
muse (15)

Understanding Content

1. When and where was the picture taken?
2. Who are the women in the photo? That is, what is their relationship to the author?
3. Why are the women together? What have they gathered to do?
4. What was the author's initial reaction to the photo?

Drawing Inferences about Thesis and Purpose

1. What reaction does Tan want readers to have after they read her
   descriptions of the women? What do the women share, other than
   family connections?
2. Explain the last line of the essay.

Analyzing Strategies and Style

1. What details do you consider to be especially important? Why do you select them?
2. Tan gives each woman's Chinese name and then its meaning in English. What does she gain from this strategy?
3. Tan uses a metaphor in paragraph 5. Explain the metaphor.

Thinking Critically

1. Do you have stories to tell about your family? If you have a family album, find a picture in it that you think holds a secret or tells a story, and write that story in your journal.
2. Why is it important to write the stories of these women? What does Tan gain for herself? For others?
3. Why is it important for humans generally to tell stories? What does each culture, each age, gain from making stories?

Remembering Lobo

PAT MORA

Educated at Texas Western College and the University of Texas at El Paso, Pat Mora (b. 1942) has published several children's books and volumes of poetry. Her essays have been collected in *Nepantla: Essays from the Land in the Middle* (1993), from which "Remembering Lobo" comes. Look for the telling details that Mora presents to develop and reveal the character of her aunt.

Questions to Guide Your Reading

1. What is Mora's purpose in writing? What does she want to share with readers?
2. What are some of the details of Lobo's life: Where was she born? Where did she live? What did she do?

1   We called her *Lobo*. The word means "wolf" in Spanish, an odd name for a generous and loving aunt. Like all names it became synonymous with her, and to this day returns me to my childself. Although the name seemed perfectly natural to us and to our friends, it did cause frowns from strangers throughout

the years. I particularly remember one hot afternoon when on a crowded streetcar between the border cities of El Paso and Juarez, I momentarily lost sight of her. "Lobo! Lobo!" I cried in panic. Annoyed faces peered at me, disappointed at such disrespect to a white-haired woman. Actually the fault was hers. She lived with us for years, and   2 when she arrived home from work in the evening, she'd knock on our front door and ask, "*¿Dónde están mis lobitos?*" "Where are my little wolves?"

Gradually she became our *lobo,* a spinster aunt who gathered   3 the four of us around her, tying us to her for life by giving us all she had. Sometimes to tease her we would call her by her real name. "*¿Dónde está Ignacia?*" we would ask. Lobo would laugh and say, "She is a ghost."

To all of us in nuclear families today, the notion of an extend-   4 ed family under one roof seems archaic, complicated. We treasure our private space. I will always marvel at the generosity of my parents, who opened their door to both my grandmother and Lobo. No doubt I am drawn to the elderly because I grew up with two entirely different white-haired women who worried about me, tucked me in at night, made me tomato soup or hot *hierbabuena* (mint tea) when I was ill.

Lobo grew up in Mexico, the daughter of a circuit judge, my   5 grandfather. She was a wonderful storyteller and over and over told us about the night her father, a widower, brought his grown daughters on a flatbed truck across the Rio Grande at the time of the Mexican Revolution. All their possessions were left in Mexico. Lobo had not been wealthy, but she had probably never expected to have to find a job and learn English.

When she lived with us, she worked in the linens section of   6 a local department store. Her area was called "piece goods and bedding." Lobo never sewed, but she would talk about materials she sold, using words I never completely understood, such as *pique* and *broadcloth.* Sometimes I still whisper such words just to remind myself of her. I'll always savor the way she would order "sweet milk" at restaurants. The precision of a speaker new to the language.

Lobo saved her money to take us out to dinner and a movie,   7 to take us to Los Angeles in the summer, to buy us shiny black shoes for Christmas. Though she never married and never bore children, Lobo taught me much about one of our greatest challenges as human beings: loving well. I don't think she ever discussed the subject with me, but through the years she lived her love, and I was privileged to watch.

8   She died at ninety-four. She was no sweet, docile Mexican woman dying with perfect resignation. Some of her last words before drifting into semiconsciousness were loud words of annoyance at the incompetence of nurses and doctors.

9   *"No sirven."* "They're worthless," she'd say to me in Spanish.

10   "They don't know what they're doing. My throat is hurting and they're taking X rays. Tell them to take care of my throat first."

11   I was busy striving for my cherished middle-class politeness. "Shh, shh," I'd say. "They're doing the best they can."

12   "Well, it's not good enough," she'd say, sitting up in anger.

13   Lobo was a woman of fierce feelings, of strong opinions. She was a woman who literally whistled while she worked. The best way to cheer her when she'd visit my young children was to ask for her help. Ask her to make a bed, fold laundry, set the table or dry dishes, and the whistling would begin as she moved about her task. Like all of us, she loved being needed. Understandable, then, that she muttered in annoyance when her body began to fail her. She was a woman who found self-definition and joy in visibly showing her family her love for us by bringing us hot *té de canela* (cinnamon tea) in the middle of the night to ease a cough, by bringing us comics and candy whenever she returned home. A life of giving.

14   One of my last memories of her is a visit I made to her on November 2, *El Día de los Muertos*, or All Souls' Day. She was sitting in her rocking chair, smiling wistfully. The source of the smile may seem a bit bizarre to a U.S. audience. She was fondly remembering past visits to the local cemetery on this religious feast day.

15   "What a silly old woman I have become," she said. "Here I sit in my rocking chair all day on All Souls' Day, sitting when I should be out there. At the cemetery. Taking good care of *mis muertos*, my dead ones.

16   "What a time I used to have. I'd wake while it was still dark outside. I'd hear the first morning birds, and my fingers would almost itch to begin. By six I'd be having a hot bath, dressing

carefully in black, wanting *mis muertos* to be proud of me, proud
to have me looking respectable and proud to have their graves
taken care of. I'd have my black coffee and plenty of toast. You
know the way I like it. Well browned and well buttered. I wanted to be ready to work hard.

"The bus ride to the other side of town was a long one, but 17
I'd say a rosary and plan my day. I'd hope that my perfume
wasn't too strong and yet would remind others that I was a lady.

"The air at the cemetery gates was full of chrysanthemums: 18
that strong, sharp, fall smell. I'd buy tin cans full of the gold and
wine flowers. How I liked seeing aunts and uncles who were
also there to care for the graves of their loved ones. We'd hug.
Happy together.

"Then it was time to begin. The smell of chrysanthemums 19
was like a whiff of pure energy. I'd pull the heavy hose and
wash the gravestones over and over, listening to the water pelt-
ing away the desert sand. I always brought newspaper. I'd kneel
on the few patches of grass, and I'd scrub and scrub, shining the
gray stones, leaning back on my knees to rest for a bit and then
scrubbing again. Finally a relative from nearby would say, *'Ya,
ya, Nacha,'* and laugh. Enough. I'd stop, blink my eyes to return
from my trance. Slightly dazed, I'd stand slowly, place a can
of chrysanthemums before each grave.

"Sometimes I would just stand there in the desert sun and lis- 20
ten. I'd hear the quiet crying of people visiting new graves; I'd
hear families exchanging gossip while they worked.

"One time I heard my aunt scolding her dead husband. She'd 21
sweep his gravestone and say, *'¿Porqué?* Why did you do this,
you thoughtless man? Why did you go and leave me like this?
You know I don't like to be alone. Why did you stop living?'
Such a sight to see my aunt with her proper black hat and her
fine dress and her carefully polished shoes muttering away for
all to hear.

"To stifle my laughter, I had to cover my mouth with my 22
hands."

Expanding Vocabulary

Examine the following words in their contexts in the essay. Then write
a brief definition or synonym for each one. (Do not use a dictionary;

try to guess each word's meaning from its context.) The number in parentheses is the number of the paragraph in which the word appears.

synonymous (1)	semiconsciousness (8)
spinster (3)	bizaare (14)
nuclear (4)	pelting (19)
archaic (4)	trance (19)
precision (6)	

Understanding Content

1. How did the author know her "Lobo"?
2. What are some of the telling details of Lobo's character? What activities or moments in her life reveal these character traits?

Drawing Inferences about Thesis and Purpose

1. When the author and her siblings called Lobo by her real name, Lobo answered that "she is a ghost." Why did she say that to the children?
2. What does Mora mean by "loving well"? What can we infer to be the characteristics of a person who loves well?

Analyzing Strategies and Style

1. Several times Mora uses Spanish words or phrases, which she then translates into English. What does she gain by including the Spanish?
2. Mora ends with Lobo's own account of visiting family graves. What does the author accomplish by ending with Lobo's own words?

Thinking Critically

1. Do you live in an extended family? If so, do you have an older family member whom you especially care for? What do we gain from extended families? What do we lose? Do the advantages outweigh the disadvantages?
2. What do you think are the marks of a meaningful life?
3. Without having read this essay, would you have included "loving well" as a mark of a meaningful life? Do you think it should be on everyone's list? Why or why not?

Let It Snow!

DIANE ACKERMAN

Diane Ackerman has been a staff writer at *The New Yorker* and a
writer in residence at several colleges. She has published books of
poetry and natural history, including a book on bats. Her latest book
is *Cultivating Delights: A Natural History of My Garden* (2001), from
which the following excerpt is taken, having appeared as an essay
in *Parade* magazine, where she is a contributing editor.

Questions to Guide Your Reading

1. What is Ackerman's purpose in writing? What does she
   want readers to see?
2. How does Ackerman want readers to feel about her topic?

It's snowing like white pepper. At noon, several hours ago,   1
it was 60 degrees. Now the bench drips a thin white glaze, the
quaking aspens keen and sway. As a steady sift of snow falls
straight down and sticks, the wire fence begins to look crocheted.
The wind poofs a snowdrift until it sprays flour. Powder snow,
they call it—the skier's friend. To me, it just looks like small
white grains, but I know it's really a blend of column- and plate-
shaped crystals that prevent the snow from packing down.

The shape of the crystal determines whether the snow will stick   2
or pack down hard. Crystals clustered together form snowflakes,
and there are many crystalline shapes. The best known are "den-
dritic," or branching—the classic star snowflake design that one
finds on sweaters and many Christmas ornaments.

But snow crystals form many shapes that aren't always visi-   3
ble to the naked eye. Most people didn't know what snowflakes
looked like until the 19th-century publication of *Cloud Crystals*,
with sketches by "A Lady," who realized she could catch flakes
on a black background and peer at them through a magnifying
glass. Then, in 1931, Wilson Alwyn Bentley published an atlas of
thousands of crystals he had photographed through a microscope, calling it simply *Snow Crystals*.

Depending on temperature, humidity and wind, snow crystals   4
can develop into stars, columns, plates, needles, asymmetricals,

No Two Are Alike...

Though unique, a snow crystal falls into a category of shapes: here, examples of the type "stellar plates."

Most people didn't know what snow crystals looked like until a book of sketches, *Cloud Crystals*, appeared in 1855, In 1931, Wison Alwyn Bentley published an atlas of crystals he had photographed through a microscope.

Photo: Camazine/Photo Researchers

capped columns or strange combinations, such as "bullets," variants of columns topped by pyramids or "stellar dendrites," which are six-pointed stars.

5   Columns are hollow crystals, spatial dendrites are three-dimensional crystals, and needles are solid crystals. As they fall, they hit other crystals, break apart, build new forms, and soon a flurry thickens into heavy snow.

6   When I was little, my mother would turn off the lights in the house, and she and I would sit on the rug in the living room, watching snowflakes dance like dervishes under the porch light. As flurry became blizzard, I knew there was a good chance I'd be staying home from school and building a snow house.

7   I like snow's odd quality of pouring over and around things without breaking up, so that it creates pockets of air, overhanging eaves and accidental igloos where garden animals huddle to keep warm. I like how solidly snow packs, and how tiny flakes of it can bring a large city to a halt when snow is nothing but water and air, mostly air. I like how well snow insulates, despite its essential coldness.

I like the many names people have given snow. With each   8
name, I learn to see snow in a slightly different way. The Inuits (a group of northern indigenous people also called Eskimos),
famous for a vocabulary of snow, have words for drifting snow
(*siqoq*), falling snow (*aniu*), wind-whipped snow (*upsik*), crusty
melting freeze snow (*siqoqtoaq*), fine smooth snow (*saluma roaq*)
and even the place where snow has blown away (*sich*), among
many others.

Soon snow quilts the ground and talcs the trees, muffling   9
sound and stifling scent. For many people, gardeners included,
winter can be a challenge. I like the contrast of hot and cold: the
warm-blooded animals trekking across the snow; the heat of a
furnace or fire keeping one snug through a blizzard; tropical
plants, such as amaryllis and orchids, blooming on the win-
dowsill while snow falls invitingly beyond the panes of glass.

Expanding Vocabulary

Write a definition for each of the following words. Then select five of
the words and use each one of those in a separate sentence of your
own. The number in parentheses is the number of the paragraph in
which the word appears.

quaking (1)	insulates (7)
crocheted (1)	indigenous (8)
asymmetricals (3)	stifling (9)
dervishes (6)	trekking (9)

Understanding Content

1. What scene does the author describe at the beginning?
2. What kind of snow is falling?
3. What are some of the kinds of shapes that snow crystals form?
   Which shape do we most commonly see at Christmas?
4. Who first explained the many shapes of snowflakes?
5. What other details of snow does Ackerman provide in addition to
   appearance?

Drawing Inferences about Thesis and Purpose

1. Ackerman begins and ends with descriptive details, but within the
   essay she includes scientific information about snowflakes. How
   would you state her subject?

2. What is the essay's thesis? Try to write a sentence or two that covers the several purposes that the author has.

Analyzing Strategies and Style

1. Ackerman begins with a metaphor. Find two other metaphors in the essay and then explain all three metaphors.
2. How does the author move from describing a scene of snow falling to presenting information about the various shapes of snowflakes? What makes her transition an effective one?
3. Where does Ackerman place us as we look at the falling snow— both at the beginning and end of her essay? How does that placement contribute to the feelings she wants readers to have?
4. Look again at her final three paragraphs. What does she repeat that helps to convey her attitude toward snow?

Thinking Critically

1. Why do you suppose that Inuits have so many names for snow?
2. When you see snow falling, what do you usually think about? Do you picture the various shapes of snow crystals? Do you find metaphors to describe to yourself the scene created by the falling snow? Something else?
3. What role does attitude play in how we respond to a situation or event?

Africa

LANCE MORROW

Journalist Lance Morrow (b. 1939) is a senior writer at *Time* magazine who contributes to cover stories and the *Time* essay section. Morrow has also written several books, including *The Chief: A Memoir of Fathers and Sons* (1985), a study of the author's relationship with his famous journalist father Hugh Morrow. In 1981, Morrow received the National Magazine Award for his *Time* essays. In "Africa," published in the February 23, 1987, issue of *Time*, Morrow re-creates in words what he saw, felt, and reflected about while on safari in East Africa.

Questions to Guide Your Reading

1. What is Morrow's purpose in writing?

2. Morrow uses many images of light and dark—"blinding clarities" and "shadows." How do these images help him portray the landscape and its animal inhabitants?

The animals stand motionless in gold-white grasses—zebras 1
and impala, Thomson's gazelles and Cape buffalo and harte-
beests and waterbuck and giraffes, and wildebeests by the thousands, all fixed in art naïf, in a smiting equatorial light. They
stand in the shadowless clarity of creation.

Now across the immense African landscape, from the distant 2
escarpment, a gray-purple rainstorm blows. It encroaches upon
the sunlight, moving through the air like a dark idea. East Africa
has a genius for such moments. Wildlife and landscape here
have about them a force of melodrama and annunciation. They
are the *Book of Genesis* enacted as an afternoon dream.

In Amboseli,[1] under the snow-covered dome of Mount Kil- 3
imanjaro, a herd of elephants moves like a dense gray cloud,
slow motion, in lumbering solidity: a mirage of floating boulders. Around them dust devils rise spontaneously out of the
desert, like tornadoes that swirl up on the thermals and go jit-
tering and rushing among the animals like evil spirits busy in
the primal garden.

Later, in the sweet last light of the afternoon, a lion prowls 4
in lion-colored grasses and vanishes into the perfect camouflage—setting off for the hunt, alert, indolent and somehow
abstracted, as cats are. A rhinoceros disappears: the eye loses
it among gray boulders and thorn trees. . . .

To the human eye, the animals so often seem mirages: now 5
you see them, now you don't. Later, just after dusk, Abyssin-
ian nightjars discover the magic wash of the headlight beams.
The birds flit in and out of the barrels of light, like dolphins
frisking before a boat's prow. The Land Cruiser jostles, in four-
wheel drive, across black volcanic stones toward the camp, the
driver steering by the distant light-speck of the cooking fire.

And then the African night, which, more than elsewhere, 6
seems an abnegation of the conscious world. MMBA, "miles and
miles of bloody Africa," and it all falls into black magic void.

The world stills, for the longest time. Then, at the edge of 7
sleep, hyenas come to giggle and whoop. Peering from the tent

---

[1]A game reserve in Kenya.—Ed.

flap, one catches in the shadows their sidelong criminal slouch. Their eyes shine like evil flashlight bulbs, a disembodied horror-movie yellow, phosphorescent, glowing like the children of the damned. In the morning, one finds their droppings: white dung, like a photographic negative. Hyenas not only eat the meat of animals but grind up and digest the bones. The hyenas' dung is white with the calcium of powdered bones.

8   Africa has its blinding clarities and its shadows. The clarities proclaim something primal, the first days of life. The shadows lie at the other extreme of time: in the premonition of last days, of extinction. Now you see the animals. Soon, perhaps, you won't.

9   Africa is comprehensive: great birth, great death, the beginning and the end. The themes are drawn, like the vivid, abstract hide of the zebra, in patterns of the absolute.

10   The first question to ask is whether the wildlife of Africa can survive.

11   The second question is this: If the wild animals of Africa vanish from the face of the earth, what, exactly, will have been lost?

12   The Africa of the animals is a sort of dream kingdom. Carl Jung traveled to East Africa in 1925 and wrote of a "most intense sentiment of returning to the land of my youth," of a "recognition of the immemorially known." Africa, he said, has "the stillness of the eternal beginning."

13   Earliest man lived in these landscapes, among such animals, among these splendid trees that have personalities as distinct as those of the animals: the aristocratic flat-topped acacia, the gnarled and magisterial baobab. Possibly scenes from that infancy are lodged in some layer of human memory, in the brilliant but preconscious morning. . . .

14   It is easy to fall in love not only with the shapes and colors of the animals but with their motions, their curving and infinitely varied gaits. The zebra moves with a strong, short-muscled stride. It is a sleek, erotic beast with vigorous bearing. The zebra's self-possession is a likable trait. It is human habit to sort the animals almost immediately into orders of preference. The animals are arranged in people's minds as a popularity contest. Some animals are endearing, and some repulsive. One wants to see the lion first, and then the elephant and after that the leopard, then rhino . . . and so on. One wants to see some animals

because they are fierce, and some because they are lovable and soft. It is hard to explain the attractions and preferences. It is possible that human feelings about wild animals reflect the complexities of sexual attractions. Certain animals are admired for their majestic aggressions, and others for softer qualities. The lion is a sleek piece of violence, the waterbuck a sweet piece of grace.

Some of the animals move in deep slow motion, as if tra- 15 versing another medium, previous to air, and thicker—an Atlantis of time. The elephant goes sleeping that way across the spaces. The medium through which it moves can be seen as time itself, a thicker, slower time than humans inhabit, a prehistoric metabolism. The giraffe goes with undulous slow motion, a long waving that starts with the head and proceeds dreamily, curving down the endless spine. The giraffe is motion as process through time. It is delicate, intelligent and eccentric, and as Karen Blixen said, so much a lady. Each of the animals has its distinct gait. The Grant's gazelle's tail never stops switching, like a nervous windshield wiper. The hartebeest moves off, when startled, in an undulous hallumph.

For days in Masai Mara,[2] the visitor watched the wildebeests. 16 Ungainly and pewter colored, they are subject to sudden electric jolts of panic, to adrenal bursts of motion that can make them seem half crazed as a tribe. Now they were engaged not so much in migration as in vagrancy, wandering across the plain on strange but idiotically determined vectors. Wildebeests smell monsters on the afternoon breeze, take sudden fear and bolt for Tanzania or Uganda or the Indian Ocean, anywhere to get away.

Sometimes, of course, the monsters are there. The veldt is lit- 17 tered with the corpses that the lion or cheetah has killed and dined on. But sometimes the herding wildebeests seem to be caught in a collective shallow madness. A fantasy of terror shoots through a herd, and all the beasts are gone: hysteria of hooves. The wildebeests thunder by the thousands across rivers and plains, moving like a barbarian invasion. They follow their instinct for the rains, for better grass. And they mow the grass before them. If they know where rain is, the wildebeests are relentless. Otherwise, they march with an undirected rigor,

[2]A game reserve in Kenya.—Ed.

without destination, like cadets on punishment, beating a trail in the parade ground. The wildebeest's bisonlike head is too large for its body, its legs too thin and ungainly. It looks like a middle-aged hypochondriac, paltry in the loins and given to terrible anxiety attacks, the sort of creature whose hands (if it had hands) would always be clammy. God's genius for design may have faltered with the wildebeest.

18   In Masai Mara, vultures wheel dreamily in the air, like a slow motion tornado of birds. Below the swirling funnel, a cheetah has brought down a baby wildebeest. The cheetah, loner and fleet aristocrat, the upper-class version of the hyena, has opened up the wildebeest and devoured the internal organs. The cheetah's belly is swollen and its mouth is ringed with blood as it breathes heavily from the exertion of gorging. A dozen vultures flap down to take their turn. They wait 20 yards away, then waddle in a little toward the kill to test the cheetah. The cheetah, in a burst, rushes the vultures to drive them off, and then returns to the baby wildebeest. The vultures grump and readjust their feathers and wait their turn, the surly lumpen-carrion class.

19   The skeleton of an elephant lies out in the grasses near a baobab tree and a scattering of black volcanic stones. The thick-trunked, gnarled baobab gesticulates with its branches, as if trying to summon help. There are no tusks lying among the bones, of course; ivory vanishes quickly in East Africa. The elephant is three weeks dead. Poachers. Not far away, a baby elephant walks alone. That is unusual. Elephants are careful mothers and do not leave their young unattended. The skeleton is the mother, and the baby is an orphan. . . .

20   The wild animals fetch back at least 2 million years. They represent, we imagine, the first order of creation, and they are vividly marked with God's eccentric genius of design: life poured into pure forms, life unmitigated by complexities of consciousness, language, ethics, treachery, revulsion, reason, religion, premeditation or free will. A wild animal does not contradict its own nature, does not thwart itself, as man endlessly does. A wild animal never plays for the other side. The wild animals are a holiday from deliberation. They are sheer life. To behold a bright being that lives without thought is, to the complex, cross-grained human mind, profoundly liberating.

And even if they had no effect upon the human mind, still the wild animals are life—other life.

John Donne asked, "Was not the first man, by the desire of 21 knowledge, corrupted even in the whitest integrity of nature?" The animals are a last glimpse of that shadowless life, previous to time and thought. They are a pure connection to the imagination of God.

Expanding Vocabulary

1. Match each word in column A with its definition in column B. When in doubt, first find the word in the essay and look for context clues to aid your understanding of the word's meaning. Then, if necessary, use your dictionary to complete the matching exercise. The number in parentheses is the number of the paragraph in which the word appears.

Column A	*Column B*
naïf (1)	original
escarpment (2)	sensual
annunciation (2)	irregular
thermals (3)	luminous
primal (3)	directions
abnegation (6)	open grassland
phosphorescent (7)	excessively worried about
premonition (8)	health
gnarled (13)	current of warm air
magisterial (13)	unqualified or unaffected
erotic (14)	natural simplicity
Atlantis (15)	authoritative
metabolism (15)	meager
undulous (15)	forewarning
eccentric (15)	expresses through gestures
adrenal (16)	twisted and knotty
vectors (16)	mythical island
veldt (17)	worthless
hypochondriac (17)	religious significance
paltry (17)	process of generating energy in
lumpen-carrion (18)	an organism
gesticulates (19)	sudden charge of energy
unmitigated (20)	rejection
	clifflike ridge of land or rock
	wavelike

2. Morrow mentions three people he expects his readers to know. After checking a dictionary or encyclopedia, add a one-sentence biographical statement to your text for Carl Jung, Karen Blixen, and John Donne.

Understanding Content

1. In the first thirteen paragraphs, Morrow paints the East Africa game preserve landscape. What are the predominant colors of this landscape? What does the land look like?
2. Morrow devotes paragraph 7 to the hyenas. What image of this animal emerges? How does the detail of the hyenas romping in the darkness help to create Morrow's view of the hyenas?
3. In paragraphs 14 through 19 Morrow describes the animals' movements. Read these paragraphs again, picturing each animal's movements as Morrow presents them. Which animals would you want to see first? Why?
4. Morrow notes what others have also experienced when on safari in a group: members of the group have animal favorites. Morrow suggests that preferences may be connected to sexual attractions. Is this a new idea for you? Does it seem to make sense?
5. Morrow ends the section on movement with nonmovement: a dead elephant and lonely baby elephant. How does this detail contribute to the image of East Africa that he seeks to develop? If the animals become extinct, what will we have lost?

Drawing Inferences about Thesis and Purpose

1. Is there one sentence in the essay that could stand as Morrow's thesis? If you don't think so, then state the essay's thesis in your own words.
2. After several paragraphs about the wildebeests, Morrow concludes that "God's genius . . . may have faltered." Why? What details lead to this conclusion?
3. Why, in Morrow's view, are the animals "pure forms" and "sheer life"? How do they differ from humans? What do they represent in the development of life forms?

Analyzing Strategies and Style

1. Look at Morrow's opening paragraphs. What does the first paragraph accomplish? As the camera rolls on, what is added in paragraph 2? How do these two scenes announce the complex world of the game preserve that Morrow develops in the rest of the essay?

2. Examine Morrow's organization. Is it appropriate to say that Morrow first shows us photographs of his trip and then a videotape? Why?
3. How many paragraphs at the beginning of the essay give us photographs? How many separate photos are needed? What is the organizing principle of the photos?
4. Morrow presents some details as contrasts, almost contradictions. Find some examples. Is a landscape of contrasts simple or complex? Boring or awesome? What sense of this world does the author give us?
5. Morrow uses some striking metaphors to develop his description. Find three that you particularly like and explain why they are effective.

Thinking Critically

1. Has Morrow rekindled, or awakened, in you an interest in the wildlife of East Africa? If so, but you cannot afford to go on safari, what can you do to see these animals and learn more about them? List as many sources of information and experience as you can.
2. On the basis of Morrow's description—or your experiences—which of the big game is your favorite animal? Why? What attracts you to that animal? List the characteristics that you find appealing.
3. Closer to home, what domestic animal is or would be your favorite pet? Why? List the characteristics that you find appealing.
4. Should we be concerned about the possible extinction of the African elephant or rhino, the two most seriously threatened of the big game in East Africa? Why or why not? Be prepared to defend your position.

My Father

DORIS LESSING

Born in Persia (now Iran) but reared in Southern Rhodesia (now Zimbabwe), Doris Lessing (b. 1919) left school at fourteen, took various odd jobs, and began to write, first in Africa and now in London. She has steadily published short stories, plays, and novels since 1950 and is considered by critics to be one of the most significant contemporary writers. She has several short story collections, including *A Man and Two Women* (1963); several short novels, including *The Grass Is Singing* (1950); and many novels, including her most celebrated one, *The Golden Notebook* (1962). A number of essays and reviews are collected in *A Small Personal Voice* (1975). In "My Father," first published in 1963 in the London *Sunday Telegraph*, we see Lessing's commitment to portraying her father clearly and honestly, and accepting the figure in the portrait.

Questions to Guide Your Reading

1. What trait most distressed Lessing's father? What did he do about it? How does this become a telling detail of character?
2. How would you describe the tone of this essay? What seems to be Lessing's attitude toward her father? Toward the war?

1   We use our parents like recurring dreams, to be entered into when needed; they are always there for love or for hate; but it occurs to me that I was not always there for my father. I've written about him before, but novels, stories, don't have to be "true." Writing this article is difficult because it has to be "true." I knew him when his best years were over.

2   There are photographs of him. The largest is of an officer in the 1914–18 war. A new uniform—buttoned, badged, strapped, tabbed—confines a handsome, dark young man who holds himself stiffly to confront what he certainly thought of as his duty. His eyes are steady, serious, and responsible, and show no signs of what he became later. A photograph at sixteen is of a dark, introspective youth with the same intent eyes. But it is his mouth you notice—a heavily-jutting upper lip contradicts the rest of a regular face. His moustache was to hide it: "Had to do something—a damned fleshy mouth. Always made me uncomfortable, that mouth of mine."

3   Earlier a baby (eyes already alert) appears in a lace waterfall that cascades from the pillowy bosom of a fat, plain woman to her feet. It is the face of a head cook. "Lord, but my mother was a practical female—almost as bad as you!" as he used to say, or throw at my mother in moments of exasperation. Beside her stands, or droops, arms dangling, his father, the source of the dark, arresting eyes, but otherwise masked by a long beard.

4   The birth certificate says: Born 3rd August, 1886, Walton Villa, Creffield Road, S. Mary at the Wall, R.S.D. Name, Alfred

Cook. Name and surname of Father: Alfred Cook Tayler. Name
and maiden name of Mother: Caroline May Batley. Rank or Profession: Bank Clerk. Colchester, Essex.
They were very poor. Clothes and boots were a problem.   5
They "made their own amusements." Books were mostly the
Bible and *The Pilgrim's Progress.* Every Saturday night they
bathed in a hip-bath in front of the kitchen fire. No servants.
Church three times on Sundays. "Lord, when I think of those
Sundays! I dreaded them all week, like a nightmare coming at
you full tilt and no escape." But he rabbited with ferrets along
the lanes and fields, bird-nested, stole fruit, picked nuts and
mushrooms, paid visits to the blacksmith and the mill and rode
a farmer's carthorse.

They ate economically, but when he got diabetes in his for-   6
ties and subsisted on lean meat and lettuce leaves, he remembered suet puddings, treacle puddings, raisin and currant
puddings, steak and kidney puddings, bread and butter pud-
ding, "batter cooked in the gravy with the meat," potato cake,
plum cake, butter cake, porridge with treacle, fruit tarts and
pies, brawn, pig's trotters and pig's cheek and home-smoked
ham and sausages. And "lashings of fresh butter and cream and
eggs." He wondered if this diet had produced the diabetes, but
said it was worth it.

There was an elder brother described by my father as: "Too   7
damned clever by half. One of those quick, clever brains. Now
I've always had a slow brain, but I get there in the end, damn it!"

The brothers went to a local school and the elder did well,   8
but my father was beaten for being slow. They both became
bank clerks in, I think, the Westminster Bank, and one must
have found it congenial, for he became a manager, the "rich
brother," who had cars and even a yacht. But my father did
not like it, though he was conscientious. For instance, he
changed his writing, letter by letter, because a senior criticised
it. I never saw his unregenerate hand, but the one he created
was elegant, spiky, careful. Did this mean he created a new personality for himself, hiding one he did not like, as he hid his
"damned fleshy mouth"? I don't know.

Nor do I know when he left home to live in Luton or why. He   9
found family life too narrow? A safe guess—he found everything too narrow. His mother was too down-to-earth? He had
to get away from his clever elder brother?

10   Being a young man in Luton was the best part of his life. It ended in 1914, so he had a decade of happiness. His reminiscences of it were all of pleasure, the delight of physical movement, of dancing in particular. All his girls were "a beautiful dancer, light as a feather." He played billiards and ping-pong (both for his county); he swam, boated, played cricket and football, went to picnics and horse races, sang at musical evenings. One family of a mother and two daughters treated him "like a son only better. I didn't know whether I was in love with the mother or the daughters, but oh I did love going there; we had such good times." He was engaged to one daughter, then, for a time, to the other. An engagement was broken off because she was rude to a waiter. "I could not marry a woman who allowed herself to insult someone who was defenceless." He used to say to my wryly smiling mother: "Just as well I didn't marry either of *them*; they would never have stuck it out the way you have, old girl."

11   Just before he died he told me he had dreamed he was standing in a kitchen on a very high mountain holding X in his arms. "Ah, yes, that's what I've missed in my life. Now don't you let yourself be cheated out of life by the old dears. They take all the colour out of everything if you let them."

12   But in that decade—"I'd walk 10, 15 miles to a dance two or three times a week and think nothing of it. Then I'd dance every dance and walk home again over the fields. Sometimes it was moonlight, but I liked the snow best, all crisp and fresh. I loved walking back and getting into my digs just as the sun was rising. My little dog was so happy to see me, and I'd feed her, and make myself porridge and tea, then I'd wash and shave and go off to work."

13   The boy who was beaten at school, who went too much to church, who carried the fear of poverty all his life, but who nevertheless was filled with the memories of country pleasures; the young bank clerk who worked such long hours for so little money, but who danced, sang, played, flirted—this naturally vigorous, sensuous being was killed in 1914, 1915, 1916. I think the best of my father died in that war, that his spirit was crippled by it. The people I've met, particularly the women, who knew him young, speak of his high spirits, his energy, his enjoyment of life. Also of his kindness, his compassion and—a word that keeps recurring—his wisdom. "Even when he was just a

boy he understood things that you'd think even an old man would find it easy to condemn." I do not think these people would have easily recognized the ill, irritable, abstracted, hypochondriac man I knew.

He "joined up" as an ordinary soldier out of a characteristi- 14 cally quirky scruple: it wasn't right to enjoy officers' privileges when the Tommies had such a bad time. But he could not stick the communal latrines, the obligatory drinking, the collective visits to brothels, the jokes about girls. So next time he was offered a commission he took it.

His childhood and young man's memories, kept fluid, were 15 added to, grew, as living memories do. But his war memories were congealed in stories that he told again and again, with the same words and gestures, in stereotyped phrases. They were anonymous, general, as if they had come out of a communal war memoir. He met a German in no-man's-land, but both slowly lowered their rifles and smiled and walked away. The Tommies were the salt of the earth, the British fighting men the best in the world. He had never known such comradeship. A certain brutal officer was shot in a sortie[1] by his men, but the other officers, recognizing rough justice, said nothing. He had known men intimately who saw the Angels at Mons.[2] He wished he could force all the generals on both sides into the trenches for just one day, to see what the common soldiers endured—*that* would have ended the war at once.

There was an undercurrent of memories, dreams, and emo- 16 tions much deeper, more personal. This dark region in him, fate-ruled, where nothing was true but horror, was expressed inarticulately, in brief, bitter exclamations or phrases of rage, incredulity, betrayal. The men who went to fight in that war believed it when they said it was to end war. My father believed it. And he was never able to reconcile his belief in his country with his anger at the cynicism of its leaders. And the anger, the sense of betrayal, strengthened as he grew old and ill.

But in 1914 he was naïve, the German atrocities in Belgium 17 inflamed him, and he enlisted out of idealism, although he knew he would have a hard time. He knew because a fortuneteller told him. (He could be described as uncritically

---

[1]A rapid movement of besieged troops to take the offensive.—Ed.
[2]A Belgian town, site of a World War I battle.—Ed.

superstitious or as psychically gifted.) He would be in great danger twice, yet not die—he was being protected by a famous soldier who was his ancestor. "And sure enough, later I heard from the Little Aunties that the church records showed we were descended the backstairs way from the Duke of Wellington, or was it Marlborough? Damn it, I forget. But one of them would be beside me all through the war, she said." (He was romantic, not only about this solicitous ghost, but also about being a descendant of the Huguenots, on the strength of the "e" in Tayler; and about "the wild blood" in his veins from a great uncle who, sent unjustly to prison for smuggling, came out of a ten-year sentence and earned it, very efficiently, along the coasts of Cornwall until he died.)

18   The luckiest thing that ever happened to my father, he said, was getting his leg shattered by shrapnel ten days before Passchendaele.[3] His whole company was killed. He knew he was going to be wounded because of the fortuneteller, who had said he would know. "I did not understand what she meant, but both times in the trenches, first when my appendix burst and I nearly died, and then just before Passchendaele, I felt for some days as if a thick, black velvet pall was settled over me. I can't tell you what it was like. Oh, it was awful, awful, and the second time it was so bad I wrote to the old people and told them I was going to be killed."

19   His leg was cut off at mid-thigh, he was shell-shocked, he was very ill for many months, with a prolonged depression afterwards. "You should always remember that sometimes people are all seething underneath. You don't know what terrible things people have to fight against. You should look at a person's eyes, that's how you tell. . . . When I was like that, after I lost my leg, I went to a nice doctor man and said I was going mad, but he said, don't worry, everyone locks up things like that. You don't know—horrible, horrible, awful things. I was afraid of myself, of what I used to dream. I wasn't myself at all."

20   In the Royal Free Hospital was my mother, Sister McVeagh. He married his nurse which, as they both said often enough (though in different tones of voice), was just as well. That was 1919. He could not face being a bank clerk in England, he said, not after the trenches. Besides, England was too narrow and con-

---

[3]A town in Belgium, site of a bloody World War I battle.—Ed.

ventional. Besides, the civilians did not know what the soldiers had suffered, they didn't want to know, and now it wasn't done even to remember "The Great Unmentionable." He went off to the Imperial Bank of Persia, in which country I was born.

The house was beautiful, with great stone-floored high- 21 ceilinged rooms whose windows showed ranges of snow-streaked mountains. The gardens were full of roses, jasmine, pomegranates, walnuts. Kermanshalhi[4] he spoke of with liking, but soon they went to Teheran, populous with "Embassy people," and my gregarious mother created a lively social life about which he was irritable even in recollection.

Irritableness—that note was first struck here, about Persia. 22 He did not like, he said, "the graft and the corruption." But here it is time to try and describe something difficult—how a man's good qualities can also be his bad ones, or if not bad, a danger to him.

My father was honourable—he always knew exactly what 23 that word meant. He had integrity. His "one does not do that sort of thing," his "no, it is *not* right," sounded throughout my childhood and were final for all of us. I am sure it was true he wanted to leave Persia because of "the corruption." But it was also because he was already unconsciously longing for something freer, because as a bank official he could not let go into the dream-logged personality that was waiting for him. And later in Rhodesia, too, what was best in him was also what prevented him from shaking away the shadows: it was always in the name of honesty or decency that he refused to take this step or that out of the slow decay of the family's fortunes.

In 1925 there was leave from Persia. That year in London 24 there was an Empire Exhibition, and on the Southern Rhodesian stand some very fine maize cobs and a poster saying that fortunes could be made on maize at 25/- a bag. So on an impulse, turning his back forever on England, washing his hands of the corruption of the East, my father collected all his capital, £ 800, I think, while my mother packed curtains from Liberty's, clothes from Harrods,[5] visiting cards, a piano, Persian rugs, a governess and two small children.

Soon, there was my father in a cigar-shaped house of thatch 25 and mud on the top of a kopje that overlooked in all directions

---

[4]A city in western Iran (formerly Persia).—Ed.
[5]Both Liberty's and Harrods are British department stores.—Ed.

a great system of mountains, rivers, valleys, while overhead the sky arched from horizon to empty horizon. This was a couple of hundred miles south from the Zambesi,[6] a hundred or so west from Mozambique,[7] in the district of Banket, so called because certain of its reefs were of the same formation as those called *banket* on the Rand. Lomagundi[8]—gold country, tobacco country, maize country—wild, almost empty. (The Africans had been turned off it into reserves.) Our neighbours were four, five, seven miles off. In front of the house . . . no neighbours, nothing; no farms, just wild bush with two rivers but no fences to the mountains seven miles away. And beyond these mountains and bush again to the Portuguese border, over which "our boys" used to escape when wanted by the police for pass or other offences.

26   And then? There was bad luck. For instance, the price of maize dropped from 25/- to 9/- a bag. The seasons were bad, prices bad, crops failed. This was the sort of thing that made it impossible for him ever to "get off the farm," which, he agreed with my mother, was what he most wanted to do.

27   It was an absurd country, he said. A man could "own" a farm for years that was totally mortgaged to the Government and run from the Land Bank, meanwhile employing half-a-hundred Africans at 12/- a month and none of them knew how to do a day's work. Why, two farm labourers from Europe could do in a day what twenty of these ignorant black savages would take a week to do. (Yet he was proud that he had a name as a just employer, that he gave "a square deal.") Things got worse. A fortuneteller had told him that her heart ached when she saw the misery ahead for my father: this was the misery.

28   But it was my mother who suffered. After a period of neurotic illness, which was a protest against her situation, she became brave and resourceful. But she never saw that her husband was not living in a real world, that he had made a captive of her common sense. We were always about to "get off the farm." A miracle would do it—a sweepstake, a goldmine,

---

[6] A river in southeastern Africa that flows to the Indian Ocean.—Ed.
[7] A southeastern African nation that borders Zimbabwe (formerly Southern Rhodesia).—Ed.
[8] A district in Zimbabwe west of Salisbury.—Ed.

a legacy. And then? What a question! We would go to England where life would be normal with people coming in for musical evenings and nice supper parties at the Trocadero after a show. Poor woman, for the twenty years we were on the farm, she waited for when life would begin for her and for her children, for she never understood that what was a calamity for her was for them a blessing.

Meanwhile my father sank towards his death (at 61). Every- 29 thing changed in him. He had been a dandy and fastidious, now he hated to change out of shabby khaki. He had been sociable, now he was misanthropic. His body's disorders—soon diabetes and all kinds of stomach ailments—dominated him. He was brave about his wooden leg, and even went down mine shafts and climbed trees with it, but he walked clumsily and it irked him badly. He greyed fast, and slept more in the day, but would be awake half the night pondering about. . . .

It could be gold divining. For ten years he experimented on 30 private theories to do with the attractions and repulsions of metals. His whole soul went into it but his theories were wrong or he was *unlucky*—after all, if he had found a mine he would have had to leave the farm. It could be the relation between the minerals of the earth and of the moon; his decision to make infusions of all the plants on the farm and drink them himself in the interests of science; the criminal folly of the British Government in not realising that the Germans and the Russians were conspiring as Anti-Christ to . . . the inevitability of war because no one would listen to Churchill, but it would be all right because God (by then he was a British Israelite) had destined Britain to rule the world; a prophecy said 10 million dead would surround Jerusalem—how would the corpses be cleared away?; people who wished to abolish flogging should be flogged; the natives understood nothing but a good beating; hanging must not be abolished because the Old Testament said "an eye for an eye and a tooth for a tooth. . . ."

Yet, as this side of him darkened, so that it seemed all his 31 thoughts were of violence, illness, war, still no one dared to make an unkind comment in his presence or to gossip. Criticism of people, particularly of women, made him more and more uncomfortable till at last he burst out with: "It's all very well, but no one has the right to say that about another person."

32   In Africa, when the sun goes down, the stars spring up, all of
them in their expected places, glittering and moving. In the
rainy season, the sky flashed and thundered. In the dry season, the great dark hollow of night was lit by veld fires: the
mountains burned through September and October in chains of
red fire. Every night my father took out his chair to watch the
sky and the mountains, smoking, silent, a thin shabby flyaway
figure under the stars. "Makes you think—there are so many
worlds up there, wouldn't really matter if we did blow ourselves up—plenty more where we came from."

33   The Second World War, so long foreseen by him, was a bad
time. His son was in the Navy and in danger, and his daughter a sorrow to him. He became very ill. More and more often
it was necessary to drive him into Salisbury with him in a coma,
or in danger of one, on the back seat. My mother moved him
into a pretty little suburban house in town near the hospitals,
where he took to his bed and a couple of years later died. For
the most part he was unconscious under drugs. When awake he
talked obsessively (a tongue licking a nagging sore place) about
"the old war." Or he remembered his youth. "I've been dreaming—Lord, to see those horses come lickety-split down the
course with their necks stretched out and the sun on their coats
and everyone shouting. . . . I've been dreaming how I walked
along the river in the mist as the sun was rising. . . . Lord, lord,
lord, what a time that was, what good times we all had then,
before the old war."

Expanding Vocabulary

Match each word in column A with its definition in column B. When
in doubt, first find the word in the essay and look for context clues
to aid your understanding of the word's meaning. Then, if necessary,
use your dictionary to complete the matching exercise. The number in parentheses is the number of the paragraph in which the word
appears.

Column A	*Column B*
introspective (2)	friendly, pleasant personality
ferrets (5)	ironically humorous
diabetes (6)	person who worries about his or her
congenial (8)	health

conscientious (8)
wryly (10)
hypochondriac (13)
quirky (14)
scruple (14)
congealed (15)
inarticulately (16)
incredulity (16)
cynicism (16)
psychically (17)
seething (19)
gregarious (21)
kopje (25)
fastidious (29)
misanthropic (29)
veld (32)

lacking clear expression
nonrationally or supernaturally aware
doubt, skepticism
boiling with agitation or anger
variety of polecat used to catch rabbits
view of life that questions the motives
    of others
disease that limits the body's use
    of sugar
especially careful, neat
peculiar, unusual behavior
honest and scrupulous
outgoing with people
examining one's own mental state
fixed, no longer fluid
hating, distrusting people
a restraint on action because of moral
    considerations
open, bush country
a small hill

Understanding Content

1. What is most striking about her father's physical appearance?
2. Why, according to Lessing, did her father leave home when he was young? What specific motives does she suggest? What general motive?

Drawing Inferences about Thesis and Purpose

1. Lessing begins by asserting that although stories do not have to be "true," essays do. Both times she puts the word *true* in quotation marks. What is her point? In what sense is a novel true? Not true? In what sense is biography true? Not true? What is the difference between truth and fact?
2. In what ways did the war "kill" Lessing's father? How did the experience change him?
3. Lessing contrasts her father's accounts of his early life with his accounts of World War I. How did these tales differ? What do these differences reveal about her father?
4. What details of his final years in Africa can be explained by personality? By his early family life? By the war?

Analyzing Strategies and Style

1. In general, what characteristics of her writing make Lessing's portrait of interest to readers who may not already be interested in her or her father?
2. Observe Lessing's opening strategies. What does she accomplish by her opening paragraph? How does she begin her portrait? What does she not begin with? What make her strategies effective?
3. What does the author do in paragraph 6? What is effective about her strategy? What can you learn about good writing from studying this paragraph?

Thinking Critically

1. Have you thought before about Lessing's distinctions between fiction and biography and between truth and fact? Do Lessing's distinctions make sense to you? If so, why? If not, why not?
2. Do you know anyone who is a war veteran? If so, how has the person been affected by his or her war experience? Does Lessing's father's change seem fairly typical or unusual?
3. Reflect on the nature of personality or character. Are we one person consistently, or are we continually reshaped (or new-shaped) by our life experiences? How stable, or how fluid, is personality?

STUDENT ESSAY—DESCRIPTION

TIME'S TROPHY
Alexa Skandar

There is something timeless and comforting about an old face. The face of my grandmother is built of a thousand weathered wrinkles. She doesn't smile too often anymore. On those rare occasions when we are lucky enough to catch her smile, her eyes seem to completely disappear behind the folds of time, yet somehow they still radiate that light that always attracted everyone to her.

Subject introduced through details of aging.

My grandmother smells of rose oil and
lettuce cream. She keeps her yellowed
white hair permed and short and slicks it
back with water every so often. Her skin
is like the leather of her brown sandals,
and her hands reveal the years of toil she
has survived. Veins show like ancient
flowing rivers through her aged skin. The
index finger of her right hand is curved.
"It's from years of crocheting," her
daughter once explained to me in whispers.
Her small, frail body, bent like her finger by the hands of time, seems to reflect
pain and hardship in her past.

*Subject is now
identified—her
grandmother.*

*Good use of
metaphors to
describe
physical details.*

Celuta Quiroga de Skandar wears black
every day, black to mourn her dead husband. Every day she prays for him. Every
day her cloudy hazel eyes show her grief
that has been there since he passed away
close to thirty years ago. She used to
go to church every day and to visit his
grave every Sunday, but she has grown too
old for that now. Instead she sits in a
chair in the corner, rosary beads in
hand, eyes partially closed, pupils
rolled back, whispering her "Hail Mary's"
as she rocks herself back and forth.
Senile though she is, sometimes she gets
serious, and her eyes become clear, as
if she has broken out of some kind of
trance for a moment, and she admits that

*Grandmother's
name and
widowed state
revealed.*

she prays every day for God to take her to be with her husband. Then her eyes cloud over and her words become meaningless again.

My grandmother is very old now. Little matters to her anymore. She has stopped living on the same plane of existence as the rest of us. She sits down to tell us the same stories over and over. She goes to bed at eight in the evening only to wake up a few hours later, make her bed, and get dressed. She often makes her way to the kitchen and is fixing breakfast before she is found and told gently, "Abuelita, it's still nighttime. Time to sleep. Let's put you back to bed." A confused look comes over her face, but she obliges, often just to get back up and repeat the morning routine a few hours later.

Example of her senility.

She used to be a strong and active woman. "Dona Celu," as they called her in her small village, was a mother, a nurse, a midwife, a farmer, a cook, and a storyteller. People who remember how she used to be tell stories of her greatness, making me proud to be her granddaughter. They recount how she organized the building of the first swimming pool in the valley in which she lived and how she saved the lives of new mothers and

Details given to reveal the person she once was.

their infants from the complications of small-town childbirth. They tell of how she took in the neighbors' orphaned children when they had nowhere else to turn, and raised them as her own. Now her feeble attempts to sneak out of the house and stumble to church inspire pity in all of us. She has become a mere shadow of the strong and determined woman she once was. But, there is a certain strength in the lines that time has etched in her face, a kind of beauty that she has attained as a trophy for all she has been through in her years of existence. For one, a wonderful grandmother.

Thesis stated at end.

MAKING CONNECTIONS

1. Degas and Picasso both depict dancers in their paintings. (See reproductions following p. 80.) How do their paintings differ? How do the differences in presentation change the viewer's "picture" of dancers? Can one painting be said to be more realistic than the other? If so, what is meant by *realistic*?
2. In their essays both Tracy Kidder and Pat Mora create a "portrait" of a woman. How do the writers feel about their subjects? How do you know?
3. Study the essays of Kidder, Mora, and Lessing. What conclusions can you draw about effective strategies for presenting telling details of character?
4. Lessing's father was shaped both by his childhood and by World War I. Santha Rama Rau (pp. 44–50) was shaped by where she grew up and also because of her ethnicity. Elizabeth Wong (pp. 40–42) and Luis Rodriguez (pp. 55–58) are influenced by growing up as minorities in American culture.

Think about what these writers say—or imply—about the shaping of personality. Reflect: What are the strongest forces in the molding of character?

5. Select one of the painters represented in the chapter and learn more about him, using your library's reference books on going online. Learn about his life, his time, the kind of painting he is known for, and something about that style or type of painting. Be able to answer the question: What makes this painter famous in the history of art? You can do a keyword search using the artist's last name to locate books in your library's book catalog, to find current articles in your library's online databases, or to locate information online.

TOPICS AND GUIDELINES FOR WRITING

---

1. Describe a place you know well and that has a special significance for you. (Possibilities include your backyard, the path you walked to school, a favorite park, playground, vacation spot, city street.) Give the details that will let your reader see this place clearly. But also provide the telling details that will let your reader understand why this place has (or had) significance for you, why it is (or was) special. Organize details according to some spatial pattern.

2. Describe a place you have visited that produced a strong reaction in you, a place that you fell in love with (e.g., Fifth Avenue the week before Christmas), heartily disliked (e.g., Los Angeles in heavy smog), found incredibly beautiful or awe-inspiring or special in some way (e.g., the Florida Everglades, Niagara Falls, the green hills of Vermont). Give enough details to let readers who have not been there see the place, but concentrate on presenting those details so that readers will want to visit—or never visit—depending on your thesis.

3. Have you been in an earthquake or hurricane or seen a tornado? If so, re-create the event in words so that readers can see it and feel the accompanying human emotions. Do not write a narrative account; rather select a moment or two and describe that time vividly.

4. Diane Ackerman describes the snow falling outside her home. Describe a specific scene during one of the seasons. Possibilities include your garden in autumn, a city park in summer, a city center at holiday time, your campus in the spring.

5. Describe a room on your campus to develop and support the thesis that the room fulfills—or fails to fulfill—its purpose or function. Possibilities include a classroom, science lab, learning lab, writing center, cafeteria, or library. If your library is a large and separate building, select one section of it, such as the periodicals room. Resist the urge to describe a large building, such as the entire student center. Instead, focus on one place and present details to support your thesis. Organize details according to some spatial pattern.

6. Lance Morrow offers readers some detailed and moving descriptions of animals he saw in the East Africa game preserves. If you enjoy wildlife, either in the wild or in a nearby zoo, take some time to watch one of your favorite animals. Or, if you have a pet, reflect on that animal. Then write a description of the animal you have selected, giving many details but also the telling details that will support a thesis about the animal. Reflect on what is central to the animal's way of life or personality to arrive at your thesis. Is the animal funny? Endearing? Inspiring? Mean? Intelligent or clever? These are some possible ideas around which you can build your thesis.

7. How well do you see someone close to you—a family member, friend, colleague, teacher? Select telling physical and biographical details to create an interesting and thoughtful portrait of the person you select. Pay close attention to the details that shape personality.

8. Select one of the paintings reproduced in this text or find a color reproduction of a favorite painting in your library's art book collection. Explain how the details in the painting work to create the painting's dominant effect. You will need to reflect on the painting's effect, or the artist's attitude toward the subject. Then ask yourself: How is that effect achieved by the details—the objects, composition, color, and brushwork—that make up the painting? Organize thoughtfully and use spatial terms (e.g., "in the foreground," "to the left of the main figure") to guide your reader through your description.

4

Using Comparison and Contrast

Ways of Learning

When we compare we examine similarities; when we contrast we examine differences. These are strategies frequently used—whether in thinking for ourselves or communicating with others—to organize information or ideas about two (or more) similar subjects. When you think about why you like your biology course more than your chemistry course, you begin to note points of difference between them. You begin to use contrast. When shopping for a stereo system, you might read a consumer guide or gather information from friends so that you can contrast several models for cost, reliability, and sound.

When to Use Comparison and Contrast

Let's see what we have said about thinking comparatively. First, it is a strategy for organizing information and ideas. You may be able to think more clearly about problems in your chemistry course if you contrast those problems with your successes in biology. Second, you have a reason to examine similarities or differences between subjects. Your goal, in our example, is to understand why you are doing better in biology than in chemistry. Perhaps you came to college thinking that you would major in chemistry. Rethinking career goals may be aided by a careful listing of specific differences in your study of chemistry and biology. (One difference is the amount of math needed in the study of chemistry. Could that be the problem?) Third, we compare or contrast items that are similar. There seems to be little purpose in contrasting your chemistry course with doing your laundry. We compare or contrast two cities, two schools, two jobs, two dorms. We probably do not contrast living in Louisville with living in a frat house because there is no point to such a contrast. (You might have good reason, though, to contrast living at home with living away at school.) Finally, a useful comparison or contrast focuses on important similarities or differences. If you have plenty of space for your new stereo, then contrasting the sizes of different systems is unimportant. But unless you have unlimited funds, the cost of each unit is quite important, important to your purpose for choosing the best stereo for you.

Remember that an organizing principle such as comparison or contrast does not supply a purpose for writing. Rather it is a strategy that needs to grow logically out of your topic and purpose. Nancy Sakamoto contrasts American and Japanese conversations to show why sometimes Japanese and Americans have trouble communicating or being comfortable in conversation with one another. Her contrast structure is a strategy, not an end in itself.

How to Use Comparison and Contrast

Sometimes writers combine comparison and contrast, but more often their goal is to show either similarities or differences. Thus the student who asserts that there are good reasons for parents to move their children from McLean to Langley High School has a thesis that announces a contrast purpose. Although the schools certainly have some similarities—both are high schools in northern Virginia—readers will expect to learn about the significant differences between the two schools.

Organization

How should points of difference between two high schools (or any two items) be organized in an essay? You have two basic plans from which to choose. Suppose you want to show differences in the two buildings, in the courses offered, and in the extracurricular activities. If we assign "A" to McLean and "B" to Langley and number the points of difference 1, 2, and 3, we can diagram the two patterns as follows:

Whole by Whole	*Part by Part*
A. McLean	A. Physical Plant
1. McLean Physical Plant	1. McLean
2. McLean Courses	2. Langley
3. McLean Activities	B. Courses
B. Langley	1. McLean
1. Langley Physical Plant	2. Langley
2. Langley Courses	C. Activities
3. Langley Activities	1. McLean
	2. Langley

Observe that the whole-by-whole pattern organizes the essay first by school and then by points of difference, whereas the part-by-part pattern organizes the paper by the three (in this example) points of difference.

As you will see in the essays in this chapter, professional writers do not always strictly follow one plan or the other. Your instructor, however, may want you to practice using either the whole-by-whole or part-by-part structure. In fact, many instructors believe that, for most contrast topics, the part-by-part pattern is the best choice because it keeps writers focused on the business of explaining points of difference.

Transitions

When you read articles that have a comparison or contrast purpose, you may want to label the two subjects A and B and then, in the margin of your book, assign a number to each point of similarity or difference as you read. Then remember when you are writing a contrast essay that you want your reader to be able to recognize the parts of your contrast structure. This means that you will need to use appropriate transitions to mark the parts of your contrast structure. Consider these possibilities and other similar expressions to guide your reader:

by contrast	on the other hand
another difference	a third similarity

Metaphors and Analogies

When we think about the strategies of comparison and contrast, two related terms come to mind: metaphor (or simile) and analogy. We have said that we compare or contrast similar items: two schools, two courses, and so on. A *metaphor* (or a *simile*) differs in that it compares two items that are essentially unalike. When the poet writes the simile: "My love is like a red, red rose," he asks us to consider the ways that love (a feeling) can be like a rose (a flower). (To express the idea as a metaphor, the poet can write: "My love blooms.") In either case, we understand that a feeling isn't really like a flower. This is why a metaphor or a simile is called a *figure of speech*—we are speaking figuratively, not literally. The cleverness of a fresh metaphor delights us, sometimes surprises us, and affects us emotionally. You will find the poet Linda Pastan and the essayist E. B. White using metaphors effectively to express feelings about their subjects.

In the chapter's sixth essay, Liane Ellison Norman compares students to squirrels. That sounds like a metaphor because people and squirrels are not like items. But since Norman uses this figurative comparison as a way to develop her entire essay, to make a point about students, we call this strategy neither comparison nor metaphor but *analogy*. Think of an analogy as fanciful (like a metaphor) but developing a number of points of similarity or difference to support a thesis. Both metaphors and analogies, when original and thoughtful, enrich our writing. Some of this chapter's exercises will give you a chance to practice both strategies.

WRITING FOCUS:

COHERENCE IS CRUCIAL

We have noted that it is important to use transition words to guide readers through your contrast essay. But writers need to use *coherence strategies* in all of their writing, not just to show contrast. Think of each body paragraph (excluding the opening and concluding paragraphs) as a "mini"-essay; each one needs both *unity* and *coherence*.

Unity means that all sentences in each paragraph are on that paragraph's topic. *Coherence* means choosing to use strategies that *show* readers how each body paragraph holds together. Make a point to use coherence strategies. They are illustrated and labeled in the following sample paragraph.

Para-
graph's
topic
sentence

Repetition of
subject
or key
words

Clear
structure of
material—
air, sea,
land

Transition
words/
phrases

During the Cretaceous Period (about 160 million to 65 million years ago in North America) you would have found some familiar plants—for example, ferns, palm trees, and redwoods—and you would have been surprised by the mix of animals. At that time you would have found many birds, including giant flying pterosaurs. In the sea, you would have seen an interesting mix, for example, sharks and turtles along with giant marine lizards and fishlike ichthyosaurs. On land there were insects and small, furry mammals, but also the dinosaurs. Although some dinosaurs were already extinct, others still roamed North America, for instance, duck-bills, Triceratops, and the famous *Tryannosaurus rex.*

Getting Started:
Reflecting on Expectations of College

Although you may not have been at college for long, still you have probably had some experiences that were not what you expected. Reflect on what you expected college to be like and how your experiences have, in part, differed from those expectations. In your journal or class notebook make two columns—one of expectations and one of what you have actually experienced. Have most of your expectations been met? Only some of them? Is there one important difference that is bothering you? You may want to write about that difference in another journal entry, or perhaps in an essay.

Conversational Ballgames

NANCY MASTERSON SAKAMOTO

American-born Sakamoto (b. 1931) lived with her Japanese husband in Osaka and taught English to Japanese students. She

is currently a professor at Shitennoji Gakuen University in
Hawaii. "Conversational Ballgames" is a chapter from her textbook on conversational English, *Polite Fictions*, published in
1982. Her contrasts of English and Japanese styles of conversation and her strategy for developing that contrast make us
aware of the effect of cultural conditioning on the ways we
learn to use language.

Questions to Guide Your Reading

1. What strategy does the author use to explain conversation
   patterns in English and in Japanese?
2. What differences between American culture and Japanese
   culture are suggested in Sakamoto's discussion of conversation?

After I was married and had lived in Japan for a while, my   1
Japanese gradually improved to the point where I could take
part in simple conversations with my husband and his friends
and family. And I began to notice that often, when I joined in,
the others would look startled, and the conversational topic
would come to a halt. After this happened several times, it
became clear to me that I was doing something wrong. But for
a long time, I didn't know what it was.

Finally, after listening carefully to many Japanese conver-   2
sations, I discovered what my problem was. Even though I
was speaking Japanese, I was handling the conversation in a
western way.

Japanese-style conversations develop quite differently from   3
western-style conversations. And the difference isn't only
in the languages. I realized that just as I kept trying to hold
western-style conversations even when I was speaking Japanese, so my English students kept trying to hold Japanese-
style conversations even when they were speaking English.
We were unconsciously playing entirely different conversational ballgames.

A western-style conversation between two people is like a   4
game of tennis. If I introduce a topic, a conversational ball, I
expect you to hit it back. If you agree with me, I don't expect
you simply to agree and do nothing more. I expect you to add
something—a reason for agreeing, another example, or an elab-
oration to carry the idea further. But I don't expect you always

to agree. I am just as happy if you question me, or challenge me, or completely disagree with me. Whether you agree or disagree, your response will return the ball to me.

5   And then it is my turn again. I don't serve a new ball from my original starting line. I hit your ball back again from where it has bounced. I carry your idea further, or answer your questions or objections, or challenge or question you. And so the ball goes back and forth, with each of us doing our best to give it a new twist, an original spin, or a powerful smash.

6   And the more vigorous the action, the more interesting and exciting the game. Of course, if one of us gets angry, it spoils the conversation, just as it spoils a tennis game. But getting excited is not at all the same as getting angry. After all, we are not trying to hit each other. We are trying to hit the ball. So long as we attack only each other's opinions, and do not attack each other personally, we don't expect anyone to get hurt. A good conversation is supposed to be interesting and exciting.

7   If there are more than two people in the conversation, then it is like doubles in tennis, or like volleyball. There's no waiting in line. Whoever is nearest and quickest hits the ball, and if you step back, someone else will hit it. No one stops the game to give you a turn. You're responsible for taking your own turn.

8   But whether it's two players or a group, everyone does his best to keep the ball going, and no one person has the ball for very long.

9   A Japanese-style conversation, however, is not at all like tennis or volleyball. It's like bowling. You wait for your turn. And you always know your place in line. It depends on such things as whether you are older or younger, a close friend or a relative stranger to the previous speaker, in a senior or junior position, and so on.

10   When your turn comes, you step up to the starting line with your bowling ball, and carefully bowl it. Everyone else stands back and watches politely, murmuring encouragement. Everyone waits until the ball has reached the end of the alley, and watches to see if it knocks down all the pins, or only some of them, or none of them. There is a pause, while everyone registers your score.

11   Then, after everyone is sure that you have completely finished your turn, the next person in line steps up to the same

starting line, with a different ball. He doesn't return your ball, and he does not begin from where your ball stopped. There is no back and forth at all. All the balls run parallel. And there is always a suitable pause between turns. There is no rush, no excitement, no scramble for the ball.

No wonder everyone looked startled when I took part in 12 Japanese conversations. I paid no attention to whose turn it was, and kept snatching the ball halfway down the alley and throwing it back at the bowler. Of course the conversation died. I was playing the wrong game.

This explains why it is almost impossible to get a western- 13 style conversation or discussion going with English students in Japan. I used to think that the problem was their lack of English language ability. But I finally came to realize that the biggest problem is that they, too, are playing the wrong game.

Whenever I serve a volleyball, everyone just stands back 14 and watches it fall, with occasional murmurs of encouragement. No one hits it back. Everyone waits until I call on someone to take a turn. And when that person speaks, he doesn't hit my ball back. He serves a new ball. Again, everyone just watches it fall.

So I call on someone else. This person does not refer to what 15 the previous speaker has said. He also serves a new ball. Nobody seems to have paid any attention to what anyone else has said. Everyone begins again from the same starting line, and all the balls run parallel. There is never any back and forth. Everyone is trying to bowl with a volleyball.

And if I try a simpler conversation, with only two of us, then 16 the other person tries to bowl with my tennis ball. No wonder foreign English teachers in Japan get discouraged.

Now that you know about the difference in the conversa- 17 tional ballgames, you may think that all your troubles are over. But if you have been trained all your life to play one game, it is no simple matter to switch to another, even if you know the rules. Knowing the rules is not at all the same thing as playing the game.

Even now, during a conversation in Japanese I will notice 18 a startled reaction, and belatedly realize that once again I have rudely interrupted by instinctively trying to hit back the other person's bowling ball. It is no easier for me to "just listen" during a conversation than it is for my Japanese students to "just relax" when speaking with foreigners. Now I can truly sympathize with how hard they must find it to try to carry on a western-style conversation.

19   If I have not yet learned to do conversational bowling in Japanese, at least I have figured out one thing that puzzled me for a long time. After his first trip to America, my husband complained that Americans asked him so many questions and made him talk so much at the dinner table that he never had a chance to eat. When I asked him why he couldn't talk and eat at the same time, he said that Japanese do not customarily think that dinner, especially on fairly formal occasions, is a suitable time for extended conversation.

20   Since westerners think that conversation is an indispensable part of dining, and indeed would consider it impolite not to converse with one's dinner partner, I found this Japanese custom rather strange. Still, I could accept it as a cultural difference even though I didn't really understand it. But when my husband added, in explanation, that Japanese consider it extremely rude to talk with one's mouth full, I got confused. Talking with one's mouth full is certainly not an American custom. We think it very rude, too. Yet we still manage to talk a lot and eat at the same time. How do we do it?

21   For a long time, I couldn't explain it, and it bothered me. But after I discovered the conversational ballgames, I finally found the answer. Of course! In a western-style conversation, you hit the ball, and while someone else is hitting it back, you take a bite, chew, and swallow. Then you hit the ball again, and then eat some more. The more people there are in the conversation, the more chances you have to eat. But even with only two of you talking, you still have plenty of chances to eat.

22   Maybe that's why polite conversation at the dinner table has never been a traditional part of Japanese etiquette. Your turn to talk would last so long without interruption that you'd never get a chance to eat.

Expanding Vocabulary

Study definitions of each of the following words and then use each one in a separate sentence. The number in parentheses is the number of the paragraph in which the word appears.

elaboration (4)	belatedly (18)
murmuring (10)	customarily (19)
registers (10)	etiquette (22)

Understanding Content

1. When Sakamoto first participated in Japanese conversations, what happened? What was the cause of her problem?
2. What are the characteristics of an American-style conversation?
3. What are the characteristics of a Japanese-style conversation?
4. How do the Japanese feel about conversing during dinner? How do Americans feel about dinner conversation?

Drawing Inferences about Thesis and Purpose

1. How hard is it to converse in another language after one has "learned" the language?
2. What is Sakamoto's thesis? Where is it stated?

Analyzing Strategies and Style

1. What strategy does Sakamoto use as an opening? What makes it effective?
2. Explain each analogy. How is American-style conversation like a tennis game, and how is Japanese-style conversation like bowling? What other game comparison does the author use?
3. Who is Sakamoto's primary audience? (Be sure to read the headnote.) What makes her writing style appropriate for her audience and purpose?

Thinking Critically

1. Did the author's analogies help you to see the differences between American and Japanese conversational styles? If not, why not? If the analogies did help you, can you explain why?
2. Had you thought before about the way we carry on conversations? After reflection, do you agree with the author's description of American conversation patterns? Why or why not?
3. What might we conclude about the relationship between language and cultural traits and values? What do we learn when, as children, we learn our primary language?

Education

E. B. WHITE

One of the finest of modern essayists, E. B. White (1899–1985) made his name as a writer for the *New Yorker*. He also published many of his best-loved essays, including "Education," from 1938 to 1943 in *Harper's* and then collected them in *One Man's Meat* (1943). White the essayist may be best known for his now-classic children's stories: *Stuart Little, Charlotte's Web,* and *The Trumpet of the Swan*. You can learn much about essay writing by observing White's variation of contrast organization to reinforce thesis and by his use of examples and metaphors.

Questions to Guide Your Reading

1. We have to understand White's thesis from his details, organization, and style. After reading carefully, answer the question: What is White's thesis?
2. In his second sentence, White lists activities over which the country school teacher is guardian. What is White's point with this seemingly odd list?

---

1   I have an increasing admiration for the teacher in the country school where we have a third-grade scholar in attendance. She not only undertakes to instruct her charges in all the subjects of the first three grades, but she manages to function quietly and effectively as a guardian of their health, their clothes, their habits, their mothers, and their snowball engagements. She has been doing this sort of Augean task for twenty years, and is both kind and wise. She cooks for the children on the stove that heats the room and she can cool their passions or warm their soup with equal competence. She conceives their costumes, cleans up their messes, and shares their confidences. My boy already regards his teacher as his great friend, and I think tells her a great deal more than he tells us.

2   The shift from city school to country school was something we worried about quietly all last summer. I have always rather favored public school over private school, if only because in public school you meet a greater variety of children. This bias

of mine, I suspect, is partly an attempt to justify my own past (I never knew anything but public schools) and partly an involuntary defense against getting kicked in the shins by a young ceramist on his way to the kiln. My wife was unacquainted with public schools, never having been exposed (in her early life) to anything more public than the washroom of Miss Winsor's. Regardless of our backgrounds, we both knew that the change in schools was something that concerned not us but the scholar himself. We hoped it would work out all right. In New York our son went to a medium-priced private institution with semi-progressive ideas of education, and modern plumbing. He learned fast, kept well, and we were satisfied. It was an electric, colorful, regimented existence with moments of pleasurable pause and giddy incident. The day the Christmas angel fainted and had to be carried out by one of the Wise Men was educational in the highest sense of the term. Our scholar gave imitations of it around the house for weeks afterward, and I doubt if it ever goes completely out of his mind.

His days were rich in formal experience. Wearing overalls 3 and an old sweater (the accepted uniform of the private seminary), he sallied forth at morn accompanied by a nurse or a parent and walked (or was pulled) two blocks to a corner where the school bus made a flag stop. This flashy vehicle was as punctual as death: seeing us waiting at the cold curb, it would sweep to a halt, open its mouth, suck the boy in, and spring away with an angry growl. It was a good deal like a train picking up a bag of mail. At school the scholar was worked on for six or seven hours by half a dozen teachers and a nurse, and was revived on orange juice in mid-morning. In a cinder court he played games supervised by an athletic instructor, and in a cafeteria he ate lunch worked out by a dietician. He soon learned to read with gratifying facility and discernment and to make Indian weapons of a semi-deadly nature. Whenever one of his classmates fell low of a fever the news was put on the wires and there were breathless phone calls to physicians, discussing periods of incubation and allied magic.

In the country all one can say is that the situation is different, 4 and somehow more casual. Dressed in corduroys, sweatshirt, and short rubber boots, and carrying a tin dinner-pail, our scholar departs at crack of dawn for the village school, two and a half miles down the road, next to the cemetery. When the road is open and the car will start, he makes the journey by motor, courtesy of his old man. When the snow is deep or the motor is dead or both, he makes it on the hoof. In the afternoons he walks or hitches all or part of the way home in fair weather, gets transported in foul. The schoolhouse is a two-room frame building, bungalow type, shingles stained a burnt brown with weather-resistant stain. It has a chemical toilet in the basement and two teachers above stairs. One takes the first three grades, the other the fourth, fifth, and sixth. They have little or no time for individual instruction, and no time at all for the esoteric. They teach what they know themselves, just as fast and as hard as they can manage. The pupils sit still at their desks in class, and do their milling around outdoors during recess.

5   There is no supervised play. They play cops and robbers (only they call it "Jail") and throw things at one another—snowballs in winter, rose hips in fall. It seems to satisfy them. They also construct darts, pinwheels, and "pick-up sticks" (jackstraws), and the school itself does a brisk trade in penny candy, which is for sale right in the classroom and which contains "surprises." The most highly prized surprise is a fake cigarette, made of cardboard, fiendishly lifelike.

6   The memory of how apprehensive we were at the beginning is still strong. The boy was nervous about the change too. The tension, on that first fair morning in September when we drove him to school, almost blew the windows out of the sedan. And when later we picked him up on the road, wandering along with his little blue lunch-pail, and got his laconic report "All right" in answer to our inquiry about how the day had gone, our relief was vast. Now, after almost a year of it, the only difference we can discover in the two school experiences is that in the country he sleeps better at night—and *that* probably is more the air than the education. When grilled on the subject of school-in-country *vs.* school-in-city, he replied that the chief difference is that the day seems to go so much quicker in the country. "Just like lightning," he reported.

Expanding Vocabulary

Study the definitions of each of the following words in your dictionary and then write the definition that fits the word's use in White's essay.

Select five words and write a sentence for each word, using it in the same way that White does. The number in parentheses is the number of the paragraph in which the word appears.

Augean (1)	kiln (2)
conceives (1)	giddy (2)
involuntary (2)	seminary (3)
ceramist (2)	sallied (3)
dietician (3)	allied (3)
facility (3)	esoteric (4)
discernment (3)	laconic (6)
incubation (3)	

Understanding Content

1. Using "A" for the country school and "B" for the city school, outline White's organization paragraph by paragraph. Which contrast structure does White most closely follow?
2. How does White vary the contrast structure he has selected? What does he gain by this variation?
3. List the specific points of difference between the two school experiences (including travel, recess, etc.).

Drawing Inferences about Thesis and Purpose

1. Because White's son has attended only one city school and one country school, White cannot claim to be contrasting all (or most) city and country schools. What, then, is he contrasting about education?

Analyzing Strategies and Style

1. The boy remembers the fainting Christmas angel from his city-school days. Why does White give us this detail? What is its significance?
2. White reveals his implied thesis in part through contrasting details. Find several sentences that express differences between the schools. How are the sentences similar? How do they differ? How do the differences in wording emphasize the differences between the schools?
3. White's metaphors may be his best strategy for expressing attitude. Find two metaphors in paragraph 3, state the two items being compared, and explain how these metaphors express White's attitude toward the city school.

4. White chooses words carefully, not only for meaning but for sound—and the emphasis gained by repeating sounds. List all the words in paragraph 1 that begin with the same first letter. (This technique is called *alliteration*.) What does White accomplish by having these words connected through sound?

Thinking Critically

1. Which school described by White do you think you would have preferred? Why?
2. White is contrasting elementary schools. Do you think his attitude would be different if he were contrasting an old, rural high school (without a gym, cafeteria, science labs, specialized teachers) and a modern, well-equipped suburban high school with specially trained teachers? Should his attitude be different?
3. In your view, how important are a school's facilities? How important are the teachers?

Girls Are Beneficiaries of Gender Gap

DIANE RAVITCH

Holding a doctorate from Columbia University, Diane Ravitch (b. 1938) was an undersecretary for education in the George H. Bush administration and is currently a research professor of education at New York University and a senior fellow at Brookings Institution. She is the author of many articles and books on education, including *The State of American Education* (1980). In the following article from *The Wall Street Journal* (December 17, 1998), Ravitch examines opposing studies of differences in school performance by gender.

Questions to Guide Your Reading

1. This essay contains two sets of contrast. What are they? Which is the more important? Why?
2. Where are the significant gaps in education to be found, according to Ravitch?

Some of us grew up with the image of reporters as tough- 1
minded skeptics. Yet there were no tough-minded reporters in
sight in 1992, when the American Association of University
Women released its report "How Schools Shortchange Girls."
Every newsmagazine, newspaper and network television program did a major story on it, without making any attempt to
examine the underlying evidence for the AAUW's charge that
the schools were harming girls.

The schools, we were told, were heedlessly crushing girls' 2
self-esteem while teachers (70% of them female) were shower-
ing attention on boys. Worst among their faults, according to the
report, was that the schools discouraged girls from taking the
math and science courses that they would need to compete in
the future. The report unleashed a plethora of gender-equity
programs in the schools and a flood of books and articles about
the maltreatment of girls in classrooms and textbooks.

Now the U.S. Department of Education has released a report 3
on high school transcripts that demolishes the AAUW's claim
that girls were not taking as many courses in mathematics and
science as boys. This new report shows that in both 1990 and
1994, female high school graduates had higher enrollments than
boys in first- and second-year algebra and in geometry; among
the graduates of 1994, there were essentially no differences
between boys and girls in their participation in precalculus,
trigonometry, statistics and advanced placement calculus.

In science courses, the picture was much the same. Female 4
graduates in both 1990 and 1994 had higher enrollments than
boys in both biology and chemistry; the only course that had
a higher male enrollment was physics, studied by 27% of the
boys but only 22% of the girls. In every other science course, the
differences between boys and girls were slight or favored girls.
Overall, girls are much better prepared by the schools than are
boys: The latest figures show that 43% of female graduates were
taking a rigorous college-preparatory program in 1994, compared with only 35% of boys.

To make matters worse for the AAUW, all of its other charges 5
have been definitively refuted in a careful review of the research
by Judith Kleinfeld of the University of Alaska. Prof. Kleinfeld
found, for example, that there is little evidence that girls have

lower self-esteem than boys or that boys get more attention in the classroom than girls.

6 Far from shortchanging girls, the schools have been the leading edge in creating gender equity in the past generation. Girls get better grades than boys; have higher scores in reading and writing; are more likely than boys to take advanced placement examinations; and are likelier to go to college. In 1970, women were only 41% of all college students. Today, female students receive 55% of all bachelor's degrees and 55% of all master's degrees. Indeed, many university campuses have begun to worry about gender imbalance, since men are a decided minority on virtually every campus.

7 Men still get a majority of professional degrees, but even here the numbers are changing fast. In 1970, women earned only 8% of medical degrees; by 1995, that number had increased to 39%. In 1970, women received only 5% of law degrees; in 1995, 43%.

8 At the same time that the AAUW ginned up a nonexistent crisis about girls, the press totally ignored the data on boys. In school, boys are 50% more likely to repeat a grade than girls and represent more than two-thirds of the children placed in special education with physical, social and emotional problems. Boys are far more likely to be given Ritalin for attention deficit disorder. And talk about a crisis in self-esteem: young men (ages 15 to 24) are five times more likely to commit suicide than young women.

9 The shameful aspect of the AAUW's phony crisis—and of the media's gullibility in turning it into conventional wisdom—is that it diverted attention from the large and genuine gaps in American education, which are not between boys and girls, but among racial groups. African-Americans and Hispanics are far behind their white peers on every measure of school achievement. On the tests administered by the National Assessment of Educational Progress, average black and Hispanic 17-year-olds score at the same level as average white 13-year-olds. African-American boys, in particular, are at high risk of dropping out without graduating high school; among black college students, nearly two-thirds are female.

10 Alarmist rhetoric about the schools solves no problem, especially when the problem itself was invented for use in nation-

al advertisements and direct mail campaigns as a fund-raising tactic. One can only dream about what might have happened if the AAUW had focused the same amount of energy on recruiting talented women to teach in schools where minority kids are concentrated or on sponsoring charter schools for needy children.

Expanding Vocabulary

Study definitions of each of the following words and then use each one in a separate sentence. The number in parentheses is the number of the paragraph in which the word appears.

skeptics (1)   refuted (5)
plethora (2)   ginned up (8)
demolishes (3)   gullibility (9)
rigorous (4)

Understanding Content

1. What did the AAUW's report, "How Schools Shortchange Girls," say? List the key points made by this report.
2. What does the Department of Education's report say? How does it contrast with the AAUW report?
3. What does Kleinfeld's research reveal? How does her research contrast with the AAUW report?
4. What negative statistics about boys are provided?

Drawing Inferences about Thesis and Purpose

1. Ravitch seems to have several purposes in writing. Can you isolate three separate—but related—purposes? (Think about the essay's opening, middle, and conclusion.)
2. After thinking about the relative importance of each of her purposes, state Ravitch's thesis. The thesis should focus on her primary purpose but can be worded to suggest her other purposes as well.

Analyzing Strategies and Style

1. Ravitch provides many specifics to develop her article. In what form are most specifics presented? How does this strategy affect the style and tone of the essay?

Thinking Critically

1. Which statistic do you find most surprising? Which is the most upsetting? Which is the best news in your view? Explain each of your answers.
2. Ravitch gives a reason for the AAUW's report. Are you disturbed by the explanation? Would you like to hear a defense of the report by the organization? What *should* a critical thinker do after reading this essay?
3. Pick one problem referred to or implied in this essay and then offer suggestions for addressing this problem in our schools.

Boys and Girls: Anatomy and Destiny

JUDITH VIORST

Judith Viorst (b. 1931) is a poet, journalist, and author of books for both children and adults. She has published several volumes of poetry and more than a dozen books. Viorst may be best known as a contributing editor to *Redbook* magazine; she has received several awards for her *Redbook* columns. Her book *Necessary Losses* (1986) is an important book for adults about coping with the changes we experience at different times in our lives. The following is an excerpt from *Necessary Losses*.

Questions to Guide Your Reading

1. What are the incorrect beliefs about males and females, according to Maccoby and Jacklin?
2. What are the four differences between males and females that researchers consider to be established? Which two may be biological in origin?

1   It is argued that sex-linked limits have been culturally produced. It is argued that sex-linked limits are innate. What gender-identity studies seem to strongly suggest, however, is that—from the moment of birth—both boys and girls are so

clearly treated as boys or as girls, that even very early displays of "masculine" or "feminine" behavior cannot be detached from environmental influences.

For parents make a distinction between boys and girls.   2

They have different ways of holding boys and girls.   3

They have different expectations for boys and girls.   4

And as their children imitate and identify with their attitudes   5
and activities, they encourage or discourage them, depending
on whether or not they are boys or girls.

Are there, in actual fact, *real* sex-linked limits? Is there an   6
inborn male or female psychology? And is there any possible
way of exploring such tricky questions unbiased by culture,
upbringing or sexual politics? . . .

Sigmund Freud . . . went on record as saying that women are   7
more masochistic, narcissistic, jealous and envious than men,
and also less moral. He saw these qualities as the inevitable consequences of the anatomical differences between the sexes—the
result of the fact (fact?) that the original sexuality of the little girl
is masculine in character, that her clitoris is merely an unde-
veloped penis and that she correctly perceives herself as nothing more than a defective boy. It is the girl's perception of herself
as a mutilated male that irrevocably damages her self-esteem,
leading to resentments and attempts at reparation which produce all the subsequent defects in her character.

Well, as his friends say, who can be right about everything?   8

For in the years since this was written, science has established   9
that while genetic sex is determined at fertilization by our chro-
mosomes (XX for girls; XY for boys), all mammals, including
humans, *regardless of their genetic sex,* start out female in nature
and in structure. This female state persists until the production,
some time later in fetal life, of male hormones. It is only with
the appearance of these hormones, at the right time and in the
right amount, that anatomical maleness and postnatal mas-
culinity become possible.

While this may not tell us much about the psychology of   10
femaleness and maleness, it does put a permanent crimp in
Freud's phallocentricity. For, far from little girls starting out
as incomplete little boys, in the beginning all human beings
are female.

11   Despite his phallocentricity, however, Freud was smart enough to note at the time that his comments on the nature of women were "certainly incomplete and fragmentary."

12   He also said: "If you want to know more about femininity, enquire from your own experiences of life, or turn to the poets, or wait until science can give you deeper and more coherent information."

13   Two Stanford psychologists have tried to do just that in a highly regarded book called *The Psychology of Sex Differences.* Surveying and evaluating a broad range of psychological studies, authors Eleanor Maccoby and Carol Jacklin conclude that there are several widely held but dead-wrong beliefs regarding the ways in which males and females differ:

14   That girls are more "social" and more "suggestible" than boys. That girls have lower self-esteem. That girls are better at rote learning and simple repetitive tasks and boys more "analytic." That girls are more affected by heredity and boys by environment. That girls are auditory and boys are visual. And that girls lack achievement motivation.

15   Not true, say authors Maccoby and Jacklin. These are myths.

16   Some myths, however—or are they myths?—have not yet been dispelled. Some sexual mysteries remain unsolved:

17   Are girls more timid? Are they more fearful? More anxious?

18   Are boys more active, competitive and dominant?

19   And is it a female quality—in contrast to a male quality— to be nurturing and compliant and maternal?

20   The evidence, the authors say, is either too ambiguous or too thin. These tantalizing questions are still open.

21   There are, however, four differences which they believe to be fairly well established: That girls have greater verbal ability. That boys have greater math ability. That boys excel in visual-spatial ability. And that verbally and physically, boys are more aggressive.

22   Are these innate differences, or are they learned? Maccoby and Jacklin reject this distinction. They prefer to talk in terms of biological predispositions to learn a particular skill or kind of behavior. And talking in these terms, they designate only two sexual differences as clearly built upon biological factors.

23   One is boys' better visual-spatial ability, for which there is evidence of a recessive sex-linked gene.

The other is the relationship that exists between male hor- 24
mones and the readiness of males to behave aggressively.

However, even that has been disputed. Endocrinologist 25
Estelle Ramey, professor of physiology and biophysics at
Georgetown Medical School, told me:

"I think hormones are great little things and that no home 26
should be without them. But I also think that virtually all the
differences in male and female behavior are culturally, not hor-
monally, determined. It's certainly true that *in utero* sex hormones play a vital role in distinguishing male from female
babies. But soon after birth the human brain takes over and
overrides *all* systems, including the endocrine system. It is said,
for instance, that men are innately more aggressive than
women. But conditioning, not sex hormones, makes them that
way. Anyone seeing women at a bargain-basement sale—where
aggression is viewed as appropriate, even endearing—sees
aggression that would make Attila the Hun turn pale."

Although Maccoby and Jacklin's survey also concludes that 27
little girls are no more dependent than boys, the female-
dependency issue will not go away. A few years ago Colette
Dowling's best-selling book *The Cinderella Complex* struck a
responsive chord in women everywhere with its theme of a
female fear of independence.

> Here it was—the Cinderella Complex. It used to hit girls of six-
> teen or seventeen, preventing them, often, from going to college,
> hastening them into early marriages. Now it tends to hit women
> after college—after they've been out in the world a while. When
> the first thrill of freedom subsides and anxiety rises to take its
> place, they begin to be tugged by that old yearning for safety: the
> wish to be saved.

Dowling argues that women, in contrast to men, have a deep 28
desire to be taken care of and that they are unwilling to accept
the adult reality that they alone are responsible for their lives.
This tendency toward dependency, Dowling maintains, is bred
into them by the training of early childhood, which teaches
boys that they're on their own in this difficult, challenging
world and which teaches girls that they need and must seek
protection.

Girls are trained *into* dependency, says Dowling. 29

Boys are trained *out* of it. 30

31   Even in the mid-1980s, at an Eastern liberal-elite private school where the mothers of students are doctors and lawyers and government officials and the students themselves are full of feminist rhetoric, there are echoes of the Cinderella Complex. One of the teachers, who gives a course in human behavior to the high school seniors, told me that he has asked them, for the last several years, where they expect to see themselves at age thirty. The answers, he said, are consistently the same. Both boys and girls expect that the girls will be bearing and rearing children, while also engaged in some interesting *part-time* work. And although the boys express a desire to have a great deal of freedom at that age, the girls routinely place the boys in successful *full-time* jobs, supporting their families.

32   Now it surely is true that a great many women live with a someday-my-prince-will-take-care-of-me fantasy. It is true that the way girls are raised may help explain why. But we also need to consider that the source of female dependence may run deeper than the customs of early child care. And we also need to remember that dependence isn't always a dirty word.

33   For female dependence appears to be less a wish to be protected than a wish to be part of a web of human relationships, a wish not only to get—but to give—loving care. To need other people to help and console you, to share the good times and bad, to say "I understand," to be on your side—*and also to need the reverse, to need to be needed*—may lie at the heart of women's very identity. Dependence on such connections might be described as "mature dependence." It also means, however, that identity—for women—has more to do with intimacy than with separateness.

34   In a series of elegant studies, psychologist Carol Gilligan found that while male self-definitions emphasized individual achievement over attachment, women repeatedly defined themselves within a context of responsible caring relationships. Indeed, she notes that "male and female voices typically speak of the importance of different truths, the former of the role of separation as it defines and empowers the self, the latter of the ongoing process of attachment that creates and sustains the human community." It is only because we live in a world where maturity is equated with autonomy, argues Gilligan, that women's concern with relationships appears to be a weakness instead of a strength.

Perhaps it is both.   35

Claire, an aspiring physician, finds essential meaning in   36
attachment. "By yourself, there is little sense to things," she
says. "It is like the sound of one hand clapping. . . . You have
to love someone else, because while you may not like them, you
are inseparable from them. In a way, it is like loving your right
hand. *They are part of you;* that other person is part of that giant
collection of people that you are connected to."

But then there is Helen who, talking about the end of a rela-   37
tionship, reveals the risks inherent in intimacy. "What I had to
learn . . .," she says, "wasn't only that I had a Self that could survive it when Tony and I broke up; but that I had a Self *at all!* I
wasn't honestly sure that, when we two were separate, there
would be anything there that *was me.*"

Freud once observed that "we are never so defenseless   38
against suffering as when we love, never so helplessly unhappy as when we have lost our loved object or its love." Women
will find these words particularly true. For women, far more
often than men, succumb to that suffering known as depression
when important love relationships are through. The logic thus
seems to be that women's dependence on intimacy makes them,
if not the weaker sex, the more vulnerable one.

Expanding Vocabulary

Match each word in column A with its definition in column B. When
in doubt, first find the word in the essay and look for context clues
to aid your understanding of the word's meaning. Then, if necessary, use your dictionary to complete the matching exercise. The
number in parentheses is the number of the paragraph in which the
word appears.

Column A	*Column B*
masochistic (7)	impossible to retract or change
narcissistic (7)	held together, logically connected
mutilated (7)	to have a hampering effect on
irrevocably (7)	idea of the central role of the penis—or lack
reparation (7)	of one—in shaping one's psychology
crimp (10)	tending to yield to others
phallocentricity (10)	independence, self-directed
coherent (12)	getting pleasure from being dominated
auditory (14)	or abused

compliant (19)	submit or yield to something
predispositions (22)	overwhelming
autonomy (34)	easily affected
inherent (37)	deprived of a limb or essential part
succumb (38)	existing as an essential characteristic
vulnerable (38)	process of making amends
	advance inclinations to something
	excessive love of oneself
	related to sense of hearing

Understanding Content

1. What do gender-identity studies suggest about how we become masculine or feminine?
2. How did Freud explain the "defects" in women's characters?
3. How do all mammals begin their development?
4. For what myths about males and females is there still inadequate evidence?
5. What is the "Cinderella Complex"?
6. How can dependency be seen as a strength? What seems to matter more to women than to men?

Drawing Inferences about Thesis and Purpose

1. What is Viorst's subject? What is her purpose in writing?
2. What is her position on differences between males and females and on the source(s) of those differences?

Analyzing Strategies and Style

1. Examine Viorst's opening. How does it both establish her subject and get reader interest?
2. The author uses many brief paragraphs. When does she use them? What does she gain by using them?

Thinking Critically

1. How many of the myths about male and female differences have you believed? Has Viorst convinced you that most are unsupported by evidence? Why or why not?
2. Observe how the author introduces the specialists on whom she draws. Are you prepared to accept them as reliable sources? Can they be reliable and still leave readers with questions and concerns? If so, why?
3. Do you see female "dependence" or desire for close relationships as a weakness or strength? Explain your views.

4. Why do we have so much trouble sorting out similarities and differences among males and females? What are some of the issues that get in the way of understanding?

Cyber U: What's Missing

MICHELE TOLELA MYERS

Born in Morocco in 1941, Michele Tolela Myers is currently president of Sarah Lawrence College in New York. She has published in her field—sociology and communications—with coauthor Gail E. Myers, *The Dynamics of Human Communication* (a textbook), *Communicating When We Speak* (1978), and *Managing by Communication* (1982). The following article appeared in the *Washington Post* on May 21, 2000.

Questions to Guide Your Reading
1. What two ways of learning in college does Myers contrast?
2. How does the author use the book/library analogy to support her thesis?

The scramble is on to respond to the easy access to knowledge and financial opportunities that computers can provide. Earlier this year the U.S. Department of Education reported that distance education programs had almost doubled in the past three years. Every week another college, university or private individual seeks to establish online education—whether for-profit like Michael Milken's online university, Unext, or Michael Saylor's projected non-profit online university whose motto would be "free education for everyone on earth, forever." 1

If education were only as simple as reading, then libraries would have replaced schools long ago. We educators are in the business of forming minds—not just filling them. 2

Gutenberg's invention of printing in the 15th century essentially ended up removing priests as the only gatekeepers of information and knowledge. In the same way, the computer and the Web are allowing larger and larger numbers of people direct access to more information and may well take the more traditional middlemen and gatekeepers (our teachers and educators) 3 out of the system. Readily available technology is good for society and good for education because it will bring ever more information from the wider world to everyone. Every academic institution will clearly want to embrace this new technology to enhance the learning experience in the classroom and to reach those who do not have the money or time to attend school.

4 The principal role of a university or college is not, however, to transmit information. If it were, then our goal would be the most "productive" way of passing on information. Logically, the larger the auditorium the better, with one teacher lecturing hundreds of students. Distance learning and virtual education are clearly even better vehicles for transmitting information, with the computer screen delivering a prepackaged syllabus to thousands, possibly millions, at a time. It makes great economic sense, and predictions may be right that classrooms will go the way of the hand-scribed text.

5 But higher education in the 21st century is in a different business—a business made even more imperative precisely because of the ubiquity of information technology. More than ever, we need to teach our young people to learn how to learn, to sort and evaluate information, to make judgments about evidence and sources. They must learn how to separate the important from the trivial and, most important, they must learn to think analytically and creatively, to have ideas, to write and speak intelligently about ideas, and to know how to go from ideas to actions. It is not enough for our students to know; rather, they should know what to know and have the capacity to imagine.

6 There is no better way to form good minds than in one-on-one interactions. Research tells us that the two most significant factors that contribute positively to learning among college students are their interaction with each other and their interaction with teachers. Is there any doubt that for children and adolescents, face-to-face time is important? Parenting and teaching both require human physical contact and creative individual responses to a singular individual to be most effective.

7 More than ever, then, we are going to need liberal arts preparation at the undergraduate level, the kind of education liberal arts colleges are best positioned to offer. This kind of education may not be the most efficient, but it is clearly the most effective. A liberal arts college offers the most contact time

between teachers and students. It offers time for students to actually practice writing, speaking, arguing, evaluating and researching in small classes with real professors who care about them as individuals and care about their work, who will critique them and hold them accountable. It is here that students hone their skills to communicate effectively—the number one quality that corporations seek when they are interviewing candidates. No computer can sharpen the mind as well as a cross-fire discussion among students with their teacher. In human affairs, there is ultimately no substitute for real human contact.

The emergence of computers challenges us to know what our business is. We must respond that we are in the business of ideas, not information, of forming minds, not filling them.

8

Expanding Vocabulary

Select the five words you are least familiar with, study their contexts in the essay (and your dictionary if necessary), and then use each one in a separate sentence. The number in parentheses is the number of the paragraph in which the word appears.

enhance (3)	capacity (5)
imperative (5)	critique (7)
ubiquity (5)	hone (7)

Understanding Content

1. What is "the number one quality" that businesses are looking for when hiring college graduates?
2. What changes have led Myers to reaffirm her view of the purpose of higher education?
3. What are the two ways of learning in use in higher education?
4. What, according to Myers, should students be learning in college?

Drawing Inferences about Thesis and Purpose

1. What is Myers's thesis? State it to make her contrast clear.
2. Myers says that now, "more than ever," young people need to learn how to "evaluate information" and "make judgments about evidence." Why now more than ever?

Analyzing Strategies and Style

1. Observe Myers's opening and concluding paragraphs. What makes each one effective?

2. What phrases does Myers repeat, from paragraph 2, in her conclusion? How do they sum up her contrast?

Thinking Critically

1. Do you agree that higher education is not primarily about gaining knowledge? Why or why not?
2. Do you think that you are getting the kind of education that Myers describes? If not, how do you account for this?
3. Have you taken any online or distance learning courses? If yes, did you think it was a good learning experience? Why or why not? If no, would you want to? Why or why not?

Pedestrian Students and High-Flying Squirrels

LIANE ELLISON NORMAN

Liane Ellison Norman (b. 1937), author of *Hammer of Justice: Molly Rush and the Plowshares Eight* (1990), obtained a Ph.D. in literature from Brandeis University and taught journalism and literature at the University of Pittsburgh. In her essay, published in 1978 in *Center* magazine, Norman reflects on her journalism students by drawing an analogy with squirrels.

Questions to Guide Your Reading

1. What seems to be the biggest concern in the minds of Norman's students? How do they feel about job opportunities?
2. Look up the word *pedestrian* in your dictionary. What are its two main meanings? How does Norman use both meanings in her essay?

1   The squirrel is curious. He darts and edges, profile first, one bright black eye on me, the other alert for his enemies on the other side. Like a fencer, he faces both ways, for every impulse toward me an impulse away. His tail is airy. He flicks and flourishes it, taking readings of some subtle kind.

2   I am enjoying a reprieve of warm sun in a season of rain and impending frost. Around me today is the wine of the garden's

final ripening. On the zucchini, planted late, the flagrant blossoms flare and decline in a day's time.

I am sitting on the front porch thinking about my students. 3
Many of them earnestly and ardently want me to teach them
to be hacks. Give us ten tricks, they plead, ten nifty fail-safe
ways to write a news story. Don't make us think our way
through these problems, they storm (and when I am insistent
that thinking *is* the trick, "You never listen to us," they complain). Who cares about the First Amendment? they sneer. What
are John Peter Zenger and Hugo Black to us? Teach us how to
earn a living. They will be content, they explain, with knowhow and jobs, satisfied to do no more than cover the tedium
of school board and weather.

Under the rebellion, there is a plaintive panic. What if, on 4
the job—assuming there is a job to be on—they fearlessly defend
the free press against government, grand jury, and media
monopoly, but don't know how to write an obituary. Shouldn't
obituaries come first?

I hope not, but even obituaries need good information and 5
firm prose, and both, I say, require clear thought.

The squirrel does not share my meditation. He grows tired 6
of inquiring into me. His dismissive tail floats out behind as
he takes a running leap into the tree. Up the bark he goes and
onto a branch, where he crashes through the leaves. He soars
from slender perch to slender perch, shaking up the tree as if he
were the west wind. What a madcap he is, to go racing from one
twig that dips under him to another at those heights!

His acrobatic clamor loosens buckeyes in their prickly armor. 7
They drop, break open, and he is down the tree in a twinkling,
picking, choosing. He finds what he wants and carries it, an outsize nut which is burnished like a fine cello, across the lawn,
up a pole, and across the tightrope telephone line to the other
side, where he disappears in maple foliage.

Some inner clock or calendar tells him to stock his larder 8
against the deep snows and hard times that are coming. I have
heard that squirrels are fuzzy-minded, that they collect their winter groceries and store them, and then forget where they are
cached. But this squirrel is purposeful; he appears to know he'd
better look ahead. Faced with necessity, he is prudent, but not fearful. He prances and flies as he goes about his task of preparation,
and he never fails to look into whatever startles his attention.

9   Though he is not an ordinary pedestrian, crossing the street far above, I sometimes see the mangled fur of a squirrel on the street, with no flirtation left. Even a high-flying squirrel may zap himself on an aerial live wire. His days are dangerous and his winters are lean, but still he lays in provisions the way a trapeze artist goes about his work, with daring and dash.

10   For the squirrel, there is no work but living. He gathers food, reproduces, tends the children for a while, and stays out of danger. Doing these things with style is what distinguishes him. But for my students, unemployment looms as large as the horizon itself. Their anxiety has cause. And yet, what good is it? Ten tricks or no ten tricks, there are not enough jobs. The well-trained, well-educated stand in line for unemployment checks with the unfortunates and the drifters. Neither skill nor virtue holds certain promise. This being so, I wonder, why should these students not demand, for the well-being of their souls, the liberation of their minds?

11   It grieves me that they want to be pedestrians, earthbound and always careful. You ask too much, they say. What you want is painful and unfair. There are a multitude of pressures that instruct them to train, not free, themselves.

12   Many of them are the first generation to go to college; family aspirations are in their trust. Advisers and models tell them to be doctors, lawyers, engineers, cops, and public-relations people; no one ever tells them they can be poets, philosophers, farmers, inventors, or wizards. Their elders are anxious too; they reject the eccentric and the novel. And, realism notwithstanding, they cling to talismanic determination; play it safe and do things right and I, each one thinks, will get a job even though others won't.

13   I tell them fondly of my college days, which were a dizzy time (as I think the squirrel's time must be), as I let loose and pitched from fairly firm stands into the space of intellect and imagination, never quite sure what solid branch I would light on. That was the most useful thing I learned, the practical advantage (not to mention the exhilaration) of launching out to find where my propellant mind could take me.

14   A luxury? one student ponders, a little wistfully.

15   Yes, luxury, and yet necessity, and it aroused that flight, a fierce unappeasable appetite to know and to essay. The luxury

I speak of is not like other privileges of wealth and power that must be hoarded to be had. If jobs are scarce, the heady regions of treetop adventure are not. Flight and gaiety cost nothing, though of course they may cost everything.

The squirrel, my frisky analogue, is not perfectly free. He 16 must go on all fours, however nimbly he does it. Dogs are always after him, and when he barely escapes, they rant up the tree as he dodges among the branches that give under his small weight. He feeds on summer's plenty and pays the price of strontium in his bones. He is no freer of industrial ordure than I am. He lives, mates, and dies (no obituary, first or last, for him), but still he plunges and balances, risking his neck because it is his nature.

I like the little squirrel for his simplicity and bravery. He will 17 never get ahead in life, never find a good job, never settle down, never be safe. There are no sure-fire tricks to make it as a squirrel.

Expanding Vocabulary

1. Norman writes with an interesting blend of colloquial or slang words and metaphors or similes. For each of the following passages, explain the word or phrase in italics. The number in parentheses is the number of the paragraph in which the word appears.

   want me to teach them to be *hacks* (3)
   ten *nifty fail-safe* ways to write (3)
   His *dismissive* tail (6)
   What a *madcap* he is (6)
   His *acrobatic clamor* loosens buckeyes in their *prickly armor* (7)
   not an ordinary pedestrian, *crossing the street far above* (9)
   squirrel may *zap* himself on an *aerial live wire* (9)
   unemployment looms as large as the horizon itself (10)
   they cling to *talismanic determination* (12)
   luxury . . . not like other *privileges of wealth and power that
   must be hoarded to be had* (15)

2. Examine the following words in their contexts in the essay and then write a brief definition or synonym for each one. (Do not use a dictionary; try to guess the word's meaning from its context.)

   profile (1)   cached (8)
   impulse (1)   eccentric (12)

reprieve (2)
impending (2)
tedium (3)
plaintive (4)
obituary (4)

essay (15)
analogue (16)
strontium (16)
ordure (16)

Understanding Content

1. Outline the contrasts that make up Norman's analogy. Using "A" for squirrels and "B" for students, list their points of difference.
2. What do squirrels and people have in common living in this world? (See paragraphs 15 through 17.)
3. Norman also introduces herself as once a student. Does she present herself as more like her students today or more like the squirrel?
4. What does Norman gain by using herself as an example? How does this help to advance her thesis?

Drawing Inferences about Thesis and Purpose

1. What is Norman's thesis? What is she asserting about students?
2. What does the author think education is—or should be—all about?

Analyzing Strategies and Style

1. What does Norman accomplish with her opening description of the squirrel? Why not begin by announcing her subject and thesis?
2. In paragraph 1, the squirrel is described through a comparison with what athlete? Describe the squirrel's movements in your own words. Does the comparison (metaphor) work well to depict the squirrel's movements?
3. Why does Norman choose the writing of obituaries as her example of what her journalism students want to know how to do? How important is this writing to newspapers? How glamorous is the task?
4. Norman describes the squirrel in part by comparing it to what circus performer? List all the words and phrases that add to this metaphor.
5. Explain the metaphor in paragraph 13 that Norman uses to describe her college experience. What is she comparing herself to? What ideas about the educational experience are suggested by this comparison?

Thinking Critically

1. Would you describe yourself as a pedestrian student or a high-flying squirrel? If you chose the first category, are you content with that label? If you are not content, what can you do to change? If you are content, explain why.

2. In paragraph 15, Norman says that "flight and gaiety cost nothing, though of course they may cost everything." This statement is a *paradox:* It seems at first to be contradictory, but actually isn't. How can you explain the statement? In what sense are flight and gaiety free? In what sense can they "cost everything"?

3. Norman shows us how metaphors can enrich our writing by providing concrete images and by suggesting much in a few words. To practice writing an *extended* metaphor (developing several points from one comparison), complete the following sentence about someone you know and then write at least three more sentences developing the metaphor.

    If _____ were an object, he/she would be a
    _____.

    Example: If my mother were an object, she would be a table. My mother is solid and sturdy, always there, feeding us and ready to help. She can be casual or dressed, just like the dining room table, for sometimes it wears a checkered tablecloth and simple pottery, and sometimes it puts on white linen and sparkling china and crystal. Even if she is scraped or banged up, she will not collapse.

You may want to try several of these extended metaphors.

Marks

LINDA PASTAN

A graduate of Radcliffe College and Brandeis University, Linda Pastan (b. 1932) is the author of eight books of poetry. Many of her poems, such as the one that follows from *The Five Stages of Grief Poems* (1978), examine the complexity and problems of family life.

Questions to Guide Your Reading

1. Who is speaking—or more accurately thinking—the words of the poem? What relationships does the speaker refer to in the poem?

2. What does the poem's title refer to?

_____

My husband gives me an A
for last night's supper,
an incomplete for my ironing,
a B plus in bed.
My son says I am average,   5
an average mother, but if
I put my mind to it
I could improve.
My daughter believes
in Pass/Fail and tells me   10
I pass. Wait 'til they learn
I'm dropping out.

Understanding Content and Strategies

1. What marks does the speaker receive? For what activities? Who does the speaker's son sound like when he says that she "could improve" if she put her "mind to it"?
2. The poem is organized and developed, then, by using what extended metaphor? The speaker is being compared to what?
3. What is the speaker's attitude toward her situation? What lines reveal her attitude?

Drawing Inferences about Theme

1. What observations about family life is Pastan making? Whose perspective on family responsibilities and chores are we given in the poem?

Thinking Critically

1. Do you think the views of family life expressed here are fairly widespread? What evidence do you have for your opinions?
2. Have you ever felt as though you were being graded by family members or rated on a scale from 1 to 10? If so, how did that make you feel?
3. Try your hand at a short, free-verse poem similar to Pastan's. In your poem create a speaker who is a teenager being "graded" by other family members.

STUDENT ESSAY—CONTRAST

THE FADED STAIN
Denisse M. Bonilla

"The plantain stain on a 'jíbaros' back can never be erased," says an old Puerto Rican proverb. "Jíbaros," or Puerto Rican peasants, is what my compatriots fondly call each other. The proverb is most commonly used to illustrate their feeling that, regardless of where a Puerto Rican lives, a Puerto Rican always remains a Puerto Rican. But reflecting on my own experiences, I have read a different meaning into the old proverb. My compatriots could be saying that once a Puerto Rican has lived on the island, she or he can never forget it. However, in saying this, one must ponder what happens to the stain itself. Does it look like a plantain for the rest of the jíbaros' life, or does it change over time? Perhaps it starts resembling a banana, looking similar but not exactly the same.

Coming back to Puerto Rico as an adult, I found a place quite different from the one I thought I had left behind. The memories I had were those of a child who had never lived outside the island. Because I lived in Puerto Rico as an

Student uses a proverb as an attention-getting opening.

Thesis stated: What I saw on a return visit to Puerto Rico was different from my youthful memories. The thesis clearly emphasizes contrast.

insular child, I had the memories of such a child. Youth had shaped my perception when I lived there; then time further confused my memory, neutralizing the colors of the countryside, creating indistinguishable Puerto Rican cities, sharpening the soft accent of the people. When I came back as an adult, what I saw was not what I expected to see.

I remembered the trip from San Juan to Ponce, a trip crossing the island from north to south, as an incredibly long and painful ordeal. Impatient to get to my grandmother's house in Ponce, I would look out the car window, sometimes noticing the small towns or the way the sea peeked out from in-between the mountains. The mountains that I saw during the beginning of the trip were green, seeming to remain in the landscape for hours. I would anxiously await the golden mountains to the south, which to me were an indication of the end of our trip.

First difference: the trip to Ponce was not as long or unpleasant as it seemed in her memories.

When I returned as an adult, I remembered and expected the same grueling and unexciting trip, but was happily disappointed. The trip south was not as long as I remembered; it was over in two hours. Perhaps it did not seem as long as it did in my youth because I had

become accustomed to driving longer distances in the large North American continent. But I accredited my newfound
tolerance to the enchanting beauty of the
Caribbean countryside! The vegetation in
the north was a lush shade of green,
growing profusely and becoming a tangle
of startling color. The houses on the
outskirts of the small towns we passed
seemed to blossom out of the foliage,
their old-fashioned charm reminiscent of
a bygone time when the Puerto Rican economy was more dependent on agriculture. In
what seemed like a short distance, the
mountains changed to golden hues and a
softer green. The Caribbean Sea appeared
to be a watercolor painting framed by the
dry southern mountains. The beauty of the
trip bewildered me, causing me to recol-
lect in disbelief the impatience I had
felt as a young girl. Had I been color-
blind when I was young?

Student analyzes causes for the differences between youthful memories and adult realities.

The Puerto Rican cities I remembered
from my youth were **also different** when
viewed through my adult eyes. I remembered Old San Juan as a beautiful old
city, <u>comparing</u> it in my memory to places
such as Old Town Alexandria. I <u>also</u> saw
generic streets in my recollections,
remembering how as a young girl I used

Second difference: cities and streets were different than remembered.

to imagine that the bigger roads looked exactly like the ones in the United States. But in contrast to my recollections, neither Old San Juan nor the streets of the other cities were similar to those in the U.S. Taking a stroll down the narrow, cobblestoned streets of Old San Juan, I often discovered hidden parks and nicely shaded plazas in which old gentlemen sat to chat, play dominoes, or feed doves. Wooden fruit stands brimming with delectable tropical fruits stood on many corners. The pastel-colored ambiance of Old San Juan, bespeaking Spanish ancestry and Caribbean sensibility, could not be compared to the somber ambiance of the old American cities in the north. As for my recollections of Puerto Rican streets that looked exactly like the ones in the United States, to my eyes accustomed to the large, smooth highways of North America, the streets of Puerto Rico looked humble and in need of repair.

Observe transition words and phrases.

The people of Puerto Rico proved to be equally changed to my adult eyes and ears. In the memories of a young insular child, Puerto Rican manners were just like American manners and Puerto Rican Spanish was bland, without any distinguishable accent. In contrast, I found my

Third difference: the people— and their way of speaking Spanish—are different than remembered.

people to be more physically demonstrative than Americans. Their faces and bodies would remain mobile through an entire conversation, allowing someone standing a few feet away to guess what they were talking about. They spoke Spanish with a funny melodic sound, characterized by relaxed pronunciation. The Puerto Rican people were more flamboyant than I had noticed as a child.

Although the plantain stain on my back faded after I left my country, the experience of rediscovering its many hues left me with an even bigger impression. To notice the essence of a country, one must spend time outside it. My recollections were bland when compared to what I later saw. What I saw when I came back to Puerto Rico left a moist, green, ripe plantain stain on my back, a stain that will never fade.

Conclusion refers again to the proverb and extends the thesis to suggest that one's country is best understood when one spends time away from it.

MAKING CONNECTIONS

1. Ravitch and Viorst examine gender differences. Ravitch provides the statistics on performance, and Viorst gives some explanations of behavioral differences. Study both articles and see if you find any connections between the two discussions. Make a list of all connections you find.
2. Sakamoto discusses differences in American and Japanese conversational styles. What are some of the ways that cultural and class differences may affect students in the

classroom? What are some ways that instructors and students can ease some of the problems created by cultural and class differences?

3. White contrasts ways of teaching and attitudes toward how students best learn; Myers contrasts the learning environment of the liberal arts college with the environment created by distance learning. On balance, are students likely to be more damaged by ineffective educational theories or by inadequate facilities? Explain your position.

4. Norman raises the issue of student attitude toward education. How important are effort and desire to succeed? How important is intellectual curiosity? (Compare Norman, pp. 156–159 and Reid, pp. 370–376, on curiosity.) How much difference can facilities and dedicated teachers make if students are unmotivated to learn? If parents and society do not place a high value on education?

5. We know that Asian (and European) students regularly outscore American students in math and science. We also know that, as a group, students from more affluent school districts outscore students from less affluent districts. What are four strategies for improving American education that you would seek to implement if you were appointed "Education Czar"? What might be some political problems you would have trying to implement your four-point plan?

TOPICS AND GUIDELINES FOR WRITING

1. In an essay, contrast two stories, two movies, or two TV shows you know well. Select two works that have something in common but differ in important and/or interesting ways so that you have a clear purpose in writing. Organize points of difference in the part-by-part pattern *before* you draft your essay. Illustrate points of difference with details from the two works.

2. If you have attended two schools that differed significantly or if you have lived in two quite different places, draw on one of these experiences for a contrast essay. Organize by specific points of difference that together support a thesis statement that announces your contrast purpose. (Example: California

and Virginia are not just miles apart; they are worlds apart.) The chapter's introduction gives guidelines for contrasting two schools. If you contrast two places, be sure to use details that *show* the reader how the places differ.

3. Do you know a neighborhood, city, or area of the country that has changed significantly for better or worse? If so, develop an essay that contrasts specific differences between the place you once knew and the place as it is now. Your purpose is to demonstrate that the changes have made the place either better or worse. (Example: The _____ neighborhood of _____ is no longer the attractive, family-oriented community in which I grew up.)

4. You have had many teachers during your years of schooling. Think of ones you liked and ones you didn't like. Think about why you enjoyed some but not others. Then select two to contrast for the purpose of revealing traits that make a good teacher. Write about specific traits (e.g., knowledge of field, energy, clarity, fairness, humor), not just generalizations (e.g., she was nice). Illustrate each teacher's traits with examples.

5. Norman contrasts her college students with squirrels—and the squirrels win because they are more curious and daring, traits Norman would like to see in her students. How do you view today's college students—or some portion of them? What traits, characteristics, attitudes toward learning, and reasons for being in school do you see? Can you think of an animal, fantasy creature, individual, or group from history who in your view has the traits that are more appropriate for college students? If so, then you can develop an analogy along the lines of Norman's essay. Remember to have specific differences between students and the animal, creature, or historical figure you are using.

6. As a variation of topic 5, develop an analogy that compares rather than contrasts today's students with some animal, fantasy creature, or historical figure. Use specific points of similarity and establish a point to the comparison, a thesis about students that is supported through the fanciful comparison.

7. Most of us have had at least one experience that did not turn out as we thought it would. Sometimes, nervous about

a new situation, we expect the worst only to discover that we are happy or successful participating in the actual experience. Probably more often we look forward to an upcoming event only to be disappointed. Or, we have childhood memories that are inconsistent with our re-experiencing a place or person from the past. Reflect about any experience you have had that fits the pattern of contrast between perception (expectation) and reality. (Possible experiences include a first date, a special event such as Thanksgiving or a wedding, a first experience with a new sport, a recent reunion with a childhood friend, or a return to your childhood home.)

Organize your thoughts into specific points of difference and use the part-by-part structure so that you avoid writing only an autobiographical narrative. The point of your contrast is to offer some insight into why we so often have expectations that do not match reality. Why do we think it will be easy to learn to ski? Why do we remember our grandparents' old house as larger and more exciting than it appears to us today? The student essay in this chapter is an example of one student's response to this topic.

5

Explaining and Illustrating

Examining Media Images

"How do you know that?" "Where is your evidence?" "Can you be specific?" These questions are raised by the avid dinner companion who wants you to illustrate and support your ideas. As a writer, you need to keep in mind that the engaged reader is going to ask the same kinds of questions. For you to be an effective writer, you must answer these questions; you must provide examples.

Illustrating ideas and opinions with examples seems so obvious a way to develop and support views that you may wonder why the strategy warrants its own chapter. Even though providing examples may be the most frequently used writing technique, as with many "obvious truths," we can all benefit from being reminded of its importance.

When to Use Examples

The smart writer searches for examples as part of the process of generating ideas. Indeed, when brainstorming or in other ways inventing ideas for an essay, you may find that specifics come to mind more easily than general points. Whether you are a generalizer who needs to find illustrations for ideas or a generator of specifics who needs to reflect on what the examples illustrate, the end result will be a blend of general points and concrete examples. When should you select the use of examples as your primary strategy of development? When you are presenting information or discussing ideas that can best be understood and absorbed by readers with the aid of specifics. And that's just about any time you write.

How to Use Examples

To use examples effectively, think about what kinds of examples are needed to develop your thesis, about how many you need, and about how to introduce and discuss them effectively. First, the *kinds* of examples. You will need to find illustrations that clearly and logically support your generalizations. When Gloria Steinem asserts that advertisers give orders to women's magazines, we expect her to explain and illustrate those orders. And this is exactly what Steinem does. If she had not used five major companies' demands as examples, we may have doubted her claim of advertisers' control over women's magazines.

We also expect *enough* examples. If Stephanie Mencimer mentioned only one "action chick" in the movies, we would probably doubt her thesis. Occasionally, a writer will select one *extended* example rather than a number of separate examples. Jack McGarvey uses one extended example, his and his students' experience of being on TV, to show the celebrity-making power of television. To develop his example, McGarvey uses techniques of narration and description, reminding us that few pieces of writing are developed using only one strategy. Typically, though, the writer who develops a thesis primarily through illustration presents a goodly number of appropriate examples. How many make a "goodly" number will vary with each essay, but be assured that few writers include too many examples.

How many examples an essay needs depends in part on how they are introduced and discussed and on how many facets of a topic need to be covered. Gloria Steinem does not just list five advertisers but gives details of their demands. After all, if all the examples were so obvious that just a brief listing would work, we would already have reached the writer's conclusions and would not need to read the article. As common to our lives as advertising, television, movies, and song lyrics are, we still have much to learn from this chapter's writers because they are the ones who have looked closely at and listened intently to the swirl of words and images bombarding us through the media. Sometimes examples are startling enough to speak for themselves. Usually the writer's task is not only to present good illustrations but to explain how they support the essay's main ideas.

When presenting and explaining illustrations, give some thought to ordering them and to moving smoothly from one to another to create coherence. Look first for some logical basis for organizing your examples. If there is no clear reason to put one example before another, then you are probably wise to put your most important example last. Examples that add to your point can be connected by such transitions as

for instance	in addition
also	next
another example	moreover
further	finally

Ocassionally, brief examples can be listed as a series in one sentence. Examples that offer contrast need contrast connectors:

by contrast	on the other hand
however	instead

Remember that a list does not make an essay. Explain *how* your examples support your thesis.

WRITING FOCUS:
VARY YOUR SENTENCES

Effective writing stays focused on a controlling idea (thesis), is concrete and vivid, and shows a command of grammar, mechanics, and correct word choice. Yet readers recognize that although two essays may follow these guidelines, one essay will "read" better than another. What accounts for the difference? One answer is content; some writers are more insightful than others. Another answer is style, the selection and arrangement of words into sentences. Do not settle for the first way that you write down an idea or detail; revise and polish sentences for both variety and emphasis. Think about ways to restructure a series of short sentences into fewer sentences—even one sentence—creating variety but also greater power.

Liane Ellison Norman (see Chapter 4) could have opened her essay this way:

> The squirrel is curious. He darts around. He looks partially at me and stays alert for enemies. So, I see only one bright black eye.

Notice that each sentence begins with subject and verb, and all have about the same weight or feel. But, here is what Norman actually wrote:

> The squirrel is curious. He darts and edges, profile first, one bright black eye on me, the other alert for his enemies on the other side.

The first sentence is arresting in its brevity. Then the next few ideas have been gathered into one longer, more dramatic sentence.

Consider the following details: *It was a battered face. But it was a noble face. It commanded immediate respect.* There are several ways these ideas can be shaped into one sentence, one more interesting and effective than the three brief sentences. Here are two possibilities:

> It was a battered but noble face, commanding immediate respect. A battered but noble face, it commanded immediate respect.

Which of these two sentences is, in your view, the most effective? Why?

Here are some guidelines for improving your sentences:

1. Combine short sentences on the same subject into longer sentences.
2. Use more than one way to combine; instead of just joining two short sentences with "and," use a dependent clause or verbal phrases or modifying words (adjectives and adverbs).
3. Do not always begin a sentence with its subject; instead use an introductory clause or phrase (e.g., *A battered but noble face*).
4. Vary sentence lengths. Use short sentences for emphasis along with longer sentences.

5. Be sure to keep the most important idea in the main clause, putting less important ideas into modifying clauses, phrases, and words.

Getting Started: Thinking About Advertising

Here are eight questions to help you think about advertising, one of the topics of this chapter and represented by the four ads that follow. The ads can be found after page 176. Reflect on these examples of current advertising by answering the questions for each ad.

Questions

1. What are the ad's purposes? To sell a product? An idea? An image of the company? Some combination?
2. What audience is the ad designed to reach?
3. What kind of relationship does it establish with its audience?
4. What social values does it express?
5. To what degree are those values held by the target audience? To what degree are they the values of a different social class or group?
6. Does the ad use metaphors? Puns? Rhyme? Does the company establish and repeat a logo or slogan for the product? How well known are the logo, the slogan, or both?
7. Does the ad use symbols? To what extent do the symbols help express the ad's social values? How is their association with the product appropriate?
8. Is the ad's appeal primarily direct and explicit or indirect and associative?

To Be or Not to Be as Defined by TV

JACK McGARVEY

Jack McGarvey (b. 1937) completed his master's degree at the University of Connecticut and taught in the Westport, Connecticut, school system for many years. He has also published many articles, short stories, and poems in the *New York Times*, *McCall's*, *Parents*, and other newspapers and magazines. The following article, a report on his experience with the power of television, appeared in 1982 in the journal *Today's Education*.

Questions to Guide Your Reading

1. Why did a TV crew come to Bedford Junior High?
2. What is the source of part of the author's title? What does he gain by his reference to that source?

1   A couple of years ago, a television crew came to film my ninth grade English class at Bedford Junior High School in Westport, Connecticut. I'm still trying to understand what happened.

2   I was doing some work with my students, teaching them to analyze the language used in television commercials. After dissecting the advertising claims, most of the class became upset over what they felt were misleading—and in a few cases, untruthful—uses of language. We decided to write to the companies that presented their products inaccurately or offensively. Most of them responded with chirpy letters and cents-off coupons. Some did not respond at all.

3   I then decided to contact *Buyline*, a consumer advocate program aired on New York City's WNBC-TV at the time. The show and its host, Betty Furness, were well-known for their investigation of consumer complaints. I sent off a packet of the unanswered letters with a brief explanation of the class's work.

4   About a week later, the show's producer telephoned me. She said that she'd seen the letters and was interested in the class's project. Could she and her director come to Westport to have a look?

I said sure and told her about a role-playing activity I was 5
planning to do with my students. I said I was going to organize my class of 24 students into four committees—each one
consisting of two representatives from the Federal Trade Commission (FTC), the agency that monitors truth in advertising;
two advertising executives anxious to have their material used;
and two TV executives caught somewhere in the middle—
wanting to please the advertisers while not offending the FTC.
Then, I would ask each committee to assume that there had
been a complaint about the language used in a TV commercial, and that the committees had to resolve the complaint. "That
sounds great! I'll bring a crew," she said.

I obtained clearance from my school district's office, and the 6
next morning, as I was walking into the school, I met one of
my students and casually let out the word: "WNBC's coming to
film our class this afternoon."

I was totally unprepared for what happened. Word spread 7
around school within five minutes. Students who barely knew
me rushed up to squeal, "Is it true? Is it really, really true? A
TV crew is coming to Bedford to film?" A girl who was not in
my class pinned me into a corner near the magazine rack in
the library to ask me whether she could sit in my class for the
day. Another girl went to her counselor and requested an immediate change in English classes, claiming a long-standing personality conflict with her current teacher.

Later, things calmed down a bit, but as I took my regular turn 8
as cafeteria supervisor, I saw students staring wide-eyed at me,
then turning to whisper excitedly to their friends. I'd become
a celebrity simply because I was the one responsible for bringing a TV crew to school.

Right after lunch, the show's producer and director came to 9
my class to look it over and watch the role-playing activity; they
planned to tape near the end of the school day. The two women
were gracious and self-effacing, taking pains not to create any dis-
turbance; but the students, of course, knew why they were there.
There were no vacant stares, no hair brushes, no gum chewers,
and no note scribblers. It was total concentration, and I enjoyed
one of my best classes in more than 15 years of teaching.

After the class, I met with the producer and director to plan 10
the taping. They talked about some of the students they'd seen

and mentioned Susan. "She's terribly photogenic and very, very good with words." They mentioned Steve. "He really chaired his committee well. Real leadership there. Handsome boy, too." They mentioned Jim, Pete, Randy, and Jenny and their insights into advertising claims. Gradually I became aware that we were engaged in a talent hunt; we were looking for a strong and attractive group to be featured in the taping.

11   We continued the discussion, deciding on the players. We also discussed the sequencing of the taping session. First, I'd do an introduction, explaining the role-playing activity as if the class had never heard of it. Then, I'd follow with the conclusion—summarizing remarks ending with a cheery "See you tomorrow!"—and dismiss the class. The bit players would leave the school and go home. We'd then rearrange the set and film the photogenic and perceptive featured players while they discussed advertising claims as a committee. Obviously, this is not the way I'd conduct an actual class, but it made sense. After all, I wanted my students to look good, and I wanted to look good.

12   "It'll be very hard work," the producer cautioned. "I trust your students understand that."

13   "It's already been hard work," I remarked as I thought of possible jealousies and bruised feelings over our choices of featured players.

14   About a half hour before school's end, the crew set up cameras and lights in the hall near the classroom we'd be working in, a room in an isolated part of the building. But as the crew began filming background shots of the normal passing of students through the hall, near chaos broke out.

15   Hordes of students suddenly appeared. A basketball star gangled through the milling mob to do an imitation of Nureyev,[1] topping off a pirouette by feigning a couple of jump shots. A pretty girl walked back and forth in front of the cameras at least a dozen times before she was snared by a home economics teacher. Three boys did a noisy pantomime of opening jammed lockers, none of which were theirs. A faculty member, seen rarely in this part of the building, managed to work his way through the crowd, smiling broadly. And as members of

[1]Famous ballet star.—Ed.

my class struggled through the press of bodies, they were hailed, clutched at, patted on the back, and hugged.

"Knock 'em dead!" I heard a student call.   16

It took the vice-principal and five teachers 10 minutes to clear   17 the hall.

We assembled the cast, arranged the furniture, erased several   18 mild obscenities from the chalkboard, and pulled down the window shades—disappointing a clutch of spectators outside. The producers then introduced the crew and explained their work.

I was wired with a mike and the crew set up a boom micro-   19 phone, while the girls checked each other's make-up and the boys sat squirming.

Finally, the taping began. It was show business, a perfor-   20 mance, a total alteration of the reality I know as a teacher. As soon as I began the introduction, 26 pairs of eyes focused on me as if I were Billy Joel about to sing. I was instantly startled and self-conscious. When I asked a question, some of the usually quieter students leaped to respond. This so unsettled me that I forgot what I was saying and had to begin again.

The novelty of being on camera, however, soon passed. We   21 had to do retakes because the soundman missed student responses from the rear of the room. The director asked me to rephrase a question and asked a student to rephrase a response. There were delays while technicians adjusted equipment.

We all became very much aware of being performers, and   22 some of the students who had been most excited about making their TV debut began to grumble about the hard work. That pleased me, for a new reality began to creep in: Television is not altogether glamorous.

We taped for almost five hours, on more than 3,200 feet of   23 videotape. That is almost an hour-and-a-half's worth, more than double a normal class period. And out of that mass of celluloid the producer said she'd use seven minutes on the program!

Two days later, five students and I went to the NBC studios   24 at Rockefeller Center to do a taping of a final segment. The producer wanted to do a studio recreation of the role-playing game. This time, however, the game would include real executives— one from advertising, one from the NBC network, and one from the FTC. We'd be part of a panel discussion moderated by Betty

Furness. My students would challenge the TV and the advertising executives, asking them to justify some of the bothersome language used in current commercials.

25   This was the most arduous part of the experience. The taping was live, meaning that the cameras would run for no longer than eight minutes. As we ate turkey and ham during a break with Ms. Furness and the guest executives, I realized that we were with people who were totally comfortable with television. I began to worry. How could mere 14-year-olds compete in a debate with those to whom being on television is as ordinary as riding a school bus?

26   But my concern soon disappeared. As Ms. Furness began reading her TelePrompTer, Susan leaned over and whispered, "This is fun!" And it was Susan who struck first. " 'You can see how luxurious my hair feels' is a perfect example of the silly language your ad writers use," she said with all the poise of a Barbara Walters. "It's impossible to *see* how something feels," she went on.

27   That pleased me, for as an English teacher, I've always emphasized the value of striving for precision in the use of language. The work we'd done with TV commercials, where suggestibility is the rule, had taken hold, I thought, as the ad executive fumbled for a response. The tension vanished, and we did well.

28   The show aired two weeks later, and I had it taped so the class could view it together. It was a slick production, complete with music—"Hey, Big Spender"—to develop a theme for Ms. Furness' introduction. "Teens are big business these days," she said. "Does television advertising influence how they spend their money?" Then followed a shot of students in the hall—edited to show none of the wildness that actually occurred. Next, three of my students appeared in brief clips of interviews. They were asked, "Have you ever been disappointed by television advertising?" The responses were, "Yes, of course," and I was pleased with their detailed answers. Finally, the classroom appeared, and there I was, lounging against my desk, smiling calmly. I looked good—a young, unrumpled Orson Bean, with a cool blue-and-brown paisley tie. My voice was mellifluous. Gee, I thought as I saw the tape, I could have been a TV personality.

Now, I am probably no more vain than most people. But   29
television does strange things to the ego. I became so absorbed
in studying the image of myself that the whole point of the
show passed me by. I didn't even notice that I'd made a goof
analyzing a commercial until I'd seen the show three times. The
students who participated were the same; watching themselves
on videotape, they missed what they had said. I had an enormous struggle to get both them and me to recall the hard work
and to see the obvious editing. It was as if reality had been
reversed: The actual process of putting together the tape was
not real, but the product was.

I showed the tape again last year to my ninth grade class. I   30
carefully explained to this delightful gang of fault-finders how
the taping had been done. I told them about the changed
sequence, the selection of the featured players, the takes and
retakes. They themselves had just been through the same role-
playing activity, and I asked them to listen carefully to what was
said. They nodded happily and set their flinty minds to look at
things critically. But as the tape ended, they wanted to tease me
about how ugly and wrinkled I looked. They wanted to say,
"That's Randy! He goes to Compo Beach all the time." "Jenny's
eye shadow—horrible!" "When will you get us on TV?"

The visual image had worked its magic once again: They had   31
missed the point of the show altogether. And, as I dismissed
them, I felt something vibrating in their glances and voices—
the celebrity image at work again. I was no longer their mun-
dane English teacher: I was a TV personality.

I decided to show the tape again the next day. I reviewed   32
the hard work, the editing, the slick packaging. I passed out
questions so we could focus on what had been said on the program. I turned on the recorder and turned off the picture to let
them hear only the sound. They protested loudly, of course. But
I was determined to force them to respond to how effectively
the previous year's class had taken apart the language used in
the claims of commercials. This was, after all, the point of the
program. And it worked, finally.

As class ended, one of the students drifted up to me. "What   33
are we going to do next?" she asked.

"We're going to make some comparisons between TV news   34
shows and what's written in newspapers," I replied.

35   "Do they put together news shows the way they filmed your class?"

36   "It's similar and usually much quicker," I answered.

37   She smiled and shook her head. "It's getting hard to believe anything anymore."

38   In that comment lies what every TV viewer should have— a healthy measure of beautiful, glorious skepticism. But as I said, I'm still trying to understand that taping session. And I'm aware of how hard it is to practice skepticism. Every time I see the *Buyline* tape, I'm struck by how good a teacher TV made me. Am I really that warm, intelligent, creative, and good looking? Of course not. But TV made me that way. I like it, and sometimes I find myself still hoping that I am what television defined me to be.

39   I sometimes think children have superior knowledge of TV. They know, from many years of watching it, that the product in all its edited glory is the only reality. Shortly after the program aired on that February Saturday two years ago, our telephone rang. The voice belonged to my daughter's 11-year-old friend. She said, "I just saw you on TV. May I have your autograph?"

40   I was baffled. After all, this was the boisterous girl who played with my daughter just about every day and who mostly regarded me as a piece of furniture that occasionally mumbled something about lowering your voices. "Are you serious?" I croaked.

41   "May I have your autograph?" she repeated, ignoring my question. "I can come over right now." Her voice was without guile.

42   She came. And I signed while she scrutinized my face, her eyes still aglow with Chromacolor.

43   To Stephanie, television had transformed a kindly grump into something real. And there is no doubt in my mind whatsoever that in the deepest part of her soul is the fervent dream that her being, too, will someday be defined and literally affirmed by an appearance on television.

44   Lately, my ninth grade class has been growing restless. Shall I move up the TV unit and bring out the tape again? Shall I remind them what a great teacher they have? Shall I remind myself what a fine teacher I am? Shall I renew their—and my— hope?

The following ads are not part of the essay by Jack McGarvey and are not the ads studied by his students. They are a sampling of current ads for your "Getting Started" analysis. (See p. 169.)

You should see what's underneath.
The calcium in milk keeps bones strong and helps prevent osteoporosis.

got milk?

GRACE UNDER PRESSURE

GladWare's tough, like Tupperware. It stands up to everyday pressures, including the microwave, dishwasher and freezer, yet costs only a fraction of what you'd pay for a Tupperware container. All of which helps you keep your grace under pressure, too.

WOULD IT SURPRISE YOU TO KNOW THAT GROWING SOYBEANS CAN HELP THE ENVIRONMENT?

Biotech soybeans have been widely planted by American farmers and they help preserve our natural resources. Plant biotechnology makes it easier to control weeds and plow soybean fields less—which means less soil erosion.

But before those soybean seeds could be planted, it took years of research and testing to ensure that biotech crops were safe for people and the environment. Extensive testing by scientists shows foods derived from plant biotechnology are as safe to eat as traditional foods.

In fact, three government agencies share the authority to evaluate the safety of new biotech products from inception to approval—the U.S. Department of Agriculture (USDA), the Environmental Protection Agency (EPA), and the Food and Drug Administration (FDA). If you want to learn more, we invite you to call or visit our Web site.

WWW.WHYBIOTECH.COM
1-800-980-8660

Biotech
Soybean

COUNCIL FOR
BIOTECHNOLOGY
INFORMATION

good ideas are growing

To be or not to be as defined by TV? Does that question sug-   45
gest what makes television so totally unlike any other medium?

Expanding Vocabulary

Match each word in column A with its definition in column B. When
in doubt, first find the word in the essay and look for context clues to
aid your understanding of the word's meaning. Then, if necessary, use
your dictionary to complete the matching exercise. The number in
parentheses is the number of the paragraph in which the word appears.

Column A	*Column B*
dissecting (2)	smoothly flowing
advocate (3)	attractive when photographed
photogenic (10)	examined carefully
sequencing (11)	walked with long-legged awkwardness
gangled (15)	careless mistake
pirouette (15)	separating, analyzing
snared (15)	ordinary
pantomime (15)	full spin of the body on the toes or
arduous (25)	ball of the foot (in ballet)
mellifluous (28)	speak in favor of
goof (29)	act of communicating with bodily or
flinty (30)	facial expressions and gestures
mundane (31)	trapped, caught
skepticism (38)	cunning, deceit
boisterous (40)	very difficult
guile (41)	emotional, zealous
scrutinized (42)	arranging in a series
fervent (43)	hard, tough
	loud, unrestrained
	doubting, questioning attitude

Understanding Content

1. What had McGarvey's English class been studying before the TV
   crew came? What response did the class receive from their letters to companies?
2. What was the response of students to the news of the coming
   crew? How did McGarvey's students behave with the crew watching their classes?
3. How did the TV producer want to sequence the class discussion?
   On what basis did they select students to tape? How long did the

taping take? How representative of a typical class would the taped version be?

4. How did McGarvey respond when he watched the finished tape? How did his class respond? And future classes?

Drawing Inferences about Thesis and Purpose

1. What attitude, according to McGarvey, should we hold toward what we see on TV? Why did he, and his students, have trouble maintaining that attitude?
2. What is McGarvey's thesis, the main points he wants to make about television?

Analyzing Strategies and Style

1. McGarvey develops his observations about TV through one example, one event that he recounts at length. Can one long example also be an effective way to illustrate an idea?
2. McGarvey includes a clever description of students (and teachers) showing off for the TV cameras in the school hallway. Examine this passage again (paragraphs 14 and 15). What makes this an effective description? What strategies does the author use here?

Thinking Critically

1. Are you skeptical about everything you see on television? That is, do you understand that much of what is presumably "live" has been taped and carefully edited? If you aren't skeptical, should you be?
2. Do you want to be on TV? If so, why? If not, why not?
3. Is there something wrong with a society in which a seven-minute TV segment can suddenly turn an ordinary person into a celebrity? Why are celebrities so appealing? Do we put too much emphasis on them?

Sex, Lies, and Advertising

GLORIA STEINEM

Editor, writer, and lecturer, Gloria Steinem (b. 1934) has been cited in *World Almanac* as one of the twenty-five most influential women in America. She is the cofounder of *Ms.* magazine and was its editor from 1972 to 1987. She is the cofounder of the National Women's Political Caucus and is the author of a number of books, including *Outrageous Acts and Everyday Rebellions* (1983), *Revolution from Within: A Book of Self-Esteem* (1992), and *Moving Beyond Words* (1993). In "Sex, Lies, and Advertising," first published in *Ms.* in 1990, Steinem "tells all" about the strategies advertisers use to control much of the content and appearance of women's magazines.

Questions to Guide Your Reading

1. What do advertisers expect—or demand—in women's magazines?
2. What does Steinem want readers to do about the control advertisers have?

When *Ms.* began, we didn't consider *not* taking ads. But we 1 wanted to ask advertisers to come in *without* the usual quid pro quo of "complementary copy"—editorial features praising their product area.

We knew this would be hard. Food advertisers have always 2 demanded that women's magazines publish recipes and articles on entertaining (preferably ones that name their products) in return for their ads; clothing advertisers expect to be surrounded by fashion spreads (especially ones that credit their designers); and shampoo, fragrance, and beauty products insist on positive editorial coverage of beauty subjects, plus photo credits besides. That's why women's magazines look the way they do.

Advertisers who demand such "complementary copy" clear- 3 ly are operating under a double standard. The same food companies place ads in *People* with no recipes. Cosmetics companies support *The New Yorker* with no regular beauty columns.

In recent years, advertisers' control over the editorial content 4 of women's magazines has become so institutionalized that it is sometimes written into "insertion orders" or dictated to ad salespeople as official policy. The following are typical orders given to women's magazines:

- Dow's Cleaning Products stipulated that ads for its Vivid and Spray 5 'n Wash products should be adjacent to "children or fashion editorial"; ads for Bathroom Cleaner should be next to "home furnishings/family" features; and so on. "If a magazine fails for $\frac{1}{2}$ the brands or more," the Dow order warns, "it will be omitted from further consideration."

6 • C. Johnson & Son, makers of Johnson Wax, lawn and laundry products, insect sprays, hair sprays, and so on, insisted that its ads *"should not be opposite extremely controversial features or material antithetical to the nature/copy of the advertised product."* (Italics theirs.)

7 • Maidenform, manufacturer of bras and other women's apparel, left a blank for the particular product and stated: "The creative concept of the _____ campaign, and the very nature of the product itself appeal to the positive emotions of the reader/consumer. Therefore, it is imperative that all editorial adjacencies reflect that same positive tone. The editorial must not be negative in content or lend itself contrary to the _____ product imagery/message (e.g., *editorial relating to illness, disillusionment, large size fashion, etc.*)." (Italics mine.)

8 • The De Beers diamond company, a big seller of engagement rings, prohibited magazines from placing its ads with "adjacencies to hard news or anti/love-romance themed editorial."

9 • Procter & Gamble, one of this country's most powerful and diversified advertisers, stands out in the memory of Anne Summers and Sandra Yates [who ran the company that published *Ms.* in the late 1980s]: its products were not to be placed in *any* issue that included *any* material on gun control, abortion, the occult, cults, or the disparagement of religion. Caution was also demanded in any issue that included articles on sex or drugs, even for educational purposes.

10   Those are the most obvious chains around women's magazines. There are also rules so understood they needn't be written down: for instance, an overall "look" compatible with beauty and fashion ads. Even "real" nonmodel women photographed for a women's magazine are usually made up, dressed in credited clothes, and retouched out of all reality. When editors do include articles on less-than-cheerful subjects (for instance, domestic violence), they tend to keep them short and unillustrated. The point is to be "upbeat." Just as women in the street are asked, "Why don't you smile, honey?" women's magazines acquire an institutional smile.

11   Within the text itself, praise for advertisers' products has become so ritualized that fields like "beauty writing" have been invented. One of its frequent practitioners explained seriously that "It's a difficult art. How many new adjectives can you find?

How much greater can you make a lipstick sound? The FDA restricts what companies can say on labels, but we create illusion. And ad agencies are on the phone all the time pushing you to get their product in." Often, editorial becomes one giant ad. An issue of *Lear's* fea-   12 tured an elegant woman executive on the cover. On the contents page, we learn she is wearing Guerlain makeup and Samsara, a new fragrance by Guerlain. Inside are full-page ads for Samsara and Guerlain antiwrinkle cream. In the article about the cover subject, we discover she is Guerlain's director of public relations and is responsible for launching, you guessed it, the new Samsara. When the *Columbia Journalism Review* cited this example in one of the few articles to include women's magazines in a critique of ad influence, editor Frances Lear was quoted as defending her magazine because "this kind of thing is done all the time."

Advertisers are also adamant about where in a magazine   13 their ads appear. When Revlon was not placed as the first beauty ad in one Hearst magazine, for instance, Revlon pulled its ads from *all* Hearst magazines. Ruth Whitney, editor in chief of *Glamour*, attributes some of these demands to "ad agencies wanting to prove to a client that they've squeezed the last drop of blood out of a magazine." She also is, she says, "sick and tired of hearing that women's magazines are controlled by cigarette ads." Relatively speaking, she's right. To be as censoring as are many advertisers for women's products, tobacco companies would have to demand articles in praise of smoking and expect glamorous photos of beautiful women smoking their brands.

I don't mean to imply that the editors I quote here share my   14 objections to ads: most assume that women's magazines have to be the way they are. But it's also true that only former editors can be completely honest. "Most of the pressure came in the form of direct product mentions," explains Sey Chassler, who was editor in chief of *Redbook* from the sixties to the eighties. "We got threats from the big guys, the Revlons, blackmail threats. They wouldn't run ads unless we credited them.

"But it's not fair to single out the beauty advertisers because   15 these pressures come from everybody. Advertising wants to know two things: What are you going to charge me? What *else* are you going to do for me? It's a holdup. For instance, management felt that fiction took up too much space. They couldn't put any advertising in that. For the last ten years, the number of fiction entries into the National Magazine Awards has declined.

16   "I also think advertisers do this to women's magazines especially," he concluded, "because of the general disrespect they have for women."

17   What could women's magazines be like if they were as editorially free as books? as realistic as newspapers? as creative as films? as diverse as women's lives? We don't know.

18   We'll only find out if we take women's magazines seriously. If readers were to act in a concerted way to change traditional practices of *all* women's magazines and the marketing of *all* women's products, we could do it. After all, they are operating on our consumer dollars; money that we now control. You and I could:

19   • refuse to buy products whose ads have clearly dictated their surroundings, and write to tell the manufacturers why;

20   • write to editors and publishers (with copies to advertisers) that we're willing to pay *more* for magazines with editorial independence, but will *not* continue to pay for those that are just editorial extensions of ads;

21   • write to advertisers (with copies to editors and publishers) that we want fiction, political reporting, consumer reporting—whether it is, or is not, supported by their ads;

22   • put as much energy into breaking advertising's control over content as into changing the images in ads, or protesting ads for harmful products like cigarettes;

23   • support only those women's magazines and products that take us seriously as readers and consumers.

24   Those of us in the magazine world can also use the carrot-and-stick technique. The stick: if magazines were a regulated medium like television, the demands of advertisers would be against FCC rules. Payola and extortion would be penalized. As it is, there are potential illegalities. A magazine's postal rates are determined by the ratio of ad-to-edit pages, and the former costs more than the latter. Counting up all the pages that are *really* ads could make an interesting legal action.

The carrot means appealing to enlightened self-interest. 25
Many studies show that the greatest factor in determining an
ad's effectiveness is the credibility of its surroundings. The
"higher the rating of editorial believability," concluded a 1987
survey by the *Journal of Advertising Research*, "the higher the rating of the advertising." Thus, an impenetrable wall between edit
and ads would also be in the best interest of advertisers.

Even as I write this, I get a call from a writer from *Elle*, who 26
is doing a whole article on where women part their hair. Why,
she wants to know, do I part mine in the middle?

It's all so familiar. A writer trying to make something of a 27
nothing assignment; an editor laboring to think of new ways
to attract ads; readers assuming that other women must want
this ridiculous stuff; more women suffering for lack of information, insight, creativity, and laughter that could be on these
same pages.

I ask you: Can't we do better than this? 28

Expanding Vocabulary

Examine the following words in their contexts in the essay and then
write a brief definition or synonym of each one. Avoid using a dictionary; try to guess each word's meaning from its context. The number in
parentheses is the number of the paragraph in which the word appears.

stipulated (5)	adjacencies (7)
antithetical (6)	diversified (9)
ritualized (11)	extensions (20)
launching (12)	Payola (24)
critique (12)	extortion (24)
adamant (13)	impenetrable (25)
concerted (18)	

Understanding Content

1. Do advertisers make demands with other kinds of magazines similar to those with women's magazines?
2. What are some of the more subtle "understood" "rules" of advertisers in women's magazines?
3. What have advertisers done to get their way?
4. What can those in the magazine business do about the control
   advertizers have?

Drawing Inferences about Thesis and Purpose

1. Explain the idea of using a carrot-and-stick approach.
2. What is Steinem's purpose in writing? Does she have more than one? What does she want to accomplish?
3. What is Steinem's thesis?

Analyzing Strategies and Style

1. Steinem uses bullets in two places. What does she gain by using this organizational strategy?
2. The author concludes by mentioning a call from an *Elle* writer. What is effective about this example as a way to conclude?

Thinking Critically

1. How many of the controlling strategies of advertisers are new to you? What one is the most surprising or shocking to you? Why?
2. Steinem suggests that advertisers place their extreme demands on women's magazines because they lack respect for women. Does this seem a good explanation of their double standard? If you disagree, how would you account for the advertisers' demands on women's magazines?
3. Steinem lists several actions we can take to change advertisers' mistreatment of women's magazines. Which suggestion do you think is the best one? Why? Are there other suggestions you would make? Explain.

Violent Femmes

STEPHANIE MENCIMER

A former writer for *Legal Times* and *Washington City Paper*, Stephanie Mencimer has a degree in journalism from the University of Oregon. She has just left *The Washington Monthly,* where she was an editor, to return to school to seek her MA and a future teaching career. Her essay on an interesting change in action movies appeared in *The Washington Monthly* in September 2001.

Questions to Guide Your Reading

1. What is Mencimer's topic? Be specific.

2. What are some of the questions that have been raised about the success of the movies Mencimer examines?

———————

This spring, while *Lara Croft: Tomb Raider* was breaking box- 1
office records and feminists were arguing over the merits of
the female action hero, no one noticed the dogs playing in theaters elsewhere. *Exit Wounds,* the latest Steven Seagal flick,
opened with a paltry $19 million—his best in years, but a poor
showing for an action film. While he's mercifully cut off the
ponytail, Seagal is showing all of his 50 years, wearing a pas-
tiche of orange pancake makeup and sporting heft not attrib-
utable to muscle mass.

In *Exit Wounds,* the martial-arts afficionado and star of macho 2
classics *Hard to Kill* and *Out for Justice* employed Hong Kong
kung-fu-movie wire tricks made famous in *The Matrix* and now
standard fare in action-chick flicks. But where the wires only
added to the grace and agility of lithesome Zhang Zi Yi in
Crouching Tiger, Hidden Dragon, they seemed to strain just to
get Seagal off the ground.

Meanwhile, *Driven,* the latest by Sylvester Stallone, the quin- 3
tessential beefcake action hero, was dying from neglect. The car-
racing movie went almost straight to video, and so far has
grossed only $32 million, a far cry from the $47 million *Tomb
Raider* made in its very first weekend. *Driven's* returns were
actually an improvement over Stallone's last disaster, *Get Carter,*
which in 2000 earned all of $15 million, barely what his 1981
classic, *Nighthawks,* grossed back when ticket-prices were a lot
cheaper.

And then there's poor Arnold Schwarzenegger. Last fall, his 4
cloning film, *The Sixth Day,* disappeared with similar returns—
this from a guy behind one of the all-time box-office blowouts,
Terminator 2: Judgment Day. Schwarzenegger had better luck last
year playing the voice of a bug in the animated film, *Antz,*
which pulled in $90 million.

This year, the muscle-bound stars of action-film blockbusters 5
of the '80s and '90s have found themselves ungraciously drop-
kicked out of the genre by, of all things, a bunch of girls. Girl-
power flicks like *Charlie's Angels, Crouching Tiger,* and *Tomb
Raider* are topping the $100 million mark once dominated by

men like Schwarzenegger. *Charlie's Angels* has brought in $125 million; *Crouching Tiger* is up to $179 million; and *Tomb Raider*, only open since mid-June, stands at $126 million. Even last year's cheerleading movie, *Bring It On*, trumped the traditional male stars, grossing $68 million.

6   Action chicks are taking over prime time television as well. *Buffy the Vampire Slayer*, *Xena: Warrior Princess* and *La Femme Nikita*—all WB or UPN fodder—are about to be joined on a major network by *Alias*, a show about Sydney Bristow, a kung-fu-chopping female agent for a top-secret division of the CIA.

7   The enormous popularity of women as film enforcers has stirred much debate over what these films say about women, feminism, Hollywood, and violence, and whether it's progress or exploitation. But no one has answered a more interesting question: What does this say about men? After all, none of the big female hits could have achieved its staggering popularity without nabbing a significant male audience, those same guys who were once the primary consumers of *Die Hard, First Blood*, and *Commando*. If men once lived vicariously through the escapades of John Rambo and Col. Matrix—in movies where women were mainly crime victims or in need of rescue—what does it mean when they love watching Lara Croft kick some bad-boy ass? It's a pretty sharp turn from misogyny to masochism.

8   The cynics say men will watch hot babes do just about anything, whether it's Jell-O wrestling or kickboxing men, and that the dominatrix has always been part of the male fantasy. Certainly, that must be part of it. But while simple sex appeal might explain why men like Lara Croft, it doesn't explain why they no longer love Schwarzenegger, to whom they'd been so loyal, suffering through everything from *Predator* to *Junior*. Nor does the hot-babe theory explain why no obvious successors have stepped in to replace Jean Claude Van Damme and the other aging beef boys.

9   More to the point, though, the pat male-fantasy explanation doesn't answer the question: Why now? Women have been playing action heroes for more than a decade, but they have never achieved *Tomb Raider's* level of success until just last year. In fact, earlier films where women played the lead roles as strong (and sexy) action heroines dropped like bombs.

Neither Demi Moore's 1997 *G.I. Jane* nor *The Long Kiss Good-* 10
night in 1996, starring Geena Davis as a highly trained government assassin, spawned any TV spin-offs or plans for sequels.
And neither came anywhere near the $100 million box-office
benchmark of *Charlie's Angels* or *Crouching Tiger*. *The Long Kiss*
grossed only $33 million; *G.I. Jane*, despite Moore's star-power
and new breasts, garnered only $48 million.

Part of the appeal of the new action genre, of course, is that 11
the old beefcake films were getting tired and repetitive, and
their stars Reagan-era relics. It's not just that their stars are getting old—most are in their 50s now—but for men on the silver
screen these days, being buff just isn't what it used to be.

If you don't believe that studs on steroids have lost their 12
Hollywood appeal, all you have to do is watch *Copland*, the
1997 indie film in which Stallone tried to revive his flagging
career by going against character and starring as a fat guy. He
wasn't bad either, playing Freddy Hefflin, the sensitive, half-
deaf New Jersey sheriff who adores Sibelius violin concertos.
Still, there was only so much the Italian Stallion could do;
Schwarzenegger had already exhausted the cutesy roles for
inarticulate lugs (remember *Kindergarten Cop?*).

The meathead movie really flourished at a time when men 13
were desperately clinging to their traditional male roles in the
world even as those roles were quickly disappearing. The
action heroes like John Rambo or *Commando's* Col. Matrix represented an ideal, and also nostalgia for a time when men built
bridges, defended helpless broads, and were worshiped for
their physical conquests—sexual and otherwise. They thrived
during the '80s, when military might made a comeback and
Bruce Springsteen dedicated albums to steelworkers.

Technology and the sexual revolution, though, have com- 14
bined to make the muscleman—and his movie—obsolete. Wires
have allowed Lucy Liu and Cameron Diaz to high-kick, jump,
and fly better than Seagal ever could, and the girls didn't have
to become body-builders in the process. The lithe titanium bodies of Angelina Jolie and *Crouching Tiger's* Zhang Zi Yi make men
like Schwarzenegger look like lumps of heavy, slow-moving
steel. Their kind of over-tanned, sweat-sheened, macho mus-
cularity has all but disappeared from the screen. Who sweats
in action films these days? . . .

Barbarella Bites Back

15   T2 also foreshadowed the emergence of the action babe, with tank-top-clad Linda Hamilton opening the film doing very manly chin-ups. It took a while before Hollywood got the formula right—*G.I. Jane* and *The Long Kiss Goodnight* were fledgling efforts to bring a woman to the center of the action, but those films were fatally flawed in terms of the mass-marketing success formula for an action film.

16   The key to any good action film is an inverse relationship between the amount of special effects and the amount of dialogue. Talk too much and the heroine loses her mystique and starts to remind men of their ex-wives. *Tomb Raider* certainly scores on that front. Angelina Jolie couldn't have more than five lines—all snappy ones, of course, which is also a prerequisite for a good action flick.

17   The other critical requirement for a successful action movie is for the audience to be able to suspend disbelief enough to enjoy the fantasy. Even with a minimum of dialogue, it's unlikely that male movie audiences 20 years ago would have been willing to accept the preposterous idea of Angelina Jolie engaged in hand-to-hand combat with a man—and winning. With the women's movement beginning to make men uncomfortable men probably weren't eager to see women back up their political threat (or even divorce threats) with good roundhouse kicks to the head.

18   Today, women everywhere seem to be kicking ass, and men don't seem to mind, within reason. You only have to look to the tennis court to see the change. Women's tennis has never been more powerful—or popular. Venus and Serena Williams are smashing 100-mile-an-hour serves that John McEnroe would have had a hard time returning in his heyday. Lindsey Davenport could eat Lara Croft for lunch.

19   Oddly enough, while women's sports have paved the way for Lara Croft to gross $100 million at the box office, they have also made Rambo and his expression of male physical power the more laughable movie scenario. Rambo's reliance on brute force, jungle warfare, and big pipes seems so passé, especially when dorks like Bill Gates run the world. Muscles on men have become somewhat irrelevant unless the men happen to be mopping the floors

at Microsoft. (Perhaps one of the slyest commentaries on the state
of the modern American male came a few years back in the film
American Beauty, when Kevin Spacey decides to try getting in
shape and has to ask the neighborhood gay guys for workout
advice.)

The average straight American male today is the doughy 20
white guy who sits in a suburban office park most of the day
before driving his SUV home to the wife and kids and online
stock reports. Shooting hoop and bench-pressing in the garage
just don't figure into the equation. And why should they, when
women are more interested in the size of men's portfolios than
the size of their pecs anyway?

Conan the Librarian

It's easy to see how Stallone and company have lost their 21
male audience. What's harder to understand is why men aren't
more threatened by the arrival of powerful heroines. Of course,
a closer viewing of these films suggests that, for all their killer
moves and rippling muscles, the action babes still aren't really
creating a new world order. . . .

And when the action babe does meet her male match, the 22
fighting becomes more like foreplay than a duel to the death, as
with Zhang Zi Yi and Chang Chen, wrestling across the sand
dunes over a stolen comb in *Crouching Tiger*. More than just a
good martial-arts scene, the fight is fraught with the excitement
of sexual conquest that has all but disappeared with the sexual
revolution.

No doubt our action heroines have come a long way since 23
Wonder Woman, but the feminist critics are right: Women are still
only allowed to be violent within certain parameters largely pro-
scribed by what men are willing to tolerate. To be sure, what men
will tolerate has certainly changed a good deal. But in the old
action films, at the end, the male hero always walks away from
a burning building looking dirty, bleeding, sweaty yet vindi-
cated (Remember Bruce Willis' bloody feet after walking
through broken glass barefoot in *Die Hard?*).

None of today's action chicks come near that level of messi- 24
ness. The violence is sterilized—it is, after all, PG-13, aimed
mostly at 12-year-olds. They rarely mess up their hair, nor do

they really fight—or perhaps gun down—significant bad guys like, say, Rutger Hauer or Wesley Snipes, which would seriously upset the balance of power. Often they end up sparring with other women. Their motives are always pure and they never use unnecessary violence the way Arnold and the boys get to. The body count in *Commando* topped 100; *Charlie's Angels* couldn't have had a single real corpse.

25   Women playing real action figures who menace *real* men still don't sell, as Geena Davis discovered in *Long Kiss Goodnight*. In the opening scene, Davis does something unbelievably unladylike: She kills Bambi, snapping a deer's neck with her bare hands. That scene alone probably sank her movie. Men may have accepted women as action figures, but only when those action figures are a cross between Gidget and Bruce Lee. To achieve box-office success, the new action babes have to celebrate women's power without being so threatening that men would be afraid to sleep with the leading lady.

Expanding Vocabulary

Match each word in column A with its definition in column B. When in doubt, first find the word in the essay and look for context clues to aid your understanding of the word's meaning. Then, if necessary, use your dictionary to complete the matching exercise. The number in parentheses is the number of the paragraph in which the word appears.

Column A	Column B
flick (1)	form, type ✓
pastiche (1)	to use unethically, selfishly
aficionado (2)	dominating female ˅
lithesome (2)	mix, blend ˄
quintessential (3)	gave rise to ˎ
genre (5)	hatred of women ˉ
fodder (6)	pleasure from being mistreated __
exploitation (7)	or dominated
nabbing (7)	movie ╱
vicariously (7)	requirement �
misogyny (7)	purest form or version ✓
masochism (7)	reversed in order ╱
	longing for the past ˜

dominatrix (8)	one who cares deeply for something
spawned (10)	no longer in fashion; dated
lugs (12)	catching
nostalgia (13)	nerds
inverse (16)	feeling as if one were living
prerequisite (16)	another's experiences
passé (19)	moves easily and gracefully
dorks (20)	clumsy fools
	food, usually for livestock

Understanding Content

1. Who are the three male actors whose latest films are not financially competitive with "girl-power flicks"?
2. What female action movies are given as examples of this genre's success?
3. Where else do we now find "action chicks"?
4. What question does Mencimer think is the most interesting one to ask about the female action movies?
5. How do the cynics answer her key question? What is the author's response to their answer?
6. What reasons does Mercimer offer for the current popularity with men of female action movies? Why have the male actors lost their following? Why are men accepting the female action stars?

Drawing Inferences about Thesis and Purpose

1. What is Mercimer's thesis? Consider her topic, the questions she raises, and then how she answers those questions.
2. The author asserts that the action babes aren't creating a new world order. What world order did the action guys create—or help sustain and justify? How has that world changed in our time?

Analyzing Strategies and Style

1. Mercimer not only refers to many films and their leading men and women; she also includes how much money these films have made. What purpose do the money references serve? How do these facts support Mercimer's thesis?
2. The author uses a number of informal or slang terms—"lugs," "dorks," "flicks," "ass"—to mention only four. What do they contribute to the style and tone of the essay?

Thinking Critically

1. Do any of the movie earnings figures surprise you? Shock you? Why or why not?
2. What connection does Mercimer see between women's tennis and the new action movies? Is this a new idea for you? Does it make sense? Why or why not?
3. The author concludes by observing that the action chicks are actually limited in their physical dominance over men, and that's why men will watch these films. First, do you think her explanation makes sense? Second, do you think that the movies reflect our society—that is, that women can do more than 30 years ago but are still restricted in their power and in the ways they can show that power? Reflect on this issue.

Look Out Below: At the Movies, Subtext Plays a Summer Role

STEPHEN HUNTER

A *Washington Post* staff writer, Stephen Hunter (b. 1946) regularly reviews new film releases. Hunter has a degree in journalism from Northwestern University and is the author of twelve novels. The following article appeared in the *Post* on August 18, 2002.

Questions to Guide Your Reading

1. What is the meaning of the word *subtext*?
2. What do the Bogey films from the 1940s have in common?

1   What lies beneath?

2   Not *What Lies Beneath*, a somewhat mediocre summer thriller of two years ago, with Harrison Ford and Michelle Pfeiffer. No, what lies *beneath*? Beneath the movies.

3   What lies beneath is subtext. It's frequently more interesting than text.

Subtext is that idea under the surface that holds it all togeth- 4
er. It's the movie's argument, its agenda, in many cases its reason to be. It's the idea of a character, what he stands for, how
he develops and what that means. It's everything that isn't covered in the dialogue or the explosions, but that you somehow
feel.

Text is story. Text is event, performances, special effects. Sub- 5
text is ideas. It's motifs, suggestions, visual implications, subtle
comparisons. It's motives, it's psychology, it's the unconscious.
Text is talking; subtext is showing.

Is this brainwashing? Hardly. It's just the way stories work, 6
in the sense that the author is telling of events that he constructs
consciously, but those events are being shaped by his unconscious, so there are expressions of his values and beliefs in them.
And usually only an idiot misses the point when it bonks you
on the head as happens in the typical American summer movie.
But maybe not this year: We find ourselves in a summer unusu-
ally rich in unexpected subtexts, movies that seem to be about
one thing but are really about something else.

It's hardly shocking, and I don't mean this to be any big 7
exposé. The last thing I exposed was my stomach at the beach
in 1986, and never again. Too much subtext! And in the movies,
subtext isn't even new. It's been around forever.

You can look at three fabulous Bogey flicks from the '40s and 8
see it most clearly. *Casablanca, To Have and Have Not* and *Key
Largo* are set oceans apart in wildly differing political and geo-
graphical situations, are directed by three different, vivid direc-
tors, are completely unrelated, have different contexts, and are
exactly the same. That is, they feel the same, because the subtexts are the same.

The first two films follow an arc that is psychological but, 9
at least metaphorically (and politically), had direct application
to the '40s. You know that thing they had then? What was that
thing called? Ah, yes: the Second World War. All three films
are calls to arms. They begin with the figure of the Isolated Man:
He's been desolated by falling in love, then being abandoned;
he's become hard and cynical, and he plays the game of war and
politics simply for laughs or profit. In one, he's a saloonkeeper;
in the second, he's a fishing boat captain; in the third, he's an

ex-Army officer, essentially shattered by the war, unable to feel love again.

10 In each case he meets a woman: maybe it's the same woman who ruined his life, maybe it's a new woman. In any event, she stirs in him feelings he thought he didn't have, and, now awakened (unstated: "and returned to sexual potency"; it was the '40s and such things were left unsaid) he finds it in himself to face formidable odds, act heroically, defeat an evil plot, kill a particularly noxious specimen of pure rank evil, and rejoin civilization. In the last two films he gets the girl; in the first, most famously, he gives her up because where he's going, she can't go, and what's he's got to do, she can't be any part of.

11 When Howard Hawks essentially remade Michael Curtiz's *Casablanca* two years later, it was set on the French Caribbean island of Martinique, where Steve (not Rick) is a down-on-his-luck fisherman, completely apolitical. Nothing matters to him except an old drunk (Walter Brennan).

12 He becomes enmeshed in French internal politics—Vichy vs. Free France, today a forgotten struggle—when he is asked to smuggle someone into Martinique, then out of Martinique. His initial answer: No way, Pierre. But in the meantime, he meets her, and her name is Marie. It is his love for Marie that drives him back toward commitment. Is she the wife of a French patriot? No, although weirdly enough, there *is* a beautiful wife of a French patriot in the movie (played by Dolores Moran), and possibly she had a bigger role in the script than in the film, where she's all but ignored. And why is this lovely creature ignored? Simple. Hawks saw the chemistry between Bogart and the ingénue in the role of Marie, nicknamed Slim, and let the camera record history in the making: Her name was Lauren Bacall.

13 So the political subtext of the film was diminished considerably. What dominates the film is another subtext, about the power of sexually provocative young women to rescue grumpy middle-aged men from the doldrums and make them tough and young again. That this corresponded with what was going on in real life (Bogart fell in love with his co-star and dumped his wife *instantly* for her) only helped. And so Bacall became a star and stayed one for years.

14 By the time John Huston made *Key Largo* in 1948, the war was long over, yet again it is at the center of the story. In fact, again

Bogart and Ingrid Bergman in *Casablanca.*

it had to have been chosen to recall the character arc of *Casablanca* and the Bogart-Bacall magic of *To Have and Have Not.* The story is a relic from before the war. Again he's the Isolated Man; she's the Girl.

All kinds of weirdnesses are loose in this one: The play, by Maxwell Anderson, was written in 1940 and in it, the hero was a disillusioned vet of the Spanish Civil War. The struggle he was rejoining was against fascism. But by 1948, fascism was in smoldering ruins all across Europe, so in this case the subtext of the film is inappropriate to the times. To make things more twisted yet, as a climax, Huston borrowed the boat-set gunfight from Hemingway's novel *To Have and Have Not,* which Hawks had dumped (along with most of the rest of the novel) when he was making his film of it. So by this go-round, everything is scrambled except, once again, the magic of Bogart and Bacall, and the power of Robinson, which still drive the piece.

Yet in this same run of '40s pictures, there's yet another Bogie-Bacall that could never be mentioned with the first three.

That's because its subtext is completely different, though it's really no more different from them in plot and setting than they are from each other. Of course it's the fabulous *The Big Sleep*, with Bogart as Raymond Chandler's Philip Marlowe and Bacall as Vivian. But there's no fallen-idealist-restored arc to the film; in fact the secret of Marlowe, and what makes him so attractive to us, is that he still is a believer, has always been a believer, and under his cynical ways, is essentially a noble knight on a crusade. In fact, if there's any rescue, it's inverted: it's his idealism that rescues her from a life of debauchery and chaos.

17 Now it is true that you can go way over the top in deciphering subtext, particularly when politics enters the equation. Liberals, who think that Rich White Bastards run the movie companies, see encomiums to conformism and materialism everywhere. Conservatives, who think that Wiggy Femi-Nazi Tree-Huggers run the movie companies, see seductions into the counterculture or the anti-culture or the unculture everywhere.

18 Well, we'll let those two camps battle it out among themselves and try not to slip on the blood upon the floor. But as I said, this is a season rich in subtexts, only one of them political. That one is the dreary sub movie—it sank so fast, someone must have left the hatch open—*K-19: The Widowmaker*, which was nothing less than an attempt by a bunch of foggy-minded fools to reinvent the Cold War as a tragic folly on the scale of World War I and to suggest that the wonderful Russian navy saved us all from nuclear annihilation.

19 The film simply did not accept, as so many American movies since 1945 have, the centrality of the concept: Communism bad, Democracy good. Okay, that's fine. It tried to sell that message on the open market and the open market responded thus: Kersploosh. That's the sound of *K-19* being flushed down the toilet of voracious, market-driven capitalism.

20 But other subtexts are more social. There's a series of secret-agent movies, *The Bourne Identity, The Sum of All Fears* and finally *XXX*. Their subtext, universally: Move over, old guys.

21 All three movies to some degree—and *XXX* and *Sum of All Fears* to a greater extent—are trying to celebrate the passing of one generation and the coming of another. In other words, it's a contest: Who wants to be the new Clint?

22 This is great work if you can get it, but returns still aren't in. Though *XXX* did $46 million in its opening weekend at the

box office and seemed to herald the coming of the Vin Diesel era and the end of the Clint era (Eastwood's *Blood Work*, opening the same weekend, finished far down in the boxoffice take), let's wait to proclaim winners till Diesel puts together a string of hits and enters mainstream consciousness as did Clint or Arnold or Bruce or any of those other fellows who now, with their tum-tums and graying temples, look pretty silly running up stairs and machine-gunning bad guys.

Expanding Vocabulary

Match each word in column A with its definition in column B. When in doubt, first find the word in the essay and look for context clues to aid your understanding of the word's meaning. Then, if necessary, use your dictionary to complete the matching exercise. The number in parentheses is the number of the paragraph in which the word appears.

Column A	Column B
mediocre (2)	revelation
motifs (5)	terribly lonely and forlorn
bonks (6)	challenging, difficult
exposé (7)	moderate to inferior in quality
flicks (8)	hits
desolated (9)	ravenous, eager to consume
formidable (10)	moral corruption
noxious (10)	innocent young woman
apolitical (11)	something that has survived
ingénue (12)	from the past
doldrums (13)	decoding, understanding
relic (14)	lofty tributes
debauchery (16)	recurring thematic elements in a
deciphering (17)	work
encomiums (17)	having no interest in politics
voracious (19)	unhappy listlessness
	movies
	injurious to health or morals

Understanding Content

1. What are the key differences between *text* and *subtext*? How do those differences help us to understand the concept of *subtext*?
2. Explain the "arc" or subtext "movement" in *Casablanca*. Why is the subtext diminished in Hawk's version of the movie?

3. How does the subtext of *The Big Sleep* differ from the previous Bogart films?
4. What political agenda do Liberals suspect Hollywood of putting into its films? How do Conservatives see Hollywood's political agenda?
5. Why did *K-19* fail?
6. What are the social subtexts of the three summer 2002 movies?

Drawing Inferences about Thesis and Purpose

1. What is Hunter's thesis? Where does he state it?
2. Hunter introduces Liberal and Conservative "readings" of Hollywood's political agenda without choosing one perspective over the other. Why does he introduce these "readings" of subtext? What seems to be his opinion of both Liberal and Conservative readings?

Analyzing Strategies and Style

1. What strategies does Hunter use to define his key term *subtext?* What strategy do you find most helpful?
2. Is Hunter serious in defining subtext? In discussing the 1940s movies? Is he less serious in some spots? How would you describe the essay's tone?

Thinking Critically

1. Why does Hunter think that the 2002 summer action movies have not necessarily demonstrated their subtexts? What does he need to agree with their message? Do you agree that the aging action-hero movie stars are finished? Why or why not?
2. Do you think about a movie's subtext? Why or why not?
3. Have you seen *Casablanca*? It may be the most famous move ever made. If you have not seen it, do you think you will? If not, why not?

Bad Raps: Music Rebels Revel in Their Thug Life

SUZANNE FIELDS

Suzanne Fields (b. 1936) is a syndicated op-ed columnist with a twice-weekly column in the *Washington Times*. She holds a Ph.D.

in literature from Catholic University and is trained in social psychology. A collection of her columns was published by the *Washington Times* in 1996. Her article on rap music appeared on May 21, 2001, in *Insight on the News*.

Questions to Guide Your Reading:
1. How does Sinatra differ from current rappers?
2. What is Field's purpose in writing?

Nothing in the culture wars makes a stronger argument for the 1
defense of conservative values than rap music. Rap expresses the worst kind of images emanating from a postmodern society that has consigned a generation of young men and women to the darkest dramas of the desperately lost.

The megastars of this genre are not about to sing of "you and 2
me and baby makes three." Their lyrics come from a world of broken families, absent fathers, illegitimate children and matriarchal dominance, often subsidized by welfare.

For the men who denigrate women as "bitches" and "ho's," 3
this is not merely misogyny (though it is that), but alienation from common humanity and community. The lyrics employ vulgar street idioms because both the language and experience of poetry or romance are absent from the lives of the rappers and their audience as well.

Frank Sinatra grew up on the mean streets of New Jersey and 4
he knew the Mafia well, but when he sang "You're the top, You're the Tower of Pisa. . . . You're the Mona Lisa" he aspired to sophistication and wanted others to see him as debonair. (Is there a rapper alive who knows the difference between the Tower of Pisa and a towering pizza?) When Frankie was bad, literally, he didn't want his fans to hear about it. He wasn't as innocent as his lyrics, but he cultivated that impression.

Rappers Sean "Puffy" Combs and Eminem, by contrast, must 5
live like they sing. They're rich, but their attraction resides in perverse behavior on and off stage. When as adults they tap into adolescent rebellion, they dumb down both their emotions and their economic success.

Shelby Steele, a black scholar, has their number when he 6
writes that to keep their audience they can't just sing about

alienation—they had better experience it as well, either with the audience or for the audience.

7 "The rappers and promoters themselves are pressured toward a thug life, simply to stay credible," Steele writes in the *Wall Street Journal*. "A rap promoter without an arrest record can start to look a lot like Dick Clark."

8 A rapper such as Eminem, who revels in affecting a white-trash identity, has defenders, too. They find irony, satire and poetic metaphor in his lyrics, but it's difficult to see how most of his fans take those lyrics as anything but straight. Lurking in them is a cruel depravity that seeks ways to go over the line by singing of macho brutality—of raping women, holding gay men with a knife at their throats and helping a group of friends to take a little sister's virginity.

9 These lyrics are powerful, but the power resides in psychological defensiveness that provides a perverse rationalization for brutality: If you don't love you can't be rejected, so you might as well hate and rape.

10 Every generation since Elvis has driven through adolescence on popular music—looking for the new sound and sensibility that rejects what their parents liked. Elvis was the cutting edge of the sexual revolution innovative then, but tame and hardly even titillating today. It's hard to believe that for his first appearance on the *Ed Sullivan Show*, the maestro wouldn't allow the cameras to focus below the singer's waist.

11 Elvis brilliantly combined the black, blues and sex rhythms of the honky-tonks of the backroads South of his time, liberating teen-age rebels in dance and song. But nearly every music hero and heroine after him has had to push the envelope or raise the ante to be a big winner. For some teenagers the explicit meanness may provide an imaginary escape, the permission to act in a dark, forbidden drama of their imaginations. For these young men and women, the incentives to "act out" may be no more aggressive than dyeing hair purple or wearing ugly clothes. For others, "acting out" as in "men behaving badly," may be the preferred response in human relationships.

12 Rappers, rollers and rockers who tap into the big time with bite and bitterness draw millions to their records and concerts for different reasons. The teen-age and young-adult Zeitgeist

is made up of rebels with and without causes. It didn't hurt Eminem that his mother sued him for $10 million for using lyrics such as "my mom smokes more dope than I do." (It might have been Eminem's press agent's idea.) That's on the same track in which he ponders which Spice Girl he would prefer to "impregnate."

There are lots of other popular singers who get less notice by 13 being less bizarre. They make up a popular lifestyle that eventually will morph into a healthy nostalgia. The pity is that the nasty stuff of violent rap may never reach the nostalgic mode but congeal into a brutal life perspective.

In one of Eminem's hits he sings of a deranged fan. Eminem 14 suggests the fan get counseling, but the fan doesn't. Instead he kills himself and his pregnant girlfriend. Fantasy or reality?

Expanding Vocabulary

Match each word in column A with its definition in column B. When in doubt, first find the word in the essay and look for context clues to aid your understanding of the word's meaning. Then, if necessary, use your dictionary to complete the matching exercise. The number in parentheses is the number of the paragraph in which the word appears.

Column A	Column B
emanating (1)	form, type
consigned (1)	attack the reputation of, put down
megastars (2)	
genre (2)	pleasurably exciting, arousing
denigrate (3)	conductor, head of the show
misogyny (3)	the stake to be paid to play
debonair (4)	given over to, set apart
perverse (5)	coming from
titillating (10)	spirit of the times
maestro (10)	insane
honky-tonks (11)	really big stars
ante (11)	change form
Zeitgeist (12)	hatred of women
morph (13)	perverted, wrong-headed
deranged (14)	cheap, noisy bars or dance halls
	suave, cultured and urbane

Understanding Content

1. What are the subjects of rapper lyrics?
2. What does Frank Sinatra have in common with modern rappers?
3. What is the relationship between Combs and Eninem's music and their lifestyles? How are their lifestyles a series of contradictions?
4. What image does Eminem like to present? How does the author describe his image?
5. What were the sources of Elvis's music? How was he innovative for his time?
6. What, according to Fields, eventually happens to each era's adolescent music? Does she expect the same process to take place with teens growing up on rap music?

Drawing Inferences about Thesis and Purpose

1. What is Field's thesis? Where does she state it?
2. Fields asserts that rap lyrics provide a "perverse rationalization for brutality." Explain her idea.

Analyzing Strategies and Style

1. The author quotes Shelby Steele, who says that rap promoters need an arrest record so as not to be like Dick Clark. Who is Dick Clark? What makes this reference effective?
2. Fields uses two examples to contrast with today's rappers—Sinatra and Elvis. What makes these popular singers particularly useful examples to show how rappers differ from popular singers of the past?

Thinking Critically

1. Do you agree with the author that "the language and experience of poetry or romance are absent from the lives of rappers and their audiences"? Is this one of the realities of our postmodern society? Explain your views.
2. Do you agree that teens influenced by rap music will be affected into adulthood by a music that alienates them from "common humanity"? If so, how do you suggest that we keep teens from this influence?
3. Do you listen to rap music? If so, how would you defend your choice? If not, why not?

Call Hating

DAVE BARRY

A humor columnist for the *Miami Herald* since 1983, Dave Barry
(b. 1947) is now syndicated in more than 150 newspapers. A
Pulitzer Prize–winner in 1988 for commentary, Barry has several books, including *Dave Barry Slept Here* (1989), a collection
of his columns. The following column appeared in 2001.

Questions to Guide Your Reading

1. What is Barry's primary purpose in writing? Can he be said
   to have more than one purpose?
2. What kinds of examples does Barry provide? What do they
   all have in common?

It was a beautiful day at the beach—blue sky, gentle breeze, 1
calm sea. I knew these things because a man sitting five feet
from me was shouting them into his cellular telephone, like a
play-by-play announcer.

"IT'S A BEAUTIFUL DAY," he shouted. "THE SKY IS BLUE, AND 2
THERE'S A BREEZE, AND THE WATER IS CALM, AND . . ."

Behind me, a woman, her cell phone pressed to her ear, was 3
pacing back and forth.

"She DIDN'T," she was saying. "No. She DIDN'T. She DID? 4
Really? Are you SERIOUS? She did NOT. She DID? No she DIDN'T.
She DID? NO she . . ."

And so on. This woman had two children, who were frolicking 5
in the surf. I found myself watching them, because the woman
surely was not. A giant squid could have surfaced and snatched
the children, and this woman would not have noticed. Or, if she
had noticed, she'd have said, "Listen, I have to go, because a giant
squid just . . . No! She didn't! She DID? No! She . . ."

And next to me, the play-by-play man would have said: 6
". . . AND A GIANT SQUID JUST ATE TWO CHILDREN, AND I'M GET-
TING A LITTLE SUNBURNED, AND . . ."

7   It used to be that the major annoyance at the beach was the jerk who brought a boom box and cranked it up so loud that the bass notes caused sea gulls to explode. But at least you knew where these jerks were; you never know which beachgoers have cell phones. You'll settle next to what appears to be a sleeping sunbather, or even (you hope) a corpse, and you'll sprawl happily on your towel, and you'll get all the way to the second sentence of your 467-page book before you doze off to the hypnotic surge of the surf, and . . .

8   BREEP! BREEP! The corpse sits up, gropes urgently for its cell phone, and shouts, "Hello! Oh hi! I'm at the beach! Yes! The beach! Yes! It's nice! Very peaceful! Very relaxing! What? She did? No she didn't! She DID? No she . . ."

9   Loud cell-phoners never seem to get urgent calls. Just once, I'd like to hear one of them say: "Hello? Yes, this is Dr. Johnson. Oh, hello, Dr. Smith. You've opened the abdominal cavity? Good! Now the appendix should be right under the . . . What? No, that's the liver. Don't take *that* out, ha ha! Oh, you did? Whoops! Okay, now listen very, very carefully . . ."

10   The good news is, some politicians want to ban cell-phone use. The bad news is, they want to ban it in cars, which is the one place where innocent bystanders don't have to listen to it. Granted, drivers using cell phones may cause accidents ("I gotta go, because I just ran over a man, and he's bleeding from the . . . What? She DID? NO she didn't. She DID? No she . . ."). But I frankly don't believe that drivers yakking on cell phones are nearly as dangerous as drivers with babies in the back seat. I'm one of those drivers, and we're definitely a menace, especially when our baby has dropped her Elmo doll and is screaming to get it back, and we're steering with one hand while groping under the back seat with the other. ("Groping for Elmo" would be a good name for a rock band.)

11   So we should, as a long-overdue safety measure, ban babies. But that is not my point. My point is that there is good news on the cell-phone front, which is that several companies—including Image Sensing Systems and Net-Line—are selling devices that jam cell-phone signals. Yes! These devices broadcast a signal that causes every cell phone

in the immediate vicinity to play the 1974 hit song "Kung Fu Fighting."

No, that would be too wonderful. But, really, these devices, 12 which start at around $900, cause all nearby cellular phones to register NO SERVICE.

Unfortunately, there's a catch. Because of some outfit calling 13 itself the "Federal Communications Commission," the cell-phone jamming devices are illegal in the United States. I say this stinks. I say we should all contact our congresspersons and tell them that if they want to make it up to us consumers for foisting those lousy low-flow toilets on us, they should put down their interns for a minute and pass a law legalizing these devices, at least for beach use.

I realize some of you disagree with me. I realize you have 14 solid reasons—perhaps life-and-death reasons—why you *must* have your cellular phone working at all times, everywhere. If you're one of those people, please believe me when I say this: I can't hear you.

Expanding Vocabulary

Examine the following words in their contexts in the essay. Then write a brief definition or synonym for each one. (Do not use a dictionary; try to guess the word's meaning from its context.) The number in parentheses is the number of the paragraph in which the word appears.

frolicking (5)
cranked (7)
hypnotic (7)
yakking (10)
menace (10)
foisting (13)

Understanding Content

1. Where, in particular, would Barry like to see an end to cell-phone use?
2. Does Barry really want to make jamming devices legal? Explain.

Drawing Inferences about Thesis and Purpose

1. What exactly is Barry's thesis?

   2. Does the author believe that most cell-phone use is necessary, that people really have to have their phones on all the time? How do you know the answer to this question?

Analyzing Strategies and Structures

   1. At what point in your reading are you aware that Barry is using humor?
   2. What passages do you find especially funny? Why?
   3. How does Barry cleverly blend and overlap his examples of cell-phone conversations? What makes this use of repetition funny?
   4. One strategy for humor is Barry's introducing something that doesn't fit the discussion, that seems completely disconnected. Find examples of this strategy.

Thinking Critically

   1. Are you bothered by intrusive cell-phoners who talk loudly about, apparently, nothing important? If no, how would you respond to Barry? If yes, what suggestions do you have for dealing with the situation?
   2. Why do you think some people have to talk loudly and repeatedly into their cells while at the beach or in a restaurant? What may explain this behavior?
   3. What guidelines for the courteous use of cell phones would you recommend? Draw up a list to share with classmates.

MAKING CONNECTIONS

---

   1. Mencimer and Fields both write about violence in the media, whether in song lyrics or the movies. Because children and teenagers are big listeners and watchers, they are growing up exposed to a considerable amount of violence. Of course, fairy tales also contain much violence, but some experts believe that their violence is healthy for children. Are there different kinds or levels of violence? Should distinctions be made, and some kinds of violence banned or available to adults only? Consider the examples these writers use and those you know, and then try to define the kinds of violence that may be tolerated and the kinds that should be controlled in some way.

2. If violence in lyrics and on television should be controlled, who should do the controlling? Is the task one for parents, for education through the schools and TV, for voluntary control by the media, for federal guidelines and restrictions? Decide on the approaches you would take if you were "media czar."

3. McGarvey and Steinem are stating or implying the power of the media. The media create images that sanction the dress, language, and behavior presented in those images. And children are not the only ones influenced by those images, as McGarvey's experience demonstrates. How should children be instructed to understand the media, especially television, movies, and advertising, so that they can distinguish between image and reality? Consider the suggestions stated or implied in this chapter and reflect on other possibilities as well.

4. Gloria Steinem examines some ways that advertising misleads. How can we know what is accurate and reliable? Think about strategies readers can use to guide their reading of both magazines and Websites.

5. Studies show that TV programs are filled with stereotypes. What about advertising? Conduct an online search to see what you can learn about stereotyping in print or TV ads, or in television shows. Search with keywords such as "advertising and stereotyping." One useful site to visit is: *http://www.media-awareness.ca.*

TOPICS AND GUIDELINES FOR WRITING

1. What makes your favorite type of television program so good, or what makes your least favorite type of program so bad? Do you most enjoy (or least enjoy) watching news, sports, sitcoms, soaps, a movie channel? Select your most (or least) favorite type and then support a thesis with specific examples from particular shows.

2. The columnist George Will has described the names of some foods as "printed noise." (Think of the names of ice cream flavors, for example.) Are there other words or pictures that

should be labeled verbal or visual litter—words or pictures that are silly, inaccurate, overstated, childish? Think about product commercials; political advertising; repeated coverage of particular issues in the media; repeated "lectures" from teachers, parents, friends that you now simply tune out. Select your topic, decide on your thesis, and then support your thesis with plenty of examples.

3. Examine current political campaigns to see whether any use negative advertising that distorts the issues and misleads voters. For evidence, listen to radio and TV ads for specific examples with which to develop your essay. Your thesis will be that the _____ campaign uses misleading negative tactics, or the _____ campaign uses only fair and accurate campaign tactics.

4. Suzanne Fields is concerned about violence in song lyrics and in the lives of rap musicians. Are you? Examine examples of lyrics and/or TV images (e.g., MTV videos), decide on your point of view, and then support it with plenty of examples.

5. In this chapter you have read some articles about the power of advertising and image making. When a product's name is clever, that name becomes an ongoing advertisement for the product. Many product names are highly connotative or suggestive, such as *Lestoil* cleaner. Think about the names used for one type of product, such as cleaning materials, perfumes, diet foods, or cigarettes. (You may want to explore your favorite grocery store or shopping mall for ideas.) In an essay, explain the effects of the various product names, grouping the names by their different effects (their purpose or the desired impact on buyers), and illustrate those effects with specific examples. Be sure to work with enough examples to support your thesis, probably at least fifteen specific items (e.g., White Shoulders) in the product category (e.g., perfumes).

6. Writing fables or parables to make a point about human character traits or about morality can be fun. Try writing one to make some point about advertising or about what motivates humans to buy particular products. Think, for example, about the many different car models—what types of people are drawn to each model—or the array of sports

equipment or kinds of drinks. When planning your story, follow these guidelines: (a) keep your story short, no more than two or three pages; (b) make it a story—not an essay— with characters, dialogue, and a sequence of events; (c) remember that characters do not have to be human; (d) fill your story with specific details; (e) avoid any direct statement of your story's point; (f) consider using humor as a way to imply your point.

6

Using Process Analysis

How We Work and Play

How does it work? How do we do it? How did it happen? These questions are answered when you provide a process analysis. You live with process analysis every day. The directions to the library that you give to a visitor, the mechanic's explanation of how your car engine is supposed to be working, your history text's account of the planning and execution of the D-Day invasion of Normandy, the biology instructor's explanation of the steps to follow in dissecting a frog: All of these directions, accounts, and instructions are examples of process analysis.

When to Use Process Analysis

The label "process analysis" tells us about this kind of writing. It is, first, *process* because we are talking about an activity or procedure that takes us from one situation to another, that results in some change, some goal reached. You follow the instructions on the recipe card to produce the desired carrot cake, or on the box to put together the new bookcase. You listen to the instructor's guidelines carefully so that you will end with a properly dissected frog. Process is also a type of *analysis* because the good writer of process breaks down the activity into a clear series of steps or stages. Getting the steps in a process right—absolutely right!—is essential. You have come to value the person who gives clear directions, the instructor whose guidelines help you through the stages that shaped an important period in history. You value those who write process analyses well because you have probably experienced more than one occasion of frustration over directions that were unclear, incomplete, or just plain wrong. When you have a topic that can most logically be developed as steps or stages in a process, then you will want to be one of those writers who presents the steps or stages clearly and completely for your readers.

How to Use Process Analysis

To write a clear, effective process analysis you need to keep several points in mind. First, when you are assigned a process analysis—or, more accurately, topics that can best be developed by using process analysis—you are not writing a *list* of instructions. You are writing an essay. This means that you must begin the way you begin any essay—with decisions about audience and purpose. You would not give the same directions for using a camera to a fifth-grade class that you would give to an advanced photography class at an adult education center. Similarly, when planning a process essay, you must assess your readers' knowledge of the subject as a basis for deciding how much background information and explanation are appropriate. These are really two separate decisions. One answers the question: Where do I start? The other answers the question: How detailed is my discussion of each step or stage in the process? Many "how-to" books are not really written for beginners, as you may have discovered. Instead, the author assumes more background than the beginner has.

When the process is complex, the writing challenge lies in giving sufficient explanation of each step so that readers are not too confused with step one to comprehend step two. Unless you are given an assignment that calls for a particular audience, think of directing your essays to a general adult audience made up of people like your classmates. Few of them are likely to be as knowledgeable as you are about a topic you select for your process analysis. When planning the essay, take time to include the background and explanations needed by readers who are not likely to have your knowledge and expertise.

The good essay is not only directed to a clearly defined audience; it is also unified around a clear thesis. In those instructions with the bookcase pieces, the implied thesis is: If you follow these directions you will put the bookcase together correctly.

In a process essay, the thesis extends beyond the completing of the process. You must ask yourself why a reader should be interested in learning about the process topic you have selected. Ernest Hemingway wants to keep inexperienced campers from having so miserable a time that they will swear never to camp again. John Aigner explains a process for preparing for a job interview so that readers will be able to do well in their interviews and get the job.

Finally, the good essay is the interesting essay. The HTML for Dummies manual doesn't have to be interesting; it just has to be clear so that the computer user can complete the desired documents. But the essay, whatever its purpose or organizational strategy, needs to engage its reader, to make an audience for itself through clear explanations and interesting details. Be sure to guide your reader through the time sequence that is your basic organizational strategy. Search for transitions that are more lively than "the first step," "the second step," and so on. Here are some transition words that often appear in process essays:

after	following	last	second
before	later	next	then
finally	last	now	when

In addition, when you present each step or stage, provide vivid details and concrete examples. Hemingway does not tell us in general terms to fry in the frying pan and boil in the kettle. He prepares trout and pancakes and macaroni, and an apple pie. The reader, mouth watering, is ready to start packing. Make your analysis right, make it clear, but, above all, make it interesting.

WRITING FOCUS:
PUNCTUATING PROPERLY

When you punctuate sentences properly, you show readers how the parts connect and what groups of words go together. Incorrect punctuation can confuse readers— and sometimes create unintended humor. There are many rules, but only a handful cover most situations. Here they are.

1. **Use commas to separate items in a series.**
   Winston Churchill spoke of blood, sweat, toil, and tears.
   It was Mario's idea, Ruth's organization, and Brian's technical skill that produced the winning project.
2. **Use commas to separate adjectives modifying the same noun.**
   The frisky, black, floppy-eared spaniel trotted next to her youthful, happy owner.
3. **Use a comma to set off lengthy introductory phrases and clauses.**
   Struggling to get his sentences punctuated properly, the student carefully reviewed the rules.
   Although the deli's sandwiches are just okay, their pizza is really good.
   Avoid using commas to set off short introductory elements.
   No: Yesterday, a little, old lady bought a new, red Miata.
4. **Use commas to set off parenthetical material, or interrupters.**
   Chuck, who will lose his job, is lazy.
   Do not set off restrictive material:
   Workers who are lazy will lose their jobs.
5. **Use a comma with a coordinating conjunction (and, or, but, for, nor, yet, so) to separate two independent clauses. (Independent clauses can stand alone as complete sentences.)**
   Some say Woods is the greatest golfer ever, but others argue that the honor still goes to Nicklaus.
6. **Use a semicolon (NOT a comma) to separate two independent clauses not joined with a coordinating conjunction.**
   Some say Woods is the greatest golfer ever; others argue that the honor still goes to Nicklaus.
7. **DO NOT use a comma between compound words or phrases.**
   The boat sailed out of the cove⊙and into the bay.
   The football team trotted onto the field⊙ and prepared for the opening kickoff.

8. **Use a comma to prevent misreading.**
Inside, the church was dimly lit.
While the dog ate, the cat hid under the sofa.

Getting Started: Reflections on Your Favorite Game

If you were going to teach some element of your favorite game or sport to a beginner, how would you break down the element into steps to be taught in sequence? For example, if you were to teach the tennis serve, you might go through the following steps: the stance, the toss, the backswing, contact with the ball, and the follow-through. List steps in the process of teaching some movement, play, or strategy in your favorite game. Try this process analysis in your journal or prepare it for class discussion.

Say My Name, Say My Name

BENJAMIN LEVY

A professional magician, Benjamin Levy has demonstrated his incredible memory before corporate and political audiences. He has now written a book on the subject: *Remembering Every Name Every Time: Corporate America's Memory Master Reveals His Secrets* (2002). In the following brief article, Levy provides a helpful guide to learning names, a problem for many people. This article appeared September 2002 in *Incentive* magazine.

Questions to Guide Your Reading

1. What is a mnemonic device?
2. What is Levy's acronym for his strategy for learning names?

1   Admit it. At some point you've forgotten someone's name. Acronyms, a collection of letters that spell out a word, are the most common mnemonic strategy used when committing information to memory. Remembering names can be achieved using FACE, which stands for the four essential steps in the process of name recall: Focus, Ask, Comment and Employ. These steps can spur a complex reaction in the mind that makes the recall of the person's name easier.

- FOCUS. In sports they call it "putting on your game face." 2
Athletes know that a large part of the battle is mental preparation, focusing on the task at hand. Athletes concentrate
their attention on what they're about to do, engaging in
what sports psychologists call "positive imaging." When the
critical moment finally arrives—a breakaway in a hockey
game, a pass into the end zone—the athlete is mentally prepared to handle it, increasing the chances of success.

Business, too, is competition. Meeting strangers is one of the 3
critical moments when you can either score points or get shut out.
Establish a connection, or you can risk lapsing into the breezy
mode that most people use when meeting others for the first time.

- ASK. Even if you've focused on hearing the name and are 4
positive that you heard it correctly, it's crucial to ask to hear
it again. It's certainly better to make the confirmation while
meeting someone rather than waiting until you run into the
person 10 minutes later.

- COMMENT. Memory building is the forming of connec- 5
tions between new information and things the brain
already knows. Cross-referencing helps embed the new
info. One of the most crucial ties of all is what you accomplish with "Comment." This takes the name deeper into
your memory by linking it to knowledge that is already
rock-solid in your brain.

Sometimes the only thing that will occur to you is a sim- 6
ple statement or fact: "My brother's name is Simon, too," or
"Melissa—that's my wife's name." Commenting gives you the
chance to say the name aloud again.

- EMPLOY. You've spoken the name inquisitively ("Did you 7
say Ed?" "It's Ed?"). But you've never said the name in a way
that signifies to an acquaintance that you've integrated it into
memory. Now it's time to "Employ" the name.

Make the person's name the topic of your initial conversation 8
or use it once in the course of talking. Introduce the person to
others. Say goodbye to the person using their name.

Expanding Vocabulary

Study the contexts in which the following words are used, or study
their definitions in your dictionary, and then use each word in a

separate sentence. The number in parentheses is the number of the paragraph in which the word appears.

mnemonic (1)
embed (5)
inquisitively (7)
integrated (7)

Understanding Content

1. What are the four steps in the process for remembering names?
2. Explain, in your own words, what one is supposed to do at each stage.

Drawing Inferences about Thesis and Purpose

1. What is Levy's thesis?
2. How does Levy think that we best learn new information?

Analyzing Strategies and Style

1. How does Levy engage his readers? Is his strategy effective? Why?
2. Levy draws an analogy to explain the first step, FOCUS. What is the analogy? How does it help to explain the concept?

Thinking Critically

1. Do you have trouble with names? If so, do you think Levy's process will work for you?
2. If you have trouble learning names, which of the four stages gives you the most trouble? Do you fail to focus? If so, why? Do you fail to use the new name? Analyze your reason(s) for having difficulty with names.
3. Why is learning names important in business? Is it important only in business? Explain.

Putting Your Job Interview into Rehearsal

JOHN P. AIGNER

A graduate of City College of New York, John Aigner (b. 1937) is the founder and president of Network Résumés, a New York

City career services firm. Aigner has taught courses for career counselors in addition to running his company, which helps job seekers with the process of finding desired positions. His article on preparing for a job interview was originally published in the *New York Times* on August 16, 1983.

Questions to Guide Your Reading

1. What are the three broad steps in preparation for a job interview?
2. What characteristics do the first two steps share? How does the third step differ somewhat from the first two?

No actor would be so foolish as to walk onto a stage in front   1
of a first-night audience without weeks of rehearsal. Yet every day thousands of job seekers at all stages of their careers walk into interviews without even a minimum of preparation. Hours of effort and expense invested in an effective résumé that successfully obtained the interview are thrown away through lack of preparation.

There are three key areas in which preparation can pay big   2
dividends:

- Creating and rehearsing a personal script.
- Developing a "power vocabulary."
- Researching information about the job, company and industry.

Creation of a script and a power vocabulary are essentially   3
one-time projects that will likely remain useful with only minor variations throughout a job search. General industry-oriented information also has an extended utility during a search. The gathering of information about the company or opportunity will need to be repeated for each occasion.

Persons who might be uncertain about the basic shoulds and   4
shouldn'ts preliminary to successful interviewing—proper dress, on-time arrival, appropriate greeting—might try reading *Sweaty Palms*, by Anthony Medley, or *How to Win in a Job Interview*, by Nason Robertson.

Preparing the Script

Devising a strategy for handling difficult questions will enable   5
you to answer them calmly and with confidence. A particularly

successful approach is to make a list of the most feared questions (some excellent examples may be found in *How to Turn an Interview Into a Job*, by Jeffrey G. Allen, or *Outinterviewing the Interviewer*, by Steven Merman and John McLaughlin), and prepare a written answer to each. Then record your answers on a cassette, listen to yourself and practice, practice, practice.

6   Be aware that most interviewers cover the same ground, and the same basic questions will appear in most interviews. This makes it relatively simple to prepare your answers. Following are some difficult questions that job-seekers may encounter, with suggestions for answering them:

- "Why did you leave your last job?" or "Why do you want to leave your present job?" Remember to be positive, not defensive. Acceptable answers are: greater opportunity, changing conditions, seeking greater responsibility. The best answers are both honest and brief.
- "Why should we hire you?" You may say that from your research you have learned that the interviewer's company is a leader in your field and you believe that your skills and its needs are well matched.
- "What are your strengths and weaknesses?" For many interviewees this question is the most intimidating. This is where preparation and a positive approach are most rewarding. One of the best ways to deal with a weakness is to refer to it as "an area in which I am working to strengthen my skills." Some career advisers suggest responding with, "Well, I don't really have any major weaknesses, but . . ." This is not a satisfactory answer, and would annoy me if I were the interviewer.

7   One general rule is never to answer a serious or really difficult question off the top of your head. Ask for an opportunity to think the question over, and promise to get back to the interviewer the next day. This approach has the added benefit of giving you a follow-up, second opportunity to sell yourself.

8   Have a friend or relative ask you the questions as many times as necessary for you to feel comfortable with the answers. Three to six hours spent practicing in this way will result in greatly improved confidence during interviews. If you think of additional questions later or if an interviewer throws you a curve, you can update your recorded answers.

9   The interviewer controls the flow of an interview, but the interviewee controls the content. If you know what you want to say, you will be more likely to say it, and you will have provided

yourself with a powerful tool to maintain control of even a difficult interview.

The Power Vocabulary

A survey conducted among personnel executives by the   10
Bureau of National Affairs concluded that the interview was the
single most important factor in landing a job and that most
applicants were rejected because they didn't promote themselves well during the interview. They frequently preface their
description of an experience with, "Well, I only . . ." or "That
wasn't a major part of my job." By such a deprecating phrase,
they devalue their experience.

This lack of confidence about self-promotion is particularly   11
true of women, an American Management Association study
has concluded. Men, it seems, have had more practice at competition and are less reticent when it comes to advertising their
accomplishments.

You should consider the interviewer to be in the same cate-   12
gory as the tax auditor. He or she is not your friend, and you are
under no obligation to volunteer any information that won't
help you. In short, telling the truth and telling everything are
not the same thing. If you performed well at a project, such as
setting up a computer installation or devising a new method
of taking inventory, it is not necessary to volunteer, for example, that the project lasted only a short while. If asked directly,
of course answer honestly.

The words you select to describe yourself during the inter-   13
view will have a powerful effect on the outcome. These words
can be planned in advance. In the same way that you planned
a script for the interview, you can also plan a vocabulary of
"power" words that will create an accumulation of positive
impressions about you and your accomplishments.

Consider this example: "I reduced costs" versus "I trimmed   14
costs." The word "reduce" conjures up a fat person who is trying to lose weight. The word "trim" brings to mind someone
who is fit and healthy.

Or: "While at company X, I . . ." versus "I am proud of the   15
fact that while at company X, I . . ." The latter approach is much
stronger and more positive.

16 Use only positive words, ones that create strong mental images, adjectives such as accurate, dynamic, proficient, reliable, thorough, and verbs such as expedite, generate, improve, motivate, persuade, solve. These descriptors will add spice if you pepper your interview with them.

17 You can learn to develop a winning interview style by selecting ten winning words each week and writing them on index cards. Practice using them in sentences about yourself, using one word per sentence. Select words with which you feel comfortable and work them into phrases within your script. You'll quickly discover that these words affect your self-image and the image that others have of you.

18 Avoid complaints of any kind. Do not criticize your previous company, supervisor or position. A complaint is always negative, and that is not the impression you wish to create.

Gathering Information

19 Valuable information about an industry, and about particular companies within it, can be acquired through a library source such as Standard & Poor's, or annual reports, or through the trade press. This is an excellent way to learn the jargon of an industry. These special-interest professional and business publications have mushroomed like cable channels, and are frequently overlooked by job seekers because most are not available on newsstands and are not sold to the general public. There are thousands of these publications—privately circulated newsletters, weekly newspapers, slick monthlies, annual directories and everything in between. They contain a wealth of insider information—for example, industrywide trends and concerns, corporate plans, new-product announcements, trade jargon.

20 A sample copy or even a free subscription is generally available for the asking. To track down the trade press in your industry, check the *Standard Periodical Directory, Gebbe Press All-in-One Directory, The Encyclopedia of Business Information Sources, Ayers Guide to Periodicals* or *Standard Rate and Data.* For articles on particular business subjects, check the *Business Periodicals Index.*

21 Being current on industry concerns in general and company problems in particular can go a long way toward making an interview successful.

Expanding Vocabulary

Examine the following words in their contexts in the essay and then write a brief definition or synonym of each one. (Do not use a dictionary; try to guess each word's meaning from its context.) The number in parentheses is the number of the paragraph in which the word appears.

preliminary (4)   accumulation (13)
intimidating (6)   descriptors (16)
deprecating (10)   jargon (19)
devalue (10)   mushroomed (19)
reticent (11)

Understanding Content

1. List the specific steps within the first step: preparing the script. Why is it possible to prepare basically one script?
2. List the specific steps for developing a power vocabulary.
3. Why does it help to think of the interviewer as similar to a tax auditor?
4. What is the procedure for gathering information? What are the advantages beyond preparation for a specific interview?

Drawing Inferences about Thesis and Purpose

1. What is Aigner's thesis—what is the point of his process analysis?
2. When advising people on how to sell themselves, one invites the charge of encouraging misrepresentation, of "packaging" the interviewee. How does Aigner seek to avoid this charge? How does he try to balance polishing one's interview skills with a fair presentation of one's qualifications?

Analyzing Strategies and Style

1. What analogy does Aigner use throughout his article? Where does he introduce the comparison? Where does he refer to it again? Is this an effective analogy? Why or why not?
2. Aigner's introduction runs to several paragraphs, but his conclusion is only one paragraph containing one sentence. Does it seem too abrupt to you? Can you make the case that it is an effective ending?
3. Examine Aigner's metaphors in paragraphs 1, 8, and 16. How are they effective? What do they contribute to the article?

Thinking Critically

1. If you have interviewed for a job, did you think at the time to prepare in any of the ways Aigner suggests? If so, do you think the process helped you in the interview? If not, would you follow Aigner's steps the next time? Why or why not?
2. Is there one step in Aigner's process that would be especially important in your career field? If so, how would it make you a better interviewee in your career field?
3. Aigner emphasizes the similarity of most job interviews. Had you thought about this point before? Does the idea seem sensible? How can understanding this characteristic of interviews help to make the interview process a little easier?
4. Aigner gives the most space to developing a power vocabulary. Is there some good advice here that extends beyond the interview process? How important are positive attitudes about ourselves?

Learning to Act Like a Professional

WILLIAM G. NICKELS, JIM McHUGH, AND SUSAN McHUGH

Dr. Nickels is an associate professor of business at the University of Maryland and the author of several marketing textbooks. Mr. McHugh teaches at St. Louis Community College and does business consulting in the St. Louis area. Ms. McHugh has advanced degrees in education and is an adult learning theory specialist. This selection comes from the fifth edition of their textbook, *Understanding Business*.

Questions to Guide Your Reading

1. What is the essay's topic? What is the thesis?
2. When is the best time to learn the rules of professional behavior?

1   You can learn a lot about good and bad manners from watching professional sports. During the 1997 basketball playoff series, for example, Michael Jordan of the Chicago Bulls showed that true professionals accept responsibility for the team and

never give up. Whenever the game was on the line, the team turned to Michael for the important shot, and, more often than not, he made it.

You can probably think of contrasting examples of sports 2 stars who have earned a bad reputation by not acting professionally (e.g., spitting, swearing, criticizing teammates in front of others, and so on). People in professional sports are fined if they are late to meetings or refuse to follow the rules established by the team and coach. Business professionals also must follow set rules; many of these rules are not formally written anywhere, but every successful businessperson learns them through experience.

You can begin the habits now that will make for great success 3 when you start your career. Those habits include the following:

1. *Making a good first impression.* "You have seven seconds to make an impression. People see your clothes before you even open your mouth. And make no mistake, everything you say following those first few moments will be weighed by how you look," says image consultant Aleysha Proctor. You don't get a second chance to make a good first impression. Skip the fads and invest in high-quality, classic clothes. Remember, "high-quality" is not necessarily the same as "expensive." Take a clue as to what is appropriate at any specific company by studying the people there who are most successful. What do they wear? How do they act?
2. *Focusing on good grooming.* Be aware of your appearance and its impact on those around you. Consistency is essential. You can't project a good image by dressing up a few times a week and then show up looking like you're getting ready to mow a lawn. Wear appropriate, clean clothing and accessories. It is not appropriate, for example, for men to wear hats inside of buildings. It is also not appropriate, usually, to wear wrinkled shirts or to have shirttails hanging out of your pants.
3. *Being on time.* When you don't come to class or to work on time, you're sending a message to your teacher or boss. You're saying, "My time is more important than your time. I have more important things to do than be here." In addition to the lack of respect tardiness shows to your teacher or boss, it rudely disrupts the work of your colleagues. Promptness may not be a priority in

some circles, but in the workplace promptness is essential. But being punctual doesn't always mean just being on time. Executive recruiter Juan Menefee recalls a time he arrived at 7:40 A.M. for an 8:00 A.M. meeting only to discover he was the last one there. "You have to look around, pay attention to the corporate culture and corporate clock," says Menefee. To develop good work habits and get good grades, it is important to get to class on time and not leave early.

4. *Practicing considerate behavior.* Considerate behavior includes listening when others are talking, and not reading the newspaper or eating in class. Don't interrupt others when they are speaking. Wait for your turn to present your views in classroom discussions. Of course, eliminate all words of profanity from your vocabulary. Use appropriate body language by sitting up attentively and not slouching. Sitting up has the added bonus of helping you stay awake! Professors and managers get a favorable impression from those who look and act alert. That may help your grades in school and your advancement at work.

5. *Being prepared.* A businessperson would never show up for a meeting without reading the materials assigned for that meeting and being prepared to discuss the topics of the day. To become a professional, one must practice acting like a professional. For students, that means reading assigned materials before class, asking questions and responding to questions in class, and discussing the material with fellow students.

4   From the minute you enter your first job interview until the day you retire people will notice whether you follow the proper business etiquette. Just as traffic laws enable people to drive more safely, business etiquette allows people to conduct business with the appropriate amount of dignity. How you talk, how you eat, and how you dress all create an impression on others.

Expanding Vocabulary

Study the following words in their contexts in the essay and then write a brief definition or synonym for each one. Do not use a dictionary; see how many words you can understand by using context clues. The number in parentheses is the number of the paragraph in which the word appears.

consultant (3)   punctual (3)
grooming (3)   profanity (3)
accessories (3)   etiquette (3)
priority (3)   dignity (4)

Understanding Content

1. What are the five habits for success in school and career?
2. What are the two elements that create a first impression, according to the authors?
3. What is essential to good grooming? What elements of dress are considered bad grooming?
4. What are two problems created by tardiness?
5. What are the marks of good body language?

Drawing Inferences about Thesis and Purpose

1. Why do the authors give steps for students to perform, given that students are not yet in business or a profession?
2. If there are no "rules" for successful professional behavior, how do we know what the rules are?

Analyzing Strategies and Style

1. The authors begin with an analogy to professional sport. What is the purpose of their comparison? What makes this an effective opening strategy?
2. The authors end with an analogy. What comparison do they use? What is the point?

Thinking Critically

1. How many of the habits listed by the authors do you practice regularly? If the answer is fewer than all of them, do you think you will practice all of them now? Why or why not?
2. Which habits do you think are most important for businesspeople? For students? Explain your choices.
3. The authors made clear that we form an impression on others by our clothes, speech, and other behaviors, even if we do not intend to be rude or careless or unprofessional. Are you prepared to accept this reality? Why or why not?

Improving Your Body Language Skills

SUZETTE H. ELGIN

A professor emeritus in linguistics from San Diego State University, Suzette Elgin (b. 1936) is the author of several books on language use, including *Try to Feel It My Way* (1996) and *How to Disagree without Being Disagreeable* (1997). She has also written several science fiction novels. "Improving Your Body Language Skills" is a section from Elgin's book *Genderspeak* (1997). Here Elgin offers guidelines for finding the most respected way of speaking American English and for understanding the messages in body language.

Questions to Guide Your Reading

1. What are the characteristics of the ideal adult voice for American speakers of English?
2. What do people "hear" when they listen to speakers whose voices lack these characteristics?

1   Body language problems between men and women who are speakers of American Mainstream English today begin at the most basic of nonverbal levels: with the *pitch* of the voice. The admired voice for the AME culture is the adult male voice; the deeper and richer it is, and the less nasal it is, the more it is admired. Women tend to pitch their voices higher than men do, and this is a strike against them in almost every language interaction. Not because there is anything inherently wrong with high-pitched voices, but because AME speakers associate them with children. A high-pitched voice that's also nasal is heard as the voice of a *whiny* child. People know, of course, that they're hearing an adult woman (or, for the occasional man with a high-pitched voice, an adult male). But at a level below conscious awareness they tend to perceive the voice as the voice of a child. This perception, however much it is in conflict with reality, affects their response to and their behavior toward the speaker.

2   The contrast in voice pitch isn't really a *physiological* matter; the difference between adult male and female vocal tracts is too minor to account for it in the majority of people. In many other

cultures, male voices are higher than those of AME-speaking men, although the physical characteristics of the males are the same. When American adults speak to infants, they pitch their voices lower as they talk to boys, and the infants respond in the same way. Females learn, literally in the bassinet and playpen, that they are expected to make higher-pitched sounds than males are.

In addition to the difference in baseline pitch, AME-speaking 3 women's voices have more of the quality called *dynamism:* They use more varied pitch levels, they move from one pitch to another more frequently, and they are more likely than men's voices are to move from one pitch to another that's quite a bit higher or lower. In other situations the term "dynamic" is a compliment, while "monotonous," its opposite, is a negative label. But not in language; not in the AME culture. The less monotonous a woman's voice is, the more likely it is that her speech will be described by others as "emotional" or "melodramatic." Monotony in the male voice, however, is ordinarily perceived as evidence of strength and stability. (For a detailed discussion of these differences, see McConnell-Ginet 1983.)

Certainly male/female body language differences go beyond 4 the voice. There are positions and gestures and facial expressions that are more typical of one gender than of the other. But the effect one gender achieves by learning to use such items of body language from the other gender is rarely positive. A woman who hooks her thumbs into her belt, spreads her feet wide, and juts out her chin usually looks foolish, as does a man who carefully crosses his legs at the ankles. There are a few stereotypically feminine items that reinforce the "childish" perception which a woman can be careful *not* to use, such as giggling behind her hand or batting her eyelashes. But the most useful thing any woman—or man—can do to get rid of the perceptually filtered "I'm listening to a child" effect is to make the voice lower, and less nasal, and more resonant, so that it will be perceived as an *adult* voice.

This is something that anyone not handicapped by a physi- 5 cal disability that interferes with voice quality can do. One way to do it is to put yourself in the hands of a competent voice *coach.* If you have the time and money to do that, and you live where such experts are available, that's an excellent idea. On the other hand, it's also something you can do by yourself, using an ancient technique that in the *Gentle Art* system is called *simultaneous modeling.* . . .

6   Let me make one thing clear, however, before we go on. I'm not suggesting that anyone, of either gender, "should" try to change the quality of their voice. As is true for many linguistic questions, this is not a moral issue but an issue of cultural fashion. Low voices are not "better" than high voices. In the same way that some people insist on their right to wear jeans in an office where everyone else dresses more formally, people have every right to take the position that the voice they have is the voice they prefer to have. I approve of that, one hundred percent. However, because that decision can have grave consequences, people need to be aware that the consequences exist and that the choice is theirs to make.

7   It's unacceptable for someone to be unaware that the primary reason for his or her communication problems is a high-pitched voice, and to assume that the problems are caused by the lack of a "powerful vocabulary," or a thin enough body, or a sufficiently expensive blazer, or some such thing. It's also unacceptable for those who do realize what the problem is to believe they're helpless to do anything about it. Except in cases requiring medical attention, *anyone,* working alone, can change his or her voice to make it closer to what our culture perceives as the ideal and adult voice. When a medical condition complicates the issue, the potential for improvement may be less, but even limited change toward the ideal can bring about significant positive effects.

8   The facts about body language and its critical importance to communication can be frightening. We don't study body language in school, and few of us are given formal training in the subject. We read everywhere that "a more powerful vocabulary" is our ticket to communication success, and that seems easy—just buy a book or a software program and learn some new words. Improving our body language skills seems mysterious and difficult by contrast. But there's no need to be intimidated; it's simpler than you think.

9   Your internal grammar, the same one that you use to put the right endings on your words and arrange your words in the proper order in your sentences, contains all the rules for body language in your culture. You just haven't had convenient *access*

to that information that would let you use it consciously and strategically. The sections that follow will help you establish that access.

Developing Your Observational Skills

The first step in developing observational skills for nonver- 10 bal communication is simply learning to PAY ATTENTION to the speaker's body and voice. Men in the AME culture tend not to do this, and to be unaware that it matters; when they do pay attention they usually follow a rule that tells them to pay attention only to the speaker's face. Women do somewhat better, not because they have any built-in biological advantage, but because it is universally true that those having less power pay more attention to the body language of those having more power. (In the most primitive situations, this means being alert to the movements of the powerful person so that you will be able to get out of the way before the powerful person grabs or hits you.)

This gender difference is well known. In 1975 a footnote in 11 the *Virginia Law Review* suggested that perhaps women should be excluded from jury duty, because their skill at observing and interpreting nonverbal communication might make them excessively vulnerable to body language effects, interfering with the defendant's right to an independent and unbiased jury. ("Notes: Judges' Nonverbal Behavior in Jury Trials: A Threat to Judicial Impartiality," *Virginia Law Review,* 1975, 61:1266–1298. For a review of research and an account of experiments proving that the body language of trial judges has a significant impact on jury decisions, see Blanck et al. 1985.)

Sometimes this language skill is an advantage for women; 12 sometimes it's not. Like any other skill, it depends on how it is used. Nobody likes the idea that another person is able to read his or her mind. The woman who expresses in words what a man's body language tells her—with claims such as "I can tell by the look on your face that you don't want to go to St. Louis" or "Don't try to tell me you want to go to St. Louis; the way you keep wiggling your index fingers gives you away every time"— is almost sure to provoke hostility. Such remarks are equally counterproductive coming from men who have well-developed body language reading skills.

13   The only way to learn to pay attention to body language is to *practice.* You have to work at it consciously until you become so skilled that you do it automatically, just as you would work at your tennis or your golf or a favorite handicraft. If you're not accustomed to body language observation, you'll find it extremely difficult at first. You'll keep *forgetting* to do it.

14   You've probably had the experience of "coming to" as you take the last highway exit on your drive home and realizing that you have no memory of your previous ten minutes on the road. In the same way, you'll start out carefully observing someone's body language and then suddenly realize that it's been five minutes since you were consciously aware of anything but the words, and perhaps the facial expression, of the speaker. If you continue to work at it, however, you'll get past this stage. As a first practice partner, I strongly recommend your television set. Unlike living persons, the TV set doesn't get tired, doesn't wonder why you're staring at it, is always available at your convenience, and—best of all—never gets its feelings hurt.

Establishing Baseline Values—and Spotting Deviations from Them—in Body Language

15   Body language baselines are profiles of people's speech when they're relaxed, as in casual conversations with close friends. Baselines include such information as the typical pitch of the voice, rate of speed for speech, frequency of eyeblink, body posture, number of hand gestures, etc., for the individual you're interacting with, during *relaxed communication.* This information is important because a *deviation* from the baseline—a move away from these typical values—is a signal to be alert. It indicates some sort of emotional involvement, positive or negative; it indicates that something is happening; sometimes it indicates an attempt to deceive or mislead you.

16   You will have read books or listened to tapes telling you that when you see a person cross his arms or scratch her nose it *means* a particular thing. You'll read that crossed arms signal defensiveness and disagreement with what you're saying; you'll hear that scratching the nose signals anxiety. Sometimes that's true, of course; but much of the time it means the person you're observing is cold or has a nose that itches.

When such items *are* reliable, they hold for a restricted population in specific circumstances—usually for the middle class or upper class dominant white male in a business situation. Learning to establish baseline values for the other person and spotting deviations from that baseline is a great deal more reliable, and will be useful to you in every communication situation, including interactions with people from outside your own culture.

For example, one of the most reliable clues to anxiety, a lack   17 of sincere commitment to what's being said, and a possible intention to deceive is a change to a higher voice pitch. But you won't know there's been a change unless you have first learned what pitch the speaker uses in normal everyday conversation. The same thing is true for other deviations from baseline values. Here are two simple and practical ways to get the necessary information:

- Make a phone call to the individual in advance of your meeting and discuss something entirely neutral, like how to get to the meeting site.
- When you're with the other person, don't begin by talking about anything important. Instead, spend five minutes—or as long as it takes—making small talk on neutral subjects.

Now we can move on to improving your body language   18 *performance* skills, as opposed to observation alone.

Simultaneous Modeling

When students learn t'ai chi, they learn not by watching the   19 teacher and then trying out the posture or movement by themselves but by watching and then moving *with* the teacher. This technique has been successful for thousands of years. If you've studied a foreign language, you're familiar with the traditional procedure: Listen to a sequence of the foreign language, and then, during the pause provided, repeat what you've just heard. At the University of California San Diego, instead of repeating the foreign language sequence *after* the recorded model, students listen to it several times to become familiar with the content and then speak simultaneously *with* the model. This technique (developed at UCSD by linguist Leonard Newmark) consistently produces results far superior to the traditional method. And there are many cultures in which people learn to do things (weaving, for example) by first watching someone who already knows how and then sitting down beside that person and working along with her or him.

20   These are all examples of *simultaneous modeling*. They take *advantage* of the way human brains work instead of fighting against it. When you change your behavior to make it like someone else's you have to make many small adjustments all over your body, all at once. You can't do that very well *consciously*. But your brain can do it competently and successfully, if you just stay out of its way. You can use this information and your brain's built-in skills to improve the quality of your voice, by adapting Newmark's foreign language teaching method.

21   Changing voice quality requires an array of small but crucial adjustments. You have to change the tension of the muscles of your tongue and throat and chest, you have to move the parts of your vocal tract in ways that you're not used to, and so on. When you listen to a foreign language sequence and try to repeat it afterward, you not only have to make all those adjustments but you have to *remember* the sequence. The final result is that you change your speech to match the sequence you *remember* instead of the one you actually heard. When you speak *with* the model voice instead of repeating on your own, this doesn't happen. Your brain takes over and does all the adjustments, matching your voice to the model.

Working with the Tape Recorder

22   You need a tape recorder (an inexpensive one will do), a few blank tapes, and a tape about thirty minutes long by someone of your own gender whose voice sounds the way you'd like to sound. For men, I recommend television anchorman Peter Jennings, or one of the male announcers on National Public Radio's regular news programs ("Morning Edition" or "All Things Considered," for example). For women I recommend a tape of Diane Sawyer or one of the female NPR newscasters. If you prefer someone else, either a public figure or someone in your own circle, that's fine. Just be sure the voice you choose as your model is one that you and others perceive as strong, resonant, pleasant, compelling, and—above all—the voice of a *mature adult*.

Then follow the steps below, at your own convenience, at your own speed, and in privacy.

1. Make a twenty- to thirty-minute *baseline* tape of your own speech, write down the date on which it was made, and keep it for comparison with tapes you make later on. Don't read aloud, and don't say something memorized—just *talk*. Talk about your childhood, or why you have trouble communicating with people of the opposite sex, or anything else you can talk about easily and naturally. `23`

2. Listen to the tape you've chosen as a model, all the way through, to get a general idea of its content. Don't write it down, and don't try to memorize it—doing either of those things just gets in the way and keeps you from succeeding. `24`

3. Choose a sentence of average length to work with, from any point on the tape. Listen to it a couple of times, to become familiar with it. Then repeat it, SPEAKING ALONG WITH THE TAPE, SIMULTANEOUSLY. Rewind the tape and do it again, as many times as you feel are necessary—ten times is not in any way unusual. Your goal is to be able to speak smoothly and easily with the model. Don't *struggle*. Trust your brain and let it carry out its functions without interference. `25`

4. When you're bored with the sentence you chose, pick another sentence and repeat Step #3. You should also move on whenever you realize that you know a sentence so well that you've stopped needing the model voice; you aren't interested in learning to *recite* the tape. Continue in this way until you've finished the tape or achieved your goal, whichever happens first. (And go on to another model tape if you find that you need one.) `26`

5. After about ten hours of practice (and after every additional five or six hours), make a new baseline tape of your own speech. Listen to it, and compare it with the earlier ones. When you're satisfied with the change you hear, STOP. The point of this technique is to improve your *own* voice. You don't want people to think you're doing Peter Jennings or Diane Sawyer imitations when you talk; if you go on too long, that's exactly what will happen. `27`

How long this will take will depend on the amount of time you have for practice, how tired you are, whether you are a person `28` who learns well by listening, and other individual factors. Try to make each practice session at least fifteen minutes long; thirty minutes is even better. Try to practice every other day, roughly. If all you can manage is ten minutes once a week, put in those ten minutes—just be prepared for it to take you much longer to achieve results on that basis. Remember: It doesn't make any *difference* how long it takes. You're not paying by the hour when you use this technique, and there won't be a final exam. Relax and let it take as long as it takes. Some of my clients have noticed substantial improvement in six weeks; others have needed six months or more for the same results.

29   The fact that you can't just take a Voice Quality Pill and change instantly is actually a good thing. The people you interact with regularly (and especially the person or persons you live with) need to be able to get used to the change in your voice gradually. You don't want your partner to leave in the morning, accustomed to the voice you've always had, and come home that night to someone who sounds like an entirely different person. A pleasant adult voice is a powerful tool for improving your relationships, but it shouldn't come as a *shock* to those around you.

30   **Note:** You can also use this procedure to learn to speak other varieties of English—other dialects or other registers—at will. If you feel that your native accent sometimes holds you back in the American Mainstream English environment, simultaneous modeling is a good way to learn a variety of English that's more helpful. Moving back and forth among varieties—called *codeswitching*—is a valuable skill.

Working with the Television Set

31   A voice coach (or an "image" coach) may be beyond the financial limits for many of us. It's fortunate that we have our television sets available to use as free coaches. In exactly the same way that you can improve your voice quality by speaking along with a tape recorded model, you can improve the rest of your body language by *moving* simultaneously with a model on videotape. Ideally, you will also have a VCR, so that you can work with a single tape over a period of time. If you have a video camera (or can rent one), to let you make a baseline video of your body language, that's also a plus. But if those items

aren't available to you, choose as a model someone of your own gender that you can see on television several times a week, and practice moving simultaneously with that person at those times. As with voice quality, stop *before* you find yourself doing impersonations of your model.

I don't recommend that women try to learn "male body language" by working with a videotape of a male speaker, or that men work with a videotape of a woman to learn "female body language." (The fact that the latter alternative is wildly unlikely outside the entertainment field is consistent with the power relationships in our society.) Cross-gender modeling is a bad idea, full of hidden hazards and boobytraps, and it almost always backfires. If you're gifted with the sort of superb acting ability that would let you do this *well*, like Dustin Hoffman playing the heroine in the movie *Tootsie*, you're not someone who needs improved body language anyway. You will be far more successful with the body language of a strong and competent adult of your own gender. 32

If you believe you have a long way to go in acquiring satisfactory body language skills, if you feel self-conscious trying to acquire them, if your opportunities to practice them are few and far between, by all means rely on the TV set. You can move on to practice with live partners when you feel more at ease. 33

Expanding Vocabulary

Study the definitions of any of the following words that are unfamiliar to you. Then use each of the words in a separate sentence. The number in parentheses is the number of the paragraph in which the word appears.

perceptually (4)	vulnerable (11)
resonant (4)	boobytraps (31)
intimidated (8)	

Understanding Content

1. What are the characteristics of a "whiny child's" voice?
2. How hard is it to improve body language skills?
3. What is the first step to improving body language skills? What is a good way to practice?
4. What are body language baseline profiles? Why are they useful to establish?

5. How do you establish baseline profiles?
6. What is meant by simultaneous modeling? Why does it work well?
7. What can you change using simultaneous modeling?
8. Summarize the process of using a tape recorder to change your voice quality.
9. Summarize the process of working with a TV to improve your body language. What should be your standard to work with?

Drawing Inferences about Thesis and Purpose

1. What is Elgin's position on changing one's voice quality? Should the typical male voice be set as a standard for everyone?
2. What is Elgin's purpose in writing?
3. What is her thesis?

Analyzing Strategies and Style

1. What tone of voice do you "hear" in this essay? Do you respond to the author as a sympathetic teacher? Support your response.
2. Elgin uses italics and even all caps for some words. Why? What do they contribute?

Thinking Critically

1. Have you thought about the idea that the typical male voice is considered standard and that many women are perceived as talking like children? Does the idea make sense to you? Why or why not?
2. Why is it important to develop sensitivity to body-language messages?
3. Do you agree that women tend to be better at this sensitivity than men? Does Elgin's explanation for this tendency make sense? Why or why not?
4. Are you going to tape yourself and examine your voice quality and body language? Why or why not?

Restoring Recess

CAROL KRUCOFF

A journalist, Carol Krucoff (b. 1954) is a freelance writer on health and exercise topics, a syndicated health columnist, and the author of a book on health and exercise to be published in

2000. Her health column, "Bodyworks," is also available on the Internet. Krucoff runs and holds a black belt in karate. In "Restoring Recess," which appeared in the *Washington Post*'s Health Section on January 12, 1999, Krucoff encourages readers to treat daily exercise not as work but as play.

Questions to Guide Your Reading

1. What is Krucoff's purpose in writing? What does she want to accomplish?
2. How do adults who exercise regularly usually feel about it?

So here we are, just a few weeks into the new year, and if   1
you're like most Americans you're already struggling to keep your resolution to shape up. Despite good intentions, the sad fact is that half of all adults who start a new exercise program drop out within six months.

Adopting a new habit isn't easy. As Sir Isaac Newton point-   2
ed out, a body at rest will tend to remain at rest. Even the promise of better health and improved appearance won't get most people to exercise regularly.

But there is one motivator that can pry even the most con-   3
firmed "potato" off the couch. Freud called it the pleasure principle: People do things that feel good and avoid things that feel bad. Most American adults get little or no exercise and more than half are overweight because many of them consider exercise to be hard, painful work—a distasteful chore they must force themselves to endure.

Yet as children we didn't feel this way about moving our   4
bodies. Most kids see physical pursuits, like skipping and running, as exciting play to be enjoyed.

So this year, meet your fitness goals by turning exercise into   5
child's play. Scratch the resolution to work out. Instead, vow to play actively for 30 minutes most days. Think of it as recess, and try to recapture the feeling you had as a child of being released onto the playground to swing, play ball or do whatever your little heart—and body—desired. Don't worry about flattening your abs or losing weight. Just enjoy the sensations of moving your body, breathing deeply and experiencing the moment.

This is your personalized playtime, so pick any form of   6
movement that you like—a solitary walk, shooting hoops with

a friend, a dance class, gardening, ping-pong, cycling. The options are vast, and nearly anything that gets you moving is fine, since even light-to-moderate exercise can yield significant health benefits.

7   The point is to stop thinking of your workout as one more demanding task you must cram into your busy day and start viewing it as a welcome recess that frees you from the confines of your chair. Most regular exercisers will tell you that this is the reason they remain active. Yes, they exercise to lose weight, build strong bones and all those other healthy reasons. But scratch deeper and most will admit that a central reason they're out there day after day is that it's fun—their exercise satisfies body and soul, and is a cherished highlight of their lives.

8   If you think this attitude adjustment is merely a mind game, you're right. Getting in shape is, after all, a matter of mind over body. But it's also a healthy way of approaching fitness, to enjoy the journey as much as reaching the destination. Goals can be helpful motivators to shape up. But once you drop a clothing size, then what?

9   So instead of being caught up in reaching a certain scale weight, view taking care of your physical self—which can play a key role in boosting your emotional self—as an opportunity for active play. This may be difficult in our culture, which considers play a frivolous time-waster. Yet "the ability to play is one of the principal criteria of mental health," wrote anthropologist Ashley Montague in his book, *Growing Young*.

10   Just as kids need the release of recess to get the "wiggles" out of the bodies, adults also need relief from the stiffness caused by sitting and the chance to oxygenate sluggish brains.

11   Next time a problem has you stumped, take it out on a walk in the fresh air—and bring along a pencil and paper. Solutions will appear on the move that eluded you at your desk.

12   To make your play breaks happen, schedule them into your life. Lack of time is the main reason people say they don't exercise, and it's true that most of us lead very busy lives. But it's also true that we find time for things that are important to us. It's a matter of making choices.

13   You may need to get up a half hour earlier—and go to bed a half hour earlier—to make your play break happen. You might have to turn off the TV, cut short a phone call or eat lunch at your desk to squeeze in recess. But if it's fun, it won't be a ter-

rible sacrifice—it'll be a willing trade-off. Besides, as a wise person once said, "If you don't make time to exercise, you'll have to take time to be sick."

To keep your break fun, remember to: 14

1. Start slowly and progress gradually. If you've been inac- 15 tive, begin with as little as five minutes of your chosen activity. Add on five more minutes each week with the goal of playing actively for 30 minutes on most days.
2. Avoid negative talk about yourself. Instead of obsess- 16 ing about your thunder thighs, have an attitude of gratitude about your body and all that it does for you.
3. Choose a positive exercise environment. Just as fresh air 17 and music may enhance your recess, mirrors may detract from your experience if you're self-critical. If so, play outdoors or in a mirror-free room.
4. Consider a few sessions with a personal trainer if you 18 need help getting started. For a referral, call the American Council on Exercise's consumer hot line at 1-800-529-8227.
5. Vary your activity. If you like doing the same thing, day 19 after day, great. But it's fine to move in different ways on different days, depending on your mood, the weather and other factors you find relevant.
6. Focus on behaviors, not on outcomes. If you consistently 20 exercise and eat right, results will come.
7. Avoid rushing back to routine. Take a few minutes to 21 breathe deeply and bring the refreshing spirit of playfulness back to your grown-up world.

Expanding Vocabulary

Study the definitions of any of the following words that are unfamiliar to you. Then use each of the words in a separate sentence. The number in parentheses is the number of the paragraph in which the word appears.

pry (3)   oxygenate (10)
confines (7)   sluggish (10)
frivolous (9)   eluded (11)

Understanding Content

1. How many adults drop out of an exercise program within six months?

2. How many Americans are overweight?
3. How did most of us feel about movement and play when we were children?
4. How much exercise and what kinds of exercise does the author recommend?
5. What steps should we take to get back to "recess"?

Drawing Inferences about Thesis and Purpose

1. What are the advantages of exercise suggested throughout Krucoff's essay?
2. What is Krucoff's thesis?

Analyzing Strategies and Style

1. How does the author use New Year's resolutions as both an opening strategy and a way develop her essay?
2. Krucoff writes with brief paragraphs and ends with a list. What is the effect of these strategies? How does her style connect to audience and purpose?

Thinking Critically

1. Do you make New Year's resolutions to exercise more? If so, do you keep them? If not, why not?
2. Do you exercise regularly? If not, why not? How would you defend your inactivity to Krucoff?
3. Do you agree that we choose to do what is important to us? Do you think that most of us could find thirty minutes most days for exercise if we really wanted to? Explain your response.
4. Has Krucoff convinced you to treat exercise as play and to start playing more? Why or why not?

Camping Out

ERNEST HEMINGWAY

One of the most popular of twentieth-century fiction writers, Ernest Hemingway (1899–1961) is best known for his short stories and novels, especially *A Farewell to Arms*, *The Sun Also Rises*, and *The Old Man and the Sea*. Hemingway, winner of the Nobel Prize for Literature, began his writing career as a journalist and returned to journalism from time to time, most notably as a correspondent during the Spanish Civil War and World War II. His guidelines for a successful camping trip, first published in the *Toronto Star Weekly* in 1920, continue to provide good advice for today's campers.

Questions to Guide Your Reading
1. What are the three problems of camping for which Hemingway provides guidelines?
2. What is Hemingway's purpose in writing about camping? What does he want to accomplish?

Thousands of people will go into the bush this summer to cut the high cost of living. A man who gets his two weeks' salary while he is on vacation should be able to put those two weeks in fishing and camping and be able to save one week's salary clear. He ought to be able to sleep comfortably every night, to eat well every day and to return to the city rested and in good condition.

But if he goes into the woods with a frying pan, an ignorance of black flies and mosquitoes, and a great and abiding lack of knowledge about cookery, the chances are that his return will be very different. He will come back with enough mosquito bites to make the back of his neck look like a relief map of the Caucasus. His digestion will be wrecked after a valiant battle to assimilate half-cooked or charred grub. And he won't have had a decent night's sleep while he has been gone.

He will solemnly raise his right hand and inform you that he has joined the grand army of never-agains. The call of the wild may be all right, but it's a dog's life. He's heard the call of the tame with both ears. Waiter, bring him an order of milk toast.

In the first place he overlooked the insects. Black flies, no-see-ums, deer flies, gnats and mosquitoes were instituted by the devil to force people to live in cities where he could get at them better. If it weren't for them everybody would live in the bush and he would be out of work. It was a rather successful invention.

But there are lots of dopes that will counteract the pests. The simplest perhaps is oil of citronella. Two bits' worth of this purchased at any pharmacist's will be enough to last for two weeks in the worst fly- and mosquito-ridden country.

Rub a little on the back of your neck, your forehead and your wrists before you start fishing, and the blacks and skeeters will shun you. The odor of citronella is not offensive to people. It smells like gun oil. But the bugs do hate it.

7   Oil of pennyroyal and eucalyptol are also much hated by mosquitoes, and with citronella they form the basis for many proprietary preparations. But it is cheaper and better to buy the straight citronella. Put a little on the mosquito netting that covers the front of your pup tent or canoe tent at night, and you won't be bothered.

8   To be really rested and get any benefit out of a vacation a man must get a good night's sleep every night. The first requisite for this is to have plenty of cover. It is twice as cold as you expect it will be in the bush four nights out of five, and a good plan is to take just double the bedding that you think you will need. An old quilt that you can wrap up in is as warm as two blankets.

9   Nearly all outdoor writers rhapsodize over the browse bed. It is all right for the man who knows how to make one and has plenty of time. But in a succession of one-night camps on a canoe trip all you need is level ground for your tent floor and you will sleep all right if you have plenty of covers under you. Take twice as much cover as you think that you will need, and then put two-thirds of it under you. You will sleep warm and get your rest.

10   When it is clear weather you don't need to pitch your tent if you are only stopping for the night. Drive four stakes at the head of your made-up bed and drape your mosquito bar over that, then you can sleep like a log and laugh at the mosquitoes.

11   Outside of insects and bum sleeping, the rock that wrecks most camping trips is cooking. The average tyro's idea of cooking is to fry everything and fry it good and plenty. Now, a frying pan is a most necessary thing to any trip, but you also need the old stew kettle and the folding reflector baker.

12   A pan of fried trout can't be bettered and they don't cost any more than ever. But there is a good and bad way of frying them.

13   The beginner puts his trout and his bacon in and over a brightly burning fire, the bacon curls up and dries into a dry tasteless cinder, and the trout is burned outside while it is still raw inside. He eats them and it is all right if he is only out for the day and going home to a good meal at night. But if he is going to face more trout and bacon the next morning and other

equally well-cooked dishes for the remainder of two weeks, he is on the pathway to nervous dyspepsia.

The proper way is to cook over coals. Have several cans of 14 Crisco or Cotosuet or one of the vegetable shortenings along that are as good as lard and excellent for all kinds of shortening. Put the bacon in and when it is about half cooked lay the trout in the hot grease, dipping them in cornmeal first. Then put the bacon on top of the trout and it will baste them as it slowly cooks.

The coffee can be boiling at the same time and in a smaller 15 skillet pancakes being made that are satisfying the other campers while they are waiting for the trout.

With the prepared pancake flours you take a cupful of pan- 16 cake flour and add a cup of water. Mix the water and flour and as soon as the lumps are out it is ready for cooking. Have the skillet hot and keep it well greased. Drop the batter in and as soon as it is done on one side loosen it in the skillet and flip it over. Apple butter, syrup or cinnamon and sugar go well with the cakes.

While the crowd have taken the edge from their appetites with 17 flapjacks, the trout have been cooked and they and the bacon are ready to serve. The trout are crisp outside and firm and pink inside and the bacon is well done—but not too done. If there is anything better than that combination the writer has yet to taste it in a lifetime devoted largely and studiously to eating.

The stew kettle will cook you dried apricots when they have 18 resumed their predried plumpness after a night of soaking, it will serve to concoct a mulligan in, and it will cook macaroni. When you are not using it, it should be boiling water for the dishes.

In the baker, mere man comes into his own, for he can make a pie that to his bush appetite will have it all over the product 19 that mother used to make, like a tent. Men have always believed that there was something mysterious and difficult about making a pie. Here is a great secret. There is nothing to it. We've been kidded for years. Any man of average office intelligence can make at least as good a pie as his wife.

All there is to a pie is a cup and a half of flour, one-half tea- 20 spoonful of salt, one-half cup of lard and cold water. That will make piecrust that will bring tears of joy into your camping partner's eyes.

Mix the salt with the flour, work the lard into the flour, make 21 it up into a good workmanlike dough with cold water. Spread some flour on the back of a box or something flat, and pat the dough around a while. Then roll it out with whatever kind of round bottle you prefer. Put a little more lard on the surface of the sheet of dough and then slosh a little flour on and roll it up and then roll it out again with the bottle.

22   Cut out a piece of the rolled-out dough big enough to line a pie tin. I like the kind with holes in the bottom. Then put in your dried apples that have soaked all night and been sweetened, or your apricots, or your blueberries, and then take another sheet of the dough and drape it gracefully over the top, soldering it down at the edges with your fingers. Cut a couple of slits in the top dough sheet and prick it a few times with a fork in an artistic manner.

23   Put it in the baker with a good slow fire for forty-five minutes and then take it out, and if your pals are Frenchmen they will kiss you. The penalty for knowing how to cook is that the others will make you do all the cooking.

24   It is all right to talk about roughing it in the woods. But the real woodsman is the man who can be really comfortable in the bush.

Expanding Vocabulary

Examine the following words in their contexts in the essay and then write a definition for each one. (Do not use a dictionary; try to guess the word's meaning from its context.) The number in parentheses is the number of the paragraph in which the word appears.

relief map (2)	requisite (8)
Caucasus (2)	rhapsodize (9)
valiant (2)	browse bed (9)
assimilate (2)	tyro (11)
grub (2)	dyspepsia (13)
dopes (5)	concoct (18)
skeeters (6)	mulligan (18)
proprietary (7)	

Understanding Content

1. Explain the processes for coping with each of the first two problems Hemingway addresses.

2. Hemingway devotes most of his article to the third problem. Why?
3. How does he organize his guidelines for cooking?
4. When explaining pie making, what misconception does Hemingway clear up?

Drawing Inferences about Thesis and Purpose

1. Hemingway's title announces the broad subject of camping but not his specific subject. State his subject by completing the phrase: "how to _____."
2. State a thesis for the essay.

Analyzing Strategies and Style

1. Hemingway has written a lively and entertaining essay, not a list of impersonal instructions. How did he make his process essay interesting? Discuss specific passages that you think are effective.
2. When Hemingway writes, in paragraph 4, "It was a rather successful invention," what writing technique is he using? What tone do we hear in the line?
3. Who is Hemingway's anticipated audience? Who does he think are potential campers among the newspaper's readers? What passages reveal his assumption?
4. Camping out has changed since the 1920s. Writers on this topic today would not assume a male audience, and they would be careful not to write in a sexist manner. How would this essay have to be edited to eliminate sexist writing? What specific changes would you make?
5. The essay's conclusion is brief—only two sentences. Why is it effective in spite of its brevity? How does it connect to the essay's thesis?

Thinking Critically

1. What reasons for camping does Hemingway suggest? Are these still the reasons most people camp out today?
2. Are the problems Hemingway addresses—bugs, uncomfortable sleeping, bad food—still the basic problems to be solved to enjoy a camping trip? What modern equipment can help campers with these problems?
3. Many people today go "camping" in well-equipped RVs. Is this really camping? What would Hemingway say? What do you say? Why?

The Day That I Sensed a New Kind of Intelligence

GARRY KASPAROV

Garry Kasparov was born in 1963 in Baku, Azerbaijan. When he won the world title in chess in 1985, he was the youngest winner ever. He remains the highest-ranked active player in the world. In 1987 his autobiography, *Child of Change,* was published. The following column, published in *Time* in 1996, was part of a *Time* cover story on artificial intelligence.

Questions to Guide Your Reading

1. What is Kasparov's subject? To what particular event is he referring?
2. The writer places several words in quotation marks: "loose," "see," "understood," and "intelligent." Why? How are we to understand these words when they are within quotation marks?

1   I got my first glimpse of artificial intelligence on Feb. 10, 1996, at 4:45 P.M. EST, when in the first game of my match with Deep Blue, the computer nudged a pawn forward to a square where it could easily be captured. It was a wonderful and extremely human move. If I had been playing White, I might have offered this pawn sacrifice. It fractured Black's pawn structure and opened up the board. Although there did not appear to be a forced line of play that would allow recovery of the pawn, my instincts told me that with so many "loose" Black pawns and a somewhat exposed Black king, White could probably recover the material, with a better overall position to boot.

2   But a computer, I thought, would never make such a move. A computer can't "see" the long-term consequences of structural changes in the position or understand how changes in pawn formations may be good or bad.

3   Humans do this sort of thing all the time. But computers generally calculate each line of play so far as possible within the time allotted. Because chess is a game of virtually limitless possibilities, even a beast like Deep Blue, which can look at more

than 100 million positions a second, can go only so deep. When computers reach that point, they evaluate the various resulting positions and select the move leading to the best one. And because computers' primary way of evaluating chess positions is by measuring material superiority, they are notoriously materialistic. If they "understood" the game, they might act differently, but they don't understand.

So I was stunned by this pawn sacrifice. What could it mean? 4 I had played a lot of computers but had never experienced anything like this. I could feel—I could *smell*—a new kind of intelligence across the table. While I played through the rest of the game as best I could, I was lost; it played beautiful, flawless chess the rest of the way and won easily.

Later I discovered the truth. Deep Blue's computational pow- 5 ers were so great that it did in fact calculate every possible move all the way to the actual recovery of the pawn six moves later. The computer didn't view the pawn sacrifice as a sacrifice at all. So the question is, If the computer makes the same move that I would make for completely different reasons, has it made an "intelligent" move? Is the intelligence of an action dependent on who (or what) takes it?

This is a philosophical question I did not have time to 6 answer. When I understood what had happened, however, I was reassured. In fact, I was able to exploit the traditional shortcomings of computers throughout the rest of the match. At one point, for example, I changed slightly the order of a well-known opening sequence. Because it was unable to compare this new position meaningfully with similar ones in its database, it had to start calculating away and was unable to find a good plan. A human would have simply wondered, "What's Garry up to?," judged the change to be meaningless and moved on.

Indeed, my overall thrust in the last five games was to avoid 7 giving the computer any concrete goal to calculate toward; if it can't find a way to win material, attack the king or fulfill one of its other programmed priorities, the computer drifts planlessly and gets into trouble. In the end, that may have been my biggest advantage: I could figure out its priorities and adjust my play. It couldn't do the same to me. So although I think I did see some signs of intelligence, it's a weird kind, an inefficient, inflexible kind that makes me think I have a few years left.

Expanding Vocabulary

Examine the following words in their contexts in the essay and then write a brief definition or synonym for each one. (Do not use the dictionary; try to guess the word's meaning from its context.) The number in parentheses is the number of the paragraph in which the word appears.

nudged (1)   exploit (6)

Understanding Content

1. Explain the process by which Deep Blue won its match.
2. How did Kasparov win the succeeding matches with Deep Blue? How did he take advantage of Deep Blue's limitations? What primarily "motivates" Deep Blue's chess playing?

Drawing Inferences about Thesis and Purpose

1. What is Kasparov's thesis?
2. A quick reading of this essay might result in some confusion. Is Kasparov saying that computers have intelligence, or not? Look carefully at his wording and then explain how he balances his position.

Analyzing Strategies and Style

1. Examine Kasparov's opening. What is the effect of beginning with the exact time and date of Deep Blue's move? How does the second sentence contrast with the first?

Thinking Critically

1. Have you played chess—or checkers? Can you visualize the game moves that Kasparov describes? If not, are you now interested in learning the game? Why or why not? (Many people find both chess and checkers to be quite fascinating games.)
2. Have you had an experience similar to Kasparov's while playing a game or sport? Has an opponent constructed a strategy that surprised you and left you confused in response? Think of the games and sports that you know. In what kinds of games or sports might a surprise tactic, or some unusual strategy, be successful?
3. Do computers have intelligence? Part of the problem we have in answering this question comes from confusion over the word *intelligence*. How should the word be defined? Are there differences in degrees of intelligence, or are there differences in kinds as well?

MAKING CONNECTIONS

1. John Aigner, Benjamin Levy, and Nickels et al. all emphasize the importance of being prepared. Preparation is a major key to success in the workplace, they establish. Does their emphasis make sense to you? If you agree, think how you would convince unprepared students of the value of preparation. If you disagree, think how you would challenge these writers.

2. John Aigner encourages interviewees to develop a power vocabulary and learn to speak only positively about themselves. Suzette Elgin gives directions for changing one's speech to be more effective. Are these writers providing useful self-help guidelines for success? Or, are they encouraging us to misrepresent ourselves to get ahead? Or, are they implying that society fails to accept diverse styles? Be prepared to debate these issues.

3. Select a sport, game, or recreational activity that may interest you and read about it in at least one encyclopedia or other appropriate reference book. Write a two-page account of the basic process of the activity for someone unfamiliar with it. Alternatively, write a two-page explanation of the process of completing one complex part of the activity.

4. Take an informal survey of those with whom you work or those you know at school to analyze their conversational styles. Are most direct or indirect in their speech? Are there other observations about conversational styles that are useful to note?

5. Select a company (e.g., Nike) or a sports organization (e.g., the United States Tennis Association) you are interested in and visit their Web site. Analyze the Web site, looking at color and graphics and the information. Does it provide useful information? Is it organized clearly? Is it engaging visually? Be prepared to discus your Web site analysis with classmates.

6. E-mailing is an important function in today's workplace. Do an online search of "e-mail etiquette" to see what you can learn about the appropriate way to use, write, and send e-mails. Consider: Should you follow these guidelines when e-mailing your professors?

TOPICS AND GUIDELINES FOR WRITING
---

1. In an essay examine some process of change that has taken place in your life. Consider physical, emotional, intellectual, or occupational changes. Although you will use chronological order, make certain that you focus on specific *stages* or *steps* that led to the change so that you write a process analysis, not a narrative. Possible topics include: how you grew (or shrank) to the size you are now, how you developed your skill in some sport or hobby, how you changed your taste in music, how you decided on a career. Analyze the change into at least three separate stages. Explain and illustrate each stage. Remember that your essay needs a thesis. Why do you want to share this process of change with readers? You may want to show, for example, that change, although painful, is ultimately rewarding, or perhaps that some changes are just painful. Reflect on *your* reason for writing about the change in your life. Then state your thesis in your first paragraph and restate it, enlarging on it, in your concluding paragraph.

2. Select a change in human society that has occurred in stages over time and that has had a significant effect on the way we live. Your thesis is the significance of the development— significance for good or ill. Develop that thesis by analyzing the process of change, the stages in development. Be sure to analyze the change into several distinct stages of development. Possible topics include technological changes (e.g., the generations of computers), changes in the classroom or school buildings, changes in recreation, and changes in dress.

3. Do you have advice to give someone preparing for a job interview, advice that is different from or in addition to the advice given by John Aigner in "Putting Your Job Interview into Rehearsal"? If so, organize your advice into a series of specific steps and write your guide to the successful interview. Your thesis, stated or implied, is that following these steps will improve one's chances of obtaining the desired position.

4. Have you taken the same type of vacation (camping, renting a beach house, sightseeing by car, traveling abroad) sev-

eral times? If so, you may have learned the hard way what to do and what not to do to have a successful vacation. In an essay, pass your knowledge along to readers. Organize your essay into a process—a series of steps or directions—but also approach your analysis by explaining both the wrong way and the right way to complete each step. Avoid writing about your last vacation. Keep your focus on general guidelines for readers. Ernest Hemingway's "Camping Out" is your model for this topic. Your thesis is that preparing the right way will ensure a pleasant vacation.

5. Many people have misconceptions about processes or tasks they are unfamiliar with, particularly if those activities are a part of a different culture. Do you understand how to do something that others might have misconceptions about? If so, prepare a process analysis that will explain the activity and thereby clear up the reader's misconceptions. In your opening paragraph you might refer to the typical misconceptions that people have and then move on to explain how the task or activity is actually done. If your activity is part of a particular culture (how to cook with a wok, how to prepare pita bread, how to serve a Japanese dinner, how to wrap a sari), enrich your process analysis with appropriate details about that culture.

6. Some social situations can be difficult to handle successfully. If you have had success in one of them (such as asking someone for a date, meeting a close friend's or a fiancé's family, attending a large family reunion, attending the office Christmas party), then explain how to handle the situation with ease and charm. Select either a chronological ordering of steps or a list of specific instructions, including dos and don'ts. Humorous examples can be used with this topic to produce lively writing.

7. Prepare a detailed, knowledgeable explanation of a particular activity or task from your work or play for interested nonspecialists. You are the expert carefully explaining the process of, for example, bunting down the third-base line, booting up the computer, tuning an engine, building a deck, sewing a dress, or whatever you know well. Be sure to give encouragement as you give directions. Make certain that you have included all the steps, in the right order, and that you have your audience clearly in mind.

7

Using Division
and Classification

Examining Human Connections—
and Misconnections

You have probably discovered by now that your college library organizes its book collection not by the Dewey decimal system but by the Library of Congress *Classification* system. And you are probably taking courses offered by several different departments. Those departments, English for example, may be further *classified* by colleges—the college of arts of sciences. If you needed to find an apartment near campus or a part-time job, you may have looked in the newspaper's *classified* section. We *divide* or separate individual items and then group or *classify* them into logical categories because order is more convenient than disorder and because the process helps us make sense of a complex world. Just think how frustrated you would be if you had to search through a random listing of want ads rather than being able to look under several headings for specific jobs, or if you had to search up and down shelves of books because they were not grouped by any system.

When to Use Division and Classification

Division and classification are not similar but distinct strategies, as are comparison and contrast. Rather, division and classification work together; they are part of the same thinking process that brings order to a mass of items, data, ideas, forms of behavior, groups of people, or whatever else someone chooses to organize.

Division is another term for analysis, the breaking down of something into its parts. Division, or analysis, provides the plan or pattern of grouping. To devise a classification system for books, books have to be divided by type: books on history, or art, or botany. Then large categories need to be subdivided: U.S. history, British history, Russian history. Then each individual book can be given a number that is its very own but also shows into what categories it has been classified, twentieth-century U.S. history, for example. The categories have been developed after thoughtful analysis; each book can be placed in one of the established categories.

A thinking process that has served us so well solving organizational problems from the biologist's classification of the animal kingdom to the phone company's classification of businesses in the Yellow Pages must surely be a useful strategy for writers. And indeed it is. If you have written essays using examples and have sought to group examples to support different parts of your topic, you have already started working with the process of division and classification. The difference between the essays in Chapter 5 ("Explaining and Illustrating") and those in this chapter lies in the rigor of the classification system. To use classification effectively, you need a logical, consistent principle of division, and your classification needs to be complete. So, when thinking about possible topics for an essay and when thinking about purpose in writing, ask yourself: Am I interested in giving some specific examples to develop an idea, or am I interested in analyzing a topic, dividing it logically into its parts? For example, Peter Drucker does not support the idea that many companies use a team concept by using Procter & Gamble and General Motors as examples. Rather, he asserts that there are three kinds of teams used in companies, analyzes the characteristics of each type of team, and then gives examples to further explain the idea of three *categories* of teams.

How to Use Division and Classification

Thinking and Organizing

Suppose that you are asked to write about some element of campus life. Reflecting on the fun you have had getting acquainted with classmates over meals in nearby restaurants, you decide to write about the various restaurants available to college students. How many and how varied are the restaurants within walking distance of the campus? To be thorough, you may not want to trust your memory; better to walk around, making a complete list of the area restaurants. Next, analyze your list to see the possible categories into which the restaurants can be grouped. You may see more than one way to classify them, perhaps by type of food (French, Chinese, Italian) and by cost (cheap, moderate, expensive). You need to avoid overlapping categories and to classify examples according to the division you select. The following chart illustrates the general principle:

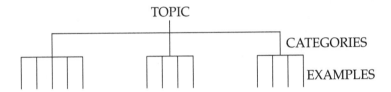

Thesis

The divisions and classifications you create must also support a thesis. What do you want to explain to your readers? This is the key question to answer in deciding on a classification pattern. If you decide to stress the variety of food available to students, for example, then you will want to classify your examples of restaurants by food type, not by cost.

In your essay on restaurants, division and classification provide an effective strategy for developing your thesis. Sometimes, though, a writer's thesis *is* the classification pattern. Put another way, what the writer has learned is that the subject can best be grasped by understanding the author's classification of that subject. Ralph Whitehead, writing about American class structure, asserts that the old categories are no longer accurate and that his new categories give us more insight into American society. Similarly, Peter Drucker wants business leaders to understand that there isn't *one* team model but *three*.

Much of what is important in your division and classification essay lies in your analysis, in the logical and perhaps new way you ask readers to examine your topic. This means that you may need to explain your categories to readers, to explain how and why you have divided your subject in your particular way and to show, if necessary, why the categories do not overlap, or how they are sometimes modified. In "The Science and Secrets of Personal Space," Curt Suplee defines the required distances for each category or zone—intimate, personal, social, and public—but then explains how various cultures modify their space requirements. Remember, too, that you need to illustrate each of your divisions. In the essay on restaurants, the student needs to name and describe sample restaurants in each of the categories.

WRITING FOCUS:
WORDS TO LIVE WITHOUT!

Student writers have been known to assure instructors that they would revise more energetically if they only knew what to look for to change or toss out. Here are several categories of words, with some examples of each, that you can watch for in your drafts and get in the habit of cutting or changing. Indeed, you can improve your writing overnight if you will commit to live without these types of words.

Unnecessary Qualifiers

How often have you written:

In my opinion, it seems to me that gun laws . . .
I believe that possibly we should have a . . .
What I got out of the poem is just that the poet . . .

Whether the goal is padding or genuine concern about "being wrong," the writing suffers. Delete these kinds of words and phrases in all of your writing.

Vague, General Language

Some words that are hard to live without in casual speech do not belong in writing. These include such words as: *thing, good, bad, nice, aspects, factor.* In your writing you have the opportunity to substitute more powerful, concrete words for these overworked and now powerless words.

Loaded Words

Avoid language that puts down someone based on gender, age, race, ethnicity, or disability. Educated writers today make every effort to write in ways that do not offend, at least when that is not the point of the writing. Here are some examples and the edits you can make: *firemen* (firefighters), *man* (human), *poetess* (poet for both genders). Also avoid all racial or ethnic slur words and be careful about political name calling as well (e.g., *radical, right wing, communist, reactionary*).

Getting Started: Classifying Recent Reading or Viewing

Make a list of all the works (books, magazines, newspapers, texts, etc.) you have read in the past three months. Study your list, thinking of several classifying principles you could use to organize your reading. Consider: Which pattern seems the most logical and complete? Could several patterns work, depending on your purpose in classifying? Alternately, complete the same exercise for all the movies or all the television shows you have seen in the past three months.

The Plot Against People

RUSSELL BAKER

A graduate of Johns Hopkins University, Russell Baker (b. 1925) began his journalism career with the *Baltimore Sun* and then moved to the *New York Times* to cover government and politics. In 1962 he began writing his "Observer" column for the *New York Times*, a column that ran for 36 years. Baker has won the Pulitzer Prize for his commentary as well as for his popular memoir *Growing Up* (1982). "The Plot Against People" was an "Observer" column in 1968.

Questions to Guide Your Reading

1. What are Baker's three categories of inanimate objects?
2. What is his primary purpose in writing?

Inanimate objects are classified scientifically into three major categories—those that break down, those that get lost, and those that don't work.　　　1

The goal of all inanimate objects is to resist man and ultimately to defeat him, and the three major classifications are based on the method each object uses to achieve its purpose. As a general rule, any object capable of breaking down at the moment when it is most needed will do so. The automobile is typical of the category.　　　2

With the cunning peculiar to its breed, the automobile never breaks down while entering a filling station which has a large staff of idle mechanics. It waits until it reaches a downtown intersection in the middle of the rush hour, or until it is fully loaded with family and luggage on the Ohio Turnpike. Thus it creates maximum inconvenience, frustration, and irritability, thereby reducing its owner's lifespan.　　　3

Washing machines, garbage disposals, lawn mowers, furnaces, TV sets, tape recorders, slide projectors—all are in league with the automobile to take their turn at breaking down whenever life threatens to flow smoothly for their enemies.　　　4

Many inanimate objects, of course, find it extremely difficult to break down. Pliers, for example, and gloves and keys are almost totally incapable of breaking down. Therefore, they have had to evolve a different technique for resisting man.　　　5

They get lost. Science has still not solved the mystery of how they do it, and no man has ever caught one of them in the act. The most plausible theory is that they have developed a secret method of locomotion which they are able to conceal from human eyes.　　　6

It is not uncommon for a pair of pliers to climb all the way from the cellar to the attic in its single-minded determination to raise its owner's blood pressure. Keys have been known to　　　7 burrow three feet under mattresses. Women's purses, despite their great weight, frequently travel through six or seven rooms to find hiding space under a couch.

8   Scientists have been struck by the fact that things that break down virtually never get lost, while things that get lost hardly ever break down. A furnace, for example, will invariably break down at the depth of the first winter cold wave, but it will never get lost. A woman's purse hardly ever breaks down; it almost invariably chooses to get lost.

9   Some persons believe this constitutes evidence that inanimate objects are not entirely hostile to man. After all, they point out, a furnace could infuriate a man even more thoroughly by getting lost than by breaking down, just as a glove could upset him far more by breaking down than by getting lost.

10   Not everyone agrees, however, that this indicates a conciliatory attitude. Many say it merely proves that furnaces, gloves and pliers are incredibly stupid.

11   The third class of objects—those that don't work—is the most curious of all. These include such objects as barometers, car clocks, cigarette lighters, flashlights and toy-train locomotives. It is inaccurate, of course, to say that they *never* work. They work once, usually for the first few hours after being brought home, and then quit. Thereafter, they never work again.

12   In fact, it is widely assumed that they are built for the purpose of not working. Some people have reached advanced ages without ever seeing some of these objects—barometers, for example—in working order.

13   Science is utterly baffled by the entire category. There are many theories about it. The most interesting holds that the things that don't work have attained the highest state possible for an inanimate object, the state to which things that break down and things that get lost can still only aspire.

14   They have truly defeated man by conditioning him never to expect anything of them. When his cigarette lighter won't light or his flashlight fails to illuminate, it does not raise his blood pressure. Objects that don't work have given man the only peace he receives from inanimate society.

Expanding Vocabulary

Be able to define each of the following words. Then, select five words and use each one in a separate sentence. The number in parentheses is the number of the paragraph in which the world appears.

inanimate (1)	hostile (9)
plausible (6)	infuriate (9)
burrow (6)	conciliatory (10)
constitutes (9)	incredibly (10)

Understanding Content

1. What is the goal of inanimate objects, despite their classification, according to Baker?
2. What are the kinds of objects that fit into the first category?
3. Why are the objects that "get lost" not in the "break down" category? What are some of Baker's examples for this second category?
4. How does the "never work" category need to be qualified?
5. What is the most interesting theory to explain the third category?

Drawing Inferences about Thesis and Purpose

1. To decide on his thesis, you need to consider Baker's purpose or purposes in writing. Is it appropriate to say that he has two purposes? If so, what are they?
2. Baker's classification system is clear. What is his thesis?
3. When Baker says that "science is utterly baffled by the entire [third] category," does he mean this seriously? Explain.

Analyzing Strategies and Style

1. Baker describes the automobile as "cunning" and pliers as having climbed "all the way from the cellar to the attic." What strategy is he using when he writes this way of these objects?
2. At what point do you recognize that one of Baker's purposes is to amuse his readers? If he does not always mean what he writes, what strategy is he using?

Thinking Critically

1. Are you often frustrated by the "behavior" of inanimate objects? Which category of objects gives you the most grief? Do you have any explanation for this?
2. What makes Baker's approach, strategies, and tone engaging and effective?
3. In what situations can humor and irony be used to good effect?

The Roles of Manners

JUDITH MARTIN

Judith Martin (b. 1938) is "Miss Manners." After graduating from Wellesley College, Martin began her career as a reporter for the *Washington Post*. She is best known now for her syndicated column, "Miss Manners." She has also published a novel, *Gilbert* (1982), *Miss Manners' Guide to Rearing Perfect Children* (1984), and *Common Courtesy* (1985). In the following, a slightly shortened version of an article that appeared in the Spring 1996 issue of *The Responsive Community*, Martin analyzes the several roles of manners.

Questions to Guide Your Reading

1. What are the three functions or roles of manners?
2. When you do not follow expected codes in society, how are you perceived? What do you appear to be doing?

1   Ritual serves one of three major functions of manners. Oddly enough, the greatest scoffers at the traditions of American etiquette, who scorn the rituals of their own society as stupid and stultifying, voice respect for the custom and folklore of Native Americans, less industrialized peoples, and other societies they find more "authentic" than their own.

2   Americans who disdain etiquette in everyday life often go into an etiquette tailspin in connection with marriage. Although the premise on which the 20th-century American wedding forms were based—that a young girl is given by the father whose protection she leaves to a husband who will perform the same function—has changed, the forms retain their emotional value. If it happens that the bride has been supporting the bridegroom for years in their own household, she may well ask their own toddler age son to "give her away" just to preserve the ritual.

3   Ritual provides a reassuring sense of social belonging far more satisfying than behavior improvised under emotionally complicated circumstances. Rituals of mourning other than funerals have been nearly abandoned, but at a great emotional cost. Not only are the bereaved unprotected from normal

social demands by customs of seclusion and symbols of vulnerability, but they are encouraged to act as if nothing had happened—only to be deemed heartless if they actually succeed. A second function of manners is the symbolic one. It is the symbolic function that confuses and upsets people who claim that etiquette is "simply a matter of common sense" when actually the symbols cannot be deduced from first principles, but must be learned in each society, and, within that society, for different times, places, ages, and social classes. 4

Because symbols are arbitrary, it can happen that opposite forms of behavior may symbolize the same idea, as when a man takes off his hat to show respect in a church, but puts on his hat to show respect in a synagogue. But once these rules are learned, they provide people with a tremendous fund of nonverbal knowledge about one another, helping them to deal appropriately with a wide range of social situations and relationships. Forms of greeting, dressing, eating, and restraining bodily functions can all be read as symbols of degrees of friendliness or hostility, respect or contempt, solidarity with the community or alienation from it. It is safe to assume that a person who advances on you with an outstretched hand is symbolizing an intent to treat you better than one who spits on the ground at the sight of you. 5

The law, the military, diplomacy, the church, and athletics have particularly strict codes of etiquette, compliance with which is taken to symbolize adherence to the particular values that these professions require: fairness, obedience, respect, piety, or valor. And following the conventions of the society is taken as a measure of respect for it—which is why people who are facing juries are advised by their own lawyers to dress and behave with the utmost convention. 6

It does not matter how arbitrary any of the violated rules may be—ignoring them is interpreted as defiance of, or indifference to, or antagonism toward, the interests of the person or community whose standard is being ignored. The person who wears blue jeans to a formal wedding, or a three-piece suit at a beach party, may protest all he likes that his choice had only to do with a clothing preference, but it is hard to imagine anyone so naive as to believe that the people whose standards he is violating will not interpret the choice as disdain. 7

In New York, a 15-year-old was shot on the street in a gang fight started over his refusal to return another teenager's high five sign of greeting. "Dissin'," the current term for showing disrespect, is cited as a leading provocation for modern murder.

8   The third function of etiquette is the regulative function, which is less troublesome to the literal-minded, because those rules can be understood functionally. Between them, etiquette and law divide the task of regulating social conduct in the interest of community harmony, with the law addressing grave conflicts, such as those threatening life or property, and administering serious punishments, while etiquette seeks to forestall such conflicts, relying on voluntary compliance with its restraints.

9   This is why etiquette restricts freedom of self-expression more than the law does (and why etiquette rejects encounter group theories of achieving harmony through total communication). It is within my legal right to tell you that you are ugly, or that your baby is, but this is likely to lead to ugly—which is to say dangerous—behavior, which it will require the law to address, no longer as a mere insult, but as a more serious charge of slander, libel, or mental cruelty.

10   But the danger of attempting to expand the dominion of the law to take over the function of etiquette—to deal with such violations as students calling one another nasty names, or protesters doing provocative things with flags—is that it may compromise our constitutional rights. For all its strictness, a generally understood community standard of etiquette is more flexible than the law and, because it depends on voluntary compliance, less threatening.

11   Jurisprudence itself cannot function without etiquette. In enforcing standards of dress, rules about when to sit and when to stand, restricting offensive language and requiring people to speak only in proper turn, courtroom etiquette overrides many of the very rights it may protect. So does the etiquette of legislatures, such as that specified in *Robert's Rules of Order*. This is necessary because the more orderly is the form of a social structure, the more conflict it can support. Etiquette requires participants in adversarial proceedings to present their opposing views in a restrained manner, to provide a disciplined and respectful ambience in which to settle conflicts peacefully.

Responding to Changing Times

That we cannot live peacefully in communities without eti- 12
quette, using only the law to prevent or resolve conflicts in
everyday life, has become increasingly obvious to the public.
And so there has been, in the last few years, a "return to etiquette," a movement for which I am not totally blameless. It has
been hampered by the idea that etiquette need not involve self-
restriction. Those who must decry rudeness in others are full
of schemes to punish those transgressors by treating them even
more rudely in return. But the well-meaning are also sometimes
stymied, because they understand "etiquette" to consist of the
social rules that were in effect approximately a generation ago,
when women rarely held significant jobs, and answering
machines and Call Waiting had not yet been invented. As the
same social conditions do not apply, they assume that there can
be no etiquette system, or that each individual may make up his
or her own rules.

One often hears that etiquette is "only a matter of being con- 13
siderate of others," and that is certainly a good basis for good
behavior. Obviously, however, it does not guide one in the
realms of symbolic or ritual etiquette. And if each individual
improvises, the variety of resulting actions would be open to
misinterpretations and conflicts, which a mutually intelligible
code of behavior seeks to prevent.

Yet many of the surface etiquette issues of today were 14
addressed under the codes of earlier times, which need only
be adapted for the present. . . . [A] system of precedence must
exist, although it need not be "ladies first." One must regulate
the access of others to one's attention—if not with a butler
announcing the conventional fiction that "Madam is not at
home," then by a machine that says, "If you leave a message
after the beep. . . ." But dropping one unfinished conversation
to begin another has always been rude, and that applies to Call
Waiting. Usually, changes happen gradually, as, for example,
most people have come to accept the unmarried couple socially, or to issue their wedding invitations in time for guests to take
advantage of bargain travel prices.

There is, of course, ideologically motivated civil disobedience 15
of etiquette, just as there is of law. But people who mean to

change the behavior of the community for its own supposed benefit by such acts must be prepared to accept the punitive consequences of their defiance. They would be well advised to disobey only the rule that offends them, carefully adhering to other conventions, if they do not wish to have their protests perceived as a general contempt for other people. Thanks to her symbolic meaning, the well-dressed, soft-spoken grandmother is a more effective agitator than the unkempt, obscenity-spouting youth.

16 Ignorance of etiquette rules is not an easily accepted excuse, except on behalf of small children or strangers to the community. An incapacity to comply is acceptable, but only if convincingly explained. To refuse to shake someone's hand will be interpreted as an insult, unless an explanation, such as that one has crippling arthritis, is provided.

17 Such excuses as "Oh, I never write letters" or "I just wasn't in the mood" or "I'm not comfortable with that" are classified as insolence and disallowed. Etiquette cannot be universally abandoned in the name of individual freedom, honesty, creativity, or comfort, without social consequences.

18 In 1978, when I began chronicling and guiding the legitimate changes in etiquette, and applying the rules in specific cases, where there may be extenuating circumstances or conflicting rules—as a judge does in considering a case—it was difficult to get people to agree that etiquette was needed. Now it is only difficult to get people to comply with its rules.

Expanding Vocabulary

Match each word in column A with its definition in column B. When in doubt, first find the word in the essay and look for context clues to aid your understanding of the word's meaning. Then, if necessary, use your dictionary to complete the matching exercise. The number in parentheses is the number of the paragraph in which the word appears.

Column A	Column B
scoffers (1)	inflicting punishment
stultifying (1)	thwarted
tailspin (2)	left desolate, especially by death

bereaved (3)	unity of sympathies or interest within a group
arbitrary (5)	
solidarity (5)	state of estrangement, feeling of separation from others
alienation (5)	
adherence (6)	sudden deep decline or slump
naive (7)	simple, lacking worldliness
provocative (10)	act of inciting anger or stirring action
adversarial (11)	special atmosphere of a particular place
ambiance (11)	those expressing scorn
decry (12)	openly condemn
stymied (12)	antagonistic, behaving as an opponent
punitive (15)	determined by chance or whim
extenuating (18)	devotion to or commitment to providing partial excuses limiting or stifling

Understanding Content

1. What is often illogical about marriage rituals today? Why do we continue with these rituals anyway?
2. Why is it incorrect to insist that manners are simply common sense?
3. When you follow the codes of etiquette, diplomacy, or athletics, what does your behavior symbolize?
4. What is the relationship between the law and etiquette? What may happen if we try to get the law to take over the role of etiquette?
5. If you want to change particular etiquette, what should you do to be most successful?
6. Why is ignorance not usually accepted as an excuse for being unmannerly?

Drawing Inferences about Thesis and Purpose

1. What is Martin's purpose in writing? Does she have more than one? Try to write a thesis that makes her purpose clear.
2. Does Martin think that people today are more—or less—likely to follow codes of etiquette? How do you know?
3. What is the author's attitude toward Call Waiting? How do you know?

Analyzing Strategies and Style

1. Think about the ordering of the three roles of manners. What does the author gain by her choice of order?

2. Why does the author put *authentic* in quotation marks in paragraph 1? What do they signify to the reader?

Thinking Critically

1. Have you thought before about the ritual and symbolic roles of manners? If not, does Martin's explanation make sense to you?
2. Why are rituals helpful? Think of ways that the rituals of etiquette can aid us—and think of specific examples to illustrate your points.
3. Do you agree that etiquette can be a better choice than laws in controlling some kinds of behavior and that we should not turn to the law as a way to make people behave? Look specifically at Martin's examples and see whether you agree or disagree with her. Explain your position.
4. Many have argued that there has been a loss of manners in our time. What do you suggest that we do about the loss?

Hot Boxes for Ex-Smokers

FRANKLIN E. ZIMRING

Franklin Zimring (b. 1942) completed his law degree at the University of Chicago in 1967 and taught there until 1985. He now teaches at the University of California at Berkeley's School of Law and directs the Earl Warren Legal Institute. Zimring has published extensively, both articles and books, usually on such legal issues as capital punishment, youth crime, the criminal justice system, and violence in society. An important recent book is *The Search for Rational Drug Control* (1992). The following article, appearing in *Newsweek* on April 20, 1987, departs from legal issues to draw on the writer's experience as an ex-smoker.

Questions to Guide Your Reading

1. What are Zimring's four categories of American ex-smokers? Into which category does the author fit?
2. How would you describe the author's tone? Is he dead serious? Poking some fun at ex-smokers? How do you know?

1   Americans can be divided into three groups—smokers, nonsmokers, and that expanding pack of us who have quit. Those

who have never smoked don't know what they're missing, but former smokers, ex-smokers, reformed smokers can never forget. We are veterans of a personal war, linked by that watershed experience of ceasing to smoke and by the temptation to have just one more cigarette. For almost all of us ex-smokers, smoking continues to play an important part in our lives. And now that it is being restricted in restaurants around the country and will be banned in almost all indoor public places in New York state starting next month, it is vital that everyone understand the different emotional states cessation of smoking can cause. I have observed four of them; and in the interest of science I have classified them as those of the zealot, the evangelist, the elect, and the serene. Each day, each category gains new recruits.   2

Not all antitobacco zealots are former smokers, but a substantial number of fire-and-brimstone opponents do come from the ranks of the reformed. Zealots believe that those who continue to smoke are degenerates who deserve scorn, not pity, and the penalties that will deter offensive behavior in public as well. Relations between these people and those who continue to smoke are strained.

One explanation for the zealot's fervor in seeking to outlaw   3 tobacco consumption is his own tenuous hold on abstaining from smoking. But I think part of the emotional force arises from sheer envy as he watches and identifies with each lung-filling puff. By making smoking in public a crime, the zealot seeks reassurance that he will not revert to bad habits; give him strong social penalties and he won't become a recidivist.

No systematic survey has been done yet, but anecdotal evi-   4 dence suggests that a disproportionate number of doctors who have quit smoking can be found among the fanatics. Just as the most enthusiastic revolutionary tends to make the most enthusiastic counterrevolutionary, many of today's vitriolic zealots include those who had been deeply committed to tobacco habits.

By contrast, the antismoking evangelist does not condemn   5 smokers. Unlike the zealot, he regards smoking as an easily curable condition, as a social disease, and not a sin. The evangelist spends an enormous amount of time seeking and preaching to the unconverted. He argues that kicking the habit is not *that* difficult. After all, *he* did it; moreover, as he describes it, the benefits of quitting are beyond measure and the disadvantages are nil.

6   The hallmark of the evangelist is his insistence that he never misses tobacco. Though he is less hostile to smokers than the zealot, he is resented more. Friends and loved ones who have been the targets of his preachments frequently greet the resumption of smoking by the evangelist as an occasion for unmitigated glee.

7   Among former smokers, the distinctions between the evangelist and the elect are much the same as the differences between proselytizing and nonproselytizing religious sects. While the evangelists preach the ease and desirability of abstinence, the elect do not attempt to convert their friends. They think that virtue is its own reward and subscribe to the Puritan theory of predestination.[1] Since they have proved themselves capable of abstaining from tobacco, they are therefore different from friends and relatives who continue to smoke. They feel superior, secure that their salvation was foreordained. These ex-smokers rarely give personal testimony on their conversion. They rarely speak about their tobacco habits, while evangelists talk about little else. Of course, active smokers find such bluenosed[2] behavior far less offensive than that of the evangelist or the zealot, yet they resent the elect simply because they are smug. Their air of self-satisfaction rarely escapes the notice of those lighting up. For active smokers, life with a member of the ex-smoking elect is less stormy than with a zealot or evangelist, but it is subtly oppressive nonetheless.

8   I have labeled my final category of former smokers the serene. This classification is meant to encourage those who find the other psychic styles of ex-smokers disagreeable. Serenity is quieter than zealotry and evangelism, and those who qualify are not as self-righteous as the elect. The serene ex-smoker accepts himself and also accepts those around him who continue to smoke. This kind of serenity does not come easily, nor does it seem to be an immediate option for those who have stopped. Rather it is a goal, an end stage in a process of development during which some former smokers progress through one or more of the less-than-positive psychological points en route. For former smokers, serenity is thus a positive

---

[1]Puritans believed that those of the elect, those saved, have been chosen by God.—Ed.
[2]Puritanical.—Ed.

possibility that exists at the end of the rainbow. But all former smokers cannot reach that promised land.

What is it that permits some former smokers to become 9 serene? I think the key is self-acceptance and gratitude. The fully mature former smoker knows he has the soul of an addict and is grateful for the knowledge. He may sit up front in an airplane, but he knows he belongs in the smoking section in back. He doesn't regret that he quit smoking, nor any of his previous adventures with tobacco. As a former smoker, he is grateful for the experience and memory of craving a cigarette.

Serenity comes from accepting the lessons of one's life. And 10 ex-smokers who have reached this point in their worldview have much to be grateful for. They have learned about the potential and limits of change. In becoming the right kind of former smoker, they developed a healthy sense of self. This former smoker, for one, believes that it is better to crave (one hopes only occasionally) and not to smoke than never to have craved at all. And by accepting that fact, the reformed smoker does not need to excoriate, envy, or dissociate himself from those who continue to smoke.

Expanding Vocabulary

Match each word in column A with its definition in column B. When in doubt, first find the word in the essay and look for context clues to aid your understanding of the word's meaning. Then, if necessary, use your dictionary to complete the matching exercise. The number in parentheses is the number of the paragraph in which the word appears.

Column A	*Column B*
watershed (1)	flimsy, uncertain
cessation (1)	deliberate self-restraint
zealot (1)	based on casual accounts rather than strong evidence
degenerates (2)	
tenuous (3)	one fanatically devoted to a cause
recidivist (3)	seeking to convert others from one belief to another
anecdotal (4)	
vitriolic (4)	self-satisfied
proselytizing (7)	turning point
sects (7)	scathing, caustic, sarcastic
abstinence (7)	mental, behavioral

foreordained (7)	declines in quality
smug (7)	denounce strongly
psychic (8)	ceasing, halt
excoriate (10)	narrowly defined religious groups
	predestined
	one who lapses into previous behavior

Understanding Content

1. How does the zealot feel about smokers? What motivates the zealot? What group of ex-smokers can often be found among the zealots?
2. What is the evangelist's attitude toward quitting? How do smokers feel about the evangelist?
3. How do the elect differ from evangelists? What attitude of the elect bothers smokers?
4. How do the serene differ from the other ex-smokers? How should ex-smokers view this category? What is the psychological state of the serene ex-smoker?

Drawing Inferences about Thesis and Purpose

1. What is Zimring's thesis, his classification of ex-smokers?

Analyzing Strategies and Style

1. Zimring draws one word (*recidivist*) from his field, the law, but many of his words come from what other field or subject area? What does he gain from using so many words from this field?
2. Zimring announces early in his essay that he is an ex-smoker. Why is it important for him to tell this to readers?

Thinking Critically

1. Are you an ex-smoker? If so, do you see yourself in one of Zimring's categories? Are there other categories that he should add?
2. Are you a smoker? If so, do you recognize Zimring's classification of ex-smokers? Which type bothers you the most? (Why are you still smoking?)
3. Is it always best to serenely accept what others do—their habits, their speech, their lifestyles? Or is there a role for zealots or evangelists? Support your position.

The Science and Secrets
of Personal Space

_____

CURT SUPLEE

Curt Suplee (b. 1945) is a science writer and editor for the *Washington Post.* He has written *Everyday Science Explained* (1996) and *Physics in the 20th Century* (1999). His analysis of personal to public spaces appeared in the *Post*'s Horizon Section on June 9, 1999.

_____

Questions to Guide Your Reading

1. How many separate spatial zones do Americans have?
2. How can the police use knowledge of personal space to aid their work?

_____

It's a free country, right? Well, not exactly. Every day, all day   1
long, the specific position of your body and the state of your mind are under the control of a powerful and authoritative force of which you are almost entirely unaware.

It's the system of personal space. Every culture has its own,   2
and some are so drastically different that they can cause friction—or at least extreme unease—when groups such as Arabs and northern Europeans get together.

Individual idiosyncracies and social context can modify the   3
rules slightly, as we shall see. But within a culture, the code usually is firmly imprinted by age 12 and remains surprisingly constant from town to town and region to region.

For the average American, according to anthropologist   4
Edward T. Hall, there are four distinctive spacial zones, each with a well-understood spectrum of appropriate behavior.

The nearest Hall calls the "intimate" zone, which extends   5
outward from the skin about 18 inches. This is the range within which lovers touch and parents communicate with infants. At that distance, it is difficult to focus on another person's face, which appears larger than your entire field of vision. That is one reason why people often kiss with their eyes closed.

6   Within this zone, the sense of smell is important; and body heat is felt immediately. For example, sexual arousal customarily floods the abdomen with blood. Many people say they can sense the condition of a partner, even during cocktail conversation or formal ballroom dancing, by feeling the radiated heat.

7   The next, or "personal," zone, extends from 18 inches to about 4 feet. Within this range, you discuss private or serious matters and confer with literally "close" friends. Touch is easy throughout the nearest part of this space, up to about 30 inches. Alternatively, you can keep someone "at arm's length."

8   (Although you may be unaware of the rules of personal space, your language is not. Many of our familiar phrases reflect our cultural code and what happens when somebody is too close for comfort.)

9   Within the personal zone, you can focus sharply on another person's face and read very subtle details of expression. But you'll probably move your eyes a lot to focus on various parts of the other person's face. Watch somebody else talking at this distance, and you'll see his or her gaze flick rapidly from one spot to another.

10   You'll also notice that personal groups larger than two or three are very rare, because it becomes difficult to maintain appropriate spacing with more people.

11   Casual acquaintances or people who just want to tell you something relatively unimportant had better stay well outside the 30-inch inner personal zone. If they don't, they'll make you very uncomfortable, and you may find yourself inadvertently backing up until you're trapped against a wall.

12   One reason that economy-class air travel frequently is so ghastly is that the strangers who are your seatmates are way inside the close personal zone. Worse yet, side-by-side seating is widely felt to be the most intimate arrangement. Men will not voluntarily choose it unless the alternative is sitting too far apart to talk.

13   In one study, American, English, Dutch, Swedish and Pakistani subjects all ranked side-by-side position as psychologically closest, followed by corner seating, face-to-face, and various diagonal arrangements.

14   The "social-consultive" zone, in which most day-to-day work and ordinary conversation occurs, starts at 4 feet and goes to

about 10 feet. In American culture, eight feet is the point at which you pretty much have to acknowledge another person's presence. Beyond that, you can ignore someone without giving obvious offense.

Usually, there are no smell or heat sensations at 4 to 10 feet, 15 and much nonverbal information is conveyed by large-scale body language. The whole body is visible as a unit at about seven feet, although you can only focus on part because the clearest vision occurs in a cone of about 15 degrees from the eyeball.

Finally, there is an all-purpose "public" zone that begins 16 at about 10 feet and extends to 25 feet. Thirty feet is the customary nearest distance for addresses by public officials or celebrities. 17

Studies have shown that people are more likely to interact with somebody who looks weird if that person stays well outside the personal zone. In one experiment, a researcher dressed as a punk rocker pretended to be looking for help from people sitting at tables in a shopping mall food court. 18

"Although only one in 15 people consented to help the punker when she sat right next to them, and 40 percent agreed to help when she sat at a medium distance," the researchers found. But "80 percent of the people agreed to help her when she took the seat farthest away."

Over the Line

When someone does something that violates the tacit rules 19 of the zone system, we are perplexed, annoyed or both. For example, if a person wanted a date with you and asked you out from 10 feet away—two feet beyond the farthest range of business conversation—you'd certainly think twice about agreeing, even if you were initially inclined to go.

On the other hand, a Latin American or French person, from 20 a culture with a much closer personal interaction distance, could seem to be too "forward" or "coming on too strong" if he or she made the request from two feet away.

Sometimes, the resulting discomfort is intentional. Psychol- 21 ogist Robert Sommer notes in his book *Personal Space* that police interrogators are taught to intrude well inside the personal zone when questioning suspects.

22   Similarly, we often decide that someone is wearing "too much" perfume or cologne if the scent extends past the distance of personal space. So if you can smell a woman's perfume 8 feet away, you may find it irritating—not just because of the odor itself but because she is making what should be an intimate olfactory statement in public space. . . .

Size Does Matter

23   Variations abound. In much of India, there are only two zones: intimate and public. Some Mediterranean cultures have personal zones that begin much closer than those typical of Americans or northern Europeans. That's why Americans sometimes feel crowded or stressed in France or Italy.

24   And, of course, some cultures simply build things differently. Japanese rooms seem too small by Western standards, and the furniture tends to be placed in the center rather than along the walls. What we don't know is that the traditional Japanese room configuration can be changed by moving the lightweight walls.

25   Thus, what we perceive as a permanent space is merely a temporary arrangement from another perspective. Conversely, our fondness for big spaces with furniture at the edges can make Western rooms look barren to the Japanese eye.

26   In 1967, Hong Kong's housing authority was constructing apartments with 35 square feet per occupant. That's 5-by-7, about the size of a modern work "cubicle." When a westerner asked why the design was so stingy, a construction supervisor replied, "With 60 square feet per person, the tenants would sublet."

Birth and Turf

27   But each culture's rules arise from the same fundamental biological impetus, which extends throughout the animal kingdom—the tendency to mark and defend one's own territory or to avoid intruding on someone else's.

28   Think about that next time you sit down in a cafeteria or library. If you find an empty table that can seat six or eight, you're probably going to sit at one of the corner chairs—an "avoidance" position, according to psychologists—and you'll

most likely face the door because some ancestral instinct says you might have to flee.

Dogs mark their territory by urinating at the boundaries. 29 Happily, human civilization has not evolved this trait. But we're constantly doing the equivalent.

Everyone has been vaguely irritated by the person in a movie 30 theater who spreads coats and bags across six seats and then goes off for popcorn. Nonetheless, we'll bypass any space that faintly appears to be "marked" by an absentee squatter. One study showed that, even in a busy and crowded library, a simple stack of magazines in front of a chair kept that seat open for more than an hour.

Analogously, you may find that when you enter someone's 31 home, you carefully avoid sitting in what seems to be the father's "personal" chair. Or you may notice how some passengers in the Metro system claim two spaces—an "aggressive" position—by putting a briefcase next to them or taking the outermost of the two side-by-side seats. . . .

Eyes Right

Space can be invaded by vision as well as another's presence, 32 and visual territories also differ from culture to culture. Unlike, say, the French, whose "frank" stares can be intimidating to outsiders, Americans rarely look directly at each other for very long, even during intense conversation.

In the animal kingdom, an averted gaze often indicates a pas- 33 sive stance. But in America, it is merely polite. We consider it an invasion of personal space to "stare" at someone, even briefly, and sensitivity varies by distance.

Thus, when the door closes on a crowded elevator, you'll 34 usually notice two behaviors. First, the occupants automatically adjust their positions to create the same amount of space between each. Then most people either look down at their feet or up at the floor indicator rather than at one another.

In fact, one experiment showed that people will sit closer to 35 a picture of a person with the eyes closed than to an otherwise identical image with the eyes open.

The English, on the other hand, regard it as rude not to look 36 directly at the other person during conversation. To do otherwise makes it appear that you're not paying attention.

37   But in order to hold the head still and the gaze steady while listening to someone, one has to be far enough away so the eyes aren't constantly shifting around the other person's face. Thus the English tend to stand near the outer limits of American personal space, making them seem aloof, reserved or literally "stand-offish."

Expanding Vocabulary

Examine the following words in their contexts in the essay and then write a brief definition or synonym of each one. Do not use a dictionary; try to guess each word's meaning from the context. The number in parentheses is the number of the paragraph in which the word appears.

idiosyncracies (3)   interrogators (21)
spectrum (15) 4   olfactory (22)
inadvertently (11)   impetus (27)
tacit (19)   Analogously (31)

Understanding Content

1. What are the characteristics of the intimate zone?
2. What are the dimensions and uses of the personal zone?
3. What terms have evolved from the dynamics of the personal zone?
4. How do most people view sitting next to strangers?
5. What are the dimensions and characteristics of the third zone? At what distance do we usually have to acknowledge another person?
6. What are the dimensions of the public zone?
7. What are some of the ways we "mark" our personal space?
8. How do American and British and French patterns differ regarding looking directly at someone?

Drawing Inferences about Thesis and Purpose

1. Why are we irritated by people who spread out their things over several chairs?
2. What is Suplee's purpose in writing? State his thesis.

Analyzing Strategies and Style

1. What are the sources of the author's information? How does he provide this information for readers?

2. Describe the strategies Suplee uses to introduce each of his four space zones.
3. What *type* of information does the author provide for each of the zones?

Thinking Critically

1. Are you familiar with this information about personal space? If not, does Suplee's analysis make sense to you? Think about your own experiences on elevators and in movie theaters.
2. What information about zones is most helpful for our personal relationships? Explain your response.
3. What information is most helpful for our dealings with people we don't know? Explain your response.

There's Three Kinds of Teams

PETER DRUCKER

Probably the most recognized name in business and management theory, Peter Drucker (b. 1909) has taught at the Claremont Graduate School since 1971 and is the author of more than twenty books on management, business organization, and economics. The following discussion of team models for companies is from a section of his book *Managing in a Time of Great Change* (1995).

Questions to Guide Your Reading

1. Who is Drucker's primary audience? What are his purposes in writing?
2. Why has the idea of creating teams in business and industry not always worked well?

"Team-building" has become a buzzword in American business. The results are not overly impressive.

Ford Motor Company began more than ten years ago to build teams to design its new models. It now reports "serious problems," and the gap in development time between Ford and its Japanese competitors has hardly narrowed. General Motors' Saturn Division was going to replace the traditional assembly line with teamwork in its "factory of the future." But the plant

278 Using Division and Classification

has been steadily moving back toward the Detroit-style assembly line. Procter and Gamble launched a team-building campaign with great fanfare several years ago. Now P&G is moving back to individual accountability for developing and marketing new products.

3   One reason—perhaps the major one—for these near-failures is the all-but-universal belief among executives that there is just one kind of team. There actually are three—each different in its structure, in the behavior it demands from its members, in its strengths, its vulnerabilities, its limitations, its requirements, but above all, in what it can do and should be used for.

4   The first kind of team is the baseball team. The surgical team that performs an open-heart operation and Henry Ford's assembly line are both "baseball teams." So is the team Detroit traditionally sets up to design a new car.

5   The players play *on* the team; they do not play *as* a team. They have fixed positions they never leave. The second baseman never runs to assist the pitcher; the anesthesiologist never comes to the aid of the surgical nurse. "Up at bat, you are totally alone," is an old baseball saying. In the traditional Detroit design team, marketing people rarely saw designers and were never consulted by them. Designers did their work and passed it on to the development engineers, who in turn did their work and passed it on to manufacturing, which in turn did its work and passed it on to marketing.

6   The second kind of team is the football team. The hospital unit that rallies around a patient who goes into shock at three a.m. is a "football team," as are Japanese automakers' design teams. The players on the football team, like those on the baseball team, have fixed positions. But on the football team players play as a team. The Japanese automakers' design teams, which Detroit and P&G rushed to imitate, are football-type teams. To use engineering terms, the designers, engineers, manufacturing people, and marketing people work "in parallel." The traditional Detroit team worked "in series."

7   Third, there is the tennis doubles team—the kind Saturn management hoped would replace the traditional assembly line. It is also the sort of team that plays in a jazz combo, the team of senior executives who form the "president's office" in big companies, or the team that is most likely to produce a genuine innovation like the personal computer fifteen years ago.

On the doubles team, players have a primary rather than a   8
fixed position. They are supposed to "cover" their teammates,
adjusting to their teammates' strengths and weaknesses and
to the changing demands of the "game."

Business executives and the management literature have lit-   9
tle good to say these days about the baseball-style team,
whether in the office or on the factory floor. There is even a
failure to recognize such teams as teams at all. But this kind of
team has enormous strengths. Each member can be evaluated
separately, can have clear and specific goals, can be held
accountable, can be measured—as witness the statistics a true
aficionado reels off about every major-leaguer in baseball history. Each member can be trained and developed to the fullest
extent of the individual's strengths. And because the members
do not have to adjust to anybody else on the team, every position can be staffed with a "star," no matter how temperamental,
jealous, or limelight-hogging each of them might be.

But the baseball team is inflexible. It works well when the   10
game has been played many times and when the sequence of its
actions is thoroughly understood by everyone. That is what
made this kind of team right for Detroit in the past.

As recently as twenty years ago, to be fast and flexible in   11
automotive design was the last thing Detroit needed or wanted. Traditional mass production required long runs with minimum changes. And since the resale value of the "good used
car"—one less than three years old—was a key factor for the
new-car buyer, it was a serious mistake to bring out a new
design (which would depreciate the old car) more than every
five years. Sales and market share took a dip on several occasions when Chrysler prematurely introduced a new, brilliant
design.

The Japanese did not invent "flexible mass production"; IBM   12
was probably the first to use it, around 1960. But when the
Japanese auto industry adopted it, it made possible the introduction of a new car model in parallel with a successful old one.
And then the baseball team did indeed become the wrong team
for Detroit, and for mass-production industry as a whole. The
design process then had to be restructured as a football team.

The football team does have the flexibility Detroit now needs.   13
But it has far more stringent requirements than the baseball
team. It needs a "score"—such as the play the coach signals to

the huddle on the field. The specifications with which the Japanese begin their design of a new car model—or a new consumer-electronics product—are far more stringent and detailed than anything Detroit is used to in respect to style, technology, performance, weight, price and so on. And they are far more closely adhered to.

14   In the traditional "baseball" design team, every position—engineering, manufacturing, marketing—does its job its own way. In the football team there is no such permissiveness. The word of the coach is law. Players are beholden to this one boss alone for their orders, their rewards, their appraisals, their promotions.

15   The individual engineer on the Japanese design team is a member of his company's engineering department. But he is on the design team because the team's leader has asked for him—not because the chief engineer sent him there. He can consult engineering and get advice. But his orders come from the design-team chief, who also appraises his performance. If there are stars on these teams, they are featured only if the team leader entrusts them with a "solo." Otherwise they subordinate themselves to the team.

16   Even more stringent are the requirements of the doubles team—the kind that GM's Saturn Division hoped to develop in its "flexible-manufacturing" plant and a flexible plant does indeed need such a team. The team must be quite small, with five to seven members at most. The members have to be trained together and must work together for quite some time before they fully function as a team. There must be one clear goal for the entire team yet considerable flexibility with respect to the individual member's work and performance. And in this kind of team only the team "performs"; individual members "contribute."

17   All three of these kinds of teams are true teams. But they are so different—in the behavior they require, in what they do best, and in what they cannot do at all—that they cannot be hybrids. One kind of team can play only one way. And it is very difficult to change from one kind of team to another.

18   Gradual change cannot work. There has to be a total break with the past, however traumatic it may be. This means that people cannot report to both their old boss and to the new coach, or team leader. And their rewards, their compensation,

their appraisals, and their promotions must be totally dependent on their performance in their new roles on their new teams. But this is so unpopular that the temptation to compromise is always great.

At Ford, for instance, the financial people have been left 19 under the control of the financial staff and report to it rather than to the new design teams. GM's Saturn Division has tried to maintain the authority of the traditional bosses—the first-line supervisors and the shop stewards—rather than hand decision-making power over to the work teams. This, however, is like playing baseball and a tennis doubles match with the same people, on the same field, and at the same time. It can only result in frustration and nonperformance. And a similar confusion seems to have prevailed at P&G.

Teams, in other words, are tools. As such, each team design 20 has its own uses, its own characteristics, its own requirements, its own limitations. Teamwork is neither "good" nor "desirable"— it is a fact. Wherever people work together or play together they do so as a team. Which team to use for what purpose is a crucial, difficult, and risky decision that is even harder to unmake. Managements have yet to learn how to make it.

Expanding Vocabulary

Examine the following words in their contexts in the essay and then write a brief definition or synonym for each one. Do not use a dictionary; try to guess the word's meaning from its context. The number in parentheses is the number of the paragraph in which the word appears.

aficionado (9)	appraisals (14)
depreciate (11)	hybrids (17)
stringent (13)	traumatic (18)

Understanding Content

1. What are the characteristics of the "baseball" team?
2. What are the characteristics of the "football" team? How does it differ from the "baseball" team?
3. What are the characteristics of the "tennis doubles" team?
4. What are the strengths of the baseball team? What is its primary weakness? Why was it a good model for car manufacture in the past?

5. Why has Detroit switched to a football-team model? What does it gain?
6. Why does General Motors want to switch to a tennis team model? What will it gain?
7. Why must change from one team model to another be total, not gradual? What are companies tempted to do?

Drawing Inferences about Thesis and Purpose

1. Who is Drucker's primary audience?
2. What are his purposes in writing?
3. What is Drucker's thesis?

Analyzing Strategies and Style

1. What primary strategy does Drucker use to explain three ways in which workers can do their work together? What makes his strategy effective?
2. What other strategy does the author use to develop and explain his classification? How are his particular choices effective, given his primary audience?

Thinking Critically

1. What are the goals of people, like Drucker, who analyze behavior on the job and try to determine how to organize workers? What do they want to accomplish?
2. Would you rather be on a baseball, football, or tennis team at work? Why?
3. Can the three team models be applied to the classroom? If so, how would each type of classroom be run? If not, explain why.

Class Acts: America's Changing Middle Class

RALPH WHITEHEAD, JR.

Beginning his career as a journalist in Chicago, Ralph Whitehead (b. 1943) became a professor of journalism at the University of Massachusetts in 1973. He is the author of many articles on social structures and public opinion and has been a consultant to political and labor groups and to the Department of Labor. His study of the changing social/economic hierarchy in American society was first published in the Jan./Feb. 1990 issue of the *Utne Reader.*

Questions to Guide Your Reading

1. What does Whitehead mean by his use of "collar," as in "bright collar" and "new collar"? What does "collar" stand for?
2. The social ladder of the 1990s has what three major categories? What is happening between the rich and the poor?

As we enter the 1990s, American society exhibits a vastly different social and economic makeup from the one that we grew accustomed to in the thirty years that followed World War II. The gap between the top and bottom is far greater now, of course, but the economic position of people in the middle is changing, too. This new social ladder is seen most vividly in the lives of our younger generations, the baby boom and the later baby bust. Because the new ladder is so much steeper than the old one, it's creating an alarming new degree of polarization in American life. 1

As it held sway for roughly the first three decades after World War II, the old social ladder was shaped largely by the continuing expansion of the middle class. For the first time, many people could afford to buy a house, a car (or two), a washer and dryer, an outdoor grill, adequate health coverage, maybe a motor boat, and possibly college for the kids. And for the first time, a growing number of blacks and Hispanics could enter the middle class. 2

Within this expanding middle class, there were a couple of fairly well-defined ways of life: white-collar life and blue-collar life. White-collar life was typified by TV characters like Ward and June Cleaver and later Mike and Carol Brady. Blue-collar life was typified by characters like Ralph and Alice Kramden and later Archie and Edith Bunker. 3

At the top of the old social ladder stood a small number of rich people. A larger but declining number of poor people stood 4 at the bottom, and the rest of the ladder was taken up by the middle-class. The old social ladder looked roughly like this:

THE RICH

THE EXPANDING MIDDLE CLASS:
White collar
Blue collar

THE POOR

5   The new social ladder is markedly different. Within the baby boom and baby bust generations, the middle class is no longer expanding. Therefore the new social ladder is shaped by—and at the same time is helping to shape—a new polarization between the haves and the have-nots. The social ladder of the 1990s looks roughly like this:

UPSCALE AMERICA:
The Rich
The Overclass

THE DIVERGING MIDDLE CLASS:
Bright collar
New collar
Blue collar

DOWNSCALE AMERICA:
The Poor
The Underclass

The rich are still on top, of course. But the new generation of rich people is typified by Donald Trump, the billionaire developer of luxury buildings for the newly rich, rather than by someone like his father, Fred Trump, a developer who made millions building modestly priced postwar homes and apartments for the expanding middle class—the kinds of homes in which the Kramdens and Bunkers lived.

6   The poor are still with us, of course, but they're no longer at the bottom. It's not because they've risen to the middle class but rather because some of them have fallen into the underclass. Because definitions of the underclass vary, so do estimates of its size. However, it does include at least two million people who lead lives that aren't typified in America's popular culture. To belong to the underclass is to be without a face and without a voice.

7   Just as an underclass has emerged, so has an overclass, which   7
occupies the rung just below the rich. Located chiefly in a dozen
metropolises and heavily concentrated in lucrative management and professional jobs, the overclass is roughly the same
size as the underclass. Its significance lies not in its numbers,
however, but in its immense power throughout American society. The overclass holds the highest level positions in the fields
of entertainment, media, marketing, advertising, real estate,
finance, and politics. It's pursued for its consumption dollars
and cajoled for its investment dollars. It is crudely typified by
the media stereotype of the yuppie.

What clearly stood out on the old social ladder that shaped   8
American society during the fifties and sixties was the dominant presence of an expanding middle class. What is notice-
able about the new social ladder is the unmistakable emergence
of distinct upper and lower rungs, and the vast social, economic,
and psychological distance between them. Together, the rich
and the overclass form Upscale America. Together, the underclass and the poor form Downscale America.

The expanding middle class, with its white and blue collars,   9
has given way in the baby boom and baby bust generations to
a diverging middle class. It consists largely of three kinds of
workers:

• **Bright collars.** Within the ranks of managerial and professional   10
workers a new category of job has emerged. The white-collar worker is receding and the bright-collar worker is advancing. The bright
collars are the 20 million knowledge workers born since 1945:
lawyers and teachers, architects and social workers, accountants
and budget analysts, engineers and consultants, rising executives
and midlevel administrators. They earn their living by taking intellectual initiatives. They face the luxury and the necessity of making
their own decisions on the job and in their personal lives.

Bright-collar people lack the touchstones that guided white-   11
collar workers like Ward Cleaver in the 1950s and 1960s. The white
collars believed in institutions; bright collars are skeptical of them.
The corporate chain of command, a strong force in white-collar life
then, is far weaker for bright collars today. They place a premium
on individuality, on standing out rather than fitting in. Although
the older white collars knew the rules and played by them, bright
collars can't be sure what the rules are and must think up their own.
The white collars were organization men and women (mostly men);
bright collars are entrepreneurs interested in building careers for
themselves outside big corporations.

12   Three quarters of the managers and professionals of the 1950s were men. Today half are women. Seven percent are black or Hispanic or Asian. Bright collars make up a third of the baby boom work force. They're typified by figures like *L.A. Law's* attorneys.

13 • **Blue Collars.** Within the manufacturing workplace, blue-collar work endures, but on a much smaller scale. Thirty years ago almost 40 percent of the adult work force did blue-collar work. Today, after the relative decline of American heavy industry, it's done by less than 25 percent of baby boom workers. During the fifties and sixties, blue-collar wages rose steadily, thus helping fuel the expansion of the middle class. In the past 15 years these wages have been relatively flat. Young blue collars often must live near the economic margins.

14   The blue-collar world is still a man's world. Roughly three quarters of today's younger blue collars are men—the same percentage as in the 1950s. Twelve percent are black, Hispanic, or Asian. Within a growing number of innovative manufacturing workplaces, new models of blue-collar work have begun to emerge, but they haven't yet advanced enough to trigger a new category of American worker. In the popular culture the new generation of blue collars finds a voice in Bruce Springsteen, but it still hasn't found a face.

15 • **New Collars.** These people aren't managers and professionals, and they don't do physical labor. Their jobs fall between those two worlds. They're secretaries, clerks, telephone operators, key-punch operators, inside salespeople, police officers. They often avoid the grime and regimentation of blue-collar work. Two thirds of the new collars are women. More than 15 percent are black, Hispanic, or Asian. The new collars make up at least 35 percent of the baby boom work force.

16   Federal Express truck drivers are typical new-collar workers. They design pickup and delivery routes, explain the company's services and fees, provide mailing supplies, and handle relatively sophisticated information technology in their trucks. They aren't traditional truck drivers so much as sales clerks in offices on wheels.

17   The rise of the new social ladder has helped to drive a number of changes in American life, but one of them, already evident, should be underscored: the dramatic shift of power within both the middle class and the society as a whole.

18   As members of the expanding middle class of the postwar years, blue collars once held considerable leverage. In the electorate, for every vote cast by the white collars in 1960, the blue collars cast two. In the workplace, they acted through powerful unions. In the marketplace, they were valued as consumers.

As a result, blue collars dealt with white collars as equals. In the fifties and sixties, whatever class lines still divided the two groups seemed to be dissolving. Within the diverging middle class today, the balance of 19 power is much different. In the electorate, for every vote cast by younger blue collars in 1988, bright collars cast two. In the workplace, younger blue-collar workers are losing union power, while bright collars exert the power of their knowledge and privilege of their status. In the marketplace, blue-collar consumers are written off as too downscale, while the bright-collar consumer is courted as an aspiring member of the overclass. Deep divisions have sprung up between bright collars and blue collars. They look a lot like class lines.

The rise of an overclass throws the decline of blue-collar life 20 into sharper relief, and vice versa. Upscale yuppie haunts spring up: the health club, the gourmet takeout shop, the pricy boutique, the atrium building. Downscale blue-collar haunts wither: the union hall, the lodge, the beauty parlor, the mill. The guys with red suspenders began showing up in the beer commercials right about the time the loggers and guys with air hammers began to disappear. The overclass's stock portfolios began to get fat just as blue-collar families were losing their pensions and health insurance. Condo prices were climbing in Atlanta just as bungalow prices fell in Buffalo. It seems that there's a battle here, a zero-sum game, whereby the rise of one comes at the expense of the other.

The contrast between the rich and the underclass is sharper 21 than ever. If you look at the new social ladder in New York, you see Donald Trump in his penthouse and the homeless people in the subways.

This situation intensifies the shift of power in society as 22 a whole. With the middle class divided, the center cannot hold. The dominant forces in society become Upscale America and Downscale America—or, more precisely, Upscale America versus Downscale America. Upscale America uses its power to secure privileges such as proposed cuts in the capital gains tax. Downscale America strikes back blindly through rising rates of crime. Through the old social ladder, the expanding middle class acted as the nation's glue. With the new social ladder, the diverging middle class is merely caught in the crossfire.

Expanding Vocabulary

Study the definitions for any of the following words that you do not know. Then select five words and use each one in a separate sentence. The number in parentheses is the number of the paragraph in which the word appears.

polarization (1)   innovative (11)
lucrative (7)   sophisticated (13)
cajoled (7)   leverage (15)
yuppie (7)   zero-sum (17)
entrepreneurs (10)

Understanding Content

1. In the social ladder for thirty years after World War II, what was happening to the middle class?
2. What were the four categories on the older social ladder?
3. What two important changes are taking place in the middle class?
4. What are the characteristics of the underclass?
5. What makes up the new overclass?
6. What are the characteristics of the three new categories of workers in the new middle class?
7. How has power changed in the new bright collar and blue collar classes?

Drawing Inferences about Thesis and Purpose

1. What is Whitehead's purpose in writing? Does he have more than one? State his thesis.
2. What does Whitehead mean when he writes of a "zero-sum game" played between upscale and downscale America (paragraph 17)?
3. What implications for America do we find in the final paragraph?

Analyzing Strategies and Style

1. What does the author gain by the visual presentation of both the former and the current class categories?
2. Whitehead uses several TV characters as examples. How are they effective? What do they imply about his expected audience?
3. The author uses contrast within his classification structure. Find several nicely balanced contrast sentences and consider why they are effective.

Thinking Critically

1. Does Whitehead's classification of contemporary American class structure seem on target? Why or why not?
2. Many Americans like to believe that we are a "classless" society; everybody is the same. Whitehead doesn't do anything to address, or counter, this attitude. What might this tell us about his expected audience?
3. Do you agree with Whitehead that the diverging middle class and the conflict between upscale and downscale America pose serious social problems for the United States? Why or why not?

STUDENT ESSAY—DIVISION AND CLASSIFICATION

BUYING TIME
Garrett Berger

Chances are you own at least one wrist-watch. Watches allow us immediate access to the correct time. They are indispensable items in our modern world, where, as the saying is, time is money. Today the primary function of a wristwatch does not necessarily guide its design; like clothes, houses, and cars, watches have become fashion statements and a way to flaunt one's wealth.

Introduction connects to reader.

To learn how watches are being sold, I surveyed all of the full-page ads from the November issues of four magazines. The first two, GQ and Vogue, are well-known fashion magazines. The Robb Report is a rather new magazine that caters to the overclass. Forbes is of course a well-known financial magazine. I was rather

Student explain his methodology of collecting ads. Paragraph concludes with his thesis.

surprised at the number of advertisements I found. After surveying 86 ads, marketing 59 brands, I have concluded that today watches are being sold through five main strategies: DESIGN/BRAND appeal, CRAFTSMANSHIP, ASSOCIATION, FASHION appeal, and EMOTIONAL appeal.

In most DESIGN/BRAND appeal ads, only a picture and the brand name are used. *Discussion of first category.* A subset of this category uses the same basic strategy with a slogan or phrases to emphasize something about the brand or product. A Mont Blanc ad shows a watch profile with a contorted metal link band, asking the question, "Is that you?" The reputation of the name and the appeal of the design sell the watch. Rolex, perhaps the best-known name in high-end watches, advertises, in Vogue, its "Oyster Perpetual Lady-Datejust Pearlmaster." A close-up of the watch face showcases the white, mother-of-pearl dial, sapphire bezel, and diamond-set band. A smaller, more complete picture crouches underneath, showing the watch on its side. The model name is displayed along a gray band that runs near the bottom. The Rolex crest anchors the bottom of the page. Forty-five ads marketing 29 brands use the DESIGN/BRAND strategy. A large picture of the product centered on a solid background is the norm.

CRAFTSMANSHIP, the second strategy, focuses on the maker, the horologer, and the technical sides of form and function. Brand heritage and a unique, hand-crafted design are major selling points. All of these ads are targeted at men, appearing in every magazine except <u>Vogue</u>. Collector pieces and limited editions were commonly sold using this strategy. The focus is on accuracy and technical excellence. Pictures of the inner works and cutaways, technical information, and explanations of movements and features are popular. Quality and exclusivity are all-important.

Discussion of second category.

A Cronoswiss ad from <u>The Robb Report</u> is a good example. The top third pictures a horologer, identified as "Gerd-R Lange, master watchmaker and founder of Cronoswiss in Munich," directly below. The middle third of the ad shows a watch, white-faced with a black leather band. The logo and slogan appear next to the watch. The bottom third contains copy beginning with the words: "My watches are a hundred years behind the times." The rest explains what that statement means. Mr. Lange apparently

Detailed examples to illustrate second category.

believes that technical perfection in
horology has already been attained. He
also offers his book, The Fascination of
Mechanics, free of charge along with the
"sole distributor for North America" at
the bottom. A "Daniel Roth" ad from the
same magazine displays the name across
the top of a white page; towards the top,
left-hand corner a gold buckle and black
band lead your eye to the center, where
a gold watch with a transparent fact displays its inner works exquisitely. Above
and to the right, copy explains the
exclusive and unique design accomplished
by inverting the movement, allowing it to
be viewed from above.

The third strategy is to sell the watch
by establishing an ASSOCIATION with an
object, experience, or person, implying
that its value and quality are beyond
question. In the six ads I found using
this approach, watches are associated
with violins, pilots, astronauts, hot air
balloons, and a hero of the free world.
This is similar to the first strategy,
but relies on a reputation other than
that of the maker. The watch is presented as being desirable for the connections
created in the ad.

Discussion of third category.

Rarmigiani ran an ad in The Robb Report
featuring a gold watch with a black face

and band illuminated by some unseen source. A blue-tinted violin rises in the background; the rest of the page is black. The brief copy reads: "For those who think a Stradivarius is only a violin. The Parmigiani Toric Chronograph is only a wristwatch." "The Moon Watch" proclaims an Omega ad from GQ. Inset on a white background is a picture of an astronaut on the moon saluting the American flag. The silver watch with a black face lies across the lower part of the page. The caption reads: "Speedmaster Professional. The first and only watch worn on the moon." Omega's logo appears at the bottom.

The fourth strategy is to present the watch simply as a FASHION statement. In this line of attack, the ads appeal to our need to be current, accepted, to fit in and be like everyone else, or to make a statement, setting us apart from others as hip and cool. The product is presented as a necessary part of our wardrobes. The watch is fashionable and will send the "right" message. Design and style are the foremost concerns; "the look" sells the watch.

Discussion of fourth category.

Techno Marine has an ad in GQ which shows a large close-up of a watch running down the entire length of the left

side of the page. Two alternate color
schemes are pictured on the right, separating small bits of copy. At the bottom on the right are the name and logo.
The first words at the top read: "Keeping time—you keep your closet up to the
minute, why not your wrist? The latest
addition to your watch wardrobe should be
the AlphaSport." Longines uses a similar
strategy in <u>Vogue</u>. Its ad is divided in
half lengthwise. On the left is a black-
and-white picture of Audrey Hepburn. The
right side is white with the Longines'
logo at the top and two ladies' watches
in the center. Near the bottom is the
phrase, "Elegance is an Attitude."
Retailers appear at the bottom. The same
ad ran in <u>GQ</u>, but with a man's watch and
a picture of Humphrey Bogart. A kind of
association is made, but quality and
value aren't the overriding concerns. The
point is to have an elegant attitude like
these fashionable stars did, one that
these watches can provide and enhance.

The fifth and final strategy is that of
EMOTIONAL appeal. The ads using this
approach strive to influence our emotional responses and allege to influence
the emotions of others towards us. Their
power and appeal are exerted through the

Discussion of fifth category.

feelings they evoke in us. Nine out of ten ads rely on a picture as the main device to trigger an emotional link between the product and the viewer. Copy is scant; words are used mainly to guide the viewer to the advertiser's desired conclusions.

A Frederique Constant ad pictures a man, wearing a watch, mulling over a chess game. Above his head are the words "Inner Passion." The man's gaze is odd; he is looking at something on the right side of the page, but a large picture of a watch superimposed over the picture hides whatever it is that he is looking at. So we are led to the watch. The bottom third is white and contains the maker's logo and the slogan "Live your Passion." An ad in <u>GQ</u> shows a man holding a woman. He leans against a rock; she reclines in his arms. Their eyes are closed, and both have peaceful, smiling expressions. He is wearing a Tommy Hilfiger watch. The ad spans two pages; a close-up of the watch is presented on the right half of the second page. The only words are the ones in the logo. This is perhaps one of those pictures that are worth a thousand words. The message is he got the girl because he's got the watch.

Even more than selling a particular watch, all of these ads focus on building the brand's image. I found many of the ads extremely effective at conveying their messages. Many of the better-known brands favor the comparatively simple DESIGN/BRAND appeal strategy, to reach a broader audience. Lesser-known, high-end makers contribute many of the more specialized strategies. We all count and mark the passing hours and minutes. And society places great importance on time, valuing punctuality. But these ads strive to convince us that having "the right time" means so much more than "the time."

Strong conclusion; the effect of watch ads.

MAKING CONNECTIONS

1. The writers in this chapter have examined many ways in which humans connect to one another. Sometimes the connections are good ones (using manners, serene ex-smokers); sometimes the connections are less than ideal (selecting the wrong team). What can you learn from these writers about human needs in relationships? What do we need to feel good? What missing needs lead to conflicts in human relationships?

2. Review the questions about advertising at the beginning of Chapter 4. Then think about what human needs are appealed to in the advertising of various products. How, for example, are perfumes (or cars) sold to us? To what specific needs do perfume (or car) ads appeal? You may want to do some reading on this subject, either in articles on advertising or in psychology texts, to review a list of basic human needs.

3. Which writer in this chapter offers the greatest insight into human connections? To answer this question, you will need to define *greatest*. The term could mean most profound, or most useful to readers, or most original or startling. You may want to classify the writers into these three categories—or others of your own—before deciding whom to select as having the greatest insight. Your initial analysis then becomes the basis for the defense of your choice.

4. Often conflicts in human relationships result from people with different personalities not understanding each other's ways of seeing the world or making decisions. Some of these conflicts can be avoided if we know ourselves better and can recognize specific traits in others we interact with. One strategy is to take the Myers/Briggs personality grid to know yourself better and to understand elements of personality. At some colleges, students can arrange to take this test and have a counselor "score" it and discuss the results with the student. You can learn more about Myers/Briggs online and see if you are interested in following through on this approach to learning about yourself. A good site to explore is: *www.teamtechnology.co.uk/ad.html.*

TOPICS AND GUIDELINES FOR WRITING

1. Look over your Getting Started exercise—your classification of recent reading, movies, or television shows. Do you think your reading (or viewing) habits are fairly typical of someone in your situation? Or are your reading (or viewing) habits unusual, reflecting, perhaps, a hobby or special interest? If you see some point—a thesis—that your classification of reading (or viewing) can support, then you have an essay topic. (Remember that division and classification is a strategy, not a purpose in writing.)

2. Reflect on the parents, teachers, or coaches you have known. Can they be divided into categories based on their ways of using discipline? Select one group (parents, teachers, or coaches), and then classify that group according to their strategies for disciplining. Be sure to have a thesis and to illustrate each division of the group with examples from

your experience. (You might want to give each type or category a label, as Zimring labels ex-smokers.)

3. Along the same lines as in topic 2, reflect on a particular group of people you know well—teachers, students, dates, workers in a particular field, athletes, and so on. Select one group and classify it according to the different types within that group. Try to make your classification complete. You are saying to your reader that these are the types of dates—or teachers—that one could conceivably know. Make your divisions clear by labeling each type, and then define and illustrate each type. Be sure to have a thesis. One possible thesis could be your view of the best and worst types in the group you are writing about.

4. Watch (and perhaps tape so that you can review) at least six evenings of the ABC, NBC, or CBS evening news. Analyze the news programs according to the types of news stories and determine the amount of time given to each type of story, to commercials, and to "what's coming" segments. What have you learned? How much serious news do we get in a half hour? How much time (in minutes or seconds) is devoted to each type of story? Report the results of your study in an essay. Introduce your topic in paragraph 1, explain how you conducted your analysis in paragraph 2, and then report on the results of your study. Illustrate your categories with specific examples from the programs you watched. (For example, if one type of story that appears regularly is what can be called "national news," then what news stories from the shows you watched fit into that category? You might explain and illustrate the category with several stories about the president or Congress.)

5. What are some of the "games" that people play in their relationships with one another? That is, what strategies are used by people to get along or get ahead? In what situations are they likely to use particular games? If you have been a careful observer of human behavior or if you have watched people behaving in one particular situation, you potentially have an essay on this topic. Take one of two approaches. (1) Write on the games people play, classifying game playing as fully as you can. Explain and illustrate each game with examples. Remember that you can use

hypothetical (made-up) examples as well as those drawn from your experience. (2) Write on the ways that people behave in a particular situation you know well. That is, how can people be classified by their behavior in a particular situation? Possible situations include the classroom, at the doctor's (or dentist's) office, in the library, at the beach, while driving, or at the movies. This second approach can be serious or humorous.

6. Think of one job category you know well (such as small business, farming, the medical profession, teaching, or banking). Then, within that one category, think of all the various workers and classify them according to Whitehead's new class divisions. Your point will be to show that not everyone in a job category is in the same class, although you may discover that not all categories are represented. For example, would anyone in teaching be placed in the underclass?

8

Using Definition

Understanding Ideas and Values

"Define your terms!" someone shouts in the middle of a heated debate. Although yelling may not be the best strategy, the advice is sound. Quite frequently the basis for a disagreement turns out to be a key word used differently by those whose discussion can now best be defined as an argument. We cannot let words mean whatever we want them to and still communicate, but, as you know from your study of vocabulary, many words have more than one dictionary definition (*denotation*). If we add to those meanings a word's *connotation* (associations and emotional suggestions), it is no wonder that we disagree over a word's meaning. To some, civil disobedience is illegal behavior; to others it is an example of patriotism. When we don't disagree over a word's generally understood meaning, we can still disagree over its connotation.

When to Use Definition

When do you need to define terms to avoid confusion? First, define words that most readers are not likely to know. If you need to use a technical term in an essay directed to nonspecialists, then you should provide a brief definition. Textbooks are, as you know, filled with definitions as the authors guide students through the vocabulary of a new subject. Second, define any word that you are using in a special way or in one of its special meanings. If you were to write: "We need to teach discrimination at an early age," you probably should add: "By discrimination I do not mean prejudice; I mean discernment, the ability to see differences." (*Sesame Street* has been teaching children this good kind of discrimination for years.)

A third occasion for using definition occurs when a writer chooses to develop a detailed explanation of the meaning of a complex, abstract, frequently debated, or emotion-laden term. Words such as *freedom, happiness, wisdom,* and *honesty* need to be reexamined, debated, and clarified in discussions that go beyond a dictionary's brief entry. We use the term *extended definition* to refer to the essay that has, as its primary purpose, the examination of a word's meaning. Sometimes the writer's purpose is to clarify our thinking: what does it mean to be *happy?* Sometimes a writer wants to reclaim a word from its current negative (or positive) connotations. This is what Robert Miller does when he argues that *discrimination* can have—and should be used with—a positive connotation.

How to Develop an Extended Definition

Extended definition describes a writing purpose. It does not suggest a particular organizational strategy. To develop an extended definition, you need to use some of the writing strategies that you have already been practicing. Suppose three Martians landed in your backyard, saw your Burmese cat, and asked, "What is that?" They are curious to know more than just the name of your pet. You could begin to answer their question with a dictionary-styled definition: a cat is a domesticated mammal (placing the object in a class) with retractable claws (distinguishing it from other members of the class—such as dogs). Your Martian friends, possibly interested in taking some cats home, want more information, so you continue with *descriptive details:* soft fur, usually long tails, padded feet, agile climbers (onto furniture, trees, and rooftops), rumbling sounds when contented. Developing your definition further, you can *contrast* cats with dogs: cats are more independent, can be trained to a box, will clean themselves. You can continue by providing *examples:* there are Siamese cats, Persian cats, tabby cats, and so on.

"This is all very interesting," the Martians respond, "but what do cats do, what are cats for?" You answer by explaining *use* or *function:* cats are pets, friends and companions, fun to play with and cuddle. Some people have even worshipped cats as gods, you add, providing *history*. A variation of providing history is to explain *word origin* or *etymology*. Often we get clues about a word's meaning by studying its origin and the changes in meaning over time. This information can be found in dictionaries that specialize in etymology, the *Oxford English Dictionary (OED)*, for example. (Your library will have the *OED*, probably both in a print format and online.)

The previous two paragraphs list and illustrate a number of strategies for developing an extended definition:

descriptive details   comparison/contrast

examples   use or function

etymology

To write a definition essay, you need to select those strategies that best suit your word and your particular purpose in defining that word. Remembering that effective writing is concrete writing, you want to include plenty of details and examples. Also give thought to the most effective organization of specifics so that the result is a unified essay, not a vocabulary exercise. Keep in mind that one of the most important strategies is contrast, for your purpose in defining is to discriminate, to explain subtle differences among words. (For example, what is the difference between wisdom and knowledge? Can one be wise without having knowledge? Or, how do self-esteem and self-respect differ? Is one better than the other?) Keep in mind that one kind of contrast, the metaphor, is especially useful because metaphors help make the abstract concrete. The Getting Started exercise below shows you how one writer used metaphors to define the concept *democracy*.

WRITING FOCUS:
USING METAPHORS, AVOIDING CLICHÉS

Just as there are colorless words—vague, general words such as *nice* and *thing*—so there are colorless expressions. These are metaphors that once had freshness but now are dulled by overuse. "In the twinkling of an eye" we become "starry-eyed" and are on "pins and needles" awaiting our true love's call. Or, in today's "fast-paced world" we have trouble avoiding "the rat race." To these expressions, called clichés, readers stop listening because they have heard them too many times before. So, when you are about to write that your friend was "as hungry as a bear," stop, ask yourself if this is *your* expression of an idea or a pat phrase you've pulled out of the air, and then erase all tuneless clichés.

Fresh metaphors, on the other hand, both delight readers and give them insight into a writer's thoughts and feelings. Here are some metaphors you will find in this chapter's essays.

> Andrew Vachss writes that a "veil of secrecy and protection then descends."
> From K. C. Cole we read: "entropy has been called the arrow of time."
> Margaret Mead and Rhoda Metraux write that a friend is someone "with whom you sparkle."
> John Ciardi writes that the concept of happiness "will not sit still for easy definition."
> Roger Rosenblatt tells us that the "way of obsessions is through the noisy night."

Find your own clever metaphors when you can. When you can't, write simply and directly, avoiding the pat phrases that so easily come to mind.

Getting Started: Reflections on E. B. White's Ideas of Democracy

E. B. White, author of "Education" (see pp. 132–134), once defined democracy largely through a series of metaphors. Three of his metaphors are

1. Democracy is "the line that forms on the right"
2. Democracy is "the hole in the stuffed shirt through which the sawdust slowly trickles"
3. Democracy is "the score at the beginning of the ninth"

First, analyze each metaphor. For each one, explain what the concrete situation is to which democracy is being compared. Ask yourself, how is that situation democratic? That is, what is White saying about democracy through the comparison? Then select the metaphor you like best and expand the idea that it suggests into a paragraph of your own on democracy. Try to include at least one metaphor of your own in your paragraph.

On Friendship

MARGARET MEAD AND RHODA METRAUX

Margaret Mead (1901–1978) may be the most famous anthropologist of our time. She revolutionized the field with the publication of her field work: *Coming of Age in Samoa* and *Growing Up in New Guinea*. Curator at the American Museum of Natural History and adjunct professor at Columbia University for many years, in later life Mead wrote and spoke often on issues in modern culture. Rhoda Metraux (b. 1914), also an anthropologist attached to the American Museum in New York City and coauthor with Mead of *Themes in French Culture*, did her field work in several Caribbean and South American countries. Mead and Metraux wrote a series of articles for *Redbook* magazine that were collected in *A Way of Seeing* in 1970. Their definition of friendship, from the *Redbook* series, reveals the cross-cultural approach of anthropology.

Questions to Guide Your Reading

1. What is the authors' primary purpose in writing? Does their discussion of cultural differences play a major or supporting role in the essay?
2. Why do American friendships confuse many Europeans?

1   Few Americans stay put for a lifetime. We move from town to city to suburb, from high school to college in a different state, from a job in one region to a better job elsewhere, from the home where we raise our children to the home where we plan to live in retirement. With each move we are forever making new friends, who become part of our new life at that time.

2   For many of us the summer is a special time for forming new friendships. Today millions of Americans vacation abroad, and they go not only to see new sights but also—in those places

where they do not feel too strange—with the hope of meeting new people. No one really expects a vacation trip to produce a close friend. But surely the beginning of a friendship is possible? Surely in every country people value friendship?

They do. The difficulty when strangers from two countries   3
meet is not a lack of appreciation of friendship, but different expectations about what constitutes friendship and how it comes into being. In those European countries that Americans are most likely to visit, friendship is quite sharply distinguished from other, more casual relations, and is differently related to family life. For a Frenchman, a German or an Englishman friendship is usually more particularized and carries a heavier burden of commitment.

But as we use the word, "friend" can be applied to a wide   4
range of relationships—to someone one has known for a few weeks in a new place, to a close business associate, to a childhood playmate, to a man or woman, to a trusted confidant. There are real differences among these relations for Americans—a friendship may be superficial, casual, situational or deep and enduring. But to a European, who sees only our surface behavior, the differences are not clear.

As they see it, people known and accepted temporarily, casu-   5
ally, flow in and out of Americans' homes with little ceremony and often with little personal commitment. They may be parents of the children's friends, house guests of neighbors, members of a committee, business associates from another town or even another country. Coming as a guest into an American   7
home, the European visitor finds no visible landmarks. The atmosphere is relaxed. Most people, old and young, are called by first names.

Who, then, is a friend?   6

Even simple translation from one language to another is dif-   7
ficult. "You see," a Frenchman explains, "if I were to say to you in France, 'This is my good friend,' that person would not be as close to me as someone about whom I said only, 'This is my friend.' Anyone about whom I have to say *more* is really less."

In France, as in many European countries, friends generally   8
are of the same sex, and friendship is seen as basically a relationship between men. Frenchwomen laugh at the idea that "women can't be friends," but they also admit sometimes that for women "it's a different thing." And many French people

doubt the possibility of a friendship between a man and a woman. There is also the kind of relationship within a group—men and women who have worked together for a long time, who may be very close, sharing great loyalty and warmth of feeling. They may call one another *copains*—a word that in English becomes "friends" but has more the feeling of "pals" or "buddies." In French eyes this is not friendship, although two members of such a group may well be friends.

9   For the French, friendship is a one-to-one relationship that demands a keen awareness of the other person's intellect, temperament and particular interests. A friend is someone who draws out your own best qualities, with whom you sparkle and become more of whatever the friendship draws upon. Your political philosophy assumes more depth, appreciation of a play becomes sharper, taste in food or wine is accentuated, enjoyment of a sport is intensified.

10   And French friendships are compartmentalized. A man may play chess with a friend for thirty years without knowing his political opinion, or he may talk politics with him for as long a time without knowing about his personal life. Different friends fill different niches in each person's life. These friendships are not made part of family life. A friend is not expected to spend evenings being nice to children or courteous to a deaf grandmother. These duties, also serious and enjoined, are primarily for relatives. Men who are friends may meet in a café. Intellectual friends may meet in larger groups for evenings of conversation. Working people may meet in the little *bistro* where they drink and talk, far from the family. Marriage does not affect such friendships; wives do not have to be taken into account.

11   In the past in France, friendships of this kind seldom were open to any but intellectual women. Since most women's lives centered on their homes, their warmest relations with other women often went back to their girlhood. The special relationship of friendship is based on what the French value most—on the mind, on compatibility of outlook, on vivid awareness of some chosen area of life.

12   Friendship heightens the sense of each person's individuality. Other relationships commanding as great loyalty and devotion have a different meaning. In World War II the first resistance groups formed in Paris were built on the foundation of *les copains*. But significantly, as time went on these little

groups, whose lives rested in one another's hands, called themselves "families." Where each had a total responsibility for all, it was kinship ties that provided the model. And even today such ties, crossing every line of class and personal interest, remain binding on the survivors of these small, secret bands.

In Germany, in contrast with France, friendship is much more   13
articulately a matter of feeling. Adolescents, boys and girls, form deeply sentimental attachments, walk and talk together—not so much to polish their wits as to share their hopes and fears and dreams, to form a common front against the world of schools and family and to join in a kind of mutual discovery of each other's and their own inner life. Within the family, the closest relationship over a lifetime is between brothers and sisters. Outside the family, men and women find in their closest friends of the same sex the devotion of a sister, the loyalty of a brother. Appropriately, in Germany friends usually are brought into the family. Children call their father's and their mother's friends "uncle" and "aunt." Between French friends, who have chosen each other for the congeniality of their point of view, lively disagreement and sharpness of argument are the breath of life. But for Germans, whose friendships are based on mutuality of feeling, deep disagreement on any subject that matters to both is regarded as a tragedy. Like ties of kinship, ties of friendship are meant to be irrevocably binding. Young Germans who come to the United States have a great difficulty in establishing such friendships with Americans. We view friendship more tentatively, subject to changes in intensity as people move, change their jobs, marry, or discover new interests.

English friendships follow still a different pattern. Their basis   14
is shared activity. Activities at different stages of life may be of very different kinds—discovering a common interest in school, serving together in the armed forces, taking part in a foreign mission, staying in the same country house during a crisis. In the midst of the activity, whatever it may be, people fall into step—sometimes two men or two women, sometimes two couples, sometimes three people—and find that they walk or play a game or tell stories or serve on a tiresome and exacting committee with the same easy anticipation of what each will do day by day or in some critical situation. Americans who have made English friends comment that, even years later, "you can take up just where you left off." Meeting after a long interval, friends

are like a couple who begin to dance again when the orchestra strikes up after a pause. English friendships are formed outside the family circle, but they are not, as in Germany, contrapuntal to the family nor are they, as in France, separated from the family. And a break in an English friendship comes not necessarily as a result of some irreconcilable difference of viewpoint or feeling but instead as a result of misjudgment, where one friend seriously misjudges how the other will think or feel or act, so that suddenly they are out of step.

15   What, then, is friendship? Looking at these different styles, including our own, each of which is related to a whole way of life, are there common elements? There is the recognition that friendship, in contrast with kinship, invokes freedom of choice. A friend is someone who chooses and is chosen. Related to this is the sense each friend gives the other of being a special individual, on whatever grounds this recognition is based. And between friends there is inevitably a kind of equality of give and take. These similarities make the bridge between societies possible, and the American's characteristic openness to different styles of relationships makes it possible for him to find new friends abroad with whom he feels at home.

Expanding Vocabulary

Mead and Metraux do not use complex terms from the social sciences, but they do use words that frequently appear in discussions of human relationships. Thus the following words are ones you want to know and use. Study their use in the essay, look up their definitions if necessary, and then use eight of the words in separate sentences of your own. The number in parentheses is the number of the paragraph in which the word appears.

particularized (3)	mutuality (13)
commitment (3)	irrevocably (13)
confidant (4)	exacting (14)
superficial (4)	kinship (12)
landmarks (5)	articulately (13)
accentuated (9)	congeniality (13)
compartmentalized (10)	contrapuntal (14)
niches (10)	invokes (15)
enjoined (10)	

Understanding Content

1. In general, how do the friendships of French, German, and English people differ from many American friendships?
2. What are the specific characteristics of friendship for the French? What sort of friendship do they think unlikely? What other term do the French use for people whom they would not consider close friends?
3. What lies at the core of friendships for Germans? How are friendships related to families? What can destroy a German friendship?
4. What is the basis for English friendships? What image best characterizes English friendships? How does this make possible a renewal of friendship after a time? What will lead to a break in friendships among the English?
5. After examining American and some European concepts of friendship, what do the authors conclude about the characteristics of friendship that extend over cultural differences?

Drawing Inferences about Thesis and Purpose

1. Do the authors make any judgments about friendships in the four countries?
2. What is their thesis? Is it stated or implied?

Analyzing Strategies and Style

1. Analyze the essay's organization. What paragraphs compose the introduction? The body of the essay? The conclusion?
2. What question indicates the shift from introduction to body? From body to conclusion?
3. Look at the use of transitions. What phrases guide readers through the paragraphs on French friendships? How is the shift to German friendship indicated? How is the shift to English friendship indicated?
4. Examine the authors' lengthy introduction. How do paragraphs 1 and 2 provide an attention-getter? How does the attention-getter lead into the authors' cross-cultural approach?

Thinking Critically

1. Do you think that the authors accurately describe American attitudes toward friendship? Why or why not?
2. Had it occurred to you that friendship might be understood somewhat differently in different cultures? Does it make sense? Do you know of other lifestyle differences between Americans and the

French, Germans, English, or those of another culture? If so, be
prepared to discuss these differences in class.
3. Is at least part of the difference in ideas of friendship a careless-
ness with words on the part of Americans? That is, do we use the
word *friend* to refer to relationships that could be more accurately described by a different word? What are some other words that
we could use? Should we use these more often than we do? Why
or why not?
4. Do you agree with the key definition of friendship offered in the
essay's final paragraph? If not, why not? Are there points you
would add? If so, what?

Is Everybody Happy?

JOHN CIARDI

A graduate of Tufts and the University of Michigan, John Ciardi
(1916–1986) was a lecturer, critic, and, primarily, a poet. Ciardi had
many collections of poetry published, including some delightful
poems for children. His major critical study is *On Poetry and the
Poetic Process* (1971). Ciardi was also for many years poetry editor of *Saturday Review*. In the following essay, from *Saturday Review*
(May 14, 1964), Ciardi defines happiness as never perfectly attain-
able and requiring effort.

Questions to Guide Your Reading
1. What seems to be the American concept of happiness?
2. What are the two extremes of happiness?

---

1   The right to pursue happiness is issued to Americans with
their birth certificates, but no one seems quite sure which way
it ran. It may be we are issued a hunting license but offered no
game. Jonathan Swift[1] seemed to think so when he attacked the
idea of happiness as "the possession of being well-deceived," the
felicity of being "a fool among knaves." For Swift saw society
as Vanity Fair, the land of false goals.

2   It is, of course, un-American to think in terms of fools and
knaves. We do, however, seem to be dedicated to the idea of buy-

---

[1]Irish-born English clergyman and satiric writer, 1667–1745.—Ed.

ing our way to happiness. We shall all have made it to Heaven when we possess enough.

And at the same time the forces of American commercial-   3
ism are hugely dedicated to making us deliberately unhappy. Advertising is one of our major industries, and advertising exists not to satisfy desires but to create them—and to create them faster than any man's budget can satisfy them. For that matter, our whole economy is based on a dedicated insatiabil-ity. We are taught that to possess is to be happy, and then we are made to want. We are even told it is our duty to want. It was only a few years ago, to cite a single example, that car dealers across the country were flying banners that read "You Auto Buy Now." They were calling upon Americans, as an act approach-ing patriotism, to buy at once, with money they did not have, automobiles they did not really need, and which they would be required to grow tired of by the time next year's models were released.

Or look at any of the women's magazines. There, as Bernard   4
DeVoto[2] once pointed out, advertising begins as poetry in the front pages and ends as pharmacopoeia and therapy in the back pages. The poetry of the front matter is the dream of perfect beauty. This is the baby skin that must be hers. These, the flaw-less teeth. This, the perfumed breath she must exhale. This, the sixteen-year-old figure she must display at forty, at fifty, at sixty, and forever.

Once past the vaguely uplifting fiction and feature articles,   5
the reader finds the other face of the dream in the back matter. This is the harness into which Mother must strap herself in order to display that perfect figure. These, the chin straps she must sleep in. This is the salve that restores all, this is her lax-ative, these are the tablets that melt away fat, these are the hor-mones of perpetual youth, these are the stockings that hide varicose veins.

Obviously no half-sane person can be completely persuaded   6
either by such poetry or by such pharmacopoeia and orthope-dics. Yet someone is obviously trying to buy the dream as offered and spending billions every year in the attempt. Clear-ly the happiness-market is not running out of customers, but what is it trying to buy?

[2]American novelist and critic, 1897–1955.—Ed.

7   The idea "happiness," to be sure, will not sit still for easy definition: the best one can do is try to set some extremes to the idea and then work in toward the middle. To think of happiness as acquisitive and competitive will do to set the materialistic extreme. To think of it as the idea one senses in, say, a holy man of India will do to set the spiritual extreme. That holy man's idea of happiness is in needing nothing from outside himself. In wanting nothing, he lacks nothing. He sits immobile, rapt in contemplation, free even of his own body. Or nearly free of it. If devout admirers bring him food he eats it; if not, he starves indifferently. Why be concerned? What is physical is an illusion to him. Contemplation is his joy and he achieves it through a fantastically demanding discipline, the accomplishment of which is itself a joy within him.

8   Is he a happy man? Perhaps his happiness is only another sort of illusion. But who can take it from him? And who will dare say it is more illusory than happiness on the installment plan?

9   But, perhaps because I am Western, I doubt such catatonic happiness, as I doubt the dreams of the happiness-market. What is certain is that his way of happiness would be torture to almost any Western man. Yet these extremes will still serve to frame the area within which all of us must find some sort of balance. Thoreau[3]—a creature of both Eastern and Western thought— had his own firm sense of that balance. His aim was to save on the low levels in order to spend on the high.

10   Possession for its own sake or in competition with the rest of the neighborhood would have been Thoreau's idea of the low levels. The active discipline of heightening one's perception of what is enduring in nature would have been his idea of the high. What he saved from the low was time and effort he could spend on the high. Thoreau certainly disapproved of starvation, but he would put into feeding himself only as much effort as would keep him functioning for more important efforts.

11   Effort is the gist of it. There is no happiness except as we take on life-engaging difficulties. Short of the impossible, as Yeats[4] put it, the satisfactions we get from a lifetime depend on how high we choose our difficulties. Robert Frost[5] was thinking in something like the same terms when he spoke of "The pleasure

[3]American author and naturalist, 1817–62.—Ed.
[4]Irish essayist, dramatist, and poet, 1865–1939.—Ed.
[5]U.S. poet, 1874–1963.—Ed.

of taking pains." The mortal flaw in the advertised version of happiness is in the fact that it purports to be effortless. We demand difficulty even in our games. We demand it 12 because without difficulty there can be no game. A game is a way of making something hard for the fun of it. The rules of the game are an arbitrary imposition of difficulty. When the spoilsport ruins the fun, he always does so by refusing to play by the rules. It is easier to win at chess if you are free, at your pleasure, to change the wholly arbitrary rules, but the fun is in winning within the rules. No difficulty, no fun.

The buyers and sellers at the happiness-market seem too 13 often to have lost their sense of pleasure of difficulty. Heaven knows what they are playing, but it seems a dull game. And the Indian holy man seems dull to us, I suppose, because he seems to be refusing to play anything at all. The Western weakness may be in the illusion that happiness can be bought. Perhaps the Eastern weakness is in the idea that there is such a thing as perfect (and therefore static) happiness.

Happiness is never more than partial. There are no pure 14 states of mankind. Whatever else happiness may be, it is neither in having nor in being, but in becoming. What the Founding Fathers declared for us as an inherent right, we should do well to remember, was not happiness but the *pursuit* of happiness. What they might have underlined, could they have foreseen the happiness-market, is the cardinal fact that happiness is in the pursuit itself, in the meaningful pursuit of what is life-engaging and life-revealing, which is to say, in the idea of *becoming*. A nation is not measured by what it possesses or wants to possess, but by what it wants to become.

By all means let the happiness-market sell us minor satis- 15 factions and even minor follies so long as we keep them in scale and buy them out of spiritual change. I am no customer for either puritanism or asceticism. But drop any real spiritual capital at those bazaars, and what you come home to will be your own poorhouse.

Expanding Vocabulary

Match each word in column A with its definition in column B. When in doubt, first find the word in the essay and look for context clues to aid your understanding of the word's meaning. Then, if necessary, use your dictionary to complete the matching exercise. The number in parentheses is the number of the paragraph in which the word appears.

Column A	Column B
insatiability (3)	ointment that soothes or heals
pharmacopoeia (4)	beliefs of Puritans who regarded
therapy (4)	pleasure as sinful
salve (5)	medical specialty dealing with injuries
varicose (5)	to the skeleton
orthopedics (6)	in a stupor, with rigid body
acquisitive (7)	stock of drugs
catatonic (9)	professes to be
purports (11)	treatment of illness
inherent (14)	intrinsic, essential characteristic
puritanism (15)	belief in life of austerity
asceticism (15)	eager to possess, grasping
	abnormally swollen or knotted
	state of not being satisfied

Understanding Content

1. How would Jonathan Swift have described people who thought they were happy?
2. Why does Ciardi reject both extremes of happiness?
3. How do the extremes help to define happiness? What must we find to begin to achieve happiness?
4. What else is essential to happiness? What role does this ingredient play in our games? Why is the advertised version of happiness flawed? Why is the Eastern version flawed?
5. Ciardi says that "happiness is never more than partial." What is another characteristic of happiness?

Drawing Inferences about Thesis and Purpose

1. What are the ingredients for happiness that Ciardi presents? State, in your own words, the key elements of his definition.

Analyzing Strategies and Style

1. In developing his definition, Ciardi refers to five writers. What do these references tell you about the author? What do they suggest about Ciardi's anticipated audience?
2. Examine Ciardi's discussion of American advertising in paragraphs 3 through 5. What is his attitude toward advertising? What

elements of style (word choice, sentence structure, examples) in these paragraphs develop and make clear his attitude?
3. Ciardi begins and ends his essay with metaphors. Explain the metaphor in his first two sentences and the metaphor in his last two sentences. What points about happiness does each metaphor suggest?
4. List all the strategies that Ciardi uses to develop his definition, giving an example of each one.

Thinking Critically

1. Ciardi thinks that happiness is a difficult term to define. Do you agree? Would you agree that it is the sort of concept that we think we understand until we are pressed to define it?
2. Ciardi asserts that "there is no happiness except as we take on life-engaging difficulties." Do you agree? Why or why not?
3. Ciardi does not think that happiness can be found in "getting the most toys," to use a modern expression. What is the relationship between money and happiness? Can some money help? Does having money make happiness more difficult to obtain? Be prepared to explain and defend your views.

Entropy

K. C. COLE

K. C. Cole (b. 1946), a graduate of Barnard College, is a journalist and freelance writer. She began her writing career focusing on Eastern European affairs but is best known for her writing about science and health issues. She has written several books about scientific subjects as a result of her work with Exploratorium, a San Francisco science museum, including *Vision: In the Eye of the Beholder* (1978) and *Order in the Universe* (1982). Currently, Cole writes a regular column for *Discover* magazine. Her ability to make scientific concepts both clear and interesting for nonspecialists is evident in the following article, which appeared in the *New York Times* in 1982.

Questions to Guide Your Reading

1. As we observe entropy in our lives, how does it make us feel?

2. Which is harder to create: order or disorder? Which is the path of least resistance?

———————

1   It was about two months ago when I realized that entropy was getting the better of me. On the same day my car broke down (again), my refrigerator conked out and I learned that I needed root-canal work in my right rear tooth. The windows in the bedroom were still leaking every time it rained and my son's baby sitter was still failing to show up every time I really needed her. My hair was turning gray and my typewriter was wearing out. The house needed paint and I needed glasses. My son's sneakers were developing holes and I was developing a deep sense of futility.

2   After all, what was the point of spending half of Saturday at the Laundromat if the clothes were dirty all over again the following Friday?

3   Disorder, alas, is the natural order of things in the universe. There is even a precise measure of the amount of disorder, called entropy. Unlike almost every other physical property (motion, gravity, energy), entropy does not work both ways. It can only increase. Once it's created it can never be destroyed. The road to disorder is a oneway street.

4   Because of its unnerving irreversibility, entropy has been called the arrow of time. We all understand this instinctively. Children's rooms, left on their own, tend to get messy, not neat. Wood rots, metal rusts, people wrinkle and flowers wither. Even mountains wear down; even the nuclei of atoms decay. In the city we see entropy in the rundown subways and worn-out sidewalks and torn-down buildings, in the increasing disorder of our lives. We know, without asking, what is old. If we were suddenly to see the paint jump back on an old building, we would know that something was wrong. If we saw an egg unscramble itself and jump back into its shell, we would laugh in the same way we laugh at a movie run backward.

5   Entropy is no laughing matter, however, because with every increase in entropy energy is wasted and opportunity is lost. Water flowing down a mountainside can be made to do some useful work on its way. But once all the water is at the same level it can work no more. That is entropy. When my refrigerator was working, it kept all the cold air ordered in one part of the kitchen and warmer air in another. Once it broke down the warm and

cold mixed into a lukewarm mess that allowed my butter to melt, my milk to rot and my frozen vegetables to decay.

Of course the energy is not really lost, but it has diffused and dissipated into a chaotic caldron of randomness that can do us no possible good. Entropy is chaos. It is loss of purpose.

People are often upset by the entropy they seem to see in the haphazardness of their own lives. Buffeted about like so many molecules in my tepid kitchen, they feel that they have lost their sense of direction, that they are wasting youth and opportunity at every turn. It is easy to see entropy in marriages, when the partners are too preoccupied to patch small things up, almost guaranteeing that they will fall apart. There is much entropy in the state of our country, in the relationships between nations—lost opportunities to stop the avalanche of disorders that seems ready to swallow us all.

Entropy is not inevitable everywhere, however. Crystals and snowflakes and galaxies are islands of incredibly ordered beauty in the midst of random events. If it was not for exceptions to entropy, the sky would be black and we would be able to see where the stars spend their days; it is only because air molecules in the atmosphere cluster in ordered groups that the sky is blue.

The most profound exception to entropy is the creation of life. A seed soaks up some soil and some carbon and some sunshine and some water and arranges it into a rose. A seed in the womb takes some oxygen and pizza and milk and transforms it into a baby.

The catch is that it takes a lot of energy to produce a baby. It also takes energy to make a tree. The road to disorder is all downhill but the road to creation takes work. Though combating entropy is possible, it also has its price. That's why it seems so hard to get ourselves together, so easy to let ourselves fall apart.

Worse, creating order in one corner of the universe always creates more disorder somewhere else. We create ordered energy from oil and coal at the price of the entropy of smog.

I recently took up playing the flute again after an absence of several months. As the uneven vibrations screeched through the house, my son covered his ears and said, "Mom, what's wrong with your flute?" Nothing was wrong with my flute, of course. It was my ability to play it that had atrophied, or entropied, as the case may be. The only way to stop that process was to practice every day, and sure enough my tone improved, though only at the price of constant work. Like anything else, abilities deteriorate when we stop applying our energies to them.

13   That's why entropy is depressing. It seems as if just breaking even is an uphill fight. There's a good reason that this should be so. The mechanics of entropy are a matter of chance. Take any ice-cold air molecule milling around my kitchen. The chances that it will wander in the direction of my refrigerator at any point are exactly 50–50. The chances that it will wander away from my refrigerator are also 50–50. But take billions of warm and cold molecules mixed together, and the chances that all the cold ones will wander toward the refrigerator and all the warm ones will wander away from it are virtually nil.

14   Entropy wins not because order is impossible but because there are always so many more paths toward disorder than toward order. There are so many more different ways to do a sloppy job than a good one, so many more ways to make a mess than to clean it up. The obstacles and accidents in our lives almost guarantee that constant collisions will bounce us on to random paths, get us off the track. Disorder is the path of least resistance, the easy but not the inevitable road.

15   Like so many others, I am distressed by the entropy I see around me today. I am afraid of the randomness of international events, of the lack of common purpose in the world; I am terrified that it will lead into the ultimate entropy of nuclear war. I am upset that I could not in the city where I live send my child to a public school; that people are unemployed and inflation is out of control; that tensions between the sexes and races seem to be increasing again; that relationships everywhere seem to be falling apart.

16   Social institutions—like atoms and stars—decay if energy is not added to keep them ordered. Friendships and families and economies fall apart unless we constantly make an effort to keep them working and well oiled. And far too few people, it seems to me, are willing to contribute to those efforts.

17   Of course, the more complex things are, the harder it is. If there were only a dozen or so air molecules in my kitchen, it would be likely—if I waited a year or so—that at some point the six coldest ones would congregate inside the freezer. But the more factors in the equation—the more players in the game—

the less likely it is that their paths will coincide in an orderly way. The more pieces in the puzzle, the harder it is to put back together once order is disturbed. "Irreversibility," said a physicist, "is the price we pay for complexity."

Expanding Vocabulary

Examine the following words in their contexts in the essay and then write a brief definition or synonym for each one. (Do not use a dictionary; try to guess the word's meanings from its context.) The number in parentheses is the number of the paragraph in which the word appears.

conked (1)	caldron (6)
futility (1)	buffeted (7)
nuclei (4)	tepid (7)
diffused (6)	atrophied (12)
dissipated (6)	

Understanding Content

1. How does entropy differ from all other physical properties?
2. When entropy increases, what is wasted?
3. Since energy cannot be lost, what is a better way to describe what happens to it?
4. What are some examples of exceptions to entropy? What is the most profound exception?
5. Does complexity make order or entropy easier? Why?

Drawing Inferences about Thesis and Purpose

1. According to Cole, what are the chief characteristics of entropy? Write a brief definition in your own words.

Analyzing Strategies and Style

1. What opening strategy does Cole use? What author voice or tone does her opening set for the rest of the essay?
2. Examine Cole's examples. What kind of range do they provide for the reader? What does Cole accomplish by using her range of examples?
3. When Cole writes about "the arrow of time" and a "caldron of randomness," what writing strategy is she using? Explain each expression.

4. Find some examples of Cole's humor. In what paragraphs does she seem particularly serious? What is her subject when she is most serious?
5. List the various strategies the author uses to define entropy.

Thinking Critically

1. Is Cole's definition of entropy your first introduction to the term? If so, have you found her definition clear and helpful? If you are familiar with the term, would you judge Cole's definition to be helpful to nonspecialist readers? Why or why not?
2. Cole seeks not just to give a "scientific" definition but to explain how the principle of *entropy* connects to our lives. What, for you, is the most telling example that makes the connection to ordinary lives? Why?
3. Select one of the other physical properties mentioned in paragraph 3, read about it in a science reference book, and then think of some examples from ordinary life that would illustrate the property.
4. Cole relates entropy not only to ordinary life but also to social institutions (see paragraph 16). There she asserts that too few of us are willing to make the effort to work at maintaining order. Do you agree with her assessment? Do you agree that this is a problem? If not, why not? If so, what can be done to withstand entropy in friendships? In families? In economies?

Discrimination Is a Virtue

ROBERT KEITH MILLER

Holding a Ph.D. from Columbia University, Robert Keith Miller (b. 1949) is a professor of English at St. Thomas University. He has published scholarly articles and books on such writers as Mark Twain, Oscar Wilde, and Willa Cather and has written for popular magazines and newspapers as well. In the following essay, which appeared in *Newsweek*'s "My Turn" column in 1980, Miller seeks to rescue the word *discrimination* from its misuse in our time.

Questions to Guide Your Reading

1. What does *discrimination* mean, as Miller defines it?
2. Why do Americans have trouble with discrimination, as Miller defines it?

When I was a child, my grandmother used to tell me a story 1
about a king who had three daughters and decided to test their
love. He asked each of them "How much do you love me?" The
first replied that she loved him as much as all the diamonds and
pearls in the world. The second said that she loved him more than
life itself. The third replied "I love you as fresh meat loves salt."
This answer enraged the king; he was convinced that his 2
youngest daughter was making fun of him. So he banished her
from his realm and left all of his property to her elder sisters.

As the story unfolded it became clear, even to a 6-year-old, 3
that the king had made a terrible mistake. The two older girls
were hypocrites, and as soon as they had profited from their
father's generosity, they began to treat him very badly. A wiser
man would have realized that the youngest daughter was the
truest. Without attempting to flatter, she had said, in effect, "We
go together naturally; we are a perfect team."

Years later, when I came to read Shakespeare, I realized that 4
my grandmother's story was loosely based upon the story of
King Lear, who put his daughters to a similar test and did not
know how to judge the results. Attempting to save the king
from the consequences of his foolishness, a loyal friend pleads,
"Come sir, arise, away! I'll teach you differences." Unfortunately, the lesson comes too late. Because Lear could not tell the
difference between true love and false, he loses his kingdom and
eventually his life.

We have a word in English which means "the ability to tell 5
differences." That word is *discrimination*. But within the last
twenty years, this word has been so frequently misused that
an entire generation has grown up believing that "discrimination" means "racism." People are always proclaiming that "discrimination" is something that should be done away with.
Should that ever happen, it would prove to be our undoing.

Discrimination means discernment; it means the ability to 6
perceive the truth, to use good judgment and to profit accordingly. The *Oxford English Dictionary* traces this understanding of
the word back to 1648 and demonstrates that, for the next 300
years, "discrimination" was a virtue, not a vice. Thus, when a
character in a nineteenth-century novel makes a happy marriage, Dickens has another character remark, "It does credit to
your discrimination that you should have found such a very
excellent young woman."

7   Of course, "the ability to tell differences" assumes that differences exist, and this is unsettling for a culture obsessed with the notion of equality. The contemporary belief that discrimination is a vice stems from the compound "discriminate against." What we need to remember, however, is that some things deserve to be judged harshly: we should not leave our kingdoms to the selfish and the wicked.

8   Discrimination is wrong only when someone or something is discriminated against because of prejudice. But to use the word in this sense, as so many people do, is to destroy its true meaning. If you discriminate against something because of general preconceptions rather than particular insights, then you are not discriminating—bias has clouded the clarity of vision which discrimination demands.

9   One of the great ironies of American life is that we manage to discriminate in the practical decisions of daily life, but usually fail to discriminate when we make public policies. Most people are very discriminating when it comes to buying a car, for example, because they realize that cars have differences. Similarly, an increasing number of people have learned to discriminate in what they eat. Some foods are better than others—and indiscriminate eating can undermine one's health.

10   Yet in public affairs, good judgment is depressingly rare. In many areas which involve the common good, we see a failure to tell differences.

11   Consider, for example, some of the thinking behind modern education. On the one hand, there is a refreshing realization that there are differences among children, and some children—be they gifted or handicapped—require special education. On the other hand, we are politically unable to accept the consequences of this perception. The trend in recent years has been to group together students of radically different ability. We call this process "mainstreaming," and it strikes me as a characteristically American response to the discovery of differences: we try to pretend that differences do not matter.

12   Similarly, we try to pretend that there is little difference between the sane and the insane. A fashionable line of argument has it that "everybody is a little mad" and that few mental patients deserve long-term hospitalization. As a consequence of such reasoning, thousands of seriously ill men and women have been evicted from their hospital beds and returned to what is

euphemistically called "the community"—which often means being left to sleep on city streets, where confused and helpless people now live out of paper bags as the direct result of our refusal to discriminate.

Or to choose a final example from a different area: how many 13 recent elections reflect thoughtful consideration of the genuine differences among candidates? Benumbed by television commercials that market aspiring officeholders as if they were a new brand of toothpaste or hair spray, too many Americans vote with only a fuzzy understanding of the issues in question. Like Lear, we seem too eager to leave the responsibility of government to others and too ready to trust those who tell us whatever we want to hear.

So as we look around us, we should recognize that "dis- 14 crimination" is a virtue which we desperately need. We must try to avoid making unfair and arbitrary distinctions, but we must not go to the other extreme and pretend that there are no distinctions to be made. The ability to make intelligent judgments is essential both for the success of one's personal life and for the functioning of society as a whole. Let us be open-minded by all means, but not so open-minded that our brains fall out.

Expanding Vocabulary

Examine the following words in their contexts in the essay and then write a brief definition or synonym for each one. (Do not use a dictionary; try to guess the word's meanings from its context.) The number in parentheses is the number of the paragraph in which the word appears

banished (2)	undermine (9)
realm (2)	evicted (12)
hypocrites (3)	euphemistically (12)
discernment (6)	benumbed (13)
preconceptions (8)	

Understanding Content

1. Currently, how is the word being used? How does the current use of the word change its connotation? (See the Glossary, if necessary, for the definition of *connotation*.)

2. When is discrimination wrong? When it is wrong, what should it be called? What has actually happened to one's ability to discriminate?
3. Under what circumstances do people usually discriminate? In what area of life do we often fail to discriminate?

Drawing Inferences about Thesis and Purpose

1. What is Miller's purpose in defining *discrimination*? What point does he want to make about the word? State his thesis.

Analyzing Strategies and Style

1. What opening strategy does Miller use? How does it lead into his subject?
2. What are Miller's examples of public policy failures in discrimination? Are they effective examples, showing a range of public policy problems?
3. Examine Miller's closing paragraph. Is it effective in its balanced language? What makes the final sentence clever?

Thinking Critically

1. Is the definition of *discrimination* that Miller wants to highlight familiar to you, or do you know the word only as it means to show prejudice? Do you see how the two meanings could develop in the same word?
2. Do you agree with Miller that we are "benumbed by television commercials" and "vote with only a fuzzy understanding of the issues"? Have you voted with a good knowledge of the candidates and the issues? (Have you voted? If not, why not?)
3. Is the American focus on equality keeping us from learning to discern differences? Explain.
4. Should differences in ability be ignored in education in favor of "mainstreaming"? Why or why not?

Still Obsessive After All These Years

ROGER ROSENBLATT

A former editor of *U.S. News and World Report*, Roger Rosenblatt (b. 1940) has continued his career in journalism as a regular contributor to magazines and newspapers. He is also the author of several books, including *Life Itself: Abortion in the American Mind* (1992). Rosenblatt's exploration of the meaning of *obsession* was published on May 20, 2002, in *Time* magazine.

Questions to Guide Your Reading

1. What is Rosenblatt "doing" in the opening paragraph? What is the paragraph's tone? That is, how should you read it?
2. What kind of "thing" is obsession?

OBSESSED? YOU SAY I'M OBSESSED? WITH WHAT, 1 OBSESSED? Oh, you mean these Studebakers. Well, in fact, they happen to be the largest collection of Studebakers in North America, if you don't count Phillips in Bismarck, N.D., with his to-say-the-least questionable "rebuilt" engines. I don't think so. How do you like these Zippo lighters—1,110, if you're counting. I certainly am. What about my Marilyn Monroe movie furniture, my Trekkie memorabilia, my Daisy Buchanan, my Holy Grail, my double helix? Call me obsessed? What do you think of this church ceiling? Took me 10 years hanging in air to get the God's-hand-to-Adam right. Do you think I did get it right? Should I start over?

But please don't characterize any of these activities as obses- 2 sions. The word has that connotation, you know: zealous, pathological—dare I say it?—dare I say it?—nuts. This, undoubtedly, is why Robert A. Caro abjures it; says, instead, that he has spent the past 27 years writing his monumental 1,000-plus-page volumes on the life of Lyndon Johnson, with many more years in both his life and Johnson's to go, because he is "interested in how power works." Interested, indeed. Captain Ahab was "interested" in Moby Dick. "Between love and madness lies" Calvin Klein's "Interest."

I am not obsessed with Caro, but I am interested in him; that 3 is, in how obsession works, because the emotion (is it an emotion?), the passion (must it always involve passion?), the mental devotion (that'll do for the moment) produces a multiplicity of applications. John W. Hinckley Jr. was obsessed with Jodie Foster; Hitler with Jews; Osama bin Laden with us.

Caro's obsession, on the other and safer hand, has produced 4 three classic works about power, four if you're counting his book on Robert Moses. I certainly am. We are not talking about an obsessive-compulsive disorder—some helpless yearning that erupts in incessant hand washing, the counting of numbers, words repeated over and over. All words and no play makes Jack a murderous boy. We are not talking about polar bears either. Young Tolstoy's brother told him to stand in the corner until he stopped thinking about the white bear. But Tolstoy was entrapped by fear of the unwanted thought, and so he thought of nothing else but white bears.

5   Psychologists like Erik Erikson and Jean Piaget (who were more than interested in how the child develops) concluded that obsession is a normal part of growing up. First, obsessed with dolls and baseball stats. Later, obsessed with political systems, religions, ideologies. In the 1970s little Stevie Jobs and Billy Gates were taken with computers. Why? Because these microcosms of interest gave them worlds they could inhabit and control? Maybe.

6   In *The Orchid Thief*, Susan Orlean comes up with a more creative, a lovelier idea. Of her eccentric Laroche, who lurched from an obsession with turtles to one with Ice Age fossils, then resilvering old mirrors, then orchids, Orlean writes: "I was starting to believe that the reason it matters to care passionately about something is that it whittles the world down to more manageable size. It makes the world seem not huge and empty, but full of possibility." In other words, the exclusionary element of an obsession also implies what the obsession includes. In other words, tunnel vision takes in the tunnel.

7   And yet obsessions are frightening too. One may feel that he is the master of the specialized universe he has glommed on to, but who is mastering whom? In truth I do not have a Studebaker or Zippo lighter to my name, but I do boast rather a large collection—one of the more extensive in North America—of random words on little pieces of paper and sundry surfaces. I could tell you that I am merely interested in how words work, but if you looked around my house—at the writing pads by the TV, the bed, on the kitchen counter, beside the bookshelves— you might deduce that something compulsive was afoot. No, I have never written on my foot. Shirts, yes.

8   The way of obsessions is through the noisy night. Why can't you sleep, Mr. Edison? And the interesting, really interesting thing is that one probably could not tell the difference in brainwave flutterings between Jeffrey Dahmer's sleepless nights and Mozart's.

I wonder if the heart of the matter isn't the heart of the mat- 9
ter—that the obsessed one detects a secret hidden in the object
of his excessive desire, the essence of the Beanie Baby, of the
orchid, of the girl. And that this secret, once unearthed, will
tell the obsessor what no one has ever been told. In his first book
on Johnson, Caro paused to note that L.B.J., through lies and
deceits, did his best to hide his life from those who went after
it. One almost hears Caro whispering, "But not from me."

My guess is that Caro has timed the production of these 10
books to make them his life's work, literally. And why not?
What would await him after the final volume is complete and
he awakens one morning to a landscape without secrets? Only
the satisfaction that he found his unique place in the universe,
drew the rest of us to it and thus defined us for a while—which,
as he has undoubtedly discovered, is how power works.

Expanding Vocabulary

Match each word in column A with its definition in column B. When
in doubt, first find the word in the essay and look for context clues
to aid your understanding of the word's meaning. Then, if necessary,
use your dictionary to complete the matching exercise. The number in
parentheses is the number of the paragraph in which the word
appears.

Column A	Column B
memorabilia (1)	deviation from the normal
zealous (2)	set of doctrines or beliefs
pathological (2)	departing from conventional patterns
abjures (2)	attached to
ideologues (5)	pares down, cuts into small pieces
microcosms (5)	objects valued for their historical
eccentric (6)	significance
whittles (6)	misrepresentations; lies
glommed (7)	disagrees; rejects
deceits (9)	fervent; especially keen
	small systems

Understanding Content

1. What is the connotation of *obsessive* that Robert Caro objects to?
2. Robert Caro is a key example for Rosenblatt. What is he famous
   for? Why is he a good example?

3. How does Rosenblatt define *obsession*? How does he qualify his definition? What is the most positive explanation of our obsessions?
4. What can make obsession frightening? What may be "the heart of the matter"?

Drawing Inferences about Thesis and Purpose

1. Does the author, finally, admire Robert Caro and his biographies of President Johnson? How do you know?
2. Explain the last sentence of the essay.

Analyzing Strategies and Style

1. Rosenblatt makes many references in his opening paragraph. Which ones can you identify? What does the author assume about his readers?
2. Rosenblatt refers to Jobs and Gates at "Stevie" and "Billy." Why? What does he gain by his word choice?

Thinking Critically

1. How would you define obsession? Would you lean to the "nuts" definition or the "control" definition or the "creative/successful" definition?
2. Has Rosenblatt altered your thinking about this word in any way? Explain.
3. Why do we have a tendency to dismiss people who are really focused on their interests/hobbies/projects as odd or pathological? Are we stereotyping? Are we rejecting those who seem different? Are we jealous of their focus/commitment/success? Reflect on these questions.

The Difference Between "Sick" and "Evil"

ANDREW VACHSS

A lawyer whose only clients are children, Andrew Vachss is also the author of more than a dozen novels. More information about Mr. Vachss, and more articles written by him, can be found at *www.vachss.com*. In response to the news coverage of Roman Catholic priests accused of child abuse, Vachss has written the following essay, which appeared in *Parade* magazine July 14, 2002.

Questions to Guide Your Reading

1. What is the context in which the author raises the question of the difference between sick and evil?
2. What is Vachss's purpose in writing?

The shock waves caused by the recent exposures of so-called 1
"pedophile priests" have reverberated throughout America. But beneath our anger and revulsion, a fundamental question pulsates: Are those who abuse positions of trust to prey upon children—a category certainly not limited to those in religious orders—sick . . . or are they evil?

We need the answer to that fundamental question. Because, 2 without the truth, we cannot act. And until we act, nothing will change.

My job is protecting children. It has taken me from big cities 3 to rural outposts, from ghettos to penthouses and from courtrooms to genocidal battlefields. But whatever the venue, the truth remains constant: Some humans intentionally hurt children. They commit unspeakable acts—for their pleasure, their profit, or both.

Many people who hear of my cases against humans who 4 rape, torture and package children for sale or rent immediately respond with, "That's sick!" Crimes against children seem so grotesquely abnormal that the most obvious explanation is that the perpetrator must be mentally ill—helpless in the grip of a force beyond his or her control.

But that very natural reaction has, inadvertently, created a spe- 5 cial category of "blameless predator." That confusion of "sick" with "sickening" is the single greatest barrier to our primary biological and ethical mandate: the protection of our children.

The difference between sick and evil cannot be dismissed with 6 facile eye-of-the-beholder rhetoric. There are specific criteria we can employ to give us the answers in every case, every time.

Some of those answers are self-evident and beyond dispute: 7 A mother who puts her baby in the oven because she hears voices commanding her to bake the devil out of the child's spirit is sick; and a mother who sells or rents her baby to child pornographers is evil. But most cases of child sexual abuse—especially those whose "nonviolent" perpetrators come from within the child's circle of trust—seem, on their surface, to be far more complex.

8   That complexity is an illusion. The truth is as simple as it is terrifying:

9   Sickness is a condition.

10   Evil is a behavior.

11   Evil is always a matter of choice. Evil is not thought; it is conduct. And that conduct is always volitional.

12   And just as evil is always a choice, sickness is always the absence of choice. Sickness happens. Evil is inflicted.

13   Until we perceive the difference clearly, we will continue to give aid and comfort to our most pernicious enemies. We, as a society, decide whether something is sick or evil. Either decision confers an obligation upon us. Sickness should be treated. Evil must be fought.

14   If a person has desires or fantasies about sexually exploiting children, that individual may be sick. (Indeed, if such desires are disturbing, as opposed to gratifying to the individual, there may even be a "cure.") But if the individual chooses to act upon those feelings, that conduct is evil. People are not what they think; they are what they do.

15   Our society distrusts the term "evil." It has an almost biblical ring to it—something we believe in (or not) but never actually understand. We prefer scientific-sounding terms, such as "sociopath." But sociopathy is not a mental condition; it is a specific cluster of behaviors. The diagnosis is only made from actual criminal conduct.

16   No reputable psychiatrist claims to be able to cure a sociopath—or, for that matter, a predatory pedophile. Even the most optimistic professionals do not aim to change such a person's thoughts and feelings. What they hope is that the predator can learn self-control, leading to a change in behavior.

17   Such hopes ignore the inescapable fact that the overwhelming majority of those who prey upon children don't want to change their behavior—they want only to minimize the consequences of being caught at it.

18   In the animal kingdom, there is a food chain—predators and prey. But among humans, there is no such natural order. Among our species, predators select themselves for that role.

Psychology has given us many insights of great value. But 19 it also has clouded our vision with euphemisms. To say a person suffers from the "disease" of pedophilia is to absolve the predator of responsibility for his behavior.

Imagine if an attorney, defending someone accused of committing a dozen holdups, told the jury his poor client was suffering from "armed-robberia." That jury would decide that the only crazy person in the courtroom was the lawyer. 20

When a perpetrator claims to be sick, the *timing* of that claim 21 is critical to discovering the truth. Predatory pedophiles carefully insinuate themselves into positions of trust. They select their prey and approach cautiously. Gradually, sometimes over a period of years, they gain greater control over their victims. Eventually, they leave dozens of permanently damaged children in their wake.

But only when they are caught do predatory pedophiles 22 declare themselves to be sick. And the higher the victim count, the sicker (and therefore less responsible) they claim to be.

In too many cases, a veil of secrecy and protection then 23 descends. The predator's own organization appoints itself judge and jury. The perpetrator is deemed sick and sent off for inhouse "treatment." The truth is never made public. And when some secret tribunal decides that a cure has been achieved, the perpetrator's rights and privileges are restored, and he or she is given a new assignment.

In fact, such privileged predators actually are assisted. They 24 enter new communities with the blessing of their own organization, their history and propensities kept secret. As a direct result, unsuspecting parents entrust their children to them. Inevitably, the predator eventually resumes his or her conduct and preys upon children again. And when that conduct comes to light, the claim of "sickness" re-emerges as well.

Too often, our society contorts itself to excuse such predators. 25 We are so eager to call those who sexually abuse children "sick," so quick to understand their demons. Why? Because sickness not only offers the possibility of finding a cure but also assures us that the predator didn't really mean it. After all, it is human nature to try to understand inhuman conduct.

Conversely, the concept of evil terrifies us. The idea that some 26 humans *choose* to prey upon our children is frightening, and their demonstrated skill at camouflage only heightens this fear.

27   For some, the question, "Does evil exist?" is philosophical. But for those who have confronted or been victimized by predatory pedophiles, there is no question at all. We are what we do.

28   Just as conduct is a choice, so is our present helplessness. We may be powerless to change the arrogance of those who believe they alone should have the authority to decide whether predatory pedophiles are "sick" or when they are "cured." But, as with the perpetrators themselves, we do have the power to change their behavior.

29   In every state, laws designate certain professions that regularly come into contact with children—such as teachers, doctors, social workers and day-care employees—as "mandated reporters." Such personnel are required to report reasonable suspicion of child abuse when it comes to their attention. Failure to do so is a crime.

30   Until now, we have exempted religious organizations from mandated-reporter laws. Recent events have proved the catastrophic consequences of this exemption. We must demand—now—that our legislators close this pathway to evil.

31   A predatory pedophile who is recycled into an unsuspecting community enters it cloaked with a protection no other sex offender enjoys. If members of religious orders were mandated reporters, we would not have to rely on their good-faith belief that a predator is cured. We could make our own informed decisions on this most vital issue.

32   Modifying the law in this way would not interfere with priest-penitent privileges: When child victims or their parents disclose abuse, they are not confessing, they are crying for help. Neither confidentiality nor religious freedom would in any way be compromised by mandatory reporting.

33   Changing the laws so that religious orders join the ranks of mandated reporters is the right thing to do. And the time is right now.

Expanding Vocabulary

Match each word in column A with its definition in column B. When in doubt, first find the word in the essay and look for context clues to aid your understanding of the word's meaning. Then, if necessary, use your dictionary to complete the matching exercise. The number in parentheses is the number of the paragraph in which the word appears.

Column A	Column B
pedophile (1)	vibrates
reverberated (1)	one who is guilty of, responsible for
revulsion (1)	site, place
pulsates (1)	psychopath with aggressive, antisocial
genocidal (3)	behavior
venue (3)	conscious choice
grotesquely (4)	destructive, cruel, evil
perpetrator (4)	select, specify
mandate (5)	echoed repeatedly; resounded
facile (6)	inoffensive terms used for offensive ones
volitional (11)	imposed on
inflicted (11)	cleverly place
pernicious (13)	hiding
sociopath (15)	command
euphemisms (19)	natural inclinations
insinuate (21)	binds and twists out of shape
tribunal (23)	one who has a preference for children
propensities (24)	freed from obligation
contorts (25)	distortedly, bizarrely
camouflage (26)	simple, easy
designate (29)	disgust; loathing
exempted (3)	court or committee giving a legal
	decision
	engaged in planned killing of a
	particular group

Understanding Content

1. Is Vachss writing only about pedophile priests? How do you know?
2. What, according to the author, is our primary mandate? In what sense is it our primary biological mandate?
3. What is the difference between *sick* and *evil*?
4. What should be our response to sickness? To evil?
5. Why do we have problems with the word *evil*?
6. How have some child abusers avoided punishment?
7. What does Vachss want to see changed? How does he think this will improve the situation—that is, help protect more children?

Drawing Inferences about Thesis and Purpose

1. What is Vachss's thesis? You may need to use more than one sentence to give a definition of evil and to connect that to the author's call for action.
2. Vachss says that psychology "has clouded our vision with euphemisms." Explain his meaning.

Analyzing Strategies and Style

1. How would you describe the author's tone? You may need to use more than one word, for example, "outrageously silly" or "deeply caring."
2. Generally, Vachss's paragraphs are short, but paragraphs 8 through 12 are especially brief. Why? What does he gain by short sentences and paragraphs in this part of his essay?

Thinking Critically

1. Do you agree with Vachss's definitions of *sick* and *evil*? Why or why not?
2. Do you agree that, today, we have trouble with the term *evil*? Why or why not?
3. Should religious organizations be covered under the mandated-reporter law? Why or why not?
4. Is our society doing an adequate job of caring for and protecting our children? Explain your views.

Curiosity

ALASTAIR REID

A Scotsman who prefers to live in Spain, Alastair Reid (b. 1926) is a poet, translator, essayist, writer of children's books, and lecturer. Holding a master's degree from Scotland's St. Andrews University, Reid has lectured at schools in England, Spain, and the United States. He has had several books of poems published, has translated much of the poetry of Latin American poet Pablo Neruda, and has been a staff writer for the *New Yorker*. "Curiosity" appeared first in the *New Yorker* and was then included in the collection *Weathering* (1959).

Curiosity

may have killed the cat. More likely,
the cat was just unlucky, or else curious
to see what death was like, having no cause
to go on licking paws, or fathering
litter on litter of kittens, predictably.   5

Nevertheless, to be curious
is dangerous enough. To distrust
what is always said, what seems,
to ask odd questions, interfere in dreams,
smell rats, leave home, have hunches,   10
does not endear cats to those doggy circles
where well-smelt baskets, suitable wives, good lunches
are the order of things, and where prevails
much wagging of incurious heads and tails.

Face it. Curiosity   15
will not cause us to die—
only lack of it will.
Never to want to see
the other side of the hill
or that improbable country   20
where living is an idyll
(although a probable hell)
would kill us all.
Only the curious
have if they live a tale   25
worth telling at all.
Dogs say cats love too much, are irresponsible,
are dangerous, marry too many wives,
desert their children, chill all dinner tables
with tales of their nine lives.   30

Well, they are lucky. Let them be
nine-lived and contradictory,
curious enough to change, prepared to pay
the cat-price, which is to die
and die again and again,   35
each time with no less pain.

A cat-minority of one
is all that can be counted on
to tell the truth; and what cats have to tell
40   on each return from hell
is this: that dying is what the living do,
that dying is what the loving do,
and that dead dogs are those who never know
that dying is what, to live, each has to do.

Understanding Content and Strategies

1. What is more likely than curiosity to have killed the cat?
2. Why is being curious "dangerous enough"?
3. What kind of people belong to "doggy circles"?
4. What do dogs say about cats? What traits do they ascribe to them? Are we to agree with the dogs' view of cats? How do you know?
5. What are the characteristics of the curious life? Given the rather negative-sounding elements of this life, why should we be like the curious cat rather than the incurious dog?
6. Notice that the title runs into the first line. How does Reid's use of punctuation (to stop us) or no punctuation (to keep us reading) parallel what he is observing about curiosity or the lack of it?
7. What is the term for poems that have the pattern—or lack of pattern—that you find in "Curiosity"?

Drawing Inferences about Theme

1. When the poet writes that "dying is what, to live, each has to do," what does he mean? The statement seems contradictory. What is the term for this strategy for gaining emphasis? For the statement to make sense, how do you have to take the word *dying?*
2. State the poem's meaning or theme. What does Reid want us to understand about the role of curiosity in life?

Thinking Critically

1. Do you find the use of cats and dogs an effective one? For the most part, do the personalities of cats and dogs seem to fit the distinction Reid wants to make?
2. Is curiosity an important trait? Why or why not? What are its virtues? What are its dangers?
3. Are most children more like cats or dogs? If they are like cats, then why are some adults so incurious? If they are like dogs, what are some ways they can be encouraged to develop curiosity?

STUDENT ESSAY—DEFINITION

PARAGON OR PARASITE?
Laura Mullins

Do you recognize this creature? He is low maintenance and often unnoticeable, a favorite companion of many. Requiring no special attention, he grows from the soil of pride and rejection, feeding regularly on a diet of ignorance and insecurity, scavenging for hurt feelings and defensiveness, gobbling up dainty morsels of lust and scandal. Like a cult leader clothed in a gay veneer, disguising himself as blameless, he wields power. Bewitching unsuspecting but devoted groupies, distracting them from honest self-examination, deceiving them into believing illusions of grandeur or, on the other extreme, unredeemable worthlessness, he breeds jealousy, hate, and fear; thus, he thrives. He is Gossip.

Attention-getting introduction

Clever extended metaphor

Subject introduced

One of my dearest friends is a gossip. She is an educated, honorable, compassionate, loving woman whose character and judgment I deeply admire and respect. After sacrificially raising six children, she went on to study medicine and become a doctor who graciously volunteers her expertise. How, you may be wondering, could a gossip deserve such praise? Then you do not understand the word. My friend is my daughter's godmother; she is my gossip, or *god-sib*, meaning sister-in-god. Derived from Middle English words *god,* meaning spiritual, and *sip/sib/syp,* meaning kinsman, this term was used to refer to a familiar acquaintance, close family friend, or intimate relation, according to the *Oxford English Dictionary.* As a male, he would have joined in fellowship and celebration with the father of the newly born; if a female, she would have been a trusted friend, a birth-attendant or midwife to the mother of the baby. The term grew to include references to the type of easy, unrestrained conversation shared by these folks.

Etymology of gossip and early meanings

As is often the case with words, the term's meaning has certainly evolved, maybe eroded from its original idea. Is it harmless, idle chat, innocuous sharing of others' personal news, or back-biting, rumor-spreading, and manipulation? Is it a beneficial activity worthy of pursuit, or a deplorable danger to be avoided?

Current meanings

In her article "Evolution, Alienation, and Gossip" (for the Social Issues Research Centre in Oxford, England), Kate Fox writes that "gossip is not a trivial pastime; it is essential to human

Good use of sources to develop definition

social, psychological, and even physical well-being." Many echo her view that gossip is a worthy activity, claiming that engaging in gossip produces endorphins, reduces stress, and aids in building intimate relationships. Gossip, seen at worst as a harmless outlet, is encouraged in the workplace. Since much of its content is not inherently critical or malicious, it is viewed as a positive activity. However, this view does nothing to encourage those speaking or listening to evaluate or examine motive or purpose; instead, it seems to reflect the "anything goes" thinking so prevalent today.

Conversely, writer and high school English and geography teacher Lennox V. Farrell of Toronto, Canada, in his essay titled "Gossip: An Urban Form of Sorcery," presents gossip as a kind of "witchcraft . . . based on using unsubstantiated accusations by those who make them, and on uncritically accepting these by those enticed into listening." Farrell uses gossip in its more widely understood definition, encompassing the breaking of confidences, inappropriate sharing of indiscretions, destructive tale-bearing, and malicious slander.

What, then, is gossip? We no longer use the term to refer to our children's

godparents. Its current definition usually comes with derogatory implications.
Imagine a backyard garden: you see a
variety of greenery, recognizing at a
glance that you are looking at different kinds of plants. Taking a closer
look, you will find the gossip vine;
inconspicuously blending in, it doesn't
appear threatening, but ultimately it
destroys. If left in the garden it will
choke and then suck out life from its
host. Zoom in on the garden scene and
follow the creeping vine up trees and
along a fence where two neighbors visit.
You can overhear one woman saying to the
other, "I know I should be the last to
tell you, but your husband is being
unfaithful to me." (Caption from a cartoon by Alan De la Nougerede!)

*Good use of
metaphor to
depict gossip as
negative*

The current popular movement to legit-
imize gossip seems an excuse to condone
the human tendency to puff-up oneself.
Compared in legal terms, gossip is to
conversation as hearsay is to eyewitness
testimony; it's not credible. Various
religious doctrines abhor the idea and
practice of gossip. An old Turkish
proverb says, "He who gossips to you will
gossip of you." From the Babylonian Tal-
mud, which calls gossip the three-pronged

*Conclusion
states view that
gossip is to be
avoided—the
writer's thesis.*

```
tongue, destroying the one talking, the
one listening, and the one being spoken
of, to the Upanishads, to the Bible, we
can conclude that no good fruit is born
from gossip. Let's tend our gardens and
check our motives when we have the urge
to gossip. Surely we can find more noble
pursuits than the self-aggrandisement we
have come to know as gossip.
```

MAKING CONNECTIONS

1. John Ciardi says that happiness is difficult to define—and to obtain. Is happiness possible without the ability to discriminate, as Robert Miller defines the term? How would each author answer this question? How would you answer the question?
2. Is happiness possible without curiosity? How would John Ciardi and Alastair Reid each answer the question? How would Liane Ellison Norman (see Chapter 4) answer the question? How would you answer the question?
3. K. C. Cole asserts that we are unwilling to work hard enough to keep disorder from displacing order. John Ciardi stresses that true happiness takes effort. Andrew Vachss suggests that we shy away from distinguishing between sick and evil because it is a difficult philosophical problem. Are we getting tired? Or lazy? As a society? Individually? Examine the three essays and then prepare your answer to these questions.
4. Robert Miller deplores our feeling that we can no longer use the word *discrimination* in its important meaning of discerning differences. Andrew Vachss is bothered by our unwillingness to call specific actions evil, to use such a strong word. Roger Rosenblatt wonders if the word *obsession* should always be seen as having a negative connotation. Have we become hemmed in by political correctness or the

attitudes of the social sciences such that we are unwilling
to use precise language? Has this become an age of indirec-
tion and "softness" in language use? If so, is this a good or
a bad situation? Think about how the authors would answer
these questions, and think about how you would answer
them.

5. Select one of the words defined in this chapter to study in
the *Oxford English Dictionary,* either in its print version in
your library or in its e-version if your library offers it among
its online references sources. Prepare a one-two page discussion of the word based on your study in the *OED.*

TOPICS AND GUIDELINES FOR WRITING

---

1. In this chapter you can find definitions of *friendship, happiness, entropy, intensity,* even *curiosity.* If you have disagreed
at least in part with one of the definitions presented here,
write your own definition of that term. Include in your
essay at least one reference to the writer with whom you
disagree, discussing his or her views and contrasting them
with your own. Make your purpose your own definition,
but use the ideas with which you disagree as one way to
develop your definition.

2. In an essay develop a definition of one of the terms below.
Use at least three of the specific strategies for developing
a definition discussed in the chapter's introduction. Try to
make one of those strategies the metaphor, including several in your essay. And use contrast as one of your strategies, contrasting the word you select with its contrasting
term in parentheses.

patriotism (chauvinism)	wisdom (knowledge)
courtesy (manners)	ghetto (neighborhood)
liberty (freedom)	hero (star)
community (subdivision)	gossip (conversation)

3. In "Curiosity," Alastair Reid plays paradoxically with the
terms *living* and *dying.* In an essay, define either *work* or
play, developing your definition in part by reflecting on
the word's relationship with its apparent opposite. In what

situations, under what conditions, can play become work? Or, in what situations, under what conditions, can work be play? We use these terms frequently to suggest opposite activities. In your definition of one of these words, show that there are some contexts in which its "opposite" is not really opposite.

4. Define a term that is currently used to label people with particular traits and values. Possibilities include: *nerd, yuppie, freak, jock, redneck, bimbo, wimp*. Reflect, before selecting this topic, on why you want to explain the meaning of the word you have chosen. One purpose might be to explain the term to someone from a different culture. Another purpose might be to defend people who are labeled negatively by one of these terms; that is, your goal is to show why the term should not have a negative connotation.

5. Select a word that you believe is currently misused. The word can be misused because it has taken on a negative (or positive) connotation that it did not once have, or because it has changed meaning and has lost something in the change. A few suggestions include *awful, fabulous, exceptional* (in education), *awesome, propaganda*. Be sure to begin with a clear understanding of the word's definitions provided by a good dictionary. You might also want to consult a dictionary of word origins.

9

Using Causal Analysis

Examining Family and Community Issues

You may know the old—and very bad—joke that asks why the chicken crossed the road. When we give up and ask for the answer, the jokester, laughing merrily at trapping us in such silliness, says: "to get to the other side." The joke isn't in the answer but on us because we expect a more profound explanation of cause. Human beings characteristically ask why things happen. The four-year-old who asks her mother why there are stars in the sky may grow up to be the astrophysicist who continues, in a more sophisticated manner, to probe the same question.

When to Use Causal Analysis

We want to know what produced past events (why did the Roman Empire collapse?), what is causing current situations (why is there an increased fear of violence in our society?), and what will happen if we act in a particular way (will inflation be avoided if the Federal Reserve lowers interest rates?). Whether the questions are about the past, the present, or the future, we are seeking a causal explanation. We usually make a distinction between a study of *causes* (what produced A) and a study of *effects* (what has happened or will happen as a result of B), but actually the distinction is more one of wording than of approach or way of thinking. If, for example, we think that inflation can be avoided (effect) by raising interest rates (cause), we are saying that low interest rates can cause inflation. So, when we want to know why, we need to explore cause, whether we approach the "connection" from the causal end or the effects end.

How to Use Causal Analysis

In the study of causes and effects, we need to stress the key word *analysis*. In Chapter 6, you learned that process analysis answers the question *how* something is done or was accomplished by determining the steps, in proper time sequence, to completing the activity. When we examine cause, we also need to analyze the situation, both present and past, to make certain that we recognize all contributing elements and that we sort out the more important from the less important. Fortunately, there are some terms for distinguishing among different kinds of causes that can help us examine cause in a thoughtful and thorough way.

Thinking about Cause

First, events do not occur in a vacuum. There are *conditions* that surround an event, making the finding of only one cause unlikely. Suppose you have decided to become a veterinarian, and you want to understand why you have made that career choice. The conditions of your family life and upbringing probably affected your decision. You grew up with a dog you loved and cared for; your parents tolerated all the frogs and wounded birds you brought home and taught you to value living things. Second, there are more specific *influences* that contribute to an event. Perhaps the family vet let you help when your dog needed shots or bandaging and by example influenced your career plans.

In addition to conditions and influences, there are the more *immediate causes* that shape an event, leading up to the *precipitating cause,* the triggering event. In your choice to become a veterinarian, these events may include your good grades in and enjoyment of high school chemistry and biology, a recognition that you like working with your hands and that you want to be your own boss, and two summers of working at an animal hospital. In short, going off to college and having to declare a major did not cause you to choose veterinary medicine. The search for cause is a search for deeper, more fundamental answers than the college's requirement that you state a major field of study.

In our need, as humans, to have explanations for what happens, we can sometimes fool ourselves into thinking that we understand events, and we can be comforted by "finding" simple explanations for complex situations. But the desire to settle for simplistic explanations or for explanations for which there is no clear evidence of a causal connection must be resisted, both in thinking about life and in writing about cause. Two all-too-common ways of generating illogical causal explanations are to mistake a *time relationship* for a causal one and a *correlation* between two events for a causal relationship. For example, you went out to dinner last night and awoke with an upset stomach this morning. Can you conclude that something you ate last night caused the stomach upset? Certainly not without further evidence. Perhaps you already had a stomach virus before you went to dinner. To understand the difference between a correlation and a cause, consider the relationship between IQ scores and college grades. Students who have high IQ scores generally get good grades in college, but scores on an IQ test do not *cause* the good grades. (Whatever skills or knowledge produce high IQ scores are certainly one cause, though, of good grades. On the other hand, IQ tests do not measure motivation or good study habits.)

Evidence and Thesis

Writing a causal analysis challenges both thinking and writing skills. Remember that readers will evaluate your logic and evidence. After all, your purpose in writing is to show readers that your analysis of cause is sound and therefore useful to them. So, resist simplistic thinking and consider the kinds of evidence needed to illustrate and support your analysis. In addition to drawing on your own experience, you may need, depending on your topic, to obtain some evidence from reading. You will discover, for example, that many writers in this chapter include statistical evidence drawn from their reading. If you plan to emphasize one cause of a situation because you believe others have overlooked that cause or have failed to understand its importance, be certain that readers understand this limited and focused purpose.

Organization

Several organizational strategies are appropriate, depending on your topic and purpose. If you are examining a series of causes, beginning with background conditions and early influences, then your basic plan will be time sequence. Use appropriate terms for types of causes you discuss and transitional words to guide your reader through the sequence of events. If you want to examine an overlooked cause, you could begin by briefly discussing the causes that are usually stressed and then go on to introduce and explain the cause you want to emphasize. If your goal is to demonstrate that the same cause has operated in several different circumstances, then you need to show how that cause is the single common denominator in each circumstance. Whatever your overall strategy, remember to illustrate your points and to explain how your examples serve as evidence in support of your thesis.

WRITING FOCUS:
REFERENCES TO AUTHORS, WORKS, AND THE WORDS OF OTHERS

Readers expect writers to follow the standard conventions for referring to authors and titles of works and for indicating when words belong to someone other than the writer. For you to be an effective writer, you need to follow these conventions both in the academic community and the workplace.

References to People
- In the first reference give the person's full name: *Amitai Etzioni, Linda J. Waite*. In all other references to that person, use the last name (surname): *Etzioni, Waite*.
- Do not use Mr., Mrs., or Ms. Special titles such as President, Chief Justice, or Doctor may be used in the first reference with the person's full name.
- Never refer to an author by his or her first name. Write *Waite*, not *Linda*.

References to Titles

- Always write titles as titles. This involves proper capitalizing of words in the title and then using either quotation marks or underlining (italics in print) depending on the work.
- Capitalizing: The first and last words are capitalized. The first word of a subtitle is capitalized. All other words are capitalized except:
  Articles (*a, an, the*)
  Coordinating conjunctions (*and, or, but, for, nor, yet, so*)
  Prepositions of five or fewer letters. Longer prepositions are capitalized.

- Titles requiring quotation marks: All works published within other works, including essays (*"Duty: The Forgotten Virtue"*), short stories, poems (*"Dream Deferred"*), chapter titles, lectures.
- Titles requiring underlining (italics in print): Works that are separate publications, including newspapers (<u>New York Times</u>), magazines (<u>Newsweek</u>), novels (<u>The Old Man and the Sea</u>), textbooks (<u>Patterns of Reflection</u>), films (<u>The Wizard of Oz</u>).

Quotations

- Put *all* words taken from a source within quotation marks. Never change any of the words within the quotation marks.
- Do not leave out any words in the quoted passage unless you use ellipses (three spaced dots: . . .). If you have to add words to make the passage clear, place them in square brackets ([]), not parentheses.
- Always provide the source of the quoted passage, preferably *before* the quoted passage.
- When working a quoted passage into your sentence, place commas and periods within the final quotation mark—even when you quote only one word: Etzioni asserts that one reason for our loss of a sense of duty is too much "me-ism."
- Place semicolons and colons outside the end quotation mark. Do not quote punctuation at the end of

a quoted passage; use only the punctuation you need for your sentence.

- Use single quotation marks (the apostrophe key on your keyboard) to identify quoted material within quoted material: Barnett and Rivers point out that "'family-friendly' corporate policies reduce burnout." *Note: There is no comma before the beginning of the quoted passage; it is smoothly worked into the sentence.*

- When a quoted passage runs to more than 3 lines of type, use a block style: indent quoted lines 10 spaces from the left margin; go to the right margin; continue to double space throughout the block quotation; do not use quotation marks—the indenting indicates a direct quotation.

- Remember your reader! Keep direct quoting to a minimum; keep quoted passages brief. You probably would not use a block quotation in a short essay, although you might use one in a research essay.

Getting Started: Reflections on Why You Are in College

Why are you in college? List the main reasons for your decision to attend college. Then reflect on some of the sources of those reasons. What people (parents, teachers, friends) and what experiences helped shape your decision? What, in other words, were the conditions and influences, as well as the more immediate causes, that led to your decision? Write in your journal on these questions or prepare responses for class discussion.

Duty: The Forgotten Virtue

AMITAI ETZIONI

Amitai Etzioni (b. 1929) is an internationally renowned sociologist. Born in Germany, he earned his Ph.D. at the University of California. He has been University Professor at George Washington University and director of the Center for Policy Research.

He is the author of many books, including *An Immodest Agenda: Rebuilding America Before the Twenty-First Century* (1983) in which he calls for an increased sense of community and decreased focus on the self. Similar ideas are expressed in his article on duty, published in 1986 in the *Washington Post.*

Questions to Guide Your Reading

1. What is Etzioni's attitude toward duty? What is his thesis?
2. What are the current ideas and values used to justify a lack of duty to society?

1   Air accidents can be viewed as random tests of the extent to which those responsible for keeping airplanes flying are doing their duty.

2   For example, the crew of an American Airlines plane recently tried to land it three times, in low visibility, with 124 people aboard, in Harlingen, Texas. On the third pass, they hit two sets of runway approach lights four feet off the ground. The collision was severe enough to deploy some oxygen masks in the passenger cabin and knock ceiling panels loose. Yet after the plane regained altitude and landed safely in San Antonio, other crews took it to Dallas-Fort Worth and then on to Denver where damage to the exterior of the plane was discovered and the plane taken out of service.

3   One may view this as nothing more than an isolated incidence of questionable judgment, but there is some evidence to suggest that Americans—always ambivalent about their duties—have been particularly loath to live up to their responsibilities in recent years.

4   A survey of young Americans found that most rank trial by jury high among their rights. However, few indicated a willingness to serve on a jury.

5   Patriotism is reported to be in vogue. However, Americans would rather pay volunteers to serve in the military than support a draft in which all would share the burden.

6   A survey conducted by H & R Block shows that Americans favor a flat tax. However, that support is offered on one troubling condition: that the respondent's favorite loophole not be closed.

7   These observations led me to ask my class at The George Washington University what the term "duty" brought to their

mind. They responded uneasily. They felt that people ought to be free to do what *they* believe in. Duties are imposed, alien, authoritarian—what the principal, the curriculum committee, the society, "they," want you to do.

I responded with a little impassioned address about the common good: If everyone goes to the forest and fells a tree, soon the hillsides will be denuded. We cannot rely on the fact that once we are out of trees, people will recognize the need to plant new ones; it takes years for trees to grow. Hence, we must, I explained, expect members of society to plant some trees now, invest in the infrastructure, trim the deficit, etc., so that the next generation will have a forest, a thriving economy, a future. We must balance the desire to focus on one's own interests with some obligation to the commons. True, duties are not fun, *otherwise there would be no need to impose them.* But a civil society cannot do without them.

Well, the students reflected aloud; they understood where I was coming from. Okay, they said, maybe there was room for duty, but—compliance ought to be voluntary, they insisted. I felt I had failed them; I never got the point across.

Americans have never been very duty-bound. The country was created by people who escaped duties imposed by authoritarian monarchies and dogmatic churches. And the ethos of the pioneers was of striking out on one's own—even if, as a matter of fact, settlement was carried out by groups very much dependent on one another.

But over the last decades the need for duty to the commons has grown as the supply diminished. Consider:

Demand Side. Practically no one expects that America can do without *some* defense. The problem is that defense requires a *continuous* willingness to dedicate resources to national security that might otherwise be used to enhance one's standard of living. As obvious as this may seem, the fact is that Americans have found it very difficult to sustain such a commitment. The defense budget typically reflects cycles of neglect followed by hysterical reactions to some real or alleged crisis. There is no well-grounded commitment.

On the domestic front, voluntarism is now supposed to replace many government services. Anyone who points to the limits of such an approach is immediately suspect of being an old-time liberal, a champion of big government. But this simple-minded dichotomy—do things privately *or* via the government—conceals the real issue: What duties to the commons *should* the government impose?

14   Most would include, aside from defense, support for basic and medical research, some environmental protection, public education and services for the deserving poor. But today these obligations to the commons are left without a moral underpinning. Most do not subscribe to a social philosophy which endorses these commitments. Instead, we celebrate *laissez faire* and a generation rich in Me-ism.

15   *Supply Side.* Americans are hardly enamored with the notion that they have duties to the social weal. They find escape in an odd concoction: a misapplication of Adam Smith mixed with surging libertarianism, pop psychology and a dash of liberation theory.

16   Americans have been brought up on a highly simplified notion of the invisible hand: Everybody goes out and tries to "maximize" himself—and the economy thrives for all. There is no need to curb self-interest, even greed; it is the propellant that fires up economies.

17   Now the reach of the invisible hand has been extended to wholly new spheres. Antismoking campaigns, pro-seatbelt moves, Social Security, environmental protection and employee safety are said to work best without "coercion"—if people are left to their own devices.

18   In this rejection of any sense that we have duties to each other, we gloss over the consequences to innocent bystanders of such a free-for-all, it's-up-to-you-Jack attitude. These range from the effect on children of those who choose not to buy insurance, to the neglect of "public goods"—goods we all need but no one is individually entrusted with procuring (e.g., highways).

19   Pop psychology is still with us. It argues that everyone ought to focus on his or her own growth. Society and its duties are viewed as standing in the way of self-fulfillment.

20   Pollster Daniel Yankelovich estimated that in the late 1970s, 17 percent of Americans were deeply committed to a philosophy of self-fulfillment and another 63 percent subscribed to it

in varying degrees. These people said they "spend a great deal of time thinking about myself" and "satisfactions come from shaping oneself rather than from home and family life." They had a strong need for excitement and sensation and tended to feel free to look, live and act however they wanted, even if this violated others' concepts of what is proper.

The significance of this is that the escape from duty reaches 21 beyond neglect of the community's needs to the neglect of one's immediate family.

Last but not least are the interest groups which elevate Me- 22 ism to a group level. True, lobbies have been around since the founding of the Republic. But in recent years their power has increased sharply. And the consequence is that service to each interest group is easily put above a concern for the general welfare.

How do we redress the balance between the "I" and the 23 "We"—so that we enhance the sense of duty?

There obviously are no simple solutions, but schools could 24 help. They could change their civics courses from teaching that the government has three branches and the Supreme Court nine members (and so on), and instead promote civility. However, since most schools are overworked and underfunded, they are unlikely to do much.

More may be achieved if the issue is put on the agenda of the 25 nationwide town-hall meetings we are, in effect, constantly conducting. The subjects vary, from civil rights to environmental protection to deficit reduction. However, the process is the same: triggered by a leading book (such as *Silent Spring*), a series of reports in leading newspapers or on television (e.g., on Vietnam), or by commissions (on education), we turn our collective attention to an issue. We debate it at length.

At first it seems nothing happens, but gradually a new con- 26 sensus arises that affects people's behavior. We agree to pollute less or drink less; we exercise more; we become more sensitive to the rights of minorities or women.

The issue of our social obligations as Americans—our 27 duties—is overdue for such a treatment. Meanwhile, we each ought to examine ourselves: What have you done for your community lately?

Expanding Vocabulary

Etzioni's essay provides a good opportunity for expanding your knowledge of terms and concepts used in discussing social and political issues.

1. In a sentence or two, explain each of the following terms or references. The number in parentheses is the number of the paragraph in which the word appears.

loophole (6)	libertarianism (15)
infrastructure (8)	pop psychology (15)
deficit (8)	liberation theory (15)
ethos (10)	invisible hand (16)
laissez faire (14)	civics (24)
Me-ism (14)	civility (24)
Adam Smith (15)	*Silent Spring* (25)

2. Be able to define each of the following words. Then, select five words and use each one in a separate sentence.

deploy (2)	alleged (12)
ambivalent (3)	dichotomy (13)
loath (3)	enamored (15)
denuded (8)	concoction (15)
dogmatic (10)	consensus (26)

Understanding Content

1. When Etzioni asked his students about the concept of duty, what was their response? Where does duty come from? Should it be imposed or voluntary?
2. In the author's view, what is the dominant value affecting the behavior of Americans?
3. What three solutions does Etzioni offer to "enhance the sense of duty"?

Drawing Inferences about Thesis and Purpose

1. The author uses two economic terms—*Demand Side* and *Supply Side*—as subheadings. How is he using these terms in this essay? What is being "demanded"? What is being "supplied"?
2. How did Etzioni feel about his students' views on duty?
3. Etzioni offers three solutions. How have his own actions shown his attempt to act on each one of them—to take his own advice?

Analyzing Strategies and Style

1. Look at the first six paragraphs. What do they provide?
2. One could say that paragraphs 7 through 9 are also part of the introduction. What does the author present in these paragraphs?
3. What is effective about Etzioni's use of specifics and his own students as an introductory strategy? Why might long introductions filled with specifics be effective openings for controversial topics?
4. The author uses a popular three-part organization for discussing a problem: (1) statement of the problem, (2) causes of the problem, (3) solutions to the problem. Analyze the essay according to this pattern, indicating the paragraphs that make up each of the three parts.
5. Now that you have marked the essay's parts, can you find sentences that signal the beginning of the second and third parts? Which sentence sums up the point of the first part?

Thinking Critically

1. If you had been in Etzioni's class, would you have responded much as his students did? If not, how would your response have differed?
2. Do you agree that most Americans are motived by the desire for self-fulfillment? Why or why not? What evidence can you offer to support your view?
3. Etzioni suggests that special-interest groups are really a form of "Me-ism." Is this a helpful way to understand these groups?
4. Is Etzioni suggesting that participating in groups is only a self-centered act, not a sign of commitment to others? What are the characteristics of the politically active groups Etzioni has in mind?
5. What is your answer to the essay's final question? Are you satisfied with your answer? Why or why not?

Family Values Go to Work

ROSALIND C. BARNETT AND CARYL RIVERS

Rosalind C. Barnett (b. 1937) is senior scientist in the women's studies program at Brandeis University and senior scholar at the Murray Research Center at Radcliffe College. A graduate of Trinity College and Columbia University, Caryl Rivers (b. 1937) is a professor of journalism at Boston University and a freelance writer. Both are authors of several books, and together they have written *Beyond Sugar and Spice* (1981) and *She Works He Works* (1996), the latter a study of how two-income families are better off. The following report of research on families, jobs, and stress—and proposals for ways to reduce the stress—appeared in the *Washington Post* on May 10, 1999.

Questions to Guide Your Reading
  1. What is now the norm for families and the workplace?
  2. What do the authors propose to reduce stress for working families?

---

1   Nearly 80 percent of couples are now working couples. Fifty-five percent of mothers of toddlers are working, and some 70 percent of all women are in the work force. Men's incomes have been flat or declining for the past decade. We are seeing the end of the era of the male breadwinner. The two-income family is now the norm, and all indications are that it will continue to be. Women now outnumber men in most college classrooms, as they prepare for a lifelong commitment to the work force.

2   Jobs that offer flexibility so that workers can meet their family needs are the top priority for men and women. Our major study of full-time-employed, two-earner couples, funded by the National Institute of Mental Health, found that the healthiest couples were those with reliable child care and flexibility in their jobs to meet family needs—such as a child's illness or an important school event. The lack of flexibility to deal with family issues was linked to stress, depression and anxiety—for men and women. And more than half the men in major surveys say they would forgo raises and advancement for more time to spend with their families.

3   In light of these facts, we would propose a "family impact initiative" as a tool to help companies deal with the family issues confronted by their workers. The concept of the Environmental Impact Statement grew out of a national concern for the health of the planet, as pollution and other hazards took their toll. We believe the time has come for an initiative to guard the health of America's working families.

4   A family impact initiative would not be a program mandated by government but one that companies could adapt in their own self-interest. Flexibility is good for the bottom line.

Research shows that "family-friendly" corporate policies reduce burnout, absenteeism and turnover while increasing employee loyalty. Employees—men as well as women—desperately want more flexibility to deal with family and community issues. A Du Pont survey showed that 56 percent of male employees favored flexible schedules that allow more family time.

These employee concerns are backed up by our study, which found that a major source of illness-producing stress for couples was not having the flexibility to deal with family issues. This stress was shared by men and women alike; there were no gender differences. Men in our study spent as many hours parenting as did their wives when the children reached school age, and men were as stressed by family problems as were women.

With a family impact initiative in place, managers would consider the effects of decisions and policies on the families of employees. Travel policies, meeting plans, relocation plans, job assignments, work hours and leave and vacation policies would be viewed in the light of family impact.

Of course, not all decisions would be made on this lone criterion, but it would be part of the mix—and a big step forward in protecting employee health and productivity. This initiative wouldn't mean that companies would have to be turned upside down. In many cases, small changes can have major effects. Ending "meeting macho" policies that make employees get to the office at 7 a.m., when parents are trying to get kids off to school, can be a big help. Giving employees enough lead time to blend travel schedules with family plans can strengthen father-child and mother-child bonds. Adequate vacation time, encouragement of parental leave and a sick-leave policy that includes fatherhood in the equation can ease stress. Maximum possible use of teleconferencing, faxes and other technology can avoid keeping employees constantly on the road. Dismantling a corporate culture that decrees that the best employee is the one who is first in the door in the morning and the last to leave at night can not only ease stress but help the bottom line. Research shows that employees with more flexibility are more productive than those who lack it.

In an era of downsizing, fewer employees are having to do more work, and our study found that in the new leaner workplace, employees are at increased health risk because of growing job demands over time. Short-term savings gained by downsizing can turn into long-term costs. Chronic exposure of workers to increasing job demands may rack up huge costs in turnover, absenteeism and workers' compensation claims. And our study showed that when one member of the dual-earner couple was experiencing high stress, so was his or her spouse.

9   Trying to anticipate such problems makes good sense for everyone. A family impact initiative could be such a forward-looking tool. It would move family concerns from the peripheral vision of business—where they too often languish—nearer to center stage. In this scenario everybody wins—workers and managers and the ever-important bottom line is enhanced in the process.

Expanding Vocabulary

Examine the following words in their contexts in the essay and then write a brief definition or synonym for each one. Do not use a dictionary; try to guess the word's meaning from its context. The number in parentheses is the number of the paragraph in which the word appears.

initiative (3)   peripheral (9)
burnout (4)   languish (9)
criterion (7)   scenario (9)
dismantling (7)   enhanced (9)
downsizing (8)

Understanding Content

1. According to the authors' study, what produced the healthiest working couples?
2. What was the effect of lack of flexibility?
3. What are the effects of flexibility for employers?
4. How would companies be affected by adopting the authors' proposal? What are some changes that can be made? How will changes affect workers and the company?
5. What happens when one worker in a two-worker family feels stress over work and family conflicts?

Drawing Inferences about Thesis and Purpose

1. What is the essay's thesis?
2. What is the authors' purpose in writing? What do they want to accomplish?

Analyzing Strategies and Style

1. The authors open with several statistics. How does this make an effective opening?
2. The writing in this article seems almost "without style"—that is, simple, direct, uncomplicated. How can such writing be an effective strategy? (What have the authors avoided with their choice of style?)

Thinking Critically

1. Which statistic in the essay is the most surprising to you? Why?
2. Are you currently one member of a two-worker family? If so, do you get stressed out trying to meet all commitments? Alternatively, do you anticipate becoming part of a two-worker family? If so, how do you expect to handle the situation?
3. Do you think the authors have a good idea for making the workplace more friendly to families? Why or why not?
4. If you do not like their proposals, what would you propose?

When Parents Are Toxic to Children

KEITH ABLOW

Keith Ablow (b. 1961), a graduate of the Johns Hopkins University Medical School, is a writer and psychiatrist who practices in the Boston area. He has published two nonfiction books, *To Wrestle with Demons* (1995) and *With Mercy* (1996), and several novels. In the following article, which appeared in the *Washington Post*'s Health Section in May 1996, Ablow examines the effects of bad parenting and argues for change.

Questions to Guide Your Reading

1. Reflect on Ablow's title. What is the key word in his title? What point is he making?
2. What are the long-term effects of abusing children?

I sat with a 15-year-old girl in the interview room where I 1
meet psychiatric inpatients for the first time, watching her as she
gazed through her long black hair at her forearm. She gingerly

traced the superficial cuts she had made with a razor the night before when she had flirted with suicide.

2 Her chart indicated that since the age of 11 she had suffered repeated bouts of severe depression that antidepressant medication didn't touch. At times she was intermittently paranoid, believing that someone was out to steal her mind or even to take her life.

3 "I'm not going back there," she finally said, looking up at me. "I'll kill myself, if they make me live with my parents."

4 "What happens there?" I asked.

5 "Constant fighting. Screaming. Swearing. Hitting. It's been like that my whole life."

6 "Do they hit you?" I asked.

7 "They used to. A lot. They don't anymore. They hit my brothers, though. And they keep telling me I'm ugly . . . and stupid. Worthless." She looked at her arm. "I don't care where I get sent. I'll go anywhere but home."

8 I was certain she would return home. Social service agencies had been involved in her case for years. No doubt there would be another family meeting during her hospitalization, perhaps more frequent home visits by a social worker afterward. But the mental health system's prejudice in favor of keeping families intact, as well as a perennial shortage of acceptable foster parents, would likely keep my young patient with her own parents and in peril.

9 I have repeatedly treated teenagers like this girl whose biological parents have inflicted irreparable psychological harm on their children. Some are the victims of sexual abuse, others of pervasive neglect. They end up in my office with symptoms that include panic attacks, severe depression and psychosis. Many are addicted to drugs before they even begin high school. Some see suicide as a reasonable way to end their pain. I prescribe them a variety of antidepressant, anti-anxiety and sometimes antipsychotic medications, hoping that their symptoms of mental illness are temporary, but worried that the damage they have suffered may be permanent. Worst of all I know that these are preventable illnesses.

10 Nor does the damage end with them. These teenage patients are tomorrow's parents. And experience has repeatedly demonstrated that many of them are likely to reenact the same destruc-

tive scenarios with their own children. Most people who harbor rage from their childhood don't expect it to surface after they become parents. Many fail to see the traumas they survived as sources of great risk for a new generation.

If we are to make a serious attempt to prevent some forms 11 of serious mental illness, parenting must no longer be seen as an inalienable right, but as a privilege that can—and will—be revoked for abuse or neglect. Society must be much less tolerant of harm to children and also must be willing to devote considerably more resources to providing alternative living situations for children and adolescents who are in danger.

Only in the most egregious cases of physical violence or emo- 12 tional neglect have I seen the state terminate parental rights. It seems that damage to children must reach the level of near catastrophe to justify cleaving a parent-child relationship that has been anything but loving.

Parents need to get a new message. If you do a lousy job par- 13 enting, you lose your job. In cases involving child custody, blood ties must be given less weight not only by the mental health system, but by the government and the court system. At the federal, state and local levels, keeping children with their parents can no longer be considered more important than keeping them safe.

Another young woman I treated had been repeatedly beaten 14 by her older brothers for years. As a girl she had been raped by her mother's boyfriend. Her moods had become erratic, and her temper unpredictable. She had turned to marijuana for relief and had been expelled from school for fighting. Yet she continued to live at home, with the blessing of the state Department of Social Services.

"She's got to get off these damn drugs," her mother com- 15 plained in my office. "That [stuff] has got her all screwed . . . "

"I'm not gonna listen to you," the girl interrupted. She turned 16 to me. "This is the woman who let me get beat on for about 10 years and let her boyfriend sneak into my bedroom, without her saying two words. How am I supposed to live as a normal human being with a mother like her?"

Privately I agreed with her. I felt hopeless about the situa- 17 tion myself. I could see that this girl was trapped in a family that was eroding her emotional resiliency, leaving her increasingly vulnerable to severe psychiatric illness. And society had no plan to rescue her from this situation. In fact, it tacitly endorsed it.

18   One of the difficulties of working as a therapist with adolescents is that they often clearly perceive the psychological dangers confronting them, but are powerless to deal with them. It's no wonder then that such experiences lay the groundwork for panic attacks, post-traumatic stress disorder, depression and paranoia that seem to come "out of the blue" later in life. The coping mechanisms of some of the teenagers I treat have short-circuited already. These patients "dissociate": They unpredictably enter altered states of consciousness in which they lose touch with reality.

19   One 17-year-old whom I treated for depression asked me plainly: "If you were me, what would you do to make sure your parents didn't get you even sicker during the next year? I mean, if I can get to 18, I can leave home, maybe join the Army or something, and they won't be able to do anything about it."

20   I told him that he needed to be less confrontational in the face of his parents' unreasonable demands for strict obedience, if only to conserve his emotional energy, not to mention avoid his father's belt. "Prisoners of war don't get in beefs every day with their captors," I told him. "They lay low until they can escape."

21   Like most of the abusive parents I have met, this young man's father, for example, made it clear to me that he too had faced traumas as a young person, including horrific beatings. He tried to do his best for his son despite severe depression and alcoholism that limited his ability to function. Doing his best, however, was not nearly good enough.

22   This is why a social policy that would raise expectations for healthy parenting and more frequently and quickly impose the loss of parental rights should include a vigorous attempt to educate parents on how to avoid harming their children. The loss of parental rights is a tragedy we should attempt to avoid.

23   Another key requirement is to recruit good foster families. Too often such families have not proven to be much better for kids than the homes they have left; sometimes they are even worse. It makes no sense to take the admittedly drastic step of removing children from bad biological parents only to place them with bad foster parents.

One 19-year-old woman I met recently had spent a decade   24
living in a foster family. She had been beaten and neglected for
the years prior to her placement and, even with obviously concerned and empathic foster parents, had required years of psy-
chotherapy to cope with her traumatic past.

With the support of a new family, however, she had achieved   25
in school, shunned drugs and made close and lasting friendships. She hoped to save money to attend college. While she
considered leaving her biological parents as one of the major
stresses in her life, she made it clear that she would have been
much worse staying with them. "I'm one of the lucky ones," she
said. "I got out."

The tragedy is that too few children do.   26

Expanding Vocabulary

Match each word in column A with its definition in column B. When
in doubt, first find the word in the essay and look for context clues
to aid your understanding of the word's meaning. Then, if necessary,
use your dictionary to complete the matching exercise. The number in
parentheses is the number of the paragraph in which the word
appears.

Column A	Column B
bouts (2)	dividing, separating
paranoid (2)	impossible to repair or fix
perennial (8)	quietly, implied rather than stated
irreparable (9)	outlines of possible future events
psychosis (9)	serious emotional shocks that may
scenarios (10)	result in lasting damage
traumas (10)	notably offensive
inalienable (11)	contests, matches
egregious (12)	destroying, eating away at
cleaving (12)	one with a disorder characterized by
eroding (17)	delusions of persecution or grandeur
resiliency (17)	ability to recover from serious problems
tacitly (17)	lasting through many years
	what cannot be transferred to another
	mental disorder marked by disconnection
	with reality and social dysfunction

Understanding Content

1. For what two reasons are abused children kept with the parents who are abusing them?
2. What problems do the abused teenagers experience; what are the effects of their situation? How does Ablow treat them?
3. How do abused adolescents view their situation?

Drawing Inferences about Thesis and Purpose

1. What is Ablow's thesis? What change in policy does he want to see? Where does he state his thesis?
2. What specific actions are needed to improve the health of abused children?

Analyzing Strategies and Style

1. The author provides several examples of abused teenagers; how do the examples help to advance his argument? Ablow begins and ends with extended examples that include dialogue. What makes these effective ways to begin and end?
2. What, in your view, is the most telling example, detail, or argument in the essay? Why?

Thinking Critically

1. Have you known any abused teens? If so, have you seen any good solutions to their problems, such as foster care or therapy? Do you know adolescents who need help? If so, what can you do?
2. Should bad parents lose their children? Why or why not?
3. Would you favor more resources to help abused children? Why or why not?
4. How can we improve education for prospective parents so that they will be prepared for good parenting? What suggestions do you have?

Social Science Finds: "Marriage Matters"

―――

LINDA J. WAITE

A former senior sociologist at the Rand Corporation, Linda Waite (b. 1947) is currently a professor at the University of Chicago. She has several books—with coauthors—including *Teenage Mother-hood* (1979) and *New Families, No Families?* (1991). In this article, published in *The Responsive Community* in 1996, Waite examines various studies of marriage to determine the effects that marriage has on those who are married.

Questions to Guide Your Reading

1. What does Waite assert about marriage; that is, what is her thesis?
2. What groups of people are the healthiest and live the longest?

As we are all too aware, the last few decades have witnessed 1 a decline in the popularity of marriage. This trend has not escaped the notice of politicians and pundits. But when critics point to the high social costs and taxpayer burden imposed by disintegrating "family values," they overlook the fact that individuals do not simply make the decisions that lead to unwed parenthood, marriage, or divorce on the basis of what is good for society. Individuals weigh the costs and benefits of each of these choices to themselves—and sometimes their children. But how much is truly known about these costs and benefits, either by the individuals making the choices or demographers like myself who study them? Put differently, what are the implications, for individuals, of the current increases in nonmarriage? If we think of marriage as an insurance policy—which it is, in some respects—does it matter if more people are uninsured, or are insured with a term rather than a whole-life policy? I shall argue that it does matter, because marriage typically provides important and substantial benefits, benefits not enjoyed by those who live alone or cohabit.

A quick look at marriage patterns today compared to, say, 2 1950 shows the extent of recent changes. Figures from the Census Bureau show that in 1950, at the height of the baby boom, about a third of white men and women were not married. Some were waiting to marry for the first time, some were divorced or widowed and not remarried. But virtually everyone married at least once at some point in their lives, generally in their early twenties.

In 1950 the proportion of black men and women not married 3 was approximately equal to the proportion unmarried among whites, but since that time the marriage behavior of blacks and whites has diverged dramatically. By 1993, 61 percent of black women and 58 percent of black men were not married, compared to 38 percent of white men and 41 percent of white women. So, in contrast to 1950 when only a little over one black adult in three was not married, now a majority of black adults are unmarried. Insofar as marriage "matters," black men and women are much less likely than whites to share in the benefits, and much less likely today than they were a generation ago.

4   The decline in marriage is directly connected to the rise in cohabitation—living with someone in a sexual relationship without being married. Although Americans are less likely to be married today than they were several decades ago, if we count both marriage and cohabitation, they are about as likely to be "coupled." If cohabitation provides the same benefits to individuals as marriage does, then we do not need to be concerned about this shift. But we may be replacing a valuable social institution with one that demands and offers less.

5   Perhaps the most disturbing change in marriage appears in its relationship to parenthood. Today a third of all births occur to women who are not married, with huge but shrinking differences between blacks and whites in this behavior. One in five births to white mothers and two-thirds of births to black mothers currently take place outside marriage. Although about a quarter of the white unmarried mothers are living with someone when they give birth, so that their children are born into two-parent—if unmarried—families, very few black children born to unmarried mothers live with fathers too.

6   I believe that these changes in marriage behavior are a cause for concern, because in a number of important ways married men and women do better than those who are unmarried. And I believe that the evidence suggests that they do better because they are married.

Marriage and Health

7   The case for marriage is quite strong. Consider the issues of longevity and health. With economist Lee Lillard, I used a large national survey to follow men and women over a 20-year period. We watched them get married, get divorced, and remarry. We

observed the death of spouses and of the individuals themselves. And we compared deaths of married men and women to those who were not married. We found that once we took other factors into account, married men and women faced lower risks of dying at any point than those who have never married or whose previous marriage has ended. Widowed women were much better off than divorced women or those who had never married, although they were still disadvantaged when compared with married women. But all men who were not currently married faced significantly higher risks of dying than married men, regardless of their marital history. Other scholars have found disadvantages in death rates for unmarried adults in a number of countries besides the United States.

How does marriage lengthen life? First, marriage appears 8 to reduce risky and unhealthy behaviors. For example, according to University of Texas sociologist Debra Umberson, married men show much lower rates of problem drinking than unmarried men. Umberson also found that both married men and women are less likely to take risks that could lead to injury than are the unmarried. Second, as we will see below, marriage increases material well-being—income, assets, and wealth. These can be used to purchase better medical care, better diet, and safer surroundings, which lengthen life. This material improvement seems to be especially important for women.

Third, marriage provides individuals—especially men—with 9 someone who monitors their health and health-related behaviors and who encourages them to drink and smoke less, to eat a healthier diet, to get enough sleep and to generally take care of their health. In addition, husbands and wives offer each other moral support that helps in dealing with stressful situations. Married men especially seem to be motivated to avoid risky behaviors and to take care of their health by the sense of meaning that marriage gives to their lives and the sense of obligation to others that it brings.

More Wealth, Better Wages—For Most

Married individuals also seem to fare better when it comes 10 to wealth. One comprehensive measure of financial well-being—household wealth—includes pension and Social Security wealth, real and financial assets, and the value of the primary residence. According to economist James Smith, in 1992 married men and women ages 51–60 had median wealth of about $66,000 per spouse, compared to $42,000 for the widowed, $35,000 for those who had never married, $34,000 among those who were divorced, and only $7,600 for those who were separated. Although married couples have higher incomes than others, this fact accounts for only about a quarter of their greater wealth.

11   How does marriage increase wealth? Married couples can share many household goods and services, such as a TV and heat, so the cost to each individual is lower than if each one purchased and used the same items individually. So the married spend less than the same individuals would for the same style of life if they lived separately. Second, married people produce more than the same individuals would if single. Each spouse can develop some skills and neglect others, because each can count on the other to take responsibility for some of the household work. The resulting specialization increases efficiency. We see below that this specialization leads to higher wages for men. Married couples also seem to save more at the same level of income than do single people.

12   The impact of marriage is again beneficial—although in this case not for all involved—when one looks at labor market outcomes. According to recent research by economist Kermit Daniel, both black and white men receive a wage premium if they are married: 4.5 percent for black men and 6.3 percent for white men. Black women receive a marriage premium of almost 3 percent. White women, however, pay a marriage penalty, in hourly wages, of over 4 percent. In addition, men appear to receive some of the benefit of marriage if they cohabit, but women do not.

13   Why should marriage increase men's wages? Some researchers think that marriage makes men more productive at work, leading to higher wages. Wives may assist husbands directly with their work, offer advice or support, or take over household tasks, freeing husbands' time and energy for work. Also, as I mentioned earlier, being married reduces drinking, substance abuse, and other unhealthy behaviors that may affect men's job performance. Finally, marriage increases men's incen-

tives to perform well at work, in order to meet obligations to family members.

For women, Daniel finds that marriage and presence of chil- 14 dren together seem to affect wages, and the effects depend on the woman's race. Childless black women earn substantially more money if they are married but the "marriage premium" drops with each child they have. Among white women only the childless receive a marriage premium. Once white women become mothers, marriage decreases their earnings compared to remaining single (with children), with very large negative effects of marriage on women's earnings for those with two children or more. White married women often choose to reduce hours of work when they have children. They also make less per hour than either unmarried mothers or childless wives.

Up to this point, all the consequences of marriage for the 15 individuals involved have been unambiguously positive—better health, longer life, more wealth, and higher earnings. But the effects of marriage and children on white women's wages are mixed, at best. Marriage and cohabitation increase women's time spent on housework; married motherhood reduces their time in the labor force and lowers their wages. Although the family as a whole might be better off with this allocation of women's time, women generally share their husbands' market earnings only when they are married. Financial well-being declines dramatically for women and their children after divorce and widowhood; women whose marriages have ended are often quite disadvantaged financially by their investment in their husbands and children rather than in their own earning power. Recent changes in divorce law—the rise in no-fault divorce and the move away from alimony—seem to have exacerbated this situation, even while increases in women's education and work experience have moderated it.

Improved Intimacy

Another benefit of married life is an improved sex life. Mar- 16 ried men and women report very active sex lives—as do those who are cohabiting. But the married appear to be more satisfied with sex than others. More married men say that they find sex with their wives to be extremely physically pleasurable than do cohabiting men or single men say the same about sex with their partners. The high levels of married men's physical satisfaction with their sex lives contradicts the popular view that sexual novelty or variety improves sex for men. Physical satisfaction with sex is about the same for married women, cohabiting women, and single women with sex partners.

17   In addition to reporting more active and more physically fulfilling sex lives than the unmarried, married men and women say that they are more emotionally satisfied with their sex lives than do those who are single or cohabiting. Although cohabitants report levels of sexual activity as high as the married, both cohabiting men and women report lower levels of emotional satisfaction with their sex lives. And those who are sexually active but single report the lowest emotional satisfaction with it.

18   How does marriage improve one's sex life? Marriage and cohabitation provide individuals with a readily available sexual partner with whom they have an established, ongoing sexual relationship. This reduces the costs—in some sense—of any particular sexual contact, and leads to higher levels of sexual activity. Since married couples expect to carry on their sex lives for many years, and since the vast majority of married couples are monogamous, husbands and wives have strong incentives to learn what pleases their partner in bed and to become good at it. But I would argue that more than "skills" are at issue here. The long-term contract implicit in marriage—which is not implicit in cohabitation—facilitates emotional investment in the relationship, which should affect both frequency of and satisfaction with sex. So the wife or husband who knows what the spouse wants is also highly motivated to provide it, both because sexual satisfaction in one's partner brings similar rewards to oneself and because the emotional commitment to the partner makes satisfying him or her important in itself.

19   To this point we have focused on the consequences of marriage for adults—the men and women who choose to marry (and stay married) or not. But such choices have consequences for the children born to these adults. Sociologists Sara McLanahan and Gary Sandefur compare children raised in intact, two-parent families with those raised in one-parent

families, which could result either from disruption of a marriage or from unmarried childbearing. They find that approximately twice as many children raised in one-parent families than children from two-parent families drop out of high school without finishing. Children raised in one-parent families are also more likely to have a birth themselves while teenagers, and to be "idle"—both out of school and out of the labor force—as young adults.

Not surprisingly, children living outside an intact marriage   20
are also more likely to be poor. McLanahan and Sandefur calculated poverty rates for children in two-parent families—including stepfamilies—and for single-parent families. They found very high rates of poverty for single-parent families, especially among blacks. Donald Hernandez, chief of marriage and family statistics at the Census Bureau, claims that the rise in mother-only families since 1959 is an important cause of increases in poverty among children.

Clearly poverty, in and of itself, is a bad outcome for children.   21
In addition, however, McLanahan and Sandefur estimate that the lower incomes of single-parent families account for only half of the negative impact for children in these families. The other half comes from children's access—or lack of access—to the time and attention of two adults in two-parent families. Children in one-parent families spend less time with their fathers (this is not surprising given that they do not live with them), but they also spend less time with their mothers than children in two-parent families. Single-parent families and stepfamilies also move much more frequently than two-parent families, disrupting children's social and academic environments. Finally, children who spend part of their childhood in a single-parent family report substantially lower quality relationships with their parents as adults and have less frequent contact with them, according to demographer Diane Lye.

Correlation Versus Causality

The obvious question, when one looks at all these "bene-   22
fits" of marriage, is whether marriage is responsible for these differences. If all, or almost all, of the benefits of marriage arise because those who enjoy better health, live longer lives, or earn

higher wages anyway are more likely to marry, then marriage is not "causing" any changes in these outcomes. In such a case, we as a society and we as individuals could remain neutral about each person's decision to marry or not, to divorce or remain married. But scholars from many fields who have examined the issues have come to the opposite conclusion. Daniel found that only half of the higher wages that married men enjoy could be explained by selectivity; he thus concluded that the other half is causal. In the area of mental health, social psychologist Catherine Ross—summarizing her own research and that of other social scientists—wrote, "The positive effect of marriage on well-being is strong and consistent, and the selection of the psychologically healthy into marriage or the psychologically unhealthy out of marriage cannot explain the effect." Thus marriage itself can be assumed to have independent positive effects on its participants.

23   So, we must ask, what is it about marriage that causes these benefits? I think that four factors are key. First, the institution of marriage involves a long-term contract—" 'til death do us part." This contract allows the partners to make choices that carry immediate costs but eventually bring benefits. The time horizon implied by marriage makes it sensible—a rational choice is at work here—for individuals to develop some skills and to neglect others because they count on their spouse to fill in where they are weak. The institution of marriage helps individuals honor this long-term contract by providing social support for the couple as a couple and by imposing social and economic costs on those who dissolve their union.

24   Second, marriage assumes a sharing of economic and social resources and what we can think of as co-insurance. Spouses act as a sort of small insurance pool against life's uncertainties, reducing their need to protect themselves—by themselves—from unexpected events.

25   Third, married couples benefit—as do cohabiting couples—from economies of scale.

26   Fourth, marriage connects people to other individuals, to their social groups (such as in-laws), and to other social institutions (such as churches and synagogues) which are themselves a source

of benefits. These connections provide individuals with a sense of 27 obligation to others, which gives life meaning beyond oneself. Cohabitation has some but not all of the characteristics of marriage and so carries some but not all of the benefits. Cohabitation does not generally imply a lifetime commitment to stay together; a significant number of cohabiting couples disagree on the future of their relationship. Frances Goldscheider and Gail Kaufman believe that the shift to cohabitation from marriage signals "declining commitment within unions, of men and women to each other and to their relationship as an enduring unit, in exchange for more freedom, primarily for men." Perhaps, as a result, many view cohabitation as an especially poor bargain for women.

The uncertainty that accompanies cohabitation makes both 28 investment in the relationship and specialization with this partner much riskier than in marriage and so reduces them. Cohabitants are much less likely than married couples to pool financial resources and more likely to assume that each partner is responsible for supporting himself or herself financially. And whereas marriage connects individuals to other important social institutions, cohabitation seems to distance them from these institutions.

Of course, all these observations concern only the average 29 benefits of marriage. Clearly, some marriages produce substantially higher benefits for those involved. Some marriages produce no benefits and even cause harm to the men, women, and children involved. That fact needs to be recognized.

Reversing the Trend

Having stated this qualification, we must still ask, if the aver- 30 age marriage produces all of these benefits for individuals, why has it declined? Although this issue remains a subject of much research and speculation, a number of factors have been mentioned as contributing. For one, because of increases in women's employment, there is less specialization by spouses now than in the past; this reduces the benefits of marriage. Clearly, employed wives have less time and energy to focus on their husbands, and are less financially and emotionally dependent on marriage than wives who work only in the home. In addition, high divorce rates decrease people's certainty about the long-run stability of their marriage, and this may reduce their willingness to invest in it, which in turn increases the chance they divorce—a sort of self-fulfilling prophecy. Also, changes in divorce laws have shifted much of the financial burden for the breakup of the marriage to women, making investment within the marriage (such as supporting a husband in medical school) a riskier proposition for them.

31   Men, in turn, may find marriage and parenthood a less attractive option when they know that divorce is common, because they may face the loss of contact with their children if their marriage dissolves. Further, women's increased earnings and young men's declining financial well-being may have made women less dependent on men's financial support and made young men less able to provide it. Finally, public policies that support single mothers and changing attitudes toward sex outside of marriage, toward unmarried childbearing, and toward divorce have all been implicated in the decline in marriage. This brief list does not exhaust the possibilities, but merely mentions some of them.

32   So how can this trend be reversed? First, as evidence accumulates and is communicated to individuals, some people will change their behavior as a result. Some will do so simply because of their new understanding of the costs and benefits, to them, of the choices involved. In addition, we have seen that attitudes frequently change toward behaviors that have been shown to have negative consequences. The attitude change then raises the social cost of the newly stigmatized behavior.

33   In addition, though, we as a society can pull some policy levers to encourage or discourage behaviors. Public policies that include asset tests (Medicaid is a good example) act to exclude the married, as do AFDC programs and most states. The "marriage penalty" in the tax code is another example. These and other policies reinforce or undermine the institution of marriage. If, as I have argued, marriage produces individuals who drink less, smoke less, abuse substances less, live longer, earn more, are wealthier, and have children who do better, we need to give more thought and effort to supporting this valuable social institution.

Expanding Vocabulary

After studying definitions of the following words, select five and use each one in a separate sentence. The number in parentheses is the number of the paragraph in which the word appears.

pundits (1)	exacerbated (15)
demographers (1)	monogamous (18)
cohabit (1)	implicit (18)
diverged (3)	disruption (19)
unambiguously (15)	stigmatized (32)

Understanding Content

1. Waite argues that most people weigh the advantages and disadvantages of marriage based on what?
2. Although marriage has declined, what has taken its place?
3. What percentage of births occur to women who are not married? What percentage of white mothers are living with someone? What percentage of black mothers are living with someone?
4. Which arrangement type has the greatest income? Which type has the least?
5. In what ways can marriage increase wealth? Who, when married, loses in hourly wages?
6. What may be causes for increased productivity for married men?
7. Which living arrangement reports having the most physical and emotional satisfaction from sex?
8. What situations increase poverty for children?
9. What are some effects of single-parent families on children?
10. Does Waite conclude that marriage itself is a cause of the improved lives of most married people? In general, who benefits the least from marriage?

Drawing Inferences about Thesis and Purpose

1. Why, if marriage has benefits, are fewer people getting married and more getting divorced?
2. What does Waite think should be done to change the movement away from marriage?

Analyzing Strategies and Style

1. This is a longish essay. What does Waite do to help readers follow her discussion?

2. What kind of evidence, primarily, does the author provide? How is this consistent with your expectations, based on your knowledge of the author?

Thinking Critically

1. Which statistic most surprises you? Why?
2. Do you think that the evidence Waite provides should encourage people to choose marriage over divorce, cohabitation, or the single life? If so, why? If not, why not?
3. What can be done to increase marriage benefits for women, the ones who have least benefited by marriage?

Will Gay Marriage Be Legal?

JOHN CLOUD

John Cloud (b. 1970) is a graduate of Harvard University and a Rhodes Scholar. He is a staff writer at *Time* magazine, which published this article on February 2, 2000.

Questions to Guide Your Reading

1. What can gay partnerships do now?
2. What is Cloud's thesis?

1   Gay marriage is already legal in some sense: Michael and I recently bought a set of All-Clad pans together. We watch *The Sopranos* and split the HBO bill every month. We shave with the same razor.

2   Slightly more important, we both work for companies that offer health insurance to their workers' sweethearts, whether legally married or not. If we wanted them to, our families would come to one of those precious pseudo-weddings you've seen on sit-coms. Ours would involve tuna tartare and Madonna remixes, followed by a trip downtown to register with New York City as "domestic partners."

3   In fact, Michael and I can't really marry—not in New York and not even in Norway or Hawaii, which have thought about allowing same-sex marriages in recent years but ultimately

decided not to. I shouldn't trivialize the perks we miss: law books at all levels contain thousands of statutes pertaining to spouses. If I were struck by a drunk driver, for instance, Michael wouldn't have the legal standing to sue the bastard or help decide on my medical treatment.

Will he in 2025? Almost certainly. In fact, within a decade, gay couples—at least those who live in progressive states—will probably enjoy all the rights, responsibilities and daily frustrations of married life, even if they don't have a marriage license. In Vermont the state supreme court has already ruled that the state must start providing the same benefits to all couples, gay and straight, except the title of marriage itself. Vermont legislators now have the option of granting same-sex couples the M word too. If they do—and it doesn't seem likely—they will ignite a federal case over whether other states have to honor Vermont's licenses. (Congress has said states can ignore others' gay marriages, but that law hasn't been tested in court.)

Ultimately, of course, the battle for gay marriage has always been about more than winning the second-driver discount at the Avis counter. In fact, the individual who has done most to push same-sex marriage—a brilliant 43-year-old lawyer-activist named Evan Wolfson—doesn't even have a boyfriend. He and the others who brought the marriage lawsuits of the past decade want nothing less than full social equality, total validation—not just the right to inherit a mother-in-law's Cadillac. As Andrew Sullivan, the (also persistently single) intellectual force behind gay marriage, has written, "Including homosexuals within marriage would be a means of conferring the highest form of social approval imaginable."

In this light, the Vermont decision looks more like *Plessy v. Ferguson*, the 1896 Supreme Court ruling that allowed "separate but equal" facilities for blacks, than *Brown v. Board of Education*, the 1954 decision that finally required meaningful equality. If that analogy stands, it will be another half-century before gay couples can, in all 50 states, stand in the same line for marriage licenses as others.

By that time, Michael and I will be in our 80s, too old to stand in line for anything but mashed peas. He and I will have had a "gay marriage," probably one without an official certificate. Tomorrow's gay kids will enjoy simply marriage—without qualifiers.

Expanding Vocabulary

Study the context for each word's meaning and then use each word in a separate sentence of your own. The number in parentheses is the number of the paragraph in which the word appears.

ultimately (3)
trivialize (3)
perks (3)
validation (5)
persistently (5)

Understanding Content

1. What are gay partnerships not able to do?
2. What will gay partnerships be able to do by 2010, according to the author?
3. By when will gays be able to get marriage licenses?

Drawing Inferences about Thesis and Purpose

1. Cloud says that the battle has always been about more than a discount at Avis. What is the battle about?
2. How optimistic is Cloud regarding legal acceptance of gay marriages? Social acceptance?

Analyzing Strategies and Structures

1. The author refers to his life partner. What effect will this have on readers? What tone does it help to create in the essay?
2. Cloud sets up a comparison with two Supreme Court decisions. What is the point of his comparison?

Thinking Critically

1. Do you think that Cloud's predictions are accurate regarding the changes ahead? If you think that he is incorrect, what evidence do you have to challenge his predictions?
2. What are your views on these predictions? Should gay partnerships have health benefits? Adoption rights as a couple? (An individual gay or lesbian person can now adopt a child.) All rights except a legally sanctioned marriage? Legally sanctioned marriage itself? Explain and support your views.

Not Much Sense in Those Census Stories

STEPHANIE COONTZ

A professor of history at Evergreen State College in Olympia, Washington, Stephanie Coontz (b. 1944) is the author of numerous articles and books, including *The Way We Never Were: American Families and the Nostalgia Trap* (1992) and *The Way We Really Are* (1997). Coontz is also national cochair of the Council on Contemporary Families (*www.contemporaryfamilies.org*); it is in this capacity that she is frequently contacted by media personnel working on stories about families. The following article was published July 15, 2001, in the *Washington Post*.

Questions to Guide Your Reading

1. What is Coontz's subject? What is her purpose in writing?
2. What has led the Census Bureau to assert an increase in children living in *traditional* family homes?

Nearly every week, the U.S. Census Bureau releases a new 1 set of figures on American families and the living arrangements they have been creating in the past decade. And each time, as the media liaison for a national association of family researchers, I'm bombarded with telephone calls from radio and television producers seeking a talking head to confirm the wildly differing—and usually wrong—conclusions they've jumped to about what those figures say about the evolving nature of family life in America.

In April, for example, Census officials announced that 56 per- 2 cent of American children were living in "traditional" nuclear families in 1996, up from 51 percent in 1991. Several prime time television shows excitedly reported this "good news" about the American family, and I heard one radio commentator declare that young couples were finally rejecting the "divorce culture" of their parents' generation.

But this supposedly dramatic reversal of a 30-year trend was 3 based on a peculiarly narrow definition of a traditional family: a two-parent household with children under 18 and no other relatives in the home. If a grandchild, grandparent or other relative were living in the house, the family was "nontraditional." (There's an obvious irony here, given that nothing is quite so traditional as an extended nuclear family that includes a grandparent!)

4   Evidently, the definition itself was largely responsible for this "trend": Enough such relatives moved to separate households during the first half of the 1990s to increase the proportion of "traditional families," even though the percentage of children living with both biological parents had stayed steady at about 62 percent, and the percentage of married couples had continued its 30-year slide. In other words, the initial reports of a resurgence in traditional families were the result of wishful thinking and a misunderstanding of the terms being used by the census.

5   But hope springs eternal among talk show producers desperate for a new angle. In mid-May, expanding on its earlier study, the Census Bureau reported that the absolute numbers of married couples with children at home had grown in 2000 after falling in two previous head counts (although the proportion of such families in the total population was still shrinking). TV producers jumped on the story, apparently ready to trumpet the return of the "Ozzie and Harriet" family of the '50s. I soon heard from several talk show hosts in the West who, state-by-state printouts in hand, were agog about the exceptionally large increase of such families in *their* regions. They wanted me to find them an expert to comment on the heartening return to traditional values.

6   Their enthusiasm dimmed, however, when I told them that this regional increase in married-couple households with children was due largely to the well-reported influx of Asian and Hispanic immigrants. Their interest evaporated entirely when I reminded them that, as immigrants assimilate, their family patterns tend to match those of the preexisting population.

7   A week later, the Census Bureau reported that the number of unmarried women with children had increased by 25 percent, dwarfing the 7 percent growth in married-couple families. This time we moved into the "bad news" cycle: Media pundits called to confirm their worst fears, looking for more figures to prove that the explosion of single motherhood was creating an ever-deepening social and cultural crisis in the land.

In fact, most of the growth in "single" motherhood during 8 the 1990s was due to an increase in births to women who, while not married, were living with the child's father. So, much of the recent increase in single motherhood simply reflected the 71 percent increase in cohabitation between 1990 and 2000. But the fact that many "single mother" families actually had fathers present didn't faze the talk show hosts who called seeking confirmation that the sky was falling because of the "collapse of marriage." This time around, they weren't the least bit interested in any good news—such as the figures, also released in May, that showed a 20 percent drop in births to teenagers over the decade.

Then, last month, the Census Bureau reported that the num- 9 ber of households headed by single fathers had increased fivefold, from 393,000 in 1970 to 2 million in 2000. I got two calls from TV producers that day, each rushing to air a show on this new trend. One asked me to explain how this reflected the increasing equality of men and women in their commitment to parenting, while the other wanted someone to tell her viewers why it represented a backlash against working mothers, who were obviously losing custody to unwed and divorced fathers.

Both producers were crushed when I told them our 10 researchers couldn't confirm either claim, and that we have no way of even knowing how many of these so-called single fathers are in fact living with the mother of their child outside of marriage, and how many are divorced dads who simply happened to have their children with them for the weekend on the day they filled out the form. When I called a Census Bureau researcher to see if he could help straighten this out, he said my guess was as good as his.

It's not that the census researchers are doing a bad job. The 11 problem is that they're asked to compress America's increasingly fluid family arrangements into one-dimensional categories that were established at a time when most single-parent households were created by death rather than by divorce, and when most people made things easy for data collectors by lying rather than admitting to "living in sin."

People's new candor about their lifestyles, combined with 12 the undeniable changes in family arrangements that have occurred over the past 40 years, makes it increasingly hard to capture new family realities in old census categories. And using such categories to talk about families has consequences.

13   Labeling people single parents, for example, when they may in fact be coparenting—either with an unmarried other parent in the home or with an exspouse in a joint custody situation—stigmatizes their children as the products of "single parenthood" and makes the uncounted parent invisible to society. This can lead teachers, school officials, neighbors and other family members to exclude the uncounted parents from activities and interactions into which they might otherwise be drawn. In fear of such marginalization, some separated parents find it hard to agree on a custody arrangement that's in the best interests of the child, because each wants to be the socially recognized parent.

14   In the past, many "intact" families had fathers who were AWOL from their children's lives. Today, conversely, many "broken" families have fathers who remain active parents. Harvard fellow Constance Ahrons, who has conducted a 20-year study of post-divorce families and their children, has certainly seen plenty of cases where the nonresident parent, usually the father, stops doing any parenting. But she has found many instances where nonresidential fathers became *more* active in their children's lives after divorce than they were during the marriage. These men need to be recognized for their support, rather than relegated to the same state of nonbeing as the deadbeat dad.

15   It's not only parents who are marginalized by outdated household categories. When I speak on work-family issues to audiences around the country, some of the biggest complaints I hear come from individuals who are described by the census as living in "non-family households." They resent the fact that their family responsibilities literally don't "count," either for society or for their employers. There is no category, for instance, for individuals who spend several days a week caring for an aging parent in the parent's separate residence. Yet one in four households in America today is providing substantial time and care to an aging relative, and more than half of all households say they expect to do so within the next 10 years.

16   It's time for our discussion of family trends to better reflect the complexities of today's family commitments. Perhaps, as

Larry McCallum, a therapist who directs the family life program at Augustana College in Rock Island, Ill., suggests, we should do for parents what we have begun to do with racial categories in the census—provide several alternative ways for people to express their overlapping identities. At the very least, we need to drop the idea that we can predict how a family functions solely by its form.

The place where we keep our clothes isn't always the only 17 place where we keep our commitments.

Expanding Vocabulary

Match each word in column A with its definition in column B. When in doubt, first find the word in the essay and look for context clues to aid your understanding of the word's meaning. Then, if necessary, use a dictionary to complete the matching exercise. The number in parentheses is the number of the paragraph in which the word appears.

Column A	*Column B*
liaison (1)	authorities
resurgence (4)	bother, concern
agog (5)	frankness, honesty
pundits (7)	full of eager excitement
cohabitation (8)	brands; labels in a negative way
faze (8)	one who maintains communication
candor (12)	between groups
stigmatizes (13)	placing on the edge of the scene;
marginalization (13)	making one less important
deadbeat (14)	one who does not pay his or her debts
	renewal or revival
	living together

Understanding Content

1. Why does the author get calls from media people asking for explanations of recent Census figures on families?
2. Why does Coontz find the Census Bureau's definition of traditional family "ironic"?
3. What number continues a 30-year decline? That is, what important change in American families continues?
4. Why did western states show an increase in "married-with-children" households?

5. What accounts for most of the growth in "single" motherhood?
6. What are the several consequences of using the old Census categories to describe today's families?

Drawing Inferences about Thesis and Purpose

1. What attitude toward the media does Coontz have—and invite readers to have? How do you know?
2. What is the author's thesis? You may need more than one sentence to present several interconnected key ideas.

Analyzing Strategies and Style

1. In paragraph 2, Coontz puts "traditional" and "good news" in quotation marks. Why? What does she want to communicate with the quotation marks?
2. The author's final paragraph is one sentence. What make it effective? What key words are connected by sound?

Thinking Critically

1. While showing the problems in using the Census Bureau's old categories, Coontz also provides readers with some interesting statistics. What data are most surprising to you? Why?
2. Have you thought about the consequences of stigmatizing and marginalizing the nonlegal father or the divorced parent without primary custody, as Coontz suggests we do with the old categories? Does this make sense to you? Do you see this as a problem we need to address?
3. Are you accepting of the various living arrangements of families today? What makes a family? Do we need to broaden our definition? Reflect on these questions.

Dream Deferred

LANGSTON HUGHES

Like many American writers, Langston Hughes (1902–1967) came from the Middle West to New York City, lived in Europe, and then returned to the United States to a career of writing. He was a journalist, fiction writer, and poet, and author of more than sixty books. Hughes was also the first African American to support himself as a professional writer. Known as "the bard of Harlem," Hughes became an important public figure and voice for black writers. "Dream Deferred," one of Hughes's best-loved poems, which comes from *The Panther and the Lash: Poems of Our Time* (1951), illustrates the effective use of metaphor to convey the poet's attitudes and emotions.

What happens to a dream deferred?

Does it dry up
like a raisin in the sun?
Or fester like a sore—
And then run?
Does it stink like rotten meat?   5
Or crust and sugar over—
like a syrupy sweet?

Maybe it just sags
like a heavy load.   10

Or does it explode?

Understanding Content and Strategies

1. How is the poem structured; that is, what is it a series of?
2. The "answers" to the poem's first question are all similes except one. Which line is a metaphor? Explain the metaphor. Why is the one metaphor an effective strategy?
3. What does Hughes mean by a "deferred" dream?
4. Explain each simile. How does each one present a response to, or the effect of, a deferred dream?
5. What do the similes and metaphor have in common?

Drawing Inferences about Theme

1. What, then, is Hughes's attitude toward his subject? What does he want us to understand about deferred dreams?
2. Might the poem also be making a social comment? If so, what?

Thinking Critically

1. Which simile do you find most effective? Why?
2. Has Hughes included most of the responses to deferred dreams? Is there any response you would add? If so, can you state it as a simile?

MAKING CONNECTIONS

1. Amatai Etzioni sees today's obsession with self-fulfillment as a major cause of social problems. Could one describe the breakdown of family as a loss of a sense of duty? Compare Etzioni's views with Linda Waite's. Will an obsession with the self bring happiness? Consider what Ciardi (see Chapter 8) has to say about happiness.
2. Linda Waite thinks that, generally, people's lives are improved by marriage. Keith Ablow is concerned with the deviance of parents that leads to abused children. Apparently not all marriages result in happier adults and children. Should we encourage marriage for everyone? Should there be testing of some kind leading to a marriage license? A parenting license?
3. Have we, in this society, chosen the search for affluence over family commitments and family joys? Does this search divide us by gender and/or class? Does it affect our compassion for those less fortunate? If the answer is yes to these questions, should we be concerned? Are these problems for society? If so, what can we do to change?
4. Perhaps one indicator of how successfully families today are coping is the rate and types of crimes committed by juveniles. Go online to gather some statistics on juvenile crime. You can look for trends (the last 10 years, for example) or look at arrest figures for one type of crime. There are many Web sites with statistical information on juvenile crime. Pick a search engine (Google or Yahoo) and type in "juvenile crime statistics."

TOPICS AND GUIDELINES FOR WRITING

1. In your prereading exercise, you reflected on your decision to attend college. Now reflect on your reasons for selecting the particular college you are attending. In an essay, explain the causes for your choice of school. You can organize according to the decision process you went through, or you can organize from least important to most

important causes. You might think of writing this essay as a feature article in your college newspaper.

2. Have you ever done something that you did not think you ought to do? If so, why did you do it? And what were the consequences of your actions? In an essay, examine the causes and effects of your action. Be sure that you have a point to make. You might want to show that you should have listened to the warning voice inside you, or you might want to show that one effect of such a situation is that we do learn something about ourselves.

3. Are you "addicted" to something? To chocolate or beer or cigarettes? To television soaps, video games, bridge, or something else? If so, reflect on why you and others like you are addicted to whatever it is that absorbs you. Drawing on your personal experience, your knowledge of others, and perhaps some reading on the topic, develop an analysis of the causes of your addiction. Organize your causes from least to most important and illustrate each one. If you use ideas from your reading, give proper credit by stating author and title.

4. Rosalind C. Barnett and Caryl Rivers, John Cloud, and Stephanie Coontz all bring up some of the problems we face with today's redefining and redesigning of the family. Drawing on your reading and your own experiences, develop an essay on one (or two related) problems that many face because of changes in family structures or lifestyles today. Give appropriate credit to any of the authors on whose essays you draw material. You may want to focus only on explaining the problems, or you may want to conclude with one or more possible solutions to the problem.

5. Do you get along well (or poorly) with a parent? If so, reflect on why you have a good (or bad) relationship with that parent. What are the causes? Are your experiences similar to those of friends? What do some of the experts say about parent/children relationships? Drawing on your personal situation, your knowledge of others, and perhaps some reading, develop an analysis of the causes for good (or bad) parent/child relationships. Organize causes from least to most important and illustrate each one. If you use ideas from your reading, give proper credit.

6. Have you experienced divorce either as a once-married person or as a child of divorced parents? If so, reflect on the effects of divorce. Drawing on your own experience, your knowledge of the experiences of others, and perhaps some reading, develop an analysis of the effects of divorce on divorced persons or their children. Follow the guidelines for organization and crediting your reading given in topic 4.

7. Amitai Etzioni feels strongly about the decline of a sense of duty in our society, and this has led him to write on the subject. Is there a current social or political problem that you are especially interested in? If so, think about the causes and effects of this problem. Then write an essay on the problem. Focus on the causes of the problem, the effects of the problem, or both causes and effects. You might want to conclude with one or more proposed solutions to the problem.

10

Using Argument and Persuasion

Preserving the Health of Our World

Losing patience with two friends, you finally moan, "Will you two *please* stop arguing! You've been bickering all evening; you're ruining the party." How often many of us have said, or wanted to say, something similar to parents, children, colleagues, or friends who seem unable to stop yelling or name calling, or quibbling over some insignificant point. In this context, the term *argument* has a negative connotation. In a classroom debate, a courtroom, a business conference, or writing, however, a sound argument is highly valued.

The Characteristics of Argument

Understanding the characteristics of good argument will help you to think critically about the arguments of others and to write better arguments of your own. Some of these characteristics may surprise you, so read thoughtfully and reflect on the following points.

- An argument makes a point. Sound reasons and relevant evidence are presented to support a claim, a main idea that the arguer keeps in focus. Collecting data on a particular topic may produce an interesting report, but unless the specifics support a point, there is no argument.
- Argument assumes an audience. The purpose of argument is not just to provide information but to change the way listeners or readers think about an issue, to move them to agree with you. Once you

accept that argument implies an audience, you have to accept the possibility of counterarguments, of listeners or readers who will not agree with you and will challenge your thinking. You have not defended your argument by simply asserting that it is *your opinion.* If you have not based your opinion on good evidence and reasons, your opinion will be challenged, and you will lose the respect of your audience.

- Good argument is based on a recognition of the complexities of most issues and the reality of opposing views. One of the greatest dangers to good argument lies in oversimplifying complex issues, or in oversimplifying reality by assuming that our claim is "clearly right" and that therefore everyone agrees with us.

- Good argument makes clear the values and beliefs that we consider relevant to the issue. Argument is not just an intellectual game. We need to recognize the values that are a part of our reasoning, our way of approaching a particular issue. For example, if you argue that abortion is wrong because it is murder, you *believe* that the fetus is a human being at the moment of conception. Your argument is convincing only to those who share your *belief.* Wanting no uncertainty about the values upon which his claim was founded, Thomas Jefferson wrote: "We hold these truths to be self-evident" and then listed such values as "all men are created equal" and "governments are instituted among men."

- In argument, we present evidence to support a claim on the *assumption* that there is a valid or logical connection between evidence and claim, what British philosopher Stephen Toulmin calls a *warrant.* When you argue that abortion is wrong because it is murder, you assume or warrant that the fetus is a human being who can be murdered. Arguments can be challenged not only on the evidence or stated reasons but also on the assumptions or warrants that support the argument's structure. Therefore, you must know what your assumptions are because you may need to defend them as part of the support for your argument.

- Argument includes the use of persuasive strategies. When you write an argumentative essay, you want to convince readers to share your views, or at least to reconsider theirs in the light of your discussion. Of course you are involved in your topic and want to affect readers. Indeed, you will write more persuasively if you write about issues that concern you. In good argument, however, emotions are tempered by logic and channeled into the energy needed to think through the topic, to gather evidence, to consider audience, and to plan the paper. Remember that one of the best *persuasive* strategies is to present yourself to readers as a reasonable person who has done your homework on the topic and who wants to find some common ground with those who disagree.

How to Use Argument and Persuasion

How can you put together a good argumentative essay? Accepting that writing an effective argument is a challenging task, you may want to give appropriate time and thought to *preparing to write* before you actually draft your essay. Use the following guidelines to aid your writing.

1. **Think about audience and purpose.** Unless you are writing about a most unusual topic, expect your readers to be aware of the issue. This does not mean that you can skip an appropriate introduction or necessary background information. It does mean that you can expect readers to know (and perhaps be a part of) the opposition, so be prepared to challenge counterarguments and consider the advantages of pointing out common ground. Also define your purpose in writing; that is, recognize the *type* of argument you are planning. Are you presenting the results of a study, perhaps the results of a questionnaire you prepared? (For example, you could do a survey of attitudes toward campus security, or proposals to eliminate the school newspaper.) Are you writing to state your position on a value-laden issue, such as euthanasia or capital punishment? Are you writing on a public-policy issue, such as whether to restrict smoking in all public buildings? Each of these types of arguments needs somewhat different support and development, so as you work on your argument's thesis or claim, think about the type of argument as well.

2. **Brainstorm about your topic to develop a tentative thesis and think about the kinds of support your thesis (claim) will need.** If you have done an investigation, you need to study your evidence to see what appropriate conclusions can be drawn. (For example, if 51 percent of the students you polled want more security on campus at night, you could say that a majority of students think that increased security is needed. But, it is more accurate to say that about half of the students polled expressed that view.)

If you are writing an argument based primarily on values rather than facts, decide on your position and then begin to list your reasons. Suppose you support euthanasia. What, exactly, are you in favor of? Physician-assisted suicide? A patient's right to refuse all life-support systems? A family-member's right to make that decision? Be sure that you state your claim so that it clearly represents your position, a position you believe you can support. Then consider why: To eliminate unnecessary suffering? To give individuals control over their deaths? If you are examining a problem in education or arguing for restricting smoking in public buildings, you may need to do some reading to locate appropriate facts and statistics. You may also need to consider the feasibility of putting your proposal into place. Will it cost money? Where will the money come from? Who may be hurt or inconvenienced? How can you bring these people to your side?

3. **Plan the organization of your essay.** Remember that any plan is just a guide so that you can get started. As you draft or when you revise, you may find that you want to switch parts around or add new ideas and examples that have come to you while writing. But remember as well that usually some plan is better than no plan. If you are writing an argument based on values, consider these steps:

a. **Begin with an introduction to get your reader's attention.** If you are writing on euthanasia, you can mention the news coverage of Dr. Kevorkian.

b. **Decide where to place your thesis.** Although typically a thesis or claim comes early in the essay, you may want to experiment with placing it at the end, after you have presented support for that claim.

c. **Organize reasons in a purposeful way.** One strategy is to move from less important to most important reasons. Another approach is to organize around counterarguments, explaining why each of the opposition's arguments does not hold up. (In this chapter, Molly Ivins uses the arguments of the gun lobby as an organizing strategy in her argument for gun control.) Consider using some of the methods of development discussed throughout this text.

Draw on your reading for statistical details, on your own experience for examples.

d. **Provide support for each reason.** You have not written an effective argument just by stating your reasons. You need to argue for them, to show why they are reasonable, or better than the opposition's reasons, or have the support of good evidence.

e. **Conclude by effectively stating or restating your claim.** As a part of your conclusion, you may want to explain to readers how this issue affects them, how they could benefit from embracing your position or your proposal for change.

4. **Revise, revise, revise.** After completing a first draft based on your tentative plan, study the draft carefully both for readability and effective argument. Examine reasons and support to be sure you have avoided logical fallacies. See where you may need to qualify statements or control your language. Be certain that you have maintained an appropriate level of seriousness so that you retain the respect of readers. As the writers in this chapter illustrate, you want to write movingly about issues that concern you without forsaking good sense and relevant evidence.

WRITING FOCUS:
LOGICAL FALLACIES

When you ignore the complexities of issues or choose emotional appeals over logic, you risk producing an essay filled with *logical fallacies*. Many arguments that could be won are ruined by those who leave reasoned debate for emotional appeals or who oversimplify the issues. Here are some frequent fallacies to avoid in your writing and to watch out for in the arguments of others.

- *ad hominem* Attacking the opponents instead of defending your position is not an effective strategy with intelligent readers. You have not supported an anti-abortion position, for example, by calling prochoice advocates "murderers" or labeling them "pro-abortion."

- **Straw Man** The straw man fallacy seeks to defend one's position by accusing opponents of holding a position that is easier to attack but is not actually what the opponents believe. To "argue" that those seeking gun registration just want to take guns away from good people and leave them in the hands of criminals is a good example. Those who want gun registration certainly do not want criminals to have guns.

- **Bandwagon** Another substitute for good argument is the appeal to join in, or join the majority, often without providing evidence that a majority holds the view of the arguer or, even more important, that the view is a sound one. Appeals to national interest or the good of the country often contain the bandwagon fallacy. For example: All good Americans want respect shown for the flag, so we need a law banning flag burning. Some "good Americans" also value free speech and see flag burning as an example of free speech.

- **Common Practice** Similar to the bandwagon fallacy, the appeal to common practice is the false logic that "everyone is doing it, so it must be a good thing." However, cheating on tests or on one's income taxes, for example, cannot be logically defended by "arguing" that everybody does it. First, it is not true that everybody does it, and second, even if that were true, it would not make cheating right.

- **Hasty Generalization or Overstatement** When drawing on your own experiences for evidence, you need to judge if your experiences are representative. For example, you may be having difficulty in calculus, but it would be illogical to conclude that the instructor is inept or that the course is too hard. These could be explanations, but they are not the only possible ones. How are other students doing in the course is a key question to ask. Even when you gather extensive evidence from reading, be cautious about generalizing. It is not true that all people on welfare are lazy or that lawyers only want to make piles of money. Qualify assertions; avoid such words as *always, never, everybody,* and *none.* (These words entice readers to find the one exception that will disprove your sweeping generalization.)

- **False Dilemma** The false dilemma is often called either/or thinking. It is the illogic of asserting that only two possibilities are available when there may be several. The effectiveness of this strategy (if you have readers who are not thinking critically) is that you can make one possibility seem a terrible choice, thereby making your choice sound good by contrast. For example: Either we pay more taxes or we will have to cut educational programs. Now these are clearly not the only two possibilities. First, there are other programs that could be cut. Second, we could find ways to save money in the running of government. Third, we can have a growing economy that brings in more government revenues without increasing taxes. Those are just three additional possibilities; there are probably others.

- **Slippery Slope** The slippery slope fallacy makes the argument that we cannot allow A to take place because if we do, then we will head down a slope all the way to Z, a place where no one wants to be. The strategy here is to make Z so awful that readers will agree with you that we should not do A. The error in logic is the unsupported assumption that if A takes place, Z will follow. For example: If the government is allowed to register guns, then before you know it they will ban handguns and then take away all guns, even hunting rifles. Unfortunately, for those who want to scare people with this illogic, there is no evidence that registration will lead to confiscation. We register cars and planes and boats; the government has not confiscated any of these items.

Getting Started: Reflections on the Challenges Facing Ourselves, Our Society, Our World

What do you consider the greatest challenge facing you in your personal life? Is it completing school? Giving up cigarettes or junk food? Reestablishing a relationship with a parent or friend? What do you consider the greatest challenge facing society? Is it reestablishing a sense of community? Improving schools? Improving race relations? Finding deterrents to crime? What do you consider the greatest challenge facing the world? Is it saving the environment? Establishing world peace? Eliminating hunger and injustice? Decide on the challenge, in one of the categories, that most troubles you and brainstorm about the reasons for the problem and possible solutions to the problem. Be prepared to discuss your reasons and proposed solutions with classmates.

Ban the Things. Ban Them All

MOLLY IVINS

Molly Ivins (b. 1944), a graduate of Smith College and Columbia University, began her career as a reporter. She has been a columnist since 1980 and is currently with the *Fort Worth Star-Telegram*. Ivins is also a contributor to magazines such as the *Nation* and *Ms.*, and she has a collection of essays published under the title *Molly Ivins Can't Say That, Can She?* An insightful political commentator, Ivins is also known for her wit and irreverent style, traits shown in the following column published March 16, 1993.

Questions to Guide Your Reading

1. What is Ivins's thesis, the claim of her argument? Where does she state it?
2. Ivins is not timid about expressing her views. As you read, note words that reveal her attitude through their negative meanings and connotations.

AUSTIN—Guns. Everywhere guns.   1

Let me start this discussion by pointing out that I am not anti-   2
gun. I'm pro-knife. Consider the merits of the knife.

In the first place, you have to catch up with someone to stab   3
him. A general substitution of knives for guns would promote
physical fitness. We'd turn into a whole nation of great runners.
Plus, knives don't ricochet. And people are seldom killed while
cleaning their knives.

As a civil libertarian, I of course support the Second Amend-   4
ment. And I believe it means exactly what it says: "A well-
regulated militia being necessary to the security of a free
state, the right of the people to keep and bear arms shall not
be infringed." Fourteen-year-old boys are not part of a well-
regulated militia. Members of wacky religious cults are not part
of a well-regulated militia. Permitting unregulated citizens to
have guns is destroying the security of this free state.

I am intrigued by the arguments of those who claim to follow   5
the judicial doctrine of original intent. How do they know it was
the dearest wish of Thomas Jefferson's heart that teenage drug
dealers should cruise the cities of this nation perforating their
fellow citizens with assault rifles? Channeling?

There is more hooey spread about the Second Amendment.   6
It says quite clearly that guns are for those who form part of a
well-regulated militia, i.e., the armed forces including the
National Guard. The reasons for keeping them away from
everyone else get clearer by the day.

The comparison most often used is that of the automobile,   7
another lethal object that is regularly used to wreak great carnage. Obviously, this society is full of people who haven't got
enough common sense to use an automobile properly. But we
haven't outlawed cars yet.

We do, however, license them and their owners, restrict their   8
use to presumably sane and sober adults and keep track of who
sells them to whom. At a minimum, we should do the same
with guns.

In truth, there is no rational argument for guns in this soci-   9
ety. This is no longer a frontier nation in which people hunt their
own food. It is a crowded, overwhelmingly urban country in
which letting people have access to guns is a continuing disaster. Those who want guns—whether for target shooting, hunting

or potting rattlesnakes (get a hoe)—should be subject to the same restrictions placed on gun owners in England—a nation in which liberty has survived nicely without an armed populace.

10   The argument that "guns don't kill people" is patent nonsense. Anyone who has ever worked in a cop shop knows how many family arguments end in murder because there was a gun in the house. Did the gun kill someone? No. But if there had been no gun, no one would have died. At least not without a good footrace first. Guns do kill. Unlike cars, that is all they do.

11   Michael Crichton makes an interesting argument about technology in his thriller *Jurassic Park*. He points out that power without discipline is making this society into a wreckage. By the time someone who studies the martial arts becomes a master—literally able to kill with bare hands—that person has also undergone years of training and discipline. But any fool can pick up a gun and kill with it.

12   "A well-regulated militia" surely implies both long training and long discipline. That is the least, the very least, that should be required of those who are permitted to have guns, because a gun is literally the power to kill. For years, I used to enjoy taunting my gun-nut friends about their psychosexual hangups—always in a spirit of good cheer, you understand. But letting the noisy minority in the National Rifle Association force us to allow this carnage to continue is just plain insane.

13   I do think gun nuts have a power hangup. I don't know what is missing in their psyches that they need to feel they have the power to kill. But no sane society would allow this to continue.

14   Ban the damn things. Ban them all.

15   You want protection? Get a dog.

Expanding Vocabulary

Study definitions of the following words and then use each of them in separate sentences. The number in parentheses is the number of the paragraph in which the word appears.

ricochet (3)	lethal (7)
wacky (4)	carnage (7)
intrigued (5)	taunting (12)
perforating (5)	psyches (13)
hooey (6)	

Understanding Content

1. What, according to Ivins, does the Second Amendment mean? How does she cleverly turn the pro-gun group's use of the Second Amendment to her advantage in this paragraph?
2. What reason does Ivins give to support the assertion that "there is no rational argument for guns in this society"? What restrictions does she want this country to adopt?
3. Why, in the author's view, is the pro-gun argument that guns don't kill people "patent nonsense"?
4. What psychological explanation does Ivins offer to account for "gun nuts"?

Drawing Inferences about Thesis and Purpose

1. When Ivins writes, in paragraph 2, that she is "not anti-gun," how do you know that she does not mean this?
2. When the author writes, in paragraph 2, "I'm pro-knife," she introduces an idea that she develops through an entire paragraph and returns to later in her essay. In what sense do knives have "merit"? In what way is she being serious? What else is she doing; that is, what does she accomplish through her discussion of the merits of the knife?

Analyzing Strategies and Style

1. Characterize Ivins's style. Consider her word choice and sentence patterns.
2. Look especially at her first two and last two paragraphs; what tone is created by her style?
3. When Ivins writes that she used to taunt friends "in a spirit of good cheer," does she mean what she says? What technique does she use in this passage?
4. How does Ivins organize her discussion of gun control? To what points is she responding as a way to develop her argument? What type of argument is this?

Thinking Critically

1. Does the author effectively challenge the "Second Amendment argument" of the gun lobby? The argument that licensing will lead to outlawing guns? The "guns don't kill" argument? Do you think that her refutation of one argument is more convincing than another? Explain and defend your evaluation of her argument.

2. What audience is likely to be offended by this column? What does your answer tell you about the audience to which her essay is targeted? Which audience do you fit into? Does that explain, at least in part, the way you responded to the first set of questions?
3. How might Ivins justify her approach of "grabbing the reader by the shoulders and shaking him or her"? Why does she think this approach is necessary?

Why Guns Matter

NED ANDREWS

A graduate of Yale University, Ned Andrews (b. 1980) was a member of the Yale Conservative Party and author of articles for both the *Yale Daily News* and *Yale Herald* while at Yale. As part of a summer internship at the *American Enterprise* magazine, Andrews posted a longer version of his article on gun control issues online. The shorter version, which follows, appeared in the September 2002 issue of the magazine.

Questions to Guide Your Reading

1. Which color represents "Gore" states and which represents "Bush" states?
2. Why were the weeks after the 2000 elections "tense"?

1   During the tense weeks that followed Election Night 2000, many Americans became familiar with the color-coded map dividing their country into patches of red and blue. Many publications, including *TAE* (see March 2002), have described the cultural differences between the primarily coastal pockets that supported Gore and the expanses of Bush territory in between. But if column inches and word counts are any indicator, few commentators have investigated the underlying philosophical difference between Blue and Red America. They might start by examining the debate over gun control.

2   Gun-control advocates frequently argue that the Second Amendment is "obsolete," that in our era the government can fulfill all our law-enforcement needs. So, how well does the gov-

ernment take care of Blue America? According to the FBI, Gore-leaning states reported one crime for every 27 residents in 2000. The situation is on the mend, but there are still plenty of holes in the Left's security blanket.

Blue America's overconfidence exemplifies the elitism and 3
insularity that characterize its culture in general. Blue America forgets that not everyone lives in cities with beat cops or in suburbs with ample law-enforcement budgets. From my east Tennessee home, the nearest police station is a good 20-minute drive away. Add the time it takes to process a 911 call and locate the offender, and it becomes evident that if my family did not own guns, criminals could wreak havoc with impunity. Apparently my situation is not unique: In Red America, those 1-in-27 odds rise to 1 in 22. Out here, the arm of the law just isn't long enough, and even liberals such as Mississippi's Mike Espy know that big government can't "go it alone" against criminals who will respect new anti-gun statues no more than the laws they break already.

Blue America holds not only that the government is a com- 4
petent agent on our behalf, but also that in forming that government we alienated our own right to fend for ourselves. Since the government is capable of defending us, it does no wrong by disarming the public. Such reasoning ignores the fact that the right to bear arms helps ensure not only our current safety but our future liberty as well.

Legal scholars disagree on whether the Second Amendment 5
merely permits states to maintain defense forces or also allows individuals to arm themselves. Yet no matter which position is correct, the goal is the same: to check the law's enforcers as well as its violators.

This is why Red America values the Second Amendment so 6
highly. Red America still evaluates the political sphere from a moral perspective: Ultimately, the role of government is not to create law but to obey it. And when government deviates from its ethical mandate, citizens have a duty to restore it to its rightful place. Red America realizes that a disarmed citizenry will be unable to stand up for what is right when its government does wrong.

Blue America has abandoned this moral point of view, 7
instead evaluating conflicts in terms of "interests." It further

relinquishes critical evaluation of those interests, assuming that all are equally worthy of satisfaction. Blue America views government not as an enforcer of duties and rights but as a facilitator of individuals' personal ends, appealing for justification not to any categorical moral code but to entirely pragmatic concerns.

8   This is why the Second Amendment is so bothersome to Blue America. The right to bear arms is the right to take a stand, to act on the belief that you are right and someone else is wrong, and as such it is a threat to the amoral collectivism that the New Left embodies. For it is our guarantee—our only guarantee—that we may transform our moral beliefs into action.

Expanding Vocabulary

Match each word in column A with its definition in column B. When is doubt, first find the word in the essay and look for context clues to aid your understanding of the word's meaning. Then, if necessary, use your dictionary to complete the matching exercise. The number in parentheses is the number of the paragraph in which the word appears.

Column A	*Column B*
exemplifies (3)	inflict widespread destruction
elitism (3)	those who compel obedience
insularity (3)	abandons, gives up
wreak havoc (3)	belief that certain persons or groups
impunity (3)	deserve favored treatment
enforcers (5)	one who assists to make things easier
deviates (6)	without punishment
relinquishes (7)	not caring about moral issues
facilitator (7)	reveals by example
amoral (8)	differs from the usual way
	narrow-mindedness, closed off
	from others

Understanding Content

1. In the discussions following the 2000 elections, what did the commentators *not* examine, in the author's view?
2. What issue will reveal differences between "Blue" and "Red" America?

3. What was the crime rate in 2000 in Blue America? What was the crime rate in Red America?
4. With what attitudes does Andrews charge Blue America?
5. Andrews argues that Red America values the Second Amendment for what two reasons?
6. By rejecting the Second Amendment, Blue America shows that it holds what beliefs about government, according to the author?

Drawing Inferences about Thesis and Purpose

1. What is Andrews's position on gun control?
2. What is his thesis?
3. What can you infer to be his political affiliation?

Analyzing Strategies and Style

1. Andrews organizes his discussion around a color-coded map revealing election results. What does he gain by this strategy? What does he expect his audience to know?
2. What word choice in paragraph 1 seems to reveal the author's political leanings?

Thinking Critically

1. Examine Andrews's argument. Has he demonstrated that those who favor gun control are elitists? That they have forgotten that not everyone lives in cities or the suburbs?
2. Andrews's crime stats indicate that the crime rate is higher in Middle America than in communities along the two coasts. Is this what you would have expected? Is this crime rate contrast clear and helpful? (Aren't there cities in Middle America and rural areas along the coasts as well?) See what crime statistics and gun-ownership statistics you can find online that might be helpful in evaluating this argument.
3. What, if any, logical fallacies do you find in this argument?

Adult Crime, Adult Time

LINDA J. COLLIER

An attorney, Linda J. Collier is currently dean of public services and social sciences at Delaware County Community College in Pennsylvania. She has been the director of student legal services

at Penn State University and special assistant for legal affairs t
o two college presidents in addition to teaching courses in sociology and criminal justice. The following essay, published in
the *Washington Post* in 1998, is written in response to the case of
a 12-year-old and a 14-year-old shooting four students and a
teacher at their school in Jonesboro, Arkansas, that same year.

Questions to Guide Your Reading
1. What is the trend in juvenile crime?
2. The juvenile justice system was designed to handle what
   kinds of cases?

1   When prosecutor Brent Davis said he wasn't sure if he could
charge 11-year-old Andrew Golden and 13-year-old Mitchell
Johnson as adults after Tuesday afternoon's slaughter in Jonesboro, Ark., I cringed. But not for the reasons you might think.
2   I knew he was formulating a judgment based on laws that
have not had a major overhaul for more than 100 years. I knew
his hands were tied by the longstanding creed that juvenile
offenders, generally defined as those under the age of 18, are
to be treated rather than punished. I knew he would have to
do legal cartwheels to get the case out of the juvenile system.
But most of all, I cringed because today's juvenile suspects—
even those who are accused of committing the most violent
crimes—are still regarded by the law as children first and criminals second.
3   As astonishing as the Jonesboro events were, this is hardly
the first time that children with access to guns and other
weapons have brought tragedy to a school. Only weeks before
the Jonesboro shootings, three girls in Paducah, Ky., were killed
in their school lobby when a 14-year-old classmate allegedly
opened fire on them. Authorities said he had several guns with
him, and the alleged murder weapon was one of seven stolen
from a neighbor's garage. And the day after the Jonesboro
shootings, a 14-year-old in Daly City, Calif., was charged as a
juvenile after he allegedly fired at his middle-school principal
with a semiautomatic handgun.
4   It's not a new or unusual phenomenon for children to commit violent crimes at younger and younger ages, but it often
takes a shocking incident to draw our attention to a trend
already in progress. According to the U.S. Department of Jus-

tice, crimes committed by juveniles have increased by 60 percent since 1984. Where juvenile delinquency was once limited to truancy or vandalism, juveniles now are more likely to be the perpetrators of serious and deadly crimes such as arson, aggravated assault, rape and murder. And these violent offenders increasingly include those as young as the Jonesboro suspects. Since 1965, the number of 12-year-olds arrested for violent crimes has doubled and the number of 13- and 14-year-olds has tripled, according to government statistics.

Those statistics are a major reason why we need to revamp   5
our antiquated juvenile justice system. Nearly every state, including Arkansas, has laws that send most youthful violent offenders to the juvenile courts, where they can only be found "delinquent" and confined in a juvenile facility (typically not past age 21). In recent years, many states have enacted changes in their juvenile crime laws, and some have lowered the age at which a juvenile can be tried as an adult for certain violent crimes. Virginia, for example, has reduced its minimum age to 14, and suspects accused of murder and aggravated malicious wounding are automatically waived to adult court. Illinois is now sending some 13-year-olds to adult court after a hearing in juvenile court. In Kansas, a 1996 law allows juveniles as young as 10 to be prosecuted as adults in some cases. These are steps in the right direction, but too many states still treat violent offenders under 16 as juveniles who belong in the juvenile system.

My views are not those of a frustrated prosecutor. I have rep-   6
resented children as a court-appointed guardian *ad litem*, or temporary guardian, in the Philadelphia juvenile justice system. Loosely defined, a guardian *ad litem* is responsible for looking after the best interest of a neglected or rebellious child who has come into the juvenile courts. It is often a humbling experience as I try to help children whose lives have gone awry, sometimes because of circumstances beyond their control.

My experience has made me believe that the system is doing   7
a poor job at treatment as well as punishment. One of my "girls," a chronic truant, was a foster child who longed to be adopted. She often talked of how she wanted a pink room, a frilly bunk bed and sisters with whom she could share her dreams. She languished in foster care from ages 2 to 13 because her drug-ravaged mother would not relinquish her parental rights. Initially, the girl refused to tolerate the half-life that the

state had maintained was in her best interest. But as it became clear that we would never convince her mother to give up her rights, the girl became a frequent runaway. Eventually she ended up pregnant, wandering from place to place and committing adult crimes to survive. No longer a child, not quite a woman, she is the kind of teenage offender for whom the juvenile system has little or nothing to offer.

8   A brief history: Proceedings in juvenile justice began in 1890 in Chicago, where the original mandate was to save wayward children and protect them from the ravages of society. The system called for children to be processed through an appendage of the family court. By design, juveniles were to be kept away from the court's criminal side, the district attorney and adult correctional institutions.

9   Typically, initial procedures are informal, non-threatening and not open to public scrutiny. A juvenile suspect is interviewed by an "intake" officer who determines the child's fate. The intake officer may issue a warning, lecture and release; he may detain the suspect; or, he may decide to file a petition, subjecting the child to juvenile "adjudication" proceedings. If the law allows, the intake officer may make a recommendation that the juvenile be transferred to adult criminal court.

10   An adjudication is similar to a hearing, rather than a trial, although the juvenile may be represented by counsel and a juvenile prosecutor will represent the interests of the community. It is important to note that throughout the proceedings, no matter which side of the fence the parties are on, the operating principle is that everyone is working in the best interests of the child. Juvenile court judges do not issue findings of guilt, but decide whether a child is delinquent. If delinquency is found, the judge must decide the child's fate. Should the child be sent back to the family—assuming there is one? Declare him or her "in need of supervision," which brings in the intense help of social services? Remove the child from the family and place him or her in foster care? Confine the child to a state institution for juvenile offenders?

11   This system was developed with truants, vandals and petty thieves in mind. But this model is not appropriate for the violent juvenile offender of today. Detaining a rapist or murderer in a juvenile facility until the age of 18 or 21 isn't even a slap on the hand. If a juvenile is accused of murdering, raping or

assaulting someone with a deadly weapon, the suspect should automatically be sent to adult criminal court. What's to ponder? With violent crime becoming more prevalent among the 12 junior set, it's a mystery why there hasn't been a major overhaul of juvenile justice laws long before now. Will the Jonesboro shootings be the incident that makes us take a hard look at the current system? When it became evident that the early release of Jesse Timmendequas—whose murder of 7-year-old Megan Kanka in New Jersey sparked national outrage—had caused unwarranted tragedy, legislative action was swift. Now New Jersey has Megan's Law, which requires the advance notification of a sexual predator's release into a neighborhood. Other states have followed suit.

It is unequivocally clear that the same type of mandate is 13 needed to establish a uniform minimum age for trying juveniles as adults. As it stands now, there is no consistency in state laws governing waivers to adult court. One reason for this lack of uniformity is the absence of direction from the federal government or Congress. The Bureau of Justice Statistics reports that adjacent states such as New York and Pennsylvania respond differently to 16-year-old criminals, with New York tending to treat offenders of that age as adults and Pennsylvania handling them in the juvenile justice system.

Federal prosecution of juveniles is not totally unheard of, but 14 it is uncommon. The Bureau of Justice Statistics estimates that during 1994, at least 65 juveniles were referred to the attorney general for transfer to adult status. In such cases, the U.S. attorney's office must certify a substantial federal interest in the case and show that one of the following is true: The state does not have jurisdiction; the state refuses to assume jurisdiction or the state does not have adequate services for juvenile offenders; the offense is a violent felony, drug trafficking or firearm offense as defined by the U.S. Code.

Exacting hurdles, but not insurmountable. In the Jonesboro 15 case, prosecutor Davis has been exploring ways to enlist the federal court's jurisdiction. Whatever happens, federal prosecutions of young offenders are clearly not the long-term answer. The states must act. So as far as I can see, the next step is clear: Children who knowingly engage in adult conduct and adult crimes should automatically be subject to adult rules and adult prison time.

Expanding Vocabulary

Match each word in column A with its definition in column B. When in doubt, first find the word in the essay and look for context clues to aid your understanding of the word's meaning. Then, if necessary, use your dictionary to complete the matching exercise. The number in parentheses is the number of the paragraph in which the word appears.

Column A	*Column B*
cringed (1)	occurrence
formulating (2)	those who are responsible for what
allegedly (3)	has happened
phenomenon (4)	obsolete, outdated
truancy (4)	revise, make over
perpetrators (4)	existed in miserable conditions
revamp (5)	claim or right given up
antiquated (5)	damages
malicious (5)	preparing in an organized way
waived (5)	hear a judicial proceeding
awry (6)	give up
languished (7)	clear examination
relinquish (7)	pulled back in fear
ravages (8)	absence without permission ·
scrutiny (9)	clearly; without question
adjudication (9)	presumably, unproven
unequivocally (13)	amiss, wrong
	desire to hurt someone

Understanding Content

1. Summarize the author's examples of recent violent juvenile crime.
2. What are some of the problems with current state laws governing juvenile crimes?
3. Briefly summarize the author's history of the juvenile justice system.
4. In addition to failing to punish properly, in the author's view, what else do juvenile court systems fail to do?
5. Where does Collier look for help in correcting the juvenile justice system?

Drawing Inferences about Thesis and Purpose

1. What is Collier's thesis? Where does she state it?

2. In paragraph 11, when she writes "What's to ponder?" what response does she want from readers?

Analyzing Strategies and Style

1. Although Collier is writing in response to the Jonesboro murders, she refers to other juvenile murders in paragraph 3. What does she seek to gain by this?
2. Collier asserts that she is not writing as a "frustrated prosecutor" and describes her experience as a court-appointed guardian. What does she gain by her discussion in paragraphs 6 and 7?

Thinking Critically

1. What are the main points of Collier's argument? Make a list of the key steps in her argument and then evaluate the argument. Has she supported her thesis convincingly?
2. Could the example of one of Collier's court-appointed "girls" be used to argue *for*, rather than against, the juvenile justice system? Explain your answer.
3. Do you think that juveniles should be tried as adults? If so, in what situations?

Kids Who Kill Are Still Kids

RICHARD COHEN

Richard Cohen (b. 1941), a *Washington Post* columnist who has been syndicated since 1976, writes about both political issues and contemporary culture. The following column appeared in newspapers on August 3, 2001.

Questions to Guide Your Reading

1. How many juveniles have been tried as adults in U.S. courts?
2. What is Cohen's thesis?

When I was about 12, I heaved a cinder block over my neighbor's fence and nearly killed her. I didn't know she was there. When I was about the same age, I started a small fire 1 in a nearby field that spread until it threatened some nearby houses. I didn't mean to do it. When I was even younger, I climbed on top of a toolshed, threw a brick in the general direction of my sister and sent her, bleeding profusely and crying so that I can still hear her, to the hospital. I didn't mean to do that, either.

2   I tell these stories to remind us all that kids are kids and to suggest that even the worst of them—even the ones who commit murder—are still kids. I would be lying if I said that I knew what to do with them—how long they should be jailed and where—but I do know that something awful has come over this country. It seems the more incomprehensible the crime, the more likely it is that a child will be treated as an adult.

3   This is what happened to Nathaniel Brazill, 14, who was recently sentenced to 28 years in prison for the murder of a teacher, Barry Grunow. Brazill was only 13 when he shot the teacher on the final day of school. Grunow, a much-beloved teacher, had stopped Brazill from talking to two girls and disrupting the class. Earlier in the day, the boy had been suspended for throwing water balloons. He had gone home, gotten a gun and returned to school. Grunow was Brazill's favorite teacher.

4   I always feel in columns of this sort the necessity to say something about the victim and how his life was taken from him. I feel a particular need to do so in this case because Grunow seemed to be an exceptional teacher, a good person. Anyway— and this is only me talking—I feel a certain awe, a humility, toward people who dedicate their lives to teaching kids instead of, say, peddling tech stocks or mouthing off on television about Gary Condit.[1]

5   But Grunow is gone and nothing can be done to bring him back. That is not merely a cliché but also an important point. Because always in these cases when it comes time to justify why a minor was treated as an adult, someone says something about sending a message to other kids. This is absurd.

Consider what Brazill did. He shot his teacher before oodles of witnesses. He shot a man he liked. He shot someone without any chance of his getting away. He shot someone for almost no reason at all. He shot someone not in the course of a robbery

[1]Californian member of Congress—Ed.

or a sex crime or because he put a move on his girlfriend but   6
because he is a screwed-up kid, damaged, full of anger and with
not much self-control. He shot someone without fully compre-
hending the consequences. He shot someone because, among
other things, he was just 13 years old.

And yet, he was prosecuted—and sentenced to three years   7
more than the mandatory minimum—as an adult. If there is
one thing he is not, it is an adult. But Brazill and, earlier, 13-
year-old Lionel Tate were sentenced as if they were button
men for some crime family. Tate was given life without parole
for the killing of a 6-year-old girl he maintained died in a
wrestling accident. These boys were tried as adults but, I'd
guess, their ability to participate in their own defense would
be labeled juvenile.

Amnesty International says about 200,000 children have been   8
tried as adults by American courts. Florida alone reports that
3,300 kids were prosecuted as adults in fiscal 1999–2000. This
sends a message—but it's to the adult community: We're getting
tough. Kids, however, are unlikely to get the message. I mean,
you know how kids are.

Where is the deterrence in this policy? Will other 13-year-olds   9
now hesitate before killing their teacher? Hardly. Who is being
punished? The child at first, but later the adult he becomes.

Brazill will be over 40 when he gets out of jail. When he's, say,   10
35, will he have anything in common with the child who pulled
the trigger? No more, I'd say, than I do with the jerk who nearly killed Richie Miller's mother with a cinder block. I didn't
set out to hurt anyone, it's true. But neither did Brazill, he says.
He just pulled the trigger and the man, somehow, died. It is,
when you think about it, a childish explanation.

Expanding Vocabulary

Study definitions of each of the following words and then use each one
in a separate sentence. The number in parentheses is the number of the
paragraph in which the word appears.

heaved (1)
profusely (1)
incomprehensible (2)
prosecuted (7)
deterrence (9)

Understanding Content

1. What is Cohen's primary example?
2. What was Brazill's sentence?
3. What is Cohen's explanation for Brazill's behavior?
4. When we try juveniles as adults, who, in Cohen's view, is being sent a message?

Drawing Inferences about Thesis and Purpose

1. Why does Cohen doubt that punishing children as adults acts as a deterrent to crime?

Analyzing Strategies and Style

1. Cohen begins by recounting stories of his childhood. Why? What point does he want to make?
2. Look at the author's concluding paragraph. What makes it effective? What is clever about the last sentence?

Thinking Critically

1. When you were young, did you do anything that could have resulted in a court case? If so, what were the consequences and how do you feel about the incident now?
2. Evaluate Cohen's argument. Are his reasons and evidence convincing? Why or why not?
3. How should the two boys used as examples by Cohen have been tried and sentenced? Take a stand.

The Myth and Math of Affirmative Action

GOODWIN LIU

A Supreme Court law clerk during the 2000–2001 term, Goodwin Liu is now an attorney in Washington, D.C., focusing on appellate litigation. Prior to his clerkship, he was senior program officer for higher education at AmeriCorps. The following article, which appeared in the *Washington Post* in September 2002, is adapted from a longer essay that was published in the same month in the *Michigan Law Review*.

Questions to Guide Your Reading

1. What does Liu mean by "the causation fallacy"?
2. What is Liu's purpose in writing?

With the arrival of spring, thousands of high school and college seniors have been anxiously checking the mail for word from the nation's most prestigious universities. Although some envelopes are thick with good news, most are thin and disappointing. For many white applicants, the disappointment will become bitterness if they suspect the reason for their rejection was affirmative action. But such suspicions, in all likelihood, are misplaced. 1

Affirmative action is widely thought to be unfair because it benefits minority applicants at the expense of more deserving whites. Yet this perception tends to inflate the cost beyond its real proportions. While it is true that affirmative action gives minority applicants a significant boost in selective admissions, it is not true that most white applicants would fare better if elite schools eliminated the practice. Understanding why is crucial to separating fact from fiction in the national debate over affirmative action. 2

Any day now, a federal appeals court in Cincinnati will issue a decision in a major test lawsuit challenging the use of race as a factor in selective admissions. In that case, the University of Michigan denied admission in 1995 to a white undergraduate applicant named Jennifer Gratz. Charging reverse discrimination, Gratz said, "I knew of people accepted to Ann Arbor who were less qualified, and my first reaction when I was rejected was, 'Let's sue.' " 3

The Michigan case will likely end up at the Supreme Court. If it does, Gratz will try to follow in the footsteps of Allan Bakke, a rejected white applicant who won admission in 1978 to the University of California at Davis's medical school after convincing the high court that the school's policy of reserving 16 of 100 seats each year for minority students was unconstitutional. For many Americans, the success of Bakke's lawsuit has long highlighted what is unfair about affirmative action: 4

Giving minority applicants a significant advantage causes deserving white applicants to lose out. But to draw such an inference in Bakke's case—or in the case of the vast majority of rejected white applicants—is to indulge in what I call "the causation fallacy."

5   There's no doubt, based on test scores and grades, that Bakke was a highly qualified applicant. Justice Lewis Powell, who authored the decisive opinion in the case, observed that Bakke's Medical College Admission Test (MCAT) scores placed him in the top tier of test-takers, whereas the average scores of the quota beneficiaries in 1974 placed them in the bottom third. Likewise, his science grade point average was 3.44 on a 4.0 scale, compared with a 2.42 average for the special admittees, and his overall GPA was similarly superior. Given these numbers, the only reason for Bakke's rejection was the school's need to make room for less qualified minority applicants, right?

6   Wrong. Although Justice Powell pointed out that minority applicants were admitted with grades and test scores much lower than Bakke's, he did not discuss what I found to be the most striking data that appeared in his opinion: Bakke's grades and scores were significantly higher than the average for the regular admittees. In other words, his academic qualifications were better than those of the majority of applicants admitted outside the racial quota. So why didn't he earn one of the 84 regular places?

7   It is clear that the medical school admitted students not only on the basis of grades and test scores, but on other factors relevant to the study and practice of medicine, such as compassion, communication skills and commitment to research. Justice Powell's opinion does not tell us exactly what qualities the regular admittees had that Bakke lacked. But it notes that the head of the admissions committee, who interviewed Bakke, found him "rather limited in his approach" to medical problems and thought he had "very definite opinions which were based more on his personal viewpoints than upon a study of the total problem."

8   Whatever Bakke's weaknesses were, there were several reasons, apart from affirmative action, that might have led the medical school to reject his application. Grades and test scores do not tell us the whole story.

Of course, affirmative action did lower Bakke's chance of 9
admission. But by how much? One way to answer this question is to compare Bakke's chance of admission had he competed for all 100 seats in the class with his chance of admission competing for the 84 seats outside of the racial quota. To simplify, let's assume none of the special applicants would have been admitted ahead of any regular candidate.

In 1974, Bakke was one of 3,109 regular applicants to the 10
medical school. With the racial quota, the average likelihood of admission for regular applicants was 2.7 percent (84 divided by 3,109). With no racial quota, the average likelihood of admission would have been 3.2 percent (100 divided by 3,109). So the quota increased the average likelihood of rejection from 96.8 percent to 97.3 percent.

To be sure, Bakke was not an average applicant. Only one-sixth 11
of regular applicants (roughly 520) received an interview. But even among these highly qualified applicants, eliminating the racial quota would have increased the average rate of admission from 16 percent (84 divided by 520) to only 19 percent (100 divided by 520). Certainly a few more regular applicants would have been admitted were it not for affirmative action. But Bakke, upon receiving his rejection letter, had no reason to believe he would have been among the lucky few.

In fact, Bakke applied in both 1973 and 1974 and, according 12
to evidence in the lawsuit, he did not even make the waiting list in either year.

The statistical pattern in Bakke's case is not an anomaly. It 13
occurs in any selection process in which the applicants who do not benefit from affirmative action greatly outnumber those who do.

Recent research confirms this point. Using 1989 data from a 14
representative sample of selective schools, former university presidents William Bowen and Derek Bok showed in their 1998 book, *The Shape of the River*, that eliminating racial preferences would have increased the likelihood of admission for white undergraduate applicants from 25 percent to only 26.5 percent.

The Mellon Foundation, which sponsored the study, pro- 15
vided me with additional data to calculate admission rates by SAT score. If the schools in the Bowen/Bok sample had admitted applicants with similar SAT scores at the same rate

regardless of race, the chance of admission for white applicants would have increased by one percentage point or less at scores 1300 and above, by three to four percentage points at scores from 1150 to 1299, and by four to seven percentage points at scores below 1150.

16   It is true that black applicants were admitted at much higher rates than white applicants with similar grades and test scores. But that fact does not prove that affirmative action imposes a substantial disadvantage on white applicants. The extent of the disadvantage depends on the number of blacks and whites in the applicant pool. Because the number of black applicants to selective institutions is relatively small, admitting them at higher rates does not significantly lower the chance of admission for the average individual in the relatively large sea of white applicants.

17   In the Bowen/Bok study, for example, 60 percent of black applicants scoring 1200–1249 on the SAT were admitted, compared with 19 percent of whites. In the 1250–1299 range, 74 percent of blacks were admitted, compared with 23 percent of whites. These data indicate—more so than proponents of affirmative action typically acknowledge—that racial preferences give minority applicants a substantial advantage. But eliminating affirmative action would have increased the admission rate for whites from 19 percent to only 21 percent in the 1200–1249 range, and from 23 percent to only 24 percent in the 1250–1299 range.

18   These figures show that rejected white applicants have every reason not to blame their misfortune on affirmative action. In selective admissions, the competition is so intense that even without affirmative action, the overwhelming majority of rejected white applicants still wouldn't get in.

19   Still, isn't it true that minority applicants are admitted at rates up to three times higher than white applicants with similar SAT scores? Isn't that unfair?

20   To answer that question, it's important to observe that racial preferences are not the only preferences that cause different groups of applicants with similar test scores to be admitted at different rates. Geographic, athletic and alumni preferences also weigh heavily, to the detriment of applicants such as Jennifer

Gratz at Michigan. Gratz hailed from a Detroit suburb, not from a rural area or the inner city. She was not a star athlete. And her working-class parents were high school graduates, not University of Michigan alumni.

Yet preferences for athletes, though occasionally criticized, have never galvanized the kind of outrage often directed at affirmative action. Similarly, there is no organized legal campaign against geographic preferences, even though where one grows up is as much an accident of circumstance as one's skin color. And neither Gratz nor her lawyers at the Washington-based Center for Individual Rights have publicly denounced alumni preferences, much less launched a moral crusade against them. 21

Such preferences reflect institutional interests that are unrelated to an applicant's grades or test scores. But the same is true of affirmative action when it is used to enhance educational diversity. The question, then, is not whether unequal treatment is unfair as a general rule, but whether unequal treatment based on race should be singled out for special condemnation. 22

As the Supreme Court said in 1954, unequal treatment based on race can inflict on members of a disfavored race "a feeling of inferiority as to their status in the community that may affect their hearts and minds in a way unlikely ever to be undone." But social stigma is not the complaint pressed by white applicants such as Bakke or Gratz. Despite 30 years of affirmative action, white students continue to dominate most of the nation's best colleges and all of the top law and medical schools. Against this backdrop, not even the most ardent foe of affirmative action would say that it stamps white applicants with a badge of racial inferiority. Indeed, just as athletic and geographic preferences do not denigrate applicants who are uncoordinated or suburban, affirmative action is not a policy of racial prejudice. 23

For white applicants, the unfairness of affirmative action lies not in its potential to displace or stigmatize, but in its potential to stereotype. Minority applicants are not the only ones who contribute to educational diversity. Were a school to use race as its sole "plus" factor in admissions, then white applicants could legitimately complain that the school failed 24 to take into account non-racial attributes essential to genuine educational diversity.

25   Putting the complaint in these terms is an important first step toward rethinking the conventional view that a race-conscious admissions policy pits whites against minorities in a zero-sum game. Instead of attacking affirmative action, white applicants such as Jennifer Gratz might do better to urge top schools committed to educational diversity to place a higher premium on first-generation college attendance or growing up in a blue-collar home. Ironically, the stories of affirmative action's "victims" could spur America's colleges to further widen the elite circles of educational opportunity. And that would be a result students of any color could applaud.

Expanding Vocabulary

Study the following words in their contexts in the essay. Then write a brief definition or synonym for each one. (Do not use a dictionary; try to guess the word's meaning from its context.) The number in parentheses is the number of the paragraph in which the word appears.

prestigious (1)   galvanized (21)
anomaly (13)   denounced (21)
imposes (16)   ardent (23)
detriment (20)   denigrate (23)

Understanding Content

1. What does affirmative action refer to with regard to college admissions?
2. How do some people see the consequences of affirmative action?
3. What does the author's discussion of the Bakke case reveal about the college selection process?
4. What are Liu's statistics designed to show?
5. What groups typically receive preferential admissions to college?

Drawing Inferences about Thesis and Purpose

1. What is the "myth" of affirmative action?
2. What is Liu's thesis?
3. What suggestion for change does he offer?

Analyzing Strategies and Style

1. Affirmative action debates are often quite heated. How would you describe Liu's tone in this essay? How is his tone consistent with his approach to the issue?
2. What does Liu gain by all the "math" that he provides?

Thinking Critically

1. What has been your view on race-based admissions to college? Has Liu affected your thinking in any way? Explain.
2. What argument would colleges make for their varied preferential admissions policies? Do you think that they have a good argument? Why or why not?

California's Big Squeeze

GREGORY RODRIGUEZ

Gregory Rodriguez is a senior fellow at Pepperdine University's Public Policy Institute and an associate editor at Pacific News Service. With the approval of Proposition 209, Californians eliminated affirmative action in the selection of students for the state's public colleges. As predicted by opponents of the proposition, its passage has resulted in some drop in minority admissions. The editors of *The Nation* magazine asked Rodriguez and another Californian to offer comments on the situation. Rodriguez's article was published in *The Nation* on October 5, 1998.

Questions to Guide Your Reading

1. What is the specific context in which Rodriguez examines affirmative action?
2. What is his purpose in writing?

The recent news that the University of California admitted 1 fewer African-American and Latino students into this fall's freshman class than it had in 1997 provoked a wave of alarmist headlines and editorials that mirrored the worst fears of opponents of the victorious Proposition 209, passed two years ago.

Prop 209, which prohibits public universities from considering race in their admissions decisions, had now borne its first fruit, and its opponents were quick to pounce on admissions data to declare that California had indeed regressed to the era of separate and unequal.

2   On *The NewsHour With Jim Lehrer*, California State Assembly Speaker Antonio Villaraigosa said he thought Prop 209 was "going to close the door of opportunity on children of California." Meanwhile, a lawyer for the NAACP publicly warned of the return of "race-exclusive" campuses.

3   National news coverage focused on the precipitate drop of 57 percent and 36 percent in black and Latino admissions at, respectively, UCLA and UC Berkeley—the two flagship campuses of the system. "Acceptance of Blacks, Latinos to UC Plunges," screamed a front-page headline in the *Los Angeles Times*. "Proposition 209 Shuts the Door" read a lead editorial in the *New York Times*. But there's been a misreading of the numbers. The elitist and narrow focus fixation on UC's two flagship campuses obscured the far less dramatic drop in minority admissions to the entire eight-campus system. When you look at numbers for the entire system, you find that the UC campuses admitted only 18 percent fewer black students and only 7 percent fewer Latinos.

4   Let's be clear. Even these reduced numbers are nothing to cheer about. On the other hand, they hardly amount to racial exclusion. Indeed, to put these statistics in context, the University of California system, with a total undergraduate enrollment of about 129,000, admitted a total of 294 fewer black and 392 fewer Latino undergraduates this year as compared with last.

5   It's lamentable that even this small number of minority students is being excluded. But the UC system has always been about exclusion—even in the heyday of affirmative action. The top level of California's public higher education system, UC has always been the destination for only a very select group of students. On average, fewer than a quarter of California students in four-year colleges attend the University of California. In 1995, before Prop 209, nearly twice as many undergraduates were enrolled in the less-celebrated California State University system, and many more attended private four-year colleges.

Despite the outcry, post-209 admissions data don't highlight 6 gross racial inequity at the University of California. If anything, the data reveal how traditional selectivity has evolved into an exclusionary elitism at the system's flagship campuses. No matter what one's background, the odds of being admitted to UC Berkeley these days are pretty slim. Fully 21,500 of the 30,000 applicants this year were rejected. Almost a third of these "rejects" had unblemished, straight-A 4.0 grade-point averages. Consider this: In 1996, before implementation of Prop 209, even students with GPAs between 3.0 and 3.99 and SATs between 1200 and 1390 had only a 33 percent chance of getting into Berkeley.

Moreover, the students with the highest rate of acceptance are not white, but Asian-American. While only 15 percent of 7 California's public high school graduates, Asian-American students made up 37 percent of UC's 129,000 undergraduates and 41 percent of the Berkeley campus last year. Twenty-eight percent of all students admitted to the UC system this year were Asian-American.

Another figure that got lost in the post-209 debate is that the 8 number of self-identified white students admitted to UC this year fell 9 percent. Another is that the percentage (14.5) of students who declined to state their ethnicity or race was nearly triple last year's rate. In other words, statistical comparisons between the two years are rendered problematic by the 8,814 rebellious applicants who opted out of the racial head count.

Affirmative action at the University of California was long a 9 cosmetic program that obscured the system's low minority retention rates and the deterioration and deeper inequities in the state's primary education system—the principal UC "feeder" schools. Post-209 admissions numbers appear to indicate that the disparities exist not so much along racial but rather class lines. Funding varies greatly from school district to district. Urban schools are falling apart. Largely middle-class districts have many more of the honors courses that give high schoolers the extra boost in their GPA necessary for UC applications.

This fall, concerned students and faculty will be spearhead- 10 ing a movement for a proposed ballot initiative to reverse Proposition 209 as far as it applies to higher education. They should also be talking about building more UC campuses— campuses that could accommodate not only the few hundred black and Latino students who were rejected this year but also the nearly 16,000 Californians of all backgrounds who are being turned away by increasingly elitist academic barriers.

Expanding Vocabulary

Examine the following words in their contexts in the essay and then write a brief definition or synonym of each one. Do not use a dictionary; try to guess each word's meaning from the context. The number in parentheses is the number of the paragraph in which the word appears.

precipitate (3)	obscured (9)
elitist (3)	deterioration (9)
exclusion (4)	disparities (9)
opted (8)	spearheading (10)

Understanding Content

1. How many fewer black and Latino students were admitted to UCLA and UC Berkeley in 1998—after the rejection of affirmative action in California?
2. How may fewer black and Latino students were admitted to the entire UC system with 129,000 students?
3. What does the author think we need to understand about the UC system in general and UC Berkeley in particular?
4. What race has the highest rate of acceptance into the UC system? What is this race's percentage at Berkeley?
5. What else is happening that makes the numbers "problematic"?

Drawing Inferences about Thesis and Purpose

1. What is Rodriguez's reaction to all the news coverage of the admissions drop?
2. How does the author want readers to react to the changes in minority enrollments?
3. How does Rodriguez want readers to think about the top schools in the UC system?

Analyzing Strategies and Style

1. Rodriguez opens by reporting many media responses to the drop in minority admissions in the UC system. Why? What does he seek to accomplish?

2. The author describes affirmative action in the UC system as a "cosmetic program." What does he mean by *cosmetic?* What attitude does the word convey to readers?

Thinking Critically

1. Instead of affirmative action, what does Rodriguez want to see? What does he think is the real problem? Does his discussion in paragraphs 9 and 10 make sense to you? Why or why not?
2. Do you think that Liu and Rodriguez could find any common ground on affirmative action? If so, what would it be? If not, why not?

Don't Wobble on Immigration

BEN WATTENBERG

A senior fellow at the American Enterprise Institute, Ben Wattenberg (b. 1933) is moderator of the weekly PBS television program *Think Tank.* He also writes a weekly syndicated newspaper column and is the author of *The Birth Dearth.* The following article on immigration was published in the *Washington Post*, March 30, 2002.

Questions to Guide Your Reading

1. What is happening to birth rates in Europe and Japan?
2. What is Wattenberg's thesis?

President Bush and others have said we are at war to save our civilization—that is, Western civilization. The events of Sept. 11 were perpetrated by Muslim radicals. All were foreigners; some were here illegally.

Understandably, many immigrants have been detained. Deportations of illegal immigrants have accelerated here and in Europe. There is speculation about an anti-immigrant backlash. The quadrennial candidate Pat Buchanan's book was high on bestseller lists. Its title says it all: *The Death of the West: How Dying Populations and Immigrant Invasions Imperil Our Country and Civilization.*

3   If we're talking about the survival and, one hopes, the extension, of Western civilization, we should be talking about immigration and demographics. Let's get some numbers straight. Birth and fertility rates in Europe and Japan are unprecedented and incredible.

4   Over time, it takes 2.1 children per woman just to keep a society at zero growth, the "replacement level," absent immigration. The total fertility rate of Europe and Japan is 1.3 children per woman—on a 50-year slide. Europe has begun "de-populating"; Japan will follow soon, according to U.N. projections, which show Europe losing 124 million people by 2050, while its median age climbs to about 50.

5   Economic markets are responsive to change, but this decline could pose a challenge. How would you like to be a home builder in a society that is losing significant population every year? Where do the public funds for the military come from when there aren't even enough worker bees to provide pensions for the senior bees? These are not the best of all possible allies. America may have to move further toward a go-it-alone position.

6   Fortunately, the other part of the West, the English-speaking settler nations—Canada, Australia and the United States—have different demographic portraits. Why? Because, in moderate numbers, they take in immigrants. And the numbers are only moderate. In our peak immigration decade of 1900–1910, America accepted immigrants amounting to 1 percent of its population, each year. The rate today is one-third that.

7   America's fertility rate has averaged about two children per woman in recent years—below replacement. Over time, if it weren't for immigration, America would stop growing and perhaps begin slowly depopulating. Such a no-growth, aging America could find it hard to lead in what may be a long struggle among civilizations, some of which, unlike the West, are projected to grow for several decades before leveling off.

8   The flash point of American immigration today concerns Mexicans. To those, such as Buchanan, who fear immigration, they appear as an inexorable Third World tan tide, intent on recapturing the American Southwest, ready to swamp Western values, the splitting wedge in a majority nonwhite America of the future.

Bunk. America takes in about a million immigrants each year, 9
of whom about 45 percent are from Latin America, of whom
Mexicans account for somewhat less than half, perhaps 25 percent to 30 percent of the total when illegals are counted. The
other 70 percent to 75 percent of immigrants to this country
come from everywhere, including 30 percent from Asia.

Nonwhite? Half of Mexicans are classified white. Third 10
World? Mexico's per capita income is above $5,000; it now has
"investment grade" bond status. Mexico is a member of the
Organization for Economic Cooperation and Development, the
"First World" economic club. It is a real democracy. Its fertility
rate has fallen from 6.5 to 2.5 children per woman in 30 years,
and it is expected to go below replacement soon.

Invasion? How many invaders compete to mow the lawns 11
and clean the dishes of those they have invaded? Mexican
Americans serve disproportionately in this country's armed
services and have won a disproportionate share of medals for
gallantry in combat.

Assimilation? By the third generation just about all Mexi- 12
can Americans speak English, and Mexican grandparents often
complain that their grandchildren speak no Spanish.

Not Western? Scholars say the *padrones* of Latin America, the 13
hegemonic roots of the culture, are language and religion. The
languages are Spanish or Portuguese, European tongues. The
religion is Catholic, with growing evangelical Protestant sects.

Now is not the time to go wobbly on immigration. It is the 14
key to American growth and prosperity. If we are indeed in for
a war to preserve Western civilization, we'll need every straight-
shooting, red-blooded, patriotic soul we can get. (Remember
immigrants *choose* the American way of life.)

Immigrants are also our best salesmen; no one tells the Amer- 15
ican story better. And we're going to need all the salesmen we
can get as we go about the business of recruiting economic, cultural and military allies—allies who believe in liberty, as we do.

Expanding Vocabulary

Match each word in column A with its definition in column B. When
in doubt, first find the word in the essay and look for context clues
to aid your understanding of the word's meaning. Then, if necessary,

use your dictionary to complete the matching exercise. The number in parentheses is the number of the paragraph in which the word appears.

Column A	Column B
perpetrated (1)	characteristics of human population
accelerated (2)	segments
quadrennial (2)	having no previous example
demographics (3)	relentless
unprecedented (3)	per person
median (4)	controlling, dominant
inexorable (8)	became faster
per capita (10)	wavering in one's beliefs
hegemonic (13)	was responsible for
wobbly (14)	located in the middle
	happening every four years

Understanding Content

1. What is America's fertility rate? Without immigration, what will happen to the United States?
2. What is the rate of immigration, per year, in the United States today?
3. What, according to the author, seems to be the problem that some see with immigration? What do people fear?
4. What percentage of yearly immigrants are Mexican? What percent are Asian?
5. What is happening in Mexico today?
6. What are Wattenberg's answers to fears of "invasion," "assimilation," and "Not Western?"

Drawing Inferences about Thesis and Purpose

1. Where does Wattenberg state his thesis?
2. Wattenberg begins paragraph 9 with the word *bunk*. What does he mean here?

Analyzing Strategies and Style

1. One could say that Wattenberg's only defense of his thesis is in his last two paragraphs. What does he do in the first 13 paragraphs to develop his thesis?
2. The author begins four paragraphs (10–13) with a one- or two-word question. What is effective about this strategy?

Thinking Critically

1. Evaluate Wattenberg's argument. Does he effectively respond to the anxieties of many who oppose immigration? Why or why not?
2. Have you thought about immigration in the context of replacing the Western depopulation trend? Is this a helpful way to examine the issue?
3. Are you a recent immigrant? If so, do you see yourself as a good salesperson for American values and culture? Why or why not?

Illegal Aliens

GEORGE J. BORJAS

An immigrant from Cuba, George Borjas (b. 1950) is a professor of public policy at Harvard University's John F. Kennedy School of Government and a research associate at the National Bureau of Economic Research. He has written numerous articles, a textbook (*Labor Economics*), and *Heaven's Door* (1999), from which the following excerpt is taken.

Questions to Guide Your Reading

1. What is Borjas's purpose in writing?
2. Who benefits the most from illegal aliens?

Five million illegal aliens lived in the United States in 1996 (see table below).[1] Their number grows by about 300,000 per year. And these numbers are on top of the three million illegal aliens who were granted amnesty in the late 1980s.

The common perception of an illegal alien is of someone who avoided inspection at the time of entry because he or she lacked the necessary documents for legal entry (such as a passport and a visa). The Immigration and Naturalization Service refers to these persons as EWIs, for "entry without inspection." The stereotypical EWI is a Mexican immigrant running across the

[1]A good description of the methodologies used to calculate the number of illegal aliens is given in U.S. General Accounting Office, *Illegal Aliens: Despite Data Limitations, Current Methods Provide Better Population Estimates*, GAO/PEMD-93–125 (Washington, D.C., August 1993).

border. Many illegal aliens, however, had a legal visa when they first entered, such as a student's visa or a tourist's visa, but simply remained in the country long after their visas expired. The illegal alien flow, therefore, can originate anywhere. And, in fact, almost half of the illegal alien population is *not* of Mexican origin.

Illegal Immigration in the United States, October 1996

	Number of illegal aliens
Total	5,000,000
"Top five" countries of origin	
Mexico	2,700,000
El Salvador	335,000
Guatemala	165,000
Canada	120,000
Haiti	105,000
"Top five" states of residence	
California	2,000,000
Texas	700,000
New York	540,000
Florida	350,000
Illinois	290,000

Source: U.S. Immigration and Naturalization Service, *Statistical Yearbook of the Immigration and Naturalization Service, 1996* (Washington, D.C., 1997), p. 198.

3   The United States attracts illegal aliens for many reasons. First, persons originating in many source countries have strong economic incentives to enter the United States—regardless of whether they can get a visa or not. Per capita income in the United States is at least three times larger than in Mexico. Even after netting out the cost of illegal immigration, such as getting to the U.S. border and payments to *coyotes* (the experienced guides who help the illegal aliens across the border), the income differential between the two countries remains exceptionally high.

4   Second, black markets arise whenever government regulations prevent people from voluntarily exchanging goods and services. Although it is illegal to buy drugs and sex, many peo-

ple still desire those goods, and black markets arise to satisfy the illicit demand. Illegal immigration is no different. Immigration policy prohibits the entry of many persons, but these persons still wish to live in the United States. As long as the potential immigrants believe that the cost of participating in this black market is relatively low, they will come. In fact, there are few penalties imposed directly on the illegal aliens who are caught by the Border Patrol. When they are apprehended, they are simply put on the first plane or bus that goes back to their source country. Once there, the aliens are free to try to reenter the United States whenever the opportunity arises.

Third, it is no secret that many American employers benefit greatly from the entry of illegal aliens. This vast pool of workers lowers wages and increases profits in the affected industries. Even though it is illegal for employers to "knowingly hire" illegal aliens, the chances of getting caught are negligible and the penalties are trivial.[2] Newly hired workers must offer proof that they are U.S. citizens, are permanent legal residents, or have visas permitting them to work in the United States. Employers must then complete forms for each new employee certifying that the relevant documents were reviewed. The statutes, however, have a huge loophole, one that essentially permits anyone to hire an illegal alien. Employers need only to certify that they reviewed the documents that described the legal status of job applicants. The employer is not required to keep copies of these documents for inspection. Hence there is practically no chance of detecting employers who decide to hire illegal aliens after "reviewing" the documents provided by willing co-conspirators.[3]

---

[2]Remarkably, it was not illegal for firms to hire illegal aliens until 1988. Even though it was illegal for some persons to be in the United States, and it was illegal for those persons to work, firms were free to hire the illegal aliens. Since 1988, first-time offenders have been liable for fines ranging from $250 to $2,000 per illegal alien hired. Criminal penalties can be imposed on repeated violators when there is a "pattern and practice" of hiring illegal aliens, including a fine of $3,000 per illegal alien and up to six months in prison.

[3]Many studies have attempted to determine if the 1986 Immigration Reform and Control Act slowed down the illegal alien flow. These studies typically conclude that the legislation was a dismal failure; see Katherine M. Donato, Jorge Durand, and Douglas S. Massy, "Stemming the Tide? Assessing the Deterrent Effects of the Immigration Reform and Control Act," *Demography* 29 (May 1992): 139–157.

6   Finally, the United States does a notoriously poor job at controlling its borders. In fact, few other countries have been so lackadaisical about border control. Although the number of agents in the Border Patrol rose rapidly in the 1990s (from about three thousand in 1990 to near ten thousand by 1998), the Mexican–U.S. border is 1,950 miles long.[4]

7   A number of highly publicized Border Patrol operations in the mid-1990s, such as Operation Hold the Line in El Paso and Operation Gatekeeper in San Diego, attempted to curtail illegal immigration by providing an around-the-clock Border Patrol presence in some of the stretches that illegal aliens typically used to cross the border.[5] These operations seem to have been effective in the targeted areas, but many observers suspect that some of the illegal aliens eventually entered the United States by crossing the border in those areas that were less heavily patrolled. A Binational Study of Migration, commissioned by the governments of Mexico and the United States, concluded that "the United States border enforcement strategies begun in 1994 are affecting migration patterns, but not preventing unauthorized entry."[6] Moreover, tighter controls on the U.S.–Mexico border do not address the problem of how to curtail the number of visa overstayers, who account for about half of the illegal aliens in the United States.

8   Any serious reform of immigration policy—and any attempt to adopt a skills-based point system—is doomed to failure unless the problem of illegal immigration is also resolved. A well-designed immigration policy may not have the desired effect on the social welfare of the United States if the border is porous. Illegal immigration can effectively unravel the social and economic effects of that policy. Illegal immigration is also unfair and unjust. Both the moral and the political legitimacy of immigration restrictions come into question if one can get to the front of the immigration queue by simply breaking the law. Finally, illegal immigration may be the root cause of substantial social

[4]Most of the illegal crossings, however, take place over a relatively small area, stretching for about 165 miles. See Robert J. Caldwell, "Grading Gatekeeper: Tougher Border Enforcement Shows Promise but Remains Incomplete," *San Diego Union-Tribune*, August 10, 1997, p. G-1.
[5]See Robert Suro, *Strangers among Us: How Latino Immigration Is Transforming America* (New York: Knopf, 1998), chap. 16, for a detailed discussion of the El Paso operation.
[6]Quoted ibid., p. 273.

and ethnic conflict, particularly in California, where the voters, fed up with government inaction on this issue, enacted Proposition 187 in 1994. This proposition denied many locally provided benefits to illegal aliens—including a public education.[7]

Proposition 187, in fact, raises fundamental questions about how far the United States can go—or *should* go—in controlling the illegal alien flow. Much has been made, for instance, about the rights and wrongs of denying a public education to the children of illegal aliens. The supporters of Proposition 187 argued that illegal aliens should not be entitled to attend public schools, that illegal immigration has unalterably lowered the quality of education in California schools, and that such a ban might reduce the incentives for illegal aliens to migrate to the United States. After all, illegal immigration from Mexico responds to the price of *tomatoes* in the United States—apprehensions rise when the price is high and American farms pay more to harvest the crops.[8] If aliens respond to the price of tomatoes, they would surely respond to the cut in education benefits.   9

The opponents of the proposition argued that it is morally wrong to kick children out of school and that, in any case, it makes economic sense to provide illegal aliens with free schooling. Preventing illegal aliens from getting a high school diploma today will only buy the United States more poverty, welfare, and crime in the future.   10

Putting the moral issues aside, barring illegal aliens from public schools may not be the most effective way of stopping the illegal flow. Many of the children who live in households headed by illegal aliens were born in the United States and are American citizens—courtesy of the Fourteenth Amendment to the Constitution.[9] The denial of public education affects a relatively small part of the illegal population, and would likely not deter the migration of single persons and childless couples.   11

---

[7]In the 1982 *Plyer v. Doe* decision, the U.S. Supreme Court ruled narrowly (on a 5-to-4 vote) that illegal aliens were entitled to a public education.

[8]S.J. Torok and Wallace E. Huffman, "U.S.–Mexican Trade in Winter Vegetables and Illegal Immigration," *American Journal of Agricultural Economics* 68 (May 1986): 246–260. See also Gordon H. Hanson and Antonio Spilimbergo, "Illegal Immigration, Border Enforcement, and Relative Wages: Evidence," *American Economic Review*, forthcoming 1999.

[9]This amendment states: "All persons born or naturalized in the United States, and subject to the jurisdiction thereof, are citizens of the United States and of the State wherein they reside." The amendment was enacted in 1868 to grant citizenship to the newly freed slave population.

12   The United States could probably deter many more illegal aliens by imposing substantial penalties on the employers who hire them. These firms—large agricultural enterprises, sweatshops, and native households that hire illegal aliens as maids or nannies—get the bulk of the gains from illegal immigration, but bear few of the costs. The demand for illegal aliens would probably drop dramatically if the government began to bill the owners of the fields where the aliens toil and the families who hire illegal servants for the expenses incurred by public schools and Medicaid.

13   There should also be some penalties assessed on the illegal aliens themselves. It is sometimes recommended that illegal aliens, when caught, should be sent for a few days to some type of detention center, so that they can pay for their crime through a short incarceration. The problem with this proposal is that it is very expensive to send a person to jail. In 1997, it cost $59.83 to send a person for one day to a federal prison.[10] If every apprehended illegal alien (and there were 1.6 million of them in 1996) were forced to spend two weeks in a federal prison, the total bill would be around $1.3 billion—assuming that no new prisons have to be built. It is unclear, therefore, whom this incarceration actually punishes, the illegal alien or the taxpayer.

14   One alternative might be to punish the illegal aliens by hitting them where it hurts the most, in the pocketbook. Federal law, for example, routinely allows the confiscation of much of the property used by drug dealers in their illegal business activities. The application of this principle to illegal immigration would imply that the aliens could be fined for their illegal activities (such as working in the United States) through the confiscation of their assets prior to deportation. The assets that would revert to the U.S. treasury could include bank accounts, cash, automobiles, and the right to collect social security benefits upon retirement (if the illegal alien had somehow been issued a valid social security number). These penalties would probably move the economic activities of the illegal alien population further into the underground economy. But the financial penalties—if accompanied by a strong effort at detecting

[10]Public Affairs Office, Federal Bureau of Prisons, telephone conversation with author.

and apprehending the aliens—could trim the economic benefits associated with migrating to the United States, and reduce the size of the illegal alien flow.

Ultimately, any serious attempt to resolve the illegal alien 15 problem faces a crucial obstacle. There must be a simple way of determining who is an illegal alien, and who is not. After all, it is unreasonable to increase the penalties on employers who hire illegal aliens if it is difficult for employers to determine the legal status of a particular job applicant. The United States has yet to grapple with this troublesome detail, which raises the specter of a national identification system.

The United States has a somewhat paradoxical attitude on 16 this issue. Most Americans probably have a libertarian streak that immediately rejects the notion of living in a country where one has to carry a card that provides information to potential employers about whether one is legally entitled to work. Yet most Americans carry credit cards that are scanned regularly whenever goods and services are purchased. The information provided by that scanning—including the type of purchase, the amount, and the location—triggers a computer "prediction" of whether the credit card actually belongs to the person who is carrying it. If, given the past consumption history of the authorized credit card holder, the computer concludes that the person at the store is buying the wrong things, or buying them in the wrong place, or going on an unexplained shopping spree, it will signal the shopkeeper to check for identification.

Regardless of one's position on the critical issue of a national 17 identification system, the basic dilemma is clear. The illegal alien problem will remain a problem as long as the United States skirts the central question of how to identify who is a legal resident and who is not.

Finally, it may be possible to encourage the parties 18 involved in the immigration debate to take illegal immigration more seriously by linking the point system for legal immigration with the size of the illegal alien flow. Suppose, for example, that the United States were to adopt a system that granted 500,000 legal visas each year. Each of these slots would become much more valuable if the government "taxed" the number of legal visas available every time an illegal alien entered the country. The Immigration and Naturalization Service might report that 200,000 illegal aliens had entered the country in any given year. The point system could then be adjusted so that only 300,000 legal visas would be granted.

19   This "tax" would introduce a number of important incentives into the enforcement of immigration policy. First, it would make the country aware of the opportunity cost of illegal immigration. In other words, by looking the other way and letting in 200,000 illegal aliens, Americans would be forgoing the economic benefits that could be provided by 200,000 well-chosen immigrants. Second, firms that employ immigrants would have to "compete" over their share of entrants. Even though some firms might benefit from the less-skilled illegal aliens, many other firms would want to see the entry of the skilled legal immigrants that they prefer to hire. Finally, the immigrant community already in the United States would have a strong incentive to stop the illegal alien flow, since each illegal alien who entered the country would make it that much harder for the relatives of current U.S. residents to enter, even if the relatives were highly skilled.

Expanding Vocabulary

Match each word in column A with its definition in column B. When in doubt, first find the word in the essay and look for context clues to aid your understanding of the word's meaning. Then, if necessary, use your dictionary to complete the matching exercise. The number in parentheses is the number of the paragraph in which the word appears.

Column A	*Column B*
amnesty (1)	amount or degree of difference
per capita (3)	with openings
differential (3)	without liveliness or interest
apprehended (4)	something that encourages action
notoriously (6)	produced, sustained by
lackadaisical (6)	imprisonment
porous (8)	general pardon
queue (8)	seizure by authority

incentives (9)	haunting prospect
incurred (12)	widely known, usually unfavorably
incarceration (13)	arrested
confiscation (14)	those who enter a competition
specter (15)	per person
entrants (19)	line of waiting people

Understanding Content

1. How do illegal aliens get into the United States? What is incorrect about the typical image of the illegal alien?
2. Why do we get so many illegal aliens?
3. What, according to Borjas, are the serious problems with illegal aliens?
4. What are the arguments for and against Proposition 187 in California?
5. What are Borjas's proposed solutions to the problem of illegal aliens?
6. What is a necessary step to implement the author's solutions? What is the problem with this step?

Drawing Inferences about Thesis and Purpose

1. How serious a problem is the illegal alien issue in Borjas's opinion?
2. What is the author's thesis? You may need more than one sentence to cover his complex topic.

Analyzing Strategies and Style

1. Why does the author begin with specifics of who illegal aliens are and where they come from? What does he want to accomplish?
2. How would you describe the tone of this essay? How does his tone help to advance his argument?

Thinking Critically

1. Has Borjas convinced you that a Proposition 187 approach is not useful? Why or why not?
2. To deal with illegals, Borjas recommends a national ID. What are your views on this proposal?
3. Evaluate the author's proposed solutions. Are they workable? Right? Why or why not?

Too Green for Their Own Good?

ANDREW GOLDSTEIN

Andrew Goldstein is a writer for *Time* magazine. His article on the environmental movement appeared in *Time*, August 26, 2002, as one of several articles exploring the topic.

Questions to Guide Your Reading

1. What does Goldstein mean by his title?
2. How successful have environmentalists been, in the author's view?

1   Here's a riddle to keep you up at night: How come, at a time when the environmental movement is stronger and richer than ever, our most pressing ecological problems just get worse? It's as though the planet has hit a Humpty-Dumpty moment in which unprecedented amounts of manpower and money are unable to put the world back together again. "Why are we losing so many battles?" wonders Gus Speth, dean of Yale's School of Forestry & Environmental Studies.

2   Of course, the issues are complicated and could require decades and trillions of dollars to resolve. But part of the problem is that it's easier to protest, to hurl venom at practices you don't like, than to find new ways to do business and create change. The dogma of traditional green activism—that business (and economic growth) is the enemy, that financial markets can't be trusted, that compromise means failure—has done little to save the planet. Which means it's fair to ask the question: Have some of the greens' tactics actually made things worse?

3   This is not to say there hasn't been progress since the environmental movement began. The air and water in the developed nations of the West are, by most measures, the cleanest they have been for decades, and the amount of land protected as national parks and preserves has quadrupled worldwide since 1970. But despite a record flow of financial resources (donations to U.S. environmental groups alone have risen 50% in the past five years, to more than $6.4 billion in 2001, according to the Amer-

ican Association of Fundraising Counsel Trust for Philanthropy),
the planet's most serious challenges—global warming, loss of
biodiversity, marine depletion—remain as intractable as ever,
making environmentalists vulnerable to charges that green
groups have prospered while the earth has not.

So it's time to look at the past tactics of many green groups   4
and identify lessons to be learned.

Business Is Not the Enemy

Thanks to scandals on Wall Street, environmentalists who   5
have been bashing "evil" corporations for years have suddenly found themselves with plenty of allies. But the planet needs
profitable, innovative businesses even more than it needs environmentalists. "It is companies, not advocacy groups, that will
create the technologies needed to save the environment," says
Jonathan Wootliff, a former Greenpeace executive turned business consultant.

So how to turn corporations into partners in preservation?   6
For starters, when companies make efforts to turn green, environmentalists shouldn't jump down their throats the minute
they see any backsliding. Wootliff says he was exasperated to
watch so many environmental groups take special aim at Ford
Motor, arguably Detroit's most environmentally friendly car-
maker, during the latest fight in Congress over fuel-efficiency
standards (in which Ford, GM and Chrysler all fought to preserve the status quo). "For goodness' sake, stop alienating your
supporters," he warns. "Going after Ford will mean fewer, not
more, CEOS will turn around and say protecting the environment
is the right thing to do."

When conservation purity is the only acceptable option, the   7
biggest polluters will have no incentive to clean up their acts.
Says Dwight Evans, executive vice president of Southern Co.,
a major U.S. energy producer: "If tomorrow we announced we
were shutting down 25% of our plants to put in new, high-tech
scrubbing devices, the headline would be, WHY NOT THE OTHER
75%? We don't get credit for what we've done, or for what we're
going to do."

This is not to suggest that environmentalists should be spine-   8
less. The threat of boycott prompted Home Depot to promise to

phase out its selling of wood from old-growth forests. The good news is that once an industry leader turns green, the rest often follow, fearful that consumers will punish them if they don't. Today every major home-improvement retailer makes an effort to sell only products certified to have come from sustainably managed forests.

Embrace the Market

9   There is a simple economic explanation for why many of China's cities have become shrouded in gray clouds of dust: it's cheap to pollute. Millions of Chinese drive mopeds and old automobiles that don't have catalytic converters, and much of the nation's electricity comes from coal-fired power plants. Technology from the 1950s, after all, is at bargain-basement prices. But that's because the prices don't reflect the hidden costs of air pollution: deaths from lung illnesses and millions of dollars wasted on health-care bills and lost worker productivity. The situation is the same the world over. The price of goods and services rarely reflects environmental costs.

10   A concerted effort to correct this basic flaw in the market could have a bigger payoff for the environment than would a thousand new national parks. But many environmental groups continue to oppose market-based environmental reforms and instead remain wedded to the "mandate, regulate and litigate" model of the past.

11   Take, for example, power-plant emissions in the U.S., which environmentalists blame for much of global warming. In the mid-1990s, the Clinton Administration was fairly close to striking a deal with the power industry that would have established a comprehensive emissions-trading program. To gain some certainty for their long-range planning, the utilities would agree to mandatory caps on emissions that included not just nitrogen oxides, sulfur dioxide and mercury but also carbon. Companies would have the flexibility of meeting targets in the most efficient manner by buying and selling emissions rights.

12   This didn't suit many of the environmental groups involved in the negotiations that believed the market was just a clever way for corporations to skirt environmental regulations. Says Katie McGinty, then chairwoman of Clinton's Council on Environmental Quality: "Practically every utility in the country

began to accept the notion that they would face legally binding carbon restrictions. But environmentalists who were opposed to doing anything consensual with industry said what we really should be doing is suing their butts under the current provisions of the Clean Air Act." Result: today the U.S. Environmental Protection Agency has no ability to regulate carbon, and the old, pollution-spewing plants are still in operation.

It's Not All or Nothing

Toward the end of a war, a simple truism applies: it is better to negotiate a surrender than to fight to the death for a losing cause. Though environmentalists may be loath to admit it, this is their choice in the battle over genetically modified foods. Despite the best attempts by European activists to seal off the Continent from what they call Frankenfoods, the new science of farming is here to stay. So if environmentalists want to help shape the future of agriculture, it's time to raise the white flag and ask the world's bioengineers for a seat at the bargaining table. 13

What could be better for the environment than a cheap, simple way for farmers to double or triple their output while using fewer pesticides on less land? According to Rockefeller University environmental scientist Jesse Ausubel, if the world's average farmer achieved the yield of the average American maize grower, the planet could feed 10 billion people on just half the crop land in use today. Of course it's possible that some genetically modified foods may carry health risks to humans (although none have so far been proved in foods that have been brought to market), and it's unclear whether agricultural companies will be able to control where their altered-gene products end up. But what's needed now are not crop tramplers and lab burners but powerful lobbyists able to negotiate for more effective safeguards and a greater humanitarian use of the technology. 14

Bioengineering has tremendous potential in the developing world. The U.S., Canada, China and Argentina contain 99% of the global area of genetically modified crops, whereas yields of sorghum and millet in sub-Saharan Africa have not increased since the 1960s. Green groups hoping to earn the trust of the developing world should lobby hard for the resources of Big 15

Agriculture to be plowed into discovering crop varieties that can handle drought and thrive on small-scale farms.

No More Exaggerations

16   A shattering piece of news came over the press wire of the Rainforest Action Network in May: "One-quarter of mammals will soon be extinct." An Associated Press story made a similar claim: "A quarter of the world's mammal species—from tigers to rhinos—could face extinction within 30 years." Problem is, the story isn't true.

17   The source of the number was a report issued by the United Nations Environment Program. It cites the World Conservation Union's most recent "Red List," which indicates that about 24% of mammals "are currently regarded as globally threatened." This figure comprises not only the approximately 4% of mammals that are "critically endangered" but also those that are merely "vulnerable," a category including animals with only a 10% chance of extinction within 100 years. The U.N. report makes this distinction clear—and even cautions against relying on species data from the Red List. But those caveats didn't make the news.

18   Fuzzy math and scare tactics might help green groups raise money, but when they, abetted by an environmentally friendly media, overplay their hand, it invites scathing critiques like that of Danish statistician Bjorn Lomborg, whose book *The Skeptical Environmentalist* debunks environmental exaggerations.

19   Even more dangerous, notes Don Melnick, head of the Center for Environmental Research and Conservation at Columbia University, is how doomsayers create a Chicken Little problem. "We need to bury the notion that the biological world is going to collapse and we're all going to be extinct," he says. "That's nonsense, and it can make people feel the situation is hopeless. We can't have people asking 'So why should we bother?' "

Expanding Vocabulary

Match each word in column A with its definition in Column B. When in doubt, first find the word in the essay and look for context clues to aid your understanding of the word's meaning. Then, if necessary, use your dictionary to complete the matching exercise. The number in parentheses is the number of the paragraph in which the word appears.

Column A	Column B
ecological (1)	exposes falsehoods to ridicule
venom (2)	stubborn
dogma (2)	wrapped, covered
quadrupled (3)	arguing in favor of a cause, idea
biodiversity (3)	reluctant, unwilling
intractable (3)	willing participation of both parties
advocacy (5)	malice, spite
boycott (8)	warnings, qualifiers
shrouded (9)	harshly critical
litigate (10)	four times as many
consensual (12)	abstain from buying or dealing with
loath (13)	as a protest
caveats (17)	relationship between organisms and
abetted (18)	their environment
scathing (18)	assisted in wrongdoing
debunks	variety of living organisms
doomsayers (19)	frequent predictor of calamity
	authoritative principle or belief
	engage in legal proceedings

Understanding Content

1. What are the three attitudes of environmentalists that Goldstein questions the value of? What fourth problem does he also examine? (Look at his subheadings.)
2. How should attitudes toward business be changed? What can environmentalists get from businesses?
3. How should environmentalists "embrace the market"?
4. What is changing the science of farming? How should environmentalists be involved?
5. What is the practical problem with exaggerations? How do people react?

Drawing Inferences about Thesis and Purpose

1. What is Goldstein's thesis?
2. What would Goldstein like to see environmental groups do?

Analyzing Strategies and Style

1. What purpose do references to Humpty-Dumpty and Chicken Little serve? How do these references help express the author's views?
2. In paragraphs 3 and 8, Goldstein recognizes successes of the green movement. What are these paragraphs designed to accomplish?

Thinking Critically

1. Evaluate Goldstein's argument. Do his examples of green tactics illustrate his points? Are they convincing evidence of flaws in the movement's approach?
2. Do you consider yourself an environmentalist? If so, on what basis? If not, why not?
3. Is it possible to make the argument that we must all be green to survive? If so, can we still allow for a debate over strategies? Explain your responses.

Lessons from Lost Worlds

JARED DIAMOND

A UCLA professor of geography and public health since 1966, Jared Diamond (b. 1937) is a director of the World Wildlife Fund and the author of the Pulitzer Prize–winning book *Guns, Germs, and Steel: The Fates of Human Societies* (1997). Diamond's article on environmental issues was a part, along with Andrew Goldstein, of a series of articles on the topic published in the August 26, 2002 issue of *Time* magazine.

Questions to Guide Your Reading

1. What is Diamond's subject? Where does he introduce it?
2. What environmental problems have led to the collapse of societies in the past?

1   Children have a wonderful ability to focus their parents' attention on the essentials. Before our twin sons were born in 1987, I had often heard about all the environmental problems projected to come to a head toward the middle of this century.

But I was born in 1937, so I would surely be dead before 2050. Hence I couldn't think of 2050 as a real date, and I couldn't grasp that the environmental risks were real.

After the birth of our kids, my wife and I proceeded to obsess about the things most parents obsess about—schools, our wills, life insurance. Then I realized with a jolt: my kids will reach my present age of 65 in 2052. That's a real date, not an unimaginable one! My kids' lives will depend on the state of the world in 2052, not just on our decisions about life insurance and schools.

I should have known that. Having lived in Europe for years, I saw that the lives of my friends also born in 1937 had been affected greatly by the state of the world around them. For many of those overseas contemporaries growing up during World War II, that state of the world left them orphaned or homeless. Their parents may have thought wisely about life insurance, but their parents' generation had not thought wisely about world conditions. Over the heads of our own children now hang other threats from world conditions, different from the threats of 1939–45.

While the risk of nuclear war between major powers still exists, it's less acute now than 15 years ago, thank God. Many people worry about terrorists, and so do I, but then I reflect that terrorists could at worst kill "only" a few tens of millions of us. The even graver environmental problems that could do in all our children are environmental ones, such as global warming and land and water degradation.

These threats interact with terrorism by breeding the desperation that drives some individuals to become terrorists and others to support terrorists. Sept. 11 made us realize that we are not immune from the environmental problems of any country, no matter how remote—not even those of Somalia and Afghanistan. Of course, in reality, that was true before Sept. 11, but we didn't think much about it then. We and the Somalis breathe and pollute the same atmosphere, are bathed by the same oceans and compete for the same global pie of shrinking resources. Before Sept. 11, though, we thought of globalization as mainly meaning "us" sending "them" good things, like the Internet and Coca-Cola. Now we understand that globalization also means "them" being in a position to send "us" bad things, like terrorist attacks, emerging diseases, illegal immigrants and situations requiring the dispatch of U.S. troops.

6   A historical perspective can help us, because ours is not the first society to face environmental challenges. Many past societies collapsed partly from their failure to solve problems similar to those we face today—especially problems of deforestation, water management, topsoil loss and climate change. The long list of victims includes the Anasazi in the U.S. Southwest, the Maya, Easter Islanders, the Greenland Norse, Mycenaean Greeks and inhabitants of the Fertile Crescent, the Indus Valley, Great Zimbabwe and Angkor Wat. The outcomes ranged from "just" a collapse of society, to the deaths of most people, to (in some cases) everyone's ending up dead. What can we learn from these events? I see four main sets of lessons.

7   First, environmental problems can indeed cause societies to collapse, even societies assaulting their environments with stone tools and far lower population densities than we have today.

8   Second, some environments are more fragile than others, making some societies more prone to collapse than others. Fragility varies even within the same country: for instance, some parts of the U.S., including Southern California, where I live, are especially at risk from low rainfall and salinization of soil from agriculture that is dependent on irrigation—the same problems that overwhelmed the Anasazi. Some nations occupy more fragile environments than do others. It's no accident that a list of the world's most environmentally devastated and/or overpopulated countries resembles a list of the world's current political tinderboxes. Both lists include Afghanistan, Haiti, Iraq, Nepal, Rwanda and Somalia.

9   Third, otherwise robust societies can be dragged down by the environmental problems of their trade partners. About 500 years ago, two Polynesian societies, on Henderson Island and Pitcairn Island, vanished because they depended for vital imports on the Polynesian society of Mangareva Island, which collapsed from deforestation. We Americans can well understand that outcome, having seen how vulnerable we are to instability in oil-exporting countries of the Middle East.

10   Fourth, we wonder, Why didn't those people see the problems developing around them and do something to avoid dis-

aster? (Future generations may ask that question about us.) One explanation is the conflicts between the short-term interests of those in power and the long-term interests of everybody: chiefs were becoming rich from processes that ultimately undermined society. That too is an acute issue today, as wealthy Americans do things that enrich themselves in the short run and harm everyone in the long run. As the Anasazi chiefs found, they could get away with those policies for a while, but ultimately they bought themselves the privilege of being merely the last to starve.

Of course, there are differences between our situation and 11 those of past societies. Our problems are more dangerous than those of the Anasazi. Today there are far more humans alive, packing far greater destructive power, than ever before. Unlike the Anasazi, a society today can't collapse without affecting societies far away. Because of globalization, the risk we face today is of a worldwide collapse, not just a local tragedy.

People often ask if I am an optimist or a pessimist about our 12 future. I answer that I'm cautiously optimistic. We face big problems that will do us in if we don't solve them. But we are capable of solving them. The risk we face isn't that of an asteroid collision beyond our ability to avoid. Instead our problems are of our own making, and so we can stop making them. The only thing lacking is the necessary political will.

The other reason for my optimism is the big advantage we 13 enjoy over the Anasazi and other past societies: the power of the media. When the Anasazi were collapsing in the U.S. Southwest, they had no idea that Easter Island was also on a downward spiral thousands of miles away, or that Mycenaean Greece had collapsed 2,400 years earlier. But we know from the media what is happening all around the world, and we know from archaeologists what happened in the past. We can learn from that understanding of remote places and times; the Anasazi didn't have that option. Knowing history, we are not doomed to repeat it.

Expanding Vocabulary

Study the definitions of each of the following words. Then select five and use each one of those in a separate sentence. The number in parentheses is the number of the paragraph in which the word appears.

obsess (2)
acute (4)
degradation (4)
immune (5)
assaulting (7)

prone (8)
fragility (8)
salinization (8)
tinderboxes (8)

Understanding Content

1. How did many Americans view globalization before 9/11?
2. Why is environmental degradation likely to be more serious than terrorism?
3. What are Diamond's examples of societies that disappeared in the past?
4. What are the four lessons from these "lost worlds"?
5. What is the important difference between the lost worlds of the past and our society today?
6. Why should we be cautiously optimistic about our survival?

Drawing Inferences about Thesis and Purpose

1. What is Diamond's thesis?
2. How does the author connect current terrorism activities and environmental dangers?

Analyzing Strategies and Style

1. Study Diamond's introductory paragraphs. What does he seek to accomplish by his approach?
2. Diamond has advanced his argument in the context of a personal essay. What characteristics of the personal essay do you find here?
3. What is the essay's tone? How do the opening and concluding paragraphs help create the tone?

Thinking Critically

1. Evaluate Diamond's argument. Are his four points clear and useful lessons? Has he convinced you that we face serious environmental problems?
2. Diamond believes that we can find the will to solve our problems before it is too late. Do you agree? Why or why not?

STUDENT ESSAY—REFUTATION

"BLAME IT ON THE MEDIA AND OTHER WAYS TO DRESS A WOLF IN SHEEP'S CLOTHING" David M. Ouellette

If an activity is legal, then people should be free to engage in that activity without fear of defamation. But smokers are being defamed, even persecuted, by a biased media bent on casting smoking as an unmitigated evil. This is Robert J. Samuelson's assertion in his September 24, 1997, Newsweek article "Do Smokers Have Rights." He says the media distort research on passive smoking's effects, demonize tobacco companies into teen-targeting drug pushers, and use these ill-founded claims as justification for punitive cigarette taxes. The result, Samuelson says, is that we "deny, ignore or minimize" the right of smokers to do something that is perfectly legal. He is mistaken on all counts.

Introduction includes author, title, publication place, and date of work to be refuted.

Attention-getter

Thesis

When it comes to the effects of passive smoking, Samuelson does not want to accept what researchers have to say. He cites a ten-year study of non-smoking nurses that reported 25 to 30 percent of their heart attacks were caused by passive

Student blends summary and direct quotation to present author's position.

smoking. No matter how you look at the
figure, it clearly states that passive
smoking is dangerous. He says, "the practical significance of this is negligible."
Ask any one of those people whose heart
attacks were caused by someone else's
smoking if what happened to them was "negligible." The practical impact is that if
smoking were eliminated, heart attacks
among nonsmokers would drop by 25 to 30
percent, according to this study.

The media, contrary to Samuelson, are
not the ones who have painted tobacco companies as purveyors of addiction to
teenagers. The tobacco industry has demo-
nized itself. Samuelson himself admits
that "the tobacco industry no doubt targets teens," but he excuses this by saying, "the ads may affect brand choices
more than the decision to smoke." However,
advertising for a brand of cigarettes is,
necessarily, at the same time advertising
for smoking. If a brand is made to look
attractive, then that also means smoking
itself is made to look attractive, for you
cannot have one without the other.

Finally, Samuelson argues that heavy
cigarette taxes actually hurt smokers
more than help them. In reality, the
taxes are intended to deter people from

*Student
analyzes the
author's logic.*

smoking by raising the price. The people who would most likely be deterred are teenagers and the poor, both of whom smoke more than any other age group or economic class. "Sin taxes," such as cigarette taxes, attempt to limit or discourage legal behavior. A high price is not tantamount to unlegislated prohibition; it is society's way of dissuading people from destructive behavior. Samuelson asks whether we have a right to limit legal behaviors, or is this infringing on individuals' rights. There is a middle ground between prohibition and unlimited right. Alcohol consumption is just such an example, a behavior so dangerous that its use is controlled yet still legal. Clearly, society has a right to prohibit or control dangerous behavior. Not only is it society's right to control the danger to which its citizens are exposed, it is its responsibility.

Student uses a comparison with alcohol to challenge the author's argument.

Samuelson's claim that the media are besmirching smokers and tobacco companies with misleading reports is false. It is the media's responsibility to report news, such as the health threat of passive smoking, and how tobacco companies target teenagers. As for the right to smoke, smoking's dangers—both to smokers

Student concludes by resisting his thesis and defending it as the responsible one.

and nonsmokers alike—demand its control.

Conceding   fist-pounding   demands   for

unlimited   rights,   regardless   of   who   gets

hurt   or   what   other   rights   get   infringed,

would   be   an   abdication   of   our   responsi-

bility   to   protect   the   health   and   welfare

of   the   nation.

MAKING CONNECTIONS

---

1. Examine the arguments in this chapter for the various
   strategies that the authors use. Then decide: (a) What particular strategy works consistently well from one essay to
   the next? And (b) What particular essay is the best argument, overall? Be prepared to defend your decisions.
2. Select one of the five pairs of arguments and study the pair
   for any common ground that you can find. You may find
   something stated directly in the essays, or you may have
   to infer some common ground based on what the authors
   have written in general. Think about how you would
   explain to the two authors that they do share some common
   ground in spite of their differences.
3. In his essay on environmental problems, Jared Diamond
   mentions a number of "lost worlds," societies that died out
   because of severe changes in their environments. Select one
   of these societies—the one you know the least about or perhaps one from a part of the world you are interested in—
   and learn more about the society and the causes of its
   disappearance. Try going online, using Yahoo or Google
   and using the name of the society as your keyword.

TOPICS AND GUIDELINES FOR WRITING

---

1. Did any one of the writers change your way of thinking
   on his or her issue? If so, write an essay in which you
   explain how that writer's argument convinced you to

rethink your position and why the writer's argument should convince other readers. Do not assume that your audience knows the essay, so provide the author, title, and publication information in your essay.

2. Select a personal problem that concerns you, perhaps because you have a friend or family member with that problem. In an essay, present and defend your view on this issue. You can write to a general audience or directly to the person involved in a letter format and tone. Possible topics include staying in school, quitting smoking or using drugs or abusing alcohol, controlling starving or binge eating, maintaining relationships with parents, selecting a career, eliminating abusive language, or other bad habits.

3. Select any writer in this chapter whose position you disagree with and prepare a refutation of the writer's argument. Do not assume that your reader has read the article you are refuting. As shown in the student essay, begin by giving author, title, publication information, and the author's position. Then present and support your position. Your argument may be developed in part by showing weaknesses in the opposing view.

4. Reflect on educational issues and problems to select a topic from this area that interests and concerns you. There are many possible topics, including censorship of books in high school libraries, control of high school and college newspapers, discrimination in sororities and fraternities, academic freedom, plagiarism, grading systems, admissions policies, and others. Definitions may play an important role in developing your argument. Be sure that you understand the arguments on both sides, acknowledge whatever common ground you share with opponents, and write in a restrained, conciliatory manner.

5. Many serious problems face our society—from drugs to taxes (and the deficit) to illegal aliens to homelessness to insider trading and other business and banking crimes to AIDs to ethical concerns such as abortion, euthanasia, and genetic engineering. Select a problem that concerns you and write an argumentative essay that presents and defends your proposed solutions to the problems. Part of your development will probably include challenging other proposed solutions

with which you disagree. You may want to do some reading so that you have current facts about the problem. (If you use sources, including Internet sources, be sure to credit them properly.)

6. Serious problems also face our world, for example, depletion of the ozone layer, acid rain, deforestation, polluted water, global warming, and possibly overpopulation. Select a problem that concerns you and prepare an argumentative essay according to the guidelines discussed in topic 5. Give thought to how you can narrow your topic to a manageable length. For example, instead of examining the problem of water pollution, write about the pollution of a lake or river or bay near where you live.

11

Works for Further Reading and Analysis

The works in this chapter demonstrate the use of a number of the strategies discussed and illustrated in previous chapters, including narration, description, definition, contrast, and argument. They also provide opportunities for exciting and challenging reading and critical thinking.

Declaration of Sentiments

ELIZABETH CADY STANTON

Elizabeth Cady Stanton (1815–1902) was one of the most important leaders of the women's rights movement. Educated at a local academy and then the Emma Willard Seminary in Troy, NY, Stanton studied law with her father before her marriage. An active reformer in the abolition and temperance movements, she later focused her attention on women's issues. At the Seneca Falls Convention in 1848, Stanton gave the opening speech and read her "Declaration of Sentiments." She founded and became president of the National Women's Suffrage Association in 1869. "The Declaration of Sentiments," patterned after the Declaration of Independence, lists the grievances of women suffering under the tyranny of men.

Keep the Declaration of Independence in mind as you read Stanton's version and use the following questions to guide your analysis.

1. What do women demand? How will they achieve their goals?

2. How have women been restricted in education, in work, if married, and psychologically?

3. What charges made by Stanton continue to be legitimate complaints, in whole or in part?

4. Consider: Do we need a new declaration of sentiments for women? If so, what specific changes would you list? Do we need a new declaration of sentiments for other groups? If so, who? For what reasons?

1   When, in the course of human events, it becomes necessary for one portion of the family of man to assume among the people of the earth a position different from that which they have hitherto occupied, but one to which the laws of nature and of nature's God entitle them, a decent respect to the opinions of mankind requires that they should declare the causes that impel them to such a course.

2   We hold these truths to be self-evident: that all men and women are created equal; that they are endowed by their Creator with certain inalienable rights; that among these are life, liberty, and the pursuit of happiness; that to secure these rights governments are instituted, deriving their just powers from the consent of the governed. Whenever any form of government becomes destructive of these ends, it is the right of those who suffer from it to refuse allegiance to it, and to insist upon the institution of a new government, laying its foundation on such principles, and organizing its powers in such form, as to them shall seem most likely to effect their safety and happiness. Prudence, indeed, will dictate that governments long established should not be changed for light and transient causes; and accordingly all experience hath shown that mankind are more disposed to suffer, while evils are sufferable, than to right themselves by abolishing the forms to which they were accustomed. But when a long train of abuses and usurpations, pursuing invariably the same object evinces a design to reduce them under absolute despotism, it is their duty to throw off such government, and to provide new guards for their future security. Such has been the patient sufferance of the women under this government, and such is now the necessity which constrains them to demand the equal station to which they are entitled.

The history of mankind is a history of repeated injuries and   3
usurpations on the part of man toward woman, having in direct
object the establishment of an absolute tyranny over her. To
prove this, let facts be submitted to a candid world.

He has never permitted her to exercise her inalienable right   4
to the elective franchise.

He has compelled her to submit to laws, in the formation of   5
which she had no voice.

He has withheld from her rights which are given to the most   6
ignorant and degraded men—both natives and foreigners.

Having deprived her of this first right of a citizen, the elective   7
franchise, thereby leaving her without representation in the halls
of legislation, he has oppressed her on all sides.

He has made her, if married, in the eye of the law, civilly   8
dead.

He has taken from her all right in property, even to the wages   9
she earns.

He has made her, morally, an irresponsible being, as she can   10
commit many crimes with impunity, provided they be done in
the presence of her husband. In the covenant of marriage, she
is compelled to promise obedience to her husband, he becoming, to all intents and purposes, her master—the law giving
him power to deprive her of her liberty, and to administer
chastisement.

He has so framed the laws of divorce, as to what shall be   11
the proper causes, and in case of separation, to whom the
guardianship of the children shall be given, as to be wholly
regardless of the happiness of women—the law, in all cases,
going upon a false supposition of the supremacy of man, and
giving all power into his hands.

After depriving her of all rights as a married woman, if sin-   12
gle, and the owner of property, he has taxed her to support a
government which recognizes her only when her property can
be made profitable to it.

He has monopolized nearly all the profitable employments,   13
and from those she is permitted to follow, she receives but a
scanty remuneration. He closes against her all the avenues
to wealth and distinction which he considers most honorable
to himself. As a teacher of theology, medicine, or law, she is
not known.

He has denied her the facilities for obtaining a thorough education, all colleges being closed against her.

He allows her in Church, as well as State, but a subordinate position, claiming Apostolic authority for her exclusion from the ministry, and, with some exceptions, from any public participation in the affairs of the Church.

16   He has created a false public sentiment by giving the world a different code of morals for men and women, by which moral delinquencies which exclude women from society, are not only tolerated, but deemed of little account in man.

17   He has usurped the prerogative of Jehovah himself, claiming it as his right to assign for her a sphere of action, when that belongs to her conscience and to her God.

18   He has endeavored, in every way that he could, to destroy her confidence in her own powers, to lessen her self-respect, and to make her willing to lead a dependent and abject life.

19   Now, in view of this entire disfranchisement of one-half the people of this country, their social and religious degradation— in view of the unjust laws above mentioned, and because women do feel themselves aggrieved, oppressed, and fraudulently deprived of their most sacred rights, we insist that they have immediate admission to all the rights and privileges which belong to them as citizens of the United States.

20   In entering upon the great work before us, we anticipate no small amount of misconception, misrepresentation, and ridicule; but we shall use every instrumentality within our power to effect our object. We shall employ agents, circulate tracts, petition the State and National legislatures, and endeavor to enlist the pulpit and the press in our behalf. We hope this Convention will be followed by a series of Conventions embracing every part of the country.

The Story of an Hour

KATE CHOPIN

Now a highly acclaimed fiction writer, Kate Chopin (1851–1904) enjoyed a decade of popularity from 1890 to 1900, and then experienced critical condemnation followed by sixty years of neglect.

Chopin began her career after her husband's death, having returned to her home in St. Louis with her six children. She saw two collections of her stories published—*Bayou Folk* in 1894 and *A Night in Acadie* in 1897—before losing her popularity with the publication of her short novel *The Awakening* in 1899, the story of a woman struggling to free herself from years of repression and subservience. "The Story of an Hour" depicts another character's struggle.

After reading, you will want to be able to summarize the story and analyze elements of the story to respond fully to it. Use these questions to aid your analysis:

1. What do the details of the scene outside Mrs. Mallard's window have in common? How do they help us understand what she experiences in her room?
2. How does Mrs. Mallard change as a result of her reflections in her room?
3. Are we to agree with the doctor's explanation for Mrs. Mallard's death? Explain the story's conclusion. What term describes the story's ending?

Knowing that Mrs. Mallard was afflicted with a heart trouble, great care was taken to break to her as gently as possible the news of her husband's death. 1

It was her sister Josephine who told her, in broken sentences; veiled hints that revealed in half concealing. Her husband's friend Richards was there, too, near her. It was he who had been in the newspaper office when intelligence of the railroad disaster was received, with Brently Mallard's name leading the list of "killed." He had only taken the time to assure himself of its truth by a second telegram, and had hastened to forestall any less careful, less tender friend in bearing the sad message. 2

She did not hear the story as many women have heard the same, with a paralyzed inability to accept its significance. She wept at once, with sudden, wild abandonment, in her sister's arms. When the storm of grief had spent itself she went away to her room alone. She would have no one follow her. 3

There stood, facing the open window, a comfortable, roomy armchair. Into this she sank, pressed down by a physical exhaustion that haunted her body and seemed to reach into her soul. 4

5   She could see in the open square before her house the tops of trees that were all aquiver with the new spring life. The delicious breath of rain was in the air. In the street below a peddler was crying his wares. The notes of a distant song which someone was singing reached her faintly, and countless sparrows were twittering in the eaves.

6   There were patches of blue sky showing here and there through the clouds that had met and piled one above the other in the west facing her window.

7   She sat with her head thrown back upon the cushion of the chair, quite motionless, except when a sob came up into her throat and shook her, as a child who has cried itself to sleep continues to sob in its dreams.

8   She was young, with a fair, calm face, whose lines bespoke repression and even a certain strength. But now there was a dull stare in her eyes, whose gaze was fixed away off yonder on one of those patches of blue sky. It was not a glance of reflection, but rather indicated a suspension of intelligent thought.

9   There was something coming to her and she was waiting for it, fearfully. What was it? She did not know; it was too subtle and elusive to name. But she felt it, creeping out of the sky, reaching toward her through the sounds, the scents, the color that filled the air.

10   Now her bosom rose and fell tumultuously. She was beginning to recognize this thing that was approaching to possess her, and she was striving to beat it back with her will—as powerless as her two white slender hands would have been.

11   When she abandoned herself a little whispered word escaped her slightly parted lips. She said it over and over under her breath: "free, free, free!" The vacant stare and the look of terror that had followed it went from her eyes. They stayed keen and bright. Her pulses beat fast, and the coursing blood warmed and relaxed every inch of her body.

12   She did not stop to ask if it were or were not a monstrous joy that held her. A clear and exalted perception enabled her to dismiss the suggestion as trivial.

13   She knew that she would weep again when she saw the kind, tender hands folded in death; the face that had never looked save with love upon her, fixed and gray and dead. But she saw beyond that bitter moment a long procession of years to come

that would belong to her absolutely. And she opened and spread her arms out to them in welcome.

There would be no one to live for her during those coming 14
years; she would live for herself. There would be no powerful will bending hers in that blind persistence with which men and women believe they have a right to impose a private will upon a fellow-creature. A kind intention or a cruel intention made the act seem no less a crime as she looked upon it in that brief moment of illumination.

And yet she had loved him—sometimes. Often she had not. 15
What did it matter! What could love, the unsolved mystery, count for in face of this possession of self-assertion which she suddenly recognized as the strongest impulse of her being!

"Free! Body and soul free!" she kept whispering. 16

Josephine was kneeling before the closed door with her lips 17
to the keyhole, imploring for admission. "Louise, open the door! I beg; open the door—you will make yourself ill. What are you doing, Louise? For heaven's sake open the door."

"Go away. I am not making myself ill." No; she was drinking 18
in a very elixir of life through that open window.

Her fancy was running riot along those days ahead of her. 19
Spring days, and summer days, and all sorts of days that would be her own. She breathed a quick prayer that life might be long. It was only yesterday she had thought with a shudder that life might be long.

She arose at length and opened the door to her sister's impor- 20
tunities. There was a feverish triumph in her eyes, and she car- ried herself unwittingly like a goddess of Victory. She clasped her sister's waist, and together they descended the stairs. Richards stood waiting for them at the bottom.

Someone was opening the front door with a latchkey. It 21
was Brently Mallard who entered, a little travel-stained, com- posedly carrying his grip-sack and umbrella. He had been far from the scene of the accident, and did not even know there had been one. He stood amazed at Josephine's piercing cry; at Richards' quick motion to screen him from the view of his wife.

But Richards was too late. 22

When the doctors came they said she had died of heart dis- 23
ease—of joy that kills.

Patterns

AMY LOWELL

Educated at private schools and widely traveled, Amy Lowell (1874–1925) was a poet and critic. Her most important critical work is a study of the British poet John Keats. Lowell frequently read her poetry and lectured on poetic techniques, defending her free verse and the work of other modern poets.

As you study "Patterns," probably her best-known poem, use the following questions as guides.

1. What is the situation of the poem? Who is the speaker, where is the speaker, and what has the speaker just learned?
2. What does the speaker imagine doing, along the garden paths, that now will not take place?
3. What do the garden paths and the speaker's gown come to represent? What patterns are repressive or destructive?
4. Is "Christ!" in the last line an oath, a prayer, or both?

I walk down the garden paths,
And all the daffodils
Are blowing, and the bright blue squills.
I walk down the patterned garden-paths
5 In my stiff, brocaded gown.
With my powdered hair and jewelled fan,
I too am a rare
Pattern. As I wander down
The garden paths.

10 My dress is richly figured,
And the train
Makes a pink and silver stain
On the gravel, and the thrift
Of the borders.
15 Just a plate of current fashion
Tripping by in high-heeled, ribboned shoes.
Not a softness anywhere about me,
Only whalebone[1] and brocade.
And I sink on a seat in the shade

---

[1]Whalebones were used to make stiff corsets for women.—Ed.

Of a lime tree. For my passion   20
Wars against the stiff brocade.
The daffodils and squills
Flutter in the breeze
As they please   25
And I weep;
For the lime-tree is in blossom
And one small flower has dropped upon my bosom.

And the plashing of waterdrops
In the marble fountain   30
Comes down the garden-paths.
The dripping never stops.
Underneath my stiffened gown
Is the softness of a woman bathing in a marble basin,
A basin in the midst of hedges grown   35
So thick, she cannot see her lover hiding,
But she guesses he is near,
And the sliding of the water
Seems the stroking of a dear
Hand upon her.   40
What is Summer in a fine brocaded gown!
I should like to see it lying in a heap upon the ground.
All the pink and silver crumpled up on the ground.

I would be the pink and silver as I ran along the paths,
And he would stumble after,
Bewildered by my laughter.   45
I should see the sun flashing from his sword-hilt and
    buckles on his shoes.
I would choose
To lead him in a maze along the patterned paths,
A bright and laughing maze for my heavy-booted lover.
Till he caught me in the shade,   50
And the buttons of his waistcoat bruised my body as he
    clasped me,
Aching, melting, unafraid.
With the shadows of the leaves and the sundrops,
And the plopping of the waterdrops,
All about us in the open afternoon—   55
I am very like to swoon
With the weight of this brocade,
For the sun sifts through the shade.

Underneath the fallen blossom
60 In my bosom,
    Is a letter I have hid.
    It was brought to me this morning by a rider from the Duke.
    "Madam, we regret to inform you that Lord Hartwell
    Died in action Thursday se'nnight.[2]
65 As I read it in the white, morning sunlight,
    The letters squirmed like snakes.
    "Any answer, Madam," said my footman.
    "No," I told him.
    "See that the messenger takes some refreshment.
70 No, no answer."
    And I walked into the garden,
    Up and down the patterned paths,
    In my stiff, correct brocade.
    The blue and yellow flowers stood up proudly in the sun,
75 Each one.
    I stood upright too,
    Held rigid to the pattern
    By the stiffness of my gown.
    Up and down I walked.
80 Up and down.

    In a month he would have been my husband.
    In a month, here, underneath this lime,
    We would have broken the pattern;
    He for me, and I for him,
85 He as Colonel, I as Lady,
    On this shady seat.
    He had a whim
    That sunlight carried blessing.
    And I answered, "It shall be as you have said."
90 Now he is dead.

    In Summer and in Winter I shall walk
    Up and down
    The patterned garden-paths
    In my stiff brocaded gown.
    The squills and daffodils

---

[2]Seven nights; hence a week ago.—Ed.

Will give place to pillared roses, and to asters, and to snow. 95
I shall go
Up and down,
In my gown.
Gorgeously arrayed,
Boned and stayed. 100
And the softness of my body will be guarded from
    embrace
By each button, hook, and lace.
For the man who should loose me is dead,
Fighting with the Duke in Flanders,[3]
In a pattern called a war. 105
Christ! What are patterns for?

Science and the Sense of Wonder

ISAAC ASIMOV

Born in Russia, Isaac Asimov (1920–1992) became a naturalized
American citizen and famous both as a scholar and writer in
physics, biochemistry, astronomy, and genetics and as a science-
fiction author. In addition to having written over 200 books, and
many more articles and short stories, Asimov was for years associate professor of biochemistry at Boston University School of
Medicine. "Science and the Sense of Wonder" first appeared in
the *Washington Post* on August 12, 1979.

*Since Asimov is writing in reaction to Whitman's poem, your
analysis needs to begin with the poem. Consider: What is the
poem's situation? What does the speaker do? What attitude
toward science does the poem convey? What attitude toward
nature? Now reflect on Asimov's response, using these
questions to direct your thinking:*

1. Asimov puts down Whitman's attitude toward science as
   "very convenient." Why?
2. When Asimov looks at what we call stars, what are some
   of the details that he understands in what he sees?

[3]Area in Belgium and France where heavy fighting occurred during World
War I—Ed.

3. Can you summarize the information about the heavens that the author provides?
4. Has Asimov convinced you that Whitman didn't know how much he was missing? Why or why not? Whose view of nature most closely resembles your own?

———————

1   One of Walt Whitman's best-known poems is this one:

When I heard the learn'd astronomer,
When the proofs, the figures, were ranged in columns before me,
When I was shown the charts and diagrams, to add, divide and measure them,
When I sitting heard the astronomer where he lectured with much applause in the lecture-room,
How soon unaccountable I became tired and sick,
Till rising and gliding out I wander'd off by myself,
In the mystical moist night-air, and from time to time,
Look'd up in perfect silence at the stars.

2   I imagine that many people reading those lines tell themselves, exultantly, "How true! Science just sucks all the beauty out of everything, reducing it all to numbers and tables and measurements! Why bother learning all that junk when I can just go out and look at the stars?"

3   That is a very convenient point of view since it makes it not only unnecessary, but downright aesthetically wrong, to try to follow all that hard stuff in science. Instead, you can just take a look at the night sky, get a quick beauty fix, and go off to a nightclub.

4   The trouble is that Whitman is talking through his hat, but the poor soul didn't know any better.

5   I don't deny that the night sky is beautiful, and I have in my time spread out on a hillside for hours looking at the stars and being awed by their beauty (and receiving bug-bites whose marks took weeks to go away).

6   But what I see—those quiet, twinkling points of light—*is not all the beauty there is.* Should I stare lovingly at a single leaf and willingly remain ignorant of the forest? Should I be satisfied to watch the sun glinting off a single pebble and scorn any knowledge of a beach?

Those bright spots in the sky that we call planets are worlds. 7
There are worlds with thick atmospheres of carbon dioxide and
sulfuric acid; worlds of red-hot liquid with hurricanes that
could gulp down the whole earth; dead worlds with quiet pock-
marks of craters; worlds with volcanoes puffing plumes of dust
into airlessness; worlds with pink and desolate deserts—each
with a weird and unearthly beauty that boils down to a mere
speck of light if we just gaze at the night sky.

Those other bright spots, which are stars rather than plan- 8
ets, are actually suns. Some of them are of incomparable
grandeur, each glowing with the light of a thousand suns like
ours; some of them are merely red-hot coals doling out their
energy stingily. Some of them are compact bodies as massive
as our sun, but with all that mass squeezed into a ball smaller
than the earth. Some are more compact still, with the mass of the
sun squeezed down into the volume of a small asteroid. And
some are more compact still, with their mass shrinking down
to a volume of zero, the site of which is marked by an intense
gravitational field that swallows up everything and gives back
nothing; with matter spiraling into that bottomless hole and giving out a wild death-scream of X-rays.

There are stars that pulsate endlessly in a great cosmic 9
breathing; and others that, having consumed their fuel, expand
and redden until they swallow up their planets, if they have any
(and someday, billions of years from now, our sun will expand
and the earth will crisp and sere and vaporize into a gas of iron
and rock with no sign of the life it once bore). And some stars
explode in a vast cataclysm whose ferocious blast of cosmic
rays, hurrying outward at nearly the speed of light, reaches
across thousands of light years to touch the earth and supply
some of the driving force of evolution through mutations.

Those paltry few stars we see as we look up in perfect silence 10
(some 2,500 or more on even the darkest and clearest night)
are joined by a vast horde we don't see, up to as many as three
hundred billion—300,000,000,000—to form an enormous pinwheel in space. This pinwheel, the Milky Way galaxy, stretches so widely that it takes light, moving at 186,282 miles each
second, a hundred thousand *years* to cross it from end to end; and
it rotates about its center in a vast and stately turn that takes two
hundred million years to complete—and the sun and the earth
and we ourselves all make that turn.

11   Beyond our Milky Way galaxy are others, a score or so of them bound to our own in a cluster of galaxies, most of them small, with no more than a few billion stars in each; but with one at least, the Andromeda galaxy, twice as large as our own.

12   Beyond our own cluster, other galaxies and other clusters exist; some clusters made up of thousands of galaxies. They stretch outward and outward as far as our best telescopes can see, with no visible sign of an end—perhaps a hundred billion of them in all.

13   And in more and more of those galaxies we are becoming aware of violence at the centers—of great explosions and out-pourings of radiation, marking the death of perhaps millions of stars. Even at the center of our own galaxy there is incredible violence masked from our own solar system far in the outskirts by enormous clouds of dust and gas that lie between us and the heaving center.

14   Some galactic centers are so bright that they can be seen from distances of billions of light-years, distances from which the galaxies themselves cannot be seen and only the bright star-like centers of ravening energy show up—as quasars. Some of these have been detected from more than ten billion light-years away.

15   All these galaxies are hurrying outward from each other in a vast universal expansion that began fifteen billion years ago, when all the matter in the universe was in a tiny sphere that exploded in the hugest conceivable shatter to form the galaxies.

16   The universe may expand forever or the day may come when the expansion slows and turns back into a contraction to re-form the tiny sphere and begin the game all over again so that the whole universe is exhaling and inhaling in breaths that are per-haps a trillion years long.

17   And all of this vision—far beyond the scale of human imag-inings—was made possible by the work of hundreds of "learn'd" astronomers. All of it; *all* of it was discovered after the death of Whitman in 1892, and most of it in the past twenty-five years, so that the poor poet never knew what a stultified and lim-ited beauty he observed when he "look'd up in perfect silence at the stars."

18   Nor can we know or imagine now the limitless beauty yet to be revealed in the future—by science.

Border Hazards: An Obsession to Become Unhealthy

RICHARD RODRIGUEZ

Richard Rodriguez (b. 1944) holds degrees in literature from Stanford and Columbia Universities and has studied at Berkeley and the Warburg Institute in London. He is an editor of Pacific News Service and an author of both articles and books, including *Days of Obligation: An Argument with My Mexican Father* (1992). He has won awards for his writing, and excerpts from his autobiography *Hunger of Memory* (1982) are frequently anthologized. In the following article, published September 20, 1998, Rodriguez examines the effects of migration to the United States and the changes in lifestyles occurring around the world.

Use these questions to guide your reading.

1. What, for Rodriguez, is ironic about the study findings by William Vega?
2. What ideas does America "sell," especially to young people?
3. In paragraph 18, the author lists specifics that American life offers. What is startling about this list? How does it help to develop Rodriguez's thesis?
4. Is America hazardous to our health?

Maybe we need to put a sign at the border and in our international airports. WARNING: AMERICA MAY BE DANGEROUS TO YOUR HEALTH. 1

It has never been easy to be an immigrant. Imagine what those 19th-century immigrants knew, leaving certainty behind, abandoning Ireland and Italy and Russia, to travel to America. (In those days, an ocean's separation from loved ones was permanent as death.) What bravery, what recklessness the journey to Ellis Island required. What a price there was to pay for leaving certain poverty. 2

A study, headed by Professor William Vega of UC Berkeley and published last week, has found that Mexican immigrants suffer increased mental stress the longer they stay in this country. Rates 3 of mental illness and other social disorders, like drug use and divorce, rise after immigration. Vega's team of researchers observed the breakdown of immigrant families within a generation, on a scale comparable to other Americans.

4   These findings are, at least, ironic. For generations, Americans have assumed moral superiority toward Latin America. Early this century, for example, citizens of San Diego traveled south, into Tijuana, whenever they wanted to sin. Just as today, Americans like to imagine that Mexican drug lords are contaminating our "innocent" youth.

5   The tables have turned. Four years ago, the Center for Science in the Public Interest in Washington warned Americans away from Mexican food. Eating a chile relleno is the equivalent of devouring a cube of butter! Now, U.S. professors warn immigrants away from burgers and fries.

6   A week before Vega's report, a panel of the National Research Council and the Institute of Medicine found that the longer an immigrant child lives in this country, the greater the chance of physical and psychological deterioration. The panel's chairman, Dr. Evan Charney of the University of Massachusetts Medical School, warned, "The longer you're in this country, the more you want to eat at McDonald's."

7   Immigrants. I see them all the time in California, their eyes filled with terror and wonder. Their jogging shoes have transported them from villages in Mexico or Central America into the postmodern city of freeways and peroxide and neon. How will they find their way?

8   Vega and his team of researchers studied the problems of Mexican immigrants in Fresno County. But the researchers would, I suspect, have come up with similar findings of social breakdown had they talked with young Mexicans in Tijuana. The poor are in movement, all over the world, from village to city, from tradition toward change.

9   Recently, in the boomtown of Monterrey, Mexico, I met teenagers, poor alongside rich, who were busy consuming drugs. Cocaine was evidence of their modernity, a habit that made them just like the Americans on TV and the movies. Monterrey has not yet turned as violent as Mexico City. But the women in the new factories, on the outskirts of town, know divorce.

10   All over the world, from Andean villages to Southeast Asia, America advertises the "I." You can drink America from a Coke

bottle; you can dance America. America is seducing the young all over the world with the idea of individual freedom. Change. Movement. Dollars.

On the line between Tijuana and San Diego tonight, you can 11 meet kids waiting for dark to run into the United States. They say they do not want to become Americans. They do not speak of Thomas Jefferson or the Bill of Rights. There is, they say, a job waiting for them in Glendale or Fresno. A job in a pizza parlor or a job as a roofer that will keep them and their families from going hungry.

The U.S. professors fret. The panelists for the National 12 Research Council advise against attempts "to push immigrant youth toward assimilation." But they might as well bemoan the jet engine or the bicycle.

Movement. America is not an easy country for either the 13 native-born or the immigrant. Everything keeps changing. In small towns in Arkansas today, Mexican immigrants arrive to pluck dead chickens because no one else will do it. They paint their houses gaudy colors, speak Spanish at the post office. Native-born Americans bemoan the change. They become foreigners in their own town.

The kid from Oaxaca ends up making pizzas in Santa Mon- 14 ica. He learns English by hearing "Hold the pepperoni!" Day after day, he breathes America. America flows into his ears— California slang, the thump of rap. There is no resisting it.

Assimilation is more a biological process than a matter of 15 choice. Immigrant kids end up breathing America, swallowing America. When you approach the counter at McDonald's, you buy more than a burger: You buy an American spirit of impatience. Immigrants end up walking like the native-born, assuming the same nervous slouch.

Drugs. Divorce. Anonymity. The religions of the world that 16 are growing today are those religions that address the sadness of the migrating poor and their longing for the abandoned, lost village. Islam spreads through U.S. prisons. Evangelical Protestantism teaches children in Lima or in Los Angeles to be reborn and cleansed of the terrible city.

Immigrant parents turn pro-choice. They chose to leave 17 Mexico, so they imagine their U.S.-born kids can choose to absent themselves from Los Angeles, "remain" Mexican despite the heaving and throbbing city around them. Papa is always grumbling that the kids are becoming disrespectful U.S. teenagers. Mama is always saying that everyone was happier—poorer, yes, but happier—in the Mexican village.

18 America is a most remarkable country, the model of modernity for people all over the world. It offers the world the possibility of individual life: the freeway onramp, the separate bedroom, the terrible loneliness, the range of choices on a TV remote.

19 The Mexican kid from Oaxaca will not go back. His dollars, and maybe something more he cannot describe, will keep him making pizzas in Santa Monica. Yes, he will regret the disrespect of his U.S.-born children. Perhaps he will even send them back to Mexico during—that most American of seasons—adolescence.

20 But the village of Mexico is not, in truth, what it used to be. It has changed. There are blond soap operas blaring from the television in the old family kitchen. Everyone in the village talks of jobs in Dallas and Guadalajara.

21 The guilt. The terrible guilt of becoming an American remains. Every child of immigrant parents knows it. It is as old as America. The scorn of a grandmother: her black dress and her face at the window. Her mutterings in Yiddish or Chinese or Swedish. Her complaint: You are turning into a gringo, goy, a stranger to her.

22 Dear Nana. Forgive us! Forgive us our love of America, this very strange country, the envy of the world. Look! Look at the fresh fruits at Ralphs. The meats and the cheeses, dear abuelita. Forgive us for transporting the 18th-century pronoun, the "I," all the way to Fresno. It has driven us mad. But it has gotten us a washer and dryer.

23 It has made your grandchildren so tall and so straight, like movie stars. Look! Who would have guessed, dear Nana, you would have grandchildren so beautiful!

Neat People vs. Sloppy People

SUZANNE BRITT

Suzanne Britt graduated from Salem Academy, has a master's degree in English, and currently teaches at Meredith College in North Carolina. She is the author of several books and many poems and articles. In the following essay, from the collection of her essays titled *Show and Tell,* Britt dishes up some kind and some cruel comments about each type of person.

As you read, think about her purpose in writing and use these questions to aid your analysis.
1. What are the differences between neat and sloppy people?
2. What is Britt's tone? Does she intend this to be funny? Does she also intend it to be serious in any way?
3. How would you argue for the superiority of neat people over sloppy people?

I've finally figured out the difference between neat people 1
and sloppy people. The distinction is, as always, moral. Neat people are lazier and meaner than sloppy people.

Sloppy people, you see, are not really sloppy. Their sloppi- 2
ness is merely the unfortunate consequence of their extreme moral rectitude. Sloppy people carry in their mind's eye a heavenly vision, a precise plan, that is so stupendous, so perfect, it can't be achieved in this world or the next.

Sloppy people live in Never-Never Land. Someday is their 3
métier. Someday they are planning to alphabetize all their books and set up home catalogs. Someday they will go through their wardrobes and mark certain items for tentative mending and certain items for passing on to relatives of similar shape and size. Someday sloppy people will make family scrapbooks into which they will put newspaper clippings, postcards, locks of hair, and the dried corsage from their senior prom. Someday they will file everything on the surface of their desks, including the cash receipts from coffee purchases at the snack shop. Someday they will sit down and read all the back issues of *The New Yorker.*

For all these noble reasons and more, sloppy people never 4
get neat. They aim too high and wide. They save everything, planning someday to file, order, and straighten out the world. But while these ambitious plans take clearer and clearer shape in their heads, the books spill from the shelves onto the floor, the clothes pile up in the hamper and closet, the family mementos accumulate in every drawer, the surface of the desk is buried under mounds of paper and the unread magazines threaten to reach the ceiling.

5   Sloppy people can't bear to part with anything. They give loving attention to every detail. When sloppy people say they're going to tackle the surface of the desk, they really mean it. Not a paper will go unturned; not a rubber band will go unboxed. Four hours or two weeks into the excavation, the desk looks exactly the same, primarily because the sloppy person is meticulously creating new piles of papers with new headings and scrupulously stopping to read all the old book catalogs before he throws them away. A neat person would just bulldoze the desk.

6   Neat people are bums and clods at heart. They have cavalier attitudes toward possessions, including family heirlooms. Everything is just another dustcatcher to them. If anything collects dust, it's got to go and that's that. Neat people will toy with the idea of throwing the children out of the house just to cut down on the clutter.

7   Neat people don't care about process. They like results. What they want to do is get the whole thing over with so they can sit down and watch the rasslin' on TV. Neat people operate on two unvarying principles: Never handle any item twice, and throw everything away.

8   The only thing messy in a neat person's house is the trash can. The minute something comes to a neat person's hand, he will look at it, try to decide if it has immediate use and, finding none, throw it in the trash.

9   Neat people are especially vicious with mail. They never go through their mail unless they are standing directly over a trash can. If the trash can is beside the mailbox, even better. All ads, catalogs, pleas for charitable contributions, church bulletins and money-saving coupons go straight into the trash can without being opened. All letters from home, postcards from Europe, bills and paychecks are opened, immediately responded to, then dropped in the trash can. Neat people keep their receipts only for tax purposes. That's it. No sentimental salvaging of birthday cards or the last letter a dying relative ever wrote. Into the trash it goes.

10 Neat people place neatness above everything, even economics. They are incredibly wasteful. Neat people throw away several toys every time they walk through the den. I knew a neat person once who threw away a perfectly good dish drainer

because it had mold on it. The drainer was too much trouble to wash. And neat people sell their furniture when they move. They will sell a La-Z-Boy recliner while you are reclining in it.

Neat people are no good to borrow from. Neat people buy   11
everything in expensive little single portions. They get their flour and sugar in two-pound bags. They wouldn't consider clipping a coupon, saving a leftover, reusing plastic nondairy whipped cream containers or rinsing off tin foil and draping it over the unmoldy dish drainer. You can never borrow a neat person's newspaper to see what's playing at the movies. Neat people have the paper all wadded up and in the trash by 7.05 A.M.

Neat people cut a clean swath through the organic as well   12
as the inorganic world. People, animals, and things are all one to them. They are so insensitive. After they've finished with the pantry, the medicine cabinet, and the attic, they will throw out the red geranium (too many leaves), sell the dog (too many fleas), and send the children off to boarding school (too many scuffmarks on the hardwood floors).

A Date to Remember

LISA MUNDY

Lisa Mundy (b. 1960) holds a master's degree in English literature from the University of Virginia and is a staff writer and columnist for the *Washington Post*, with a regular column in the paper's Sunday magazine. The following Sunday "Postmodern" column, appearing July 14, 2002, offers a thoughtful analysis of our times.

Use these questions to guide your reading of Mundy's essay.

1. How have we traditionally referred to important moments in our history?
2. What is different about our use of "9/11"?
3. How does the author explain the difference? How does 9/11 fit our times?
4. Is it troubling, in any way, to consider that a digital "short-hand" represents our era?

Photo: Brian Noyes

1   There's a Web site now that shows you how to fold the new $20 bill to create a strange little origami construction that depicts, on one side, a scene that looks uncannily like the World Trade Center on fire and, on the other, one that resembles the Pentagon with flames coming out of the center. The site, www.allbrevard.net, makes much of what it calls the "amazing $20 bill 9/11 coincidence," and goes on to explore any number of insane conspiracy theories, such as whether the U.S. government planned the attacks, whether it means anything that you can also fold the $50 bill to depict a *plume of smoke,* etc. Predictably, responders to the site alternately glom onto these nutty ideas or excoriate the site for using them to sell its own Web-hosting service. Me, I was struck by something else: the way "9/11" has entered our consciousness to the point where even on a site clearly meant to appeal to the stupidest among us, it needs no explanation. The numbers are there. Nine. Eleven. We know instantly what they signify.

2   Up to now, there was no event in American history that we designated digitally, if you will, by lining numerals up in a row. Many people continue to say "September 11," it's true, and somehow using the word, like that, seems more formal, possibly more sad. But many others use the short form, without

intending any disrespect. There are any number of Web sites and relief funds for the "victims of 9/11"; and just the other day Sen. Charles Schumer of New York used the short version in a Senate hearing, pointing out that "before 9/11, the FBI's computers were less sophisticated than the one I bought for my son for $1,400."

Up to now, the signal events of our history were known, more often than not, by place names. Pearl Harbor is the analogy everybody thought of when the attacks happened; the worst disaster the nation had known will be forever associated with a lyrically named spot in Hawaii, the very name of which conjures up images of horrified Americans hearing the news by radio, sailors tapping vainly on their ship's hull for days, it is said, before they died. It's synecdoche, the part standing for the whole, and it's how we have always remembered our major military events. Bunker Hill, Valley Forge, Gettysburg, Little Big Horn: Great and terrible moments have traditionally been evoked by the places where they happened, here and, often, around the world. Historically, battles are known by names like Hastings, Gallipoli, the Somme; treaties by names like Yalta; trials by names like Nuremberg; assassinations by names like Dallas, a word that connotes not only the shooting of a president but the end of a national innocence. Why did we not adopt, similarly, a place name for the national innocence that ended last fall? Was it because it happened in planes, in the air, everywhere and nowhere? 3

I think that's part of it. This was an assault with a strangely un-regional quality; despite the intensity with which the attacks were felt in New York and Washington, they were also experienced by those watching, live, on television. All of America was the target. The attack happened on a single day, a singular day, a day that shocked us not only with the attacks themselves but with the sudden recognition that the forces that caused them had been gathering, unknown to most of us, for a long time. In the same way, those relatively few historical events that are remembered by their dates—July 4th, Cinco de Mayo, Juneteenth—are days when something that had been coming for a long time happened; the social order had been changing, but now the change burst into the open. Nine-eleven is the dark opposite of those celebratory occasions. It's the dark opposite 4 of D-Day, too, another event we remember as just that, a day, its name evocative of the operational codes of World War II and the military determination of an era.

5   In the same way, the phrase "9/11" evokes something about our own era. We would never refer to Independence Day as 7/4; that would seem anachronistic. But 9/11 fits. We are all digital thinkers now, accustomed to looking at our calendars, our watches, and seeing numerals. Granted, there is some especially odd thing about these numerals; it *is* weird that 911 is what people punched on their cell phones, often in vain, to seek help that day. There's significance in numbers, menace in numbers. It's a ridiculous stretch when one *allbrevard.net* link points out that 9 + 11 = 20 ($20, get it?), but serious counterterrorism people have actually studied these numbers to see if there really is a pattern, a portent. Numbers involve ancient superstitions and modern habits. So do terrorists. Nine-eleven was a disaster born of an old evil, an old hatred, but one that could have happened only in the communication age, when terrorists can hook up using satellite phones and e-mail accounts and synchronized Casio watches. Funny how 9/11 exactly expresses all that: the menace, the placelessness, the precision of time. Like the event itself, our use of numbers to describe what happened signifies that something about us, and the way we think, has changed, possibly forever.

Glossary

Alliteration Repetition of initial consonant sound in two or more words. For example, the *first frost.*

Allusion Reference to lines or characters from literature or mythology or to figures or events from history. For example, if someone describes you as "an old *Scrooge,*" then, like the character in Charles Dickens's *A Christmas Carol,* you are not generous with money.

Analogy An extended comparison of two things that are essentially not alike with several points of similarity (or difference) established to support an idea or thesis. Liane Norman (Chapter 4) draws an analogy between students and squirrels to make a point about students.

Analysis The division of a work or a topic into its component parts. To analyze a writer's style is to examine the various elements that compose style, such as word choice, sentence structure, use of figurative language. (See also **Causal analysis.**)

Argumentation A form of thinking and writing in which reasons and evidence are presented to support a position on an issue. (See Chapter 10.)

Audience The readers of a piece of writing. Hence, as a writing concept, the expected or anticipated readers to whom a piece of writing is directed. A sense of audience should guide a writer's choice about approach, content, and tone for a piece of writing.

Brainstorm Prewriting strategy for generating material on a subject by jotting down all ideas and examples or details that come to mind.

Causal analysis The examination of a situation by division into and study of its several causes, or its pattern of conditions, influences, and remote and immediate causes. (See Chapter 9.)

Character   Any person in narrative and dramatic works; also, the personality traits that together shape a person's "character."

Characterization   The description of a person, either a real person or one from fiction or drama. A detailed characterization includes physical appearance, speech and behavior patterns, personality traits, and values.

Chronology   The arrangement of events in time sequence. A narrative or historical account organizes events in chronological order. A process analysis explains steps in their appropriate chronology.

Classification   A pattern of thinking and writing in which a subject is divided into logical categories, and then elements of the subject are grouped within those categories. (See Chapter 7.)

Cliché   Overused, worn-out expressions, often metaphors, that were once fresh and clever but should now be avoided in writing, except as examples or to reveal character. I'm *fit as a fiddle, hungry as a bear,* and *head over heels in love* are examples of clichés.

Coherence   A quality of good writing marked by a logical ordering of statements and by the use of words and phrases that guide readers through the material and show them how the writing hangs together. Some techniques for obtaining coherence include repetition of key words, use of pronouns, and use of transition words and phrases.

Colloquial language   Language used in conversation but usually avoided in writing, especially in academic and business writing, unless used purposely to create a particular effect.

Comparison   A pattern of writing in which similarities between two subjects (two schools, two jobs, two novels) are examined. (See Chapter 4.)

Complex sentence   Sentence containing at least one dependent or subordinate clause and one independent clause. For example, "When you come to a term about writing that you do not know, [dependent clause] you should look it up in the Glossary [independent clause]."

Compound sentence Sentence containing at least two independent clauses. For example, "A comparison develops similarities between two like things [first independent clause], but [coordinating conjunction] a metaphor expresses a similarity between two unalike things [second independent clause].

Conclusion The ending of a piece of writing; it gives the reader a sense of finish and completeness. Many strategies for concluding are available to writers, including restating and emphasizing the significance of the thesis, summarizing main points, and suggesting a course of action. Writing needs to conclude, not just stop.

Connotation The suggestions and emotional overtones conveyed by a word. Selecting the word with the appropriate connotative significance allows writers to develop subtle shades of meaning and to convey their attitudes.

Context clues The words or sentences surrounding a word that help readers to understand the meaning of that word.

Contrast A pattern of writing in which differences between two subjects (e.g., two schools, two jobs, two novels) are examined. (See Chapter 4.)

Definition Explanation of a word's meaning. It can be provided in a sentence or expanded into an essay. (See Chapter 8.)

Denotation The meanings of a word, often referred to as a word's dictionary definitions. For example, a *house* is a building used primarily for private living. A *home*, however, also connotes family, love, and security.

Description Details appealing to the five senses that help readers to "see" the writer's subject. (See Chapter 3.)

Details Specific pieces of information that range from descriptions of people and places to statistical data and that are used by writers to illustrate and support ideas and general points.

Dialect Variations in grammar, sentence patterns, and word choice that mark the particular use of a language by one group.

Dialogue Exact words spoken by people introduced in essays or by characters in litierature. The words are always set off by quotation marks, and a new paragraph is started to show a change of speaker.

Diction   A writer's choice of words. Levels of diction refer to the degree of formality or informality in word choice.

Division   A pattern of thinking and writing in which large and/or complicated subjects are separated into parts for clear and logical discussion. (See Chapter 7.)

Effects   The consequences or outcomes of events. Effects are often a part of causal analysis when writers examine both what has produced a given situation and what that situation will lead to. Writers also analyze only effects, explaining both immediate and long-term consequences. (See Chapter 9.)

E.g.   Abbreviation of the Latin words *exempli gratia,* meaning "for example."

Essay   A short prose work presenting the writer's views on a particular topic.

Evidence   Facts and examples used to support the thesis or proposition in an argument.

Example   A specific illustration used to develop a thesis or general idea. (See Chapter 6.)

Fable   A narrative written (or told) to teach a moral or lesson.

Fact   A statement that is verifiable by observation, measurement, experiment, or use of reliable reference sources such as encyclo-pedias, atlases, and almanacs.

Fiction   An imagined narrative; a story. "The Story of an Hour" by Kate Chopin is fiction. Essays are nonfiction.

Figurative language   Language containing figures of speech that extend meaning beyond the literal. A metaphor, for example, is a figure of speech.

Illustration   The use of examples to develop and support a thesis. (See Chapter 6.)

Image   The recreation in words of a sense experience. Vivid images enrich descriptive writing.

Imagery   All the images in a work. Also, a cluster of similar images creating a dominant impression in a work.

Introductions   The openings of essays; one or several paragraphs that seek to get the reader's attention and interest and to establish the writer's subject. Many strategies for good introductions are available, including using a startling statistic, stating the thesis, providing an interesting, relevant quotation, asking a question, and giving a brief anecdote or example. Introductions to avoid include sweeping generalizations that range beyond the paper's scope and purpose and statements such as "In this essay, I plan to discuss . . ."

Irony In general, the expression of incongruity or discrepancy. *Verbal irony* expresses a discrepancy between what is said and what is meant. *Dramatic irony* expresses a discrepancy between what a character says or does and what readers understand to be true. *Irony of situation* develops a discrepancy between what we expect to happen and what actually happens.

Jargon Specialized terms of a particular profession or subject area. Jargon often has a negative connotation, a reminder to writers that jargon should be avoided in essays written for general audiences who will be unfamiliar with the terms. Always define specialized terms that must be used.

Metaphor A figure of speech in which a comparison is either stated or implied between two unlike things. (E.g., "this *bud* of *love*" or "*Life's* but a *walking shadow*.")

Narration The account, usually in chronological order, of a historical event or a story (fiction). Also, a strategy for developing the main point of an essay. (See Chapter 2.)

Occasion The situation or circumstances in which a writer produces a particular work. Writers are often motivated to write in response to an event or to their reading.

Order The pattern in which the parts of an essay are arranged. This text explains many of the patterns available to writers.

Paradox A statement that seems contradictory but can be under-stood to be true, usually by taking one part of the statement figuratively rather than literally. For example, "The more money I make, the less I have."

Part by part A structure for comparison or contrast that arranges by points of difference rather than by the subjects being compared.

Point of view The perspective or angle of vision from which a story is told. Sometimes the term is used to refer to the grammatical "person" used in essay writing, that is, the first person ("I," "we"), the second person ("you"), which is rarely used except when giving directions, or the third person ("he," "she," "they"). The fiction writer's choices are: *first person* (a character tells the story using "I"), *omniscient* (the all-knowing narrator), *limited omniscient* (through the eyes of one character but in the third person), or *objective* (reporting only what can be seen and heard, not what characters are thinking).

Process analysis A pattern of writing that takes the reader through the steps or stages necessary to complete a task, perform an activity, or accomplish a goal.

Purpose One's reason for writing. General purposes include to inform, to explain, and to persuade.

Refutation A form of argument in which the primary purpose is to counter, or show weaknesses in, another's argument. (See Chapter 10.)

Reporter's questions Traditionally the questions *who, what, where, when,* and *why* are considered those a journalist should answer about each story covered. Essay writers can also use these questions in planning a topic's development.

Rhetorical question A question raised by a writer when the writer believes that readers will see only one possible answer—the answer the writer would give.

Sarcasm Bitter or cutting expression, often ironic.

Satire Work that ridicules the vices and follies of humanity, often with the purpose of bringing about change.

Setting The physical locale of the work. Can be presented to create atmosphere as well.

Simile A comparison between two essentially unalike things that is stated explicitly by using connectors such as *like, as,* or *seems.* For example, "I wandered lonely *as* a cloud," written by William Wordsworth.

Simple sentence A sentence containing only one independent clause. For example, "A simple sentence contains only one independent clause."

Style A writer's selection and arrangement of language.

Summary A brief, objective restatement of the main ideas in a work.

Symbol An object, character, or action that suggests meanings, associations, and emotions beyond what is characteristic of its nature or function. A rose is a flower, but a rose symbolically represents love and beauty.

Theme The central idea (or ideas) that a work embodies.

Thesis The main idea of an essay. It is often but not always expressed in a *thesis sentence.*

Tone The expression of a writer's attitude (e.g., playful, bitter).

Transitions Words and phrases that show readers how ideas in a work are related or connected. For example, *in addition, for example, however.*

Unity A characteristic of good writing in which everything included relates to the work's main idea and contributes to its development.

Whole by whole A structure for comparison or contrast that organizes by the two subjects being compared rather than by their specific points of similarity or difference.

Credits

Index